Monster Girls

The Illustrated Guide to

3

The Illustrated Guide to Monster Girls

3

Name: Mayoi Sadakuni
Type: automaton
Deadly sin: lust

SUZU AKEKO

YEN PRESS

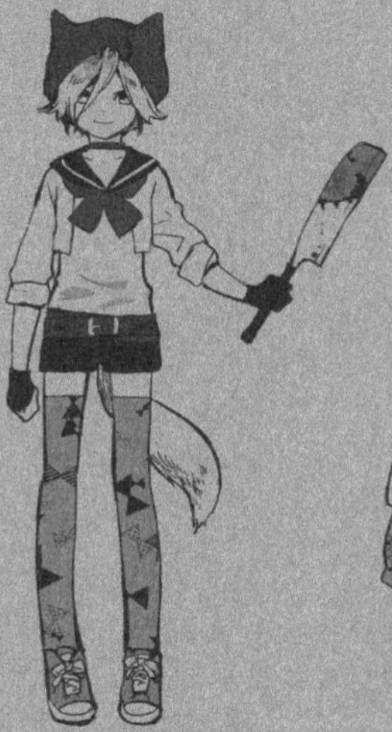

Name: Saiko Akagari
Type: ghoula
Deadly sin: gluttony

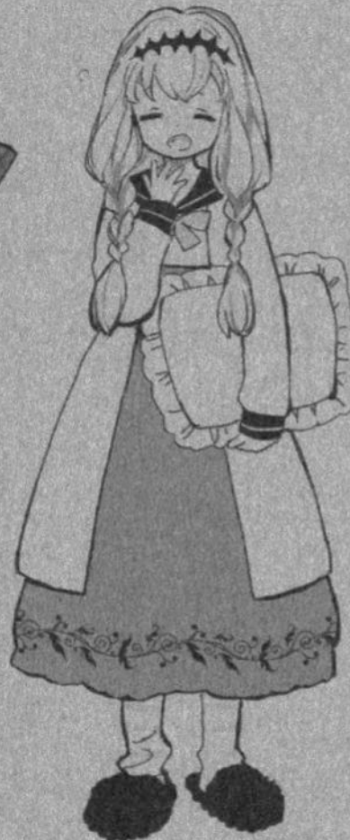

Name: Nemu Ibara
Type: vampire
Deadly sin: sloth

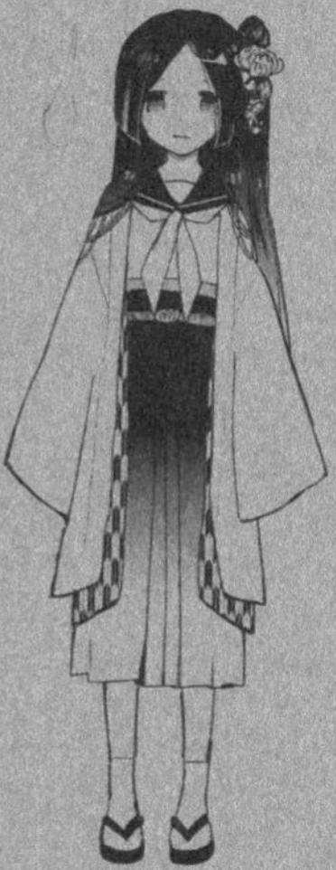

Name: Reika Kikuno
Type: ghost
Deadly sin: envy

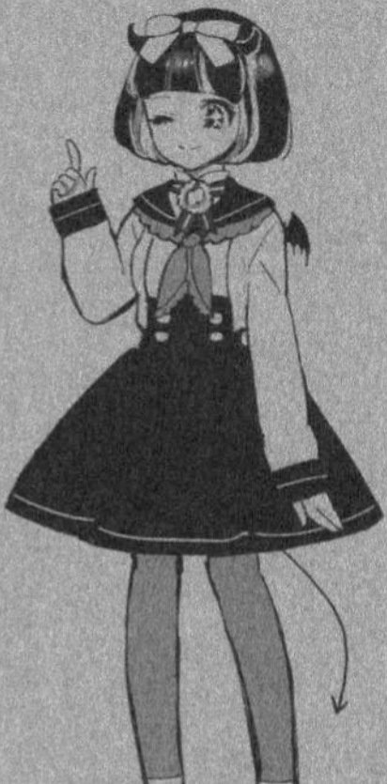

Name: Ringo Shirayuki
Type: devil
Deadly sin: pride

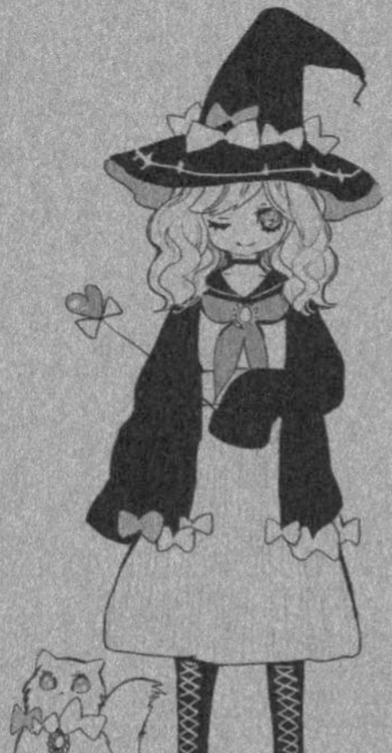

Name: Syouko Haikaburi
Type: witch
Deadly sin: greed

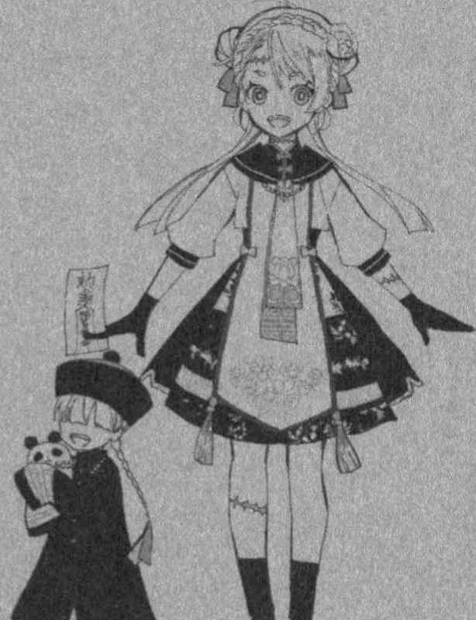

Name: Ichika Luo
Type: jiangshi
Deadly sin: wrath

YEN PRESS

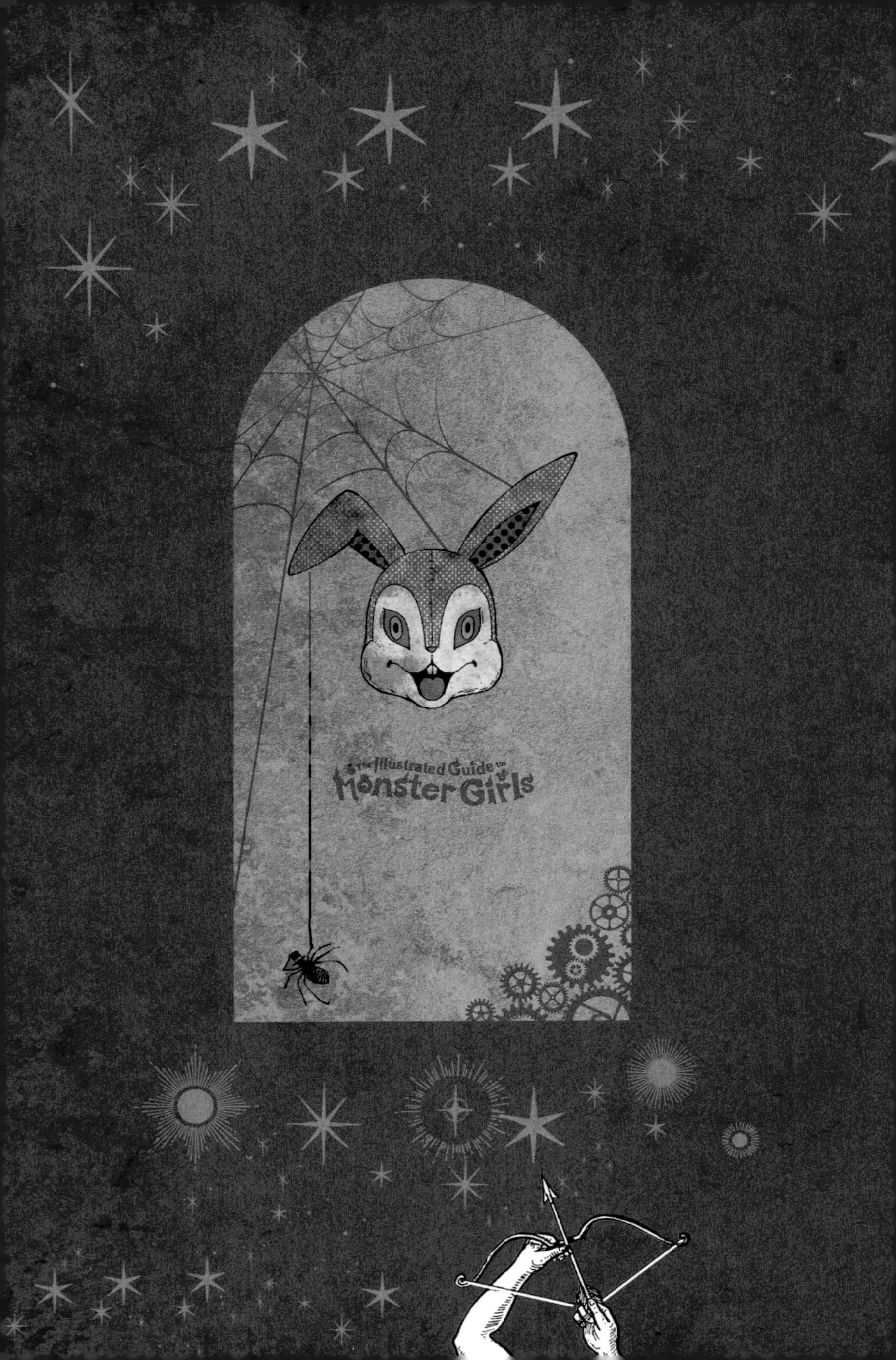
The Illustrated Guide to
Monster Girls

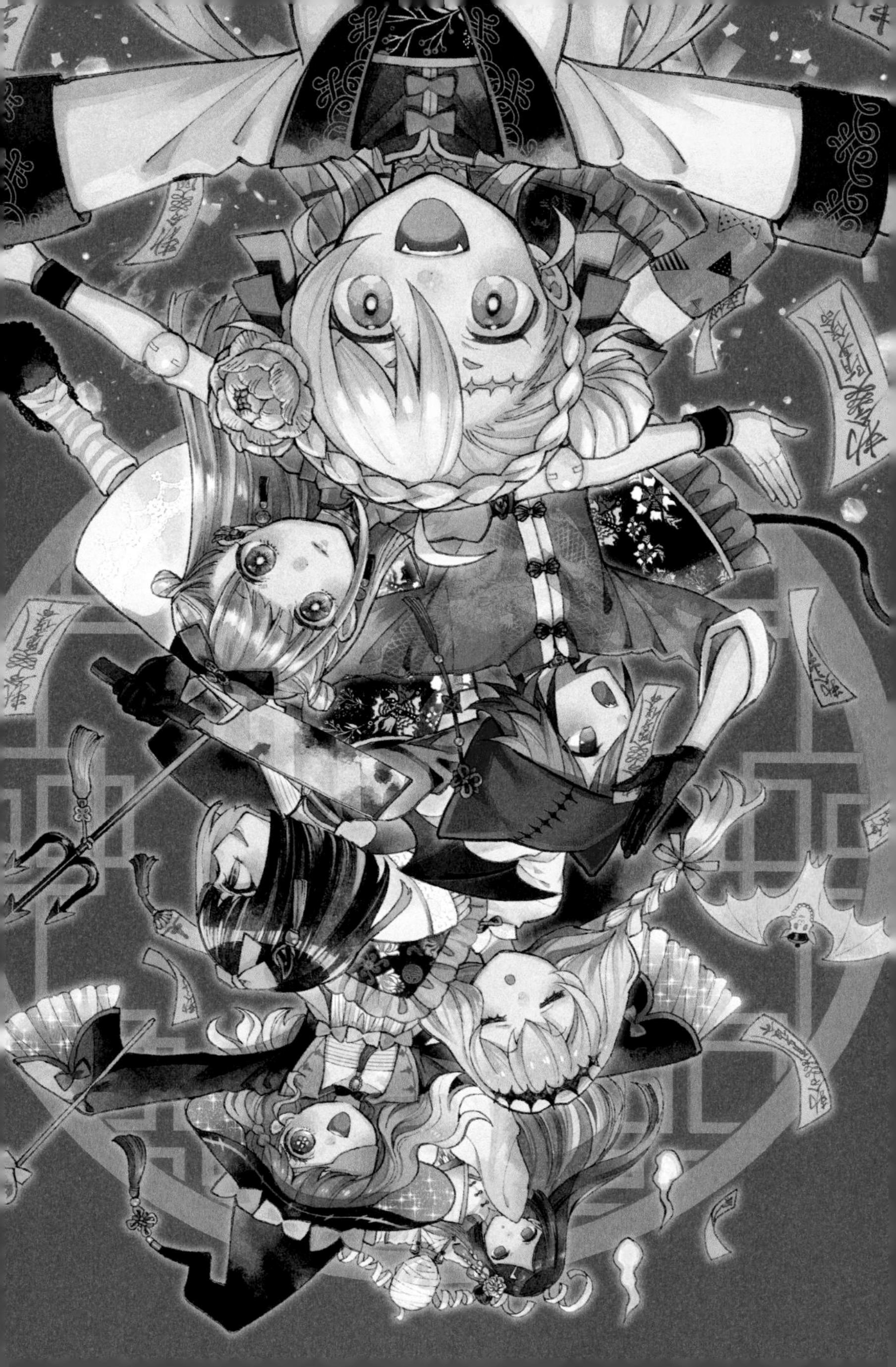

ENTRY 14 — Doubt!? You May Not Believe Me, but I Really Was There!! (9)

ENTRY 15 — Clammy! Our Household Is Social Distancing! (35)

ENTRY 16 — Sneak...Flesh and Blood plus Bloody Tears While Sister Watching! (61)

ENTRY 17 — Sliiip...Tonight I'm Coming for Your BLANK! (81)

CONTENTS

SIDE ENTRY

Leeearn...Introducing
the Students a
Little Late! 167

ENTRY 19

Poonh! The Human
Realm's Halloween Is
a Toughie! Part 1 137

ENTRY 18

Poink! The Haughty
Underdog Devil Princess
Starts Her Campaign! 111

Reika Kikuno

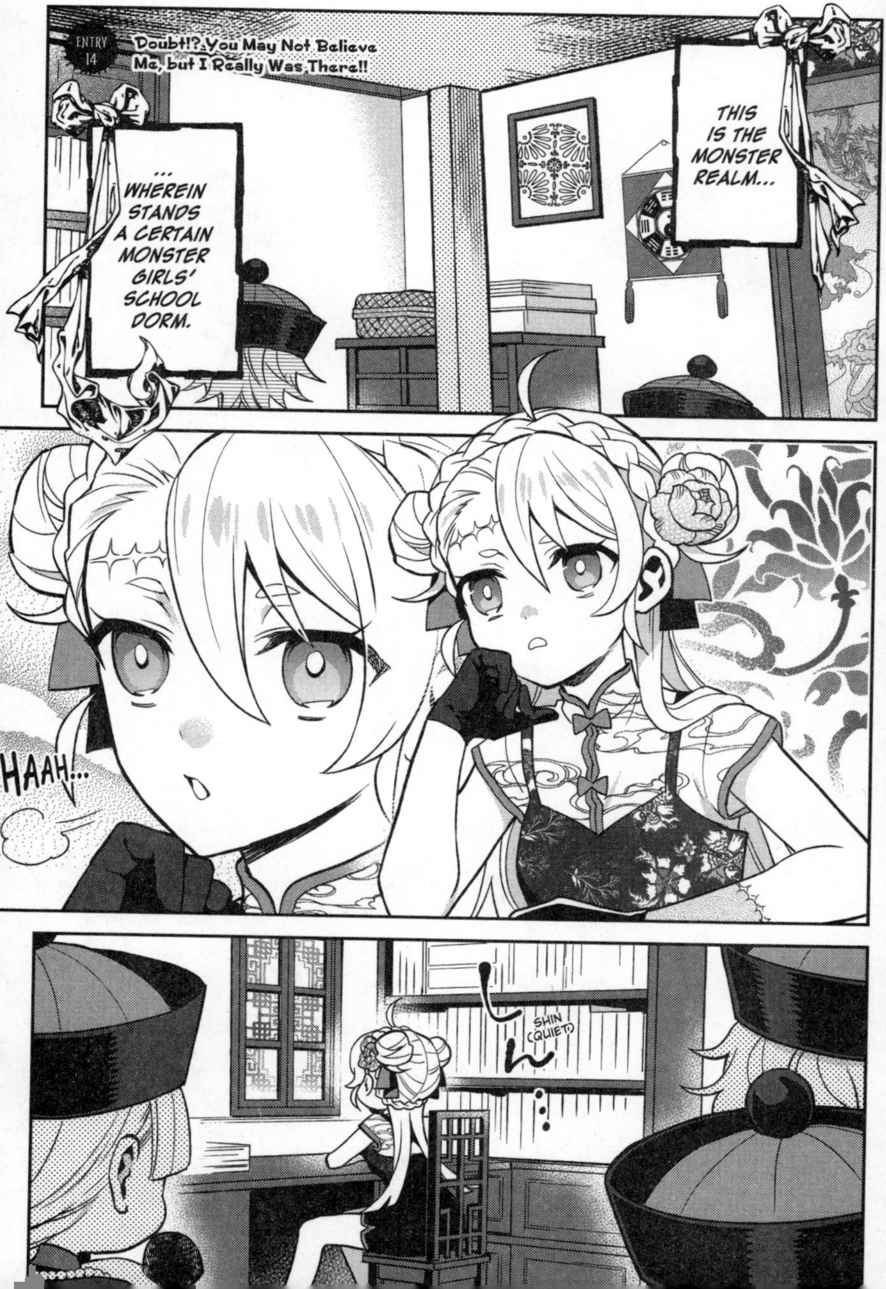
ENTRY 14
Doubt!? You May Not Believe Me, but I Really Was There!!
THIS IS THE MONSTER REALM...
... WHEREIN STANDS A CERTAIN MONSTER GIRLS' SCHOOL DORM.
HAAH...
SHIN (QUIET)
...

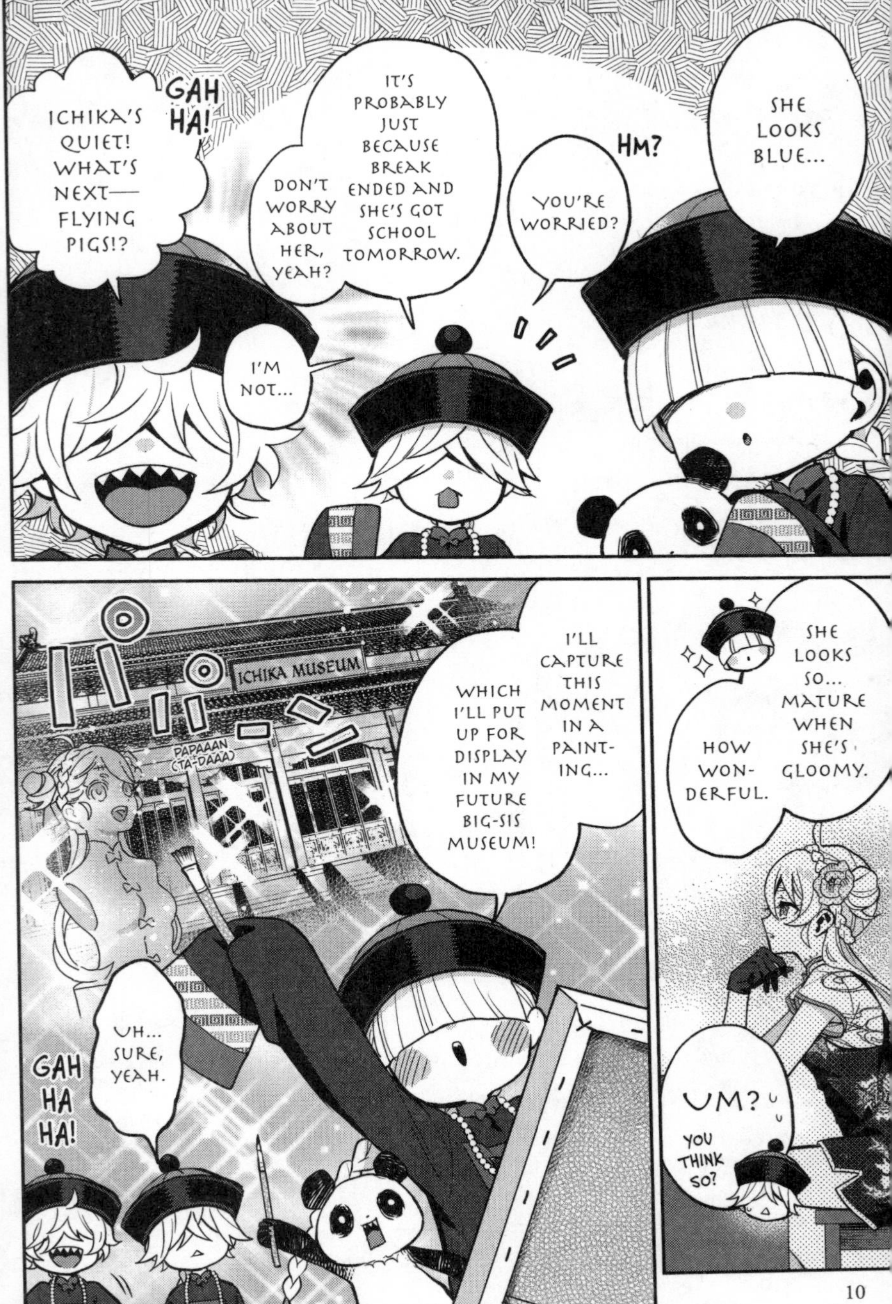
SHE LOOKS BLUE...
HM?
YOU'RE WORRIED?
IT'S PROBABLY JUST BECAUSE BREAK ENDED AND SHE'S GOT SCHOOL TOMORROW.
DON'T WORRY ABOUT HER, YEAH?
GAH HA!
ICHIKA'S QUIET! WHAT'S NEXT—FLYING PIGS!?
I'M NOT...
SHE LOOKS SO... MATURE WHEN SHE'S GLOOMY.
HOW WON-DERFUL.
UM?
YOU THINK SO?
I'LL CAPTURE THIS MOMENT IN A PAINT-ING...
WHICH I'LL PUT UP FOR DISPLAY IN MY FUTURE BIG-SIS MUSEUM!
ICHIKA MUSEUM
PAPAAAN (TA-DAAA)
UH... SURE, YEAH.
GAH HA HA!

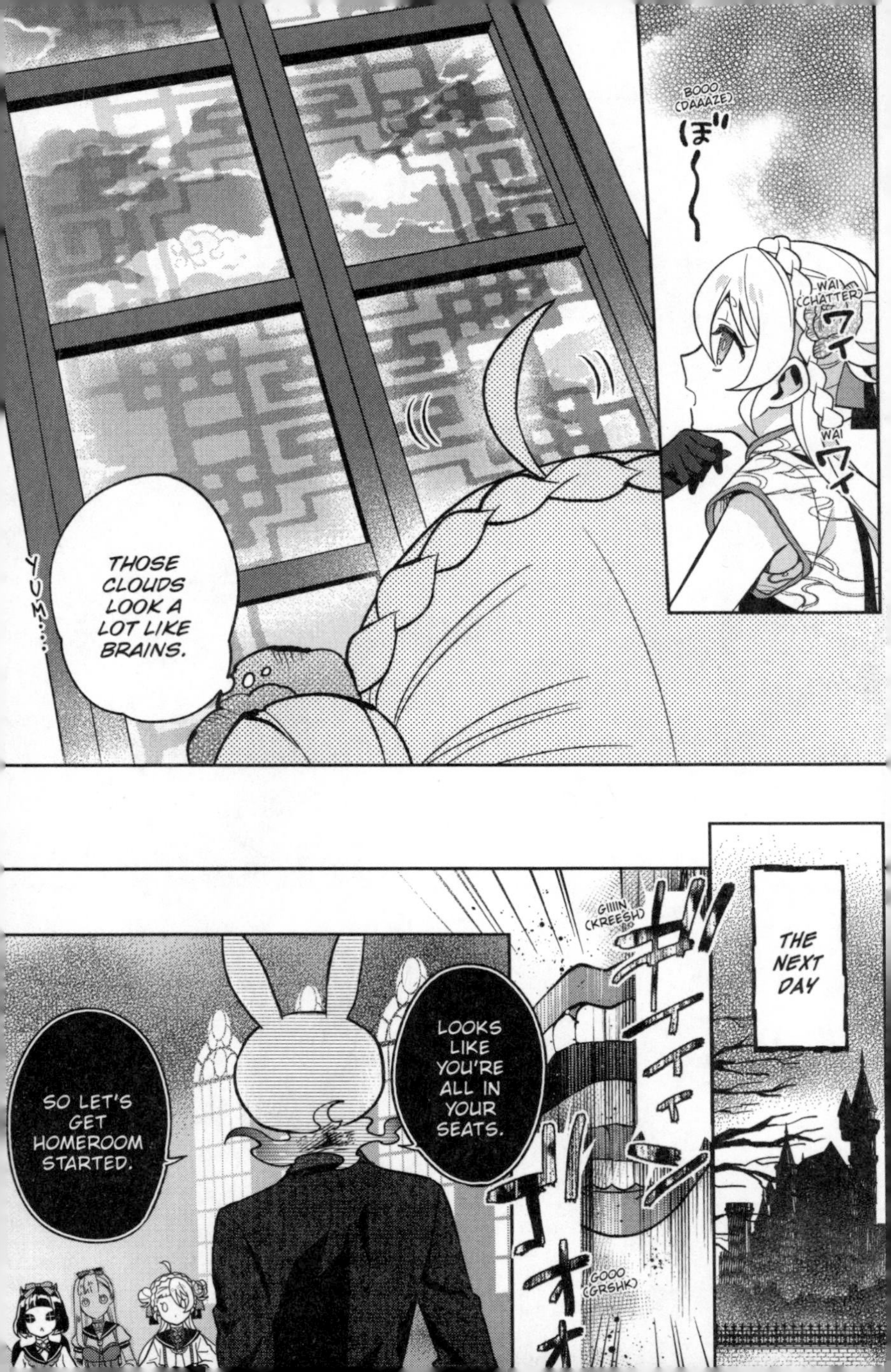
BOOO (DAAAZE)
ぼ〜〜
WAI (CHATTER) ワイ
WAI ワイ
YUM...
THOSE CLOUDS LOOK A LOT LIKE BRAINS.
THE NEXT DAY
GIIIN (KREESH)
GOOO (GRSHK)
LOOKS LIKE YOU'RE ALL IN YOUR SEATS.
SO LET'S GET HOMEROOM STARTED.

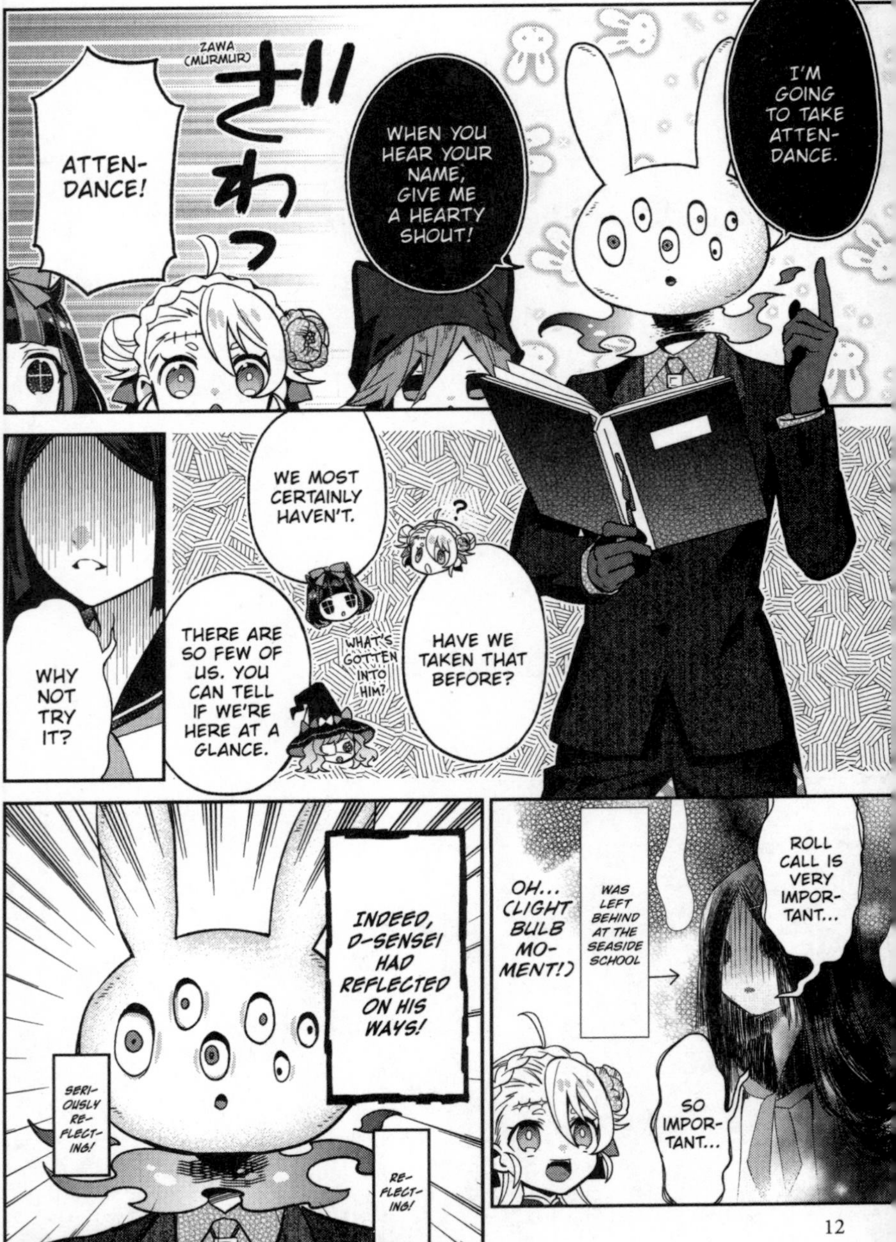

I'M GOING TO TAKE ATTEN-DANCE.
WHEN YOU HEAR YOUR NAME, GIVE ME A HEARTY SHOUT!
ざわっ
ZAWA (MURMUR)
ATTEN-DANCE!
HAVE WE TAKEN THAT BEFORE?
WE MOST CERTAINLY HAVEN'T.
WHAT'S GOTTEN INTO HIM?
?
THERE ARE SO FEW OF US. YOU CAN TELL IF WE'RE HERE AT A GLANCE.
WHY NOT TRY IT?
ROLL CALL IS VERY IMPOR-TANT...
WAS LEFT BEHIND AT THE SEASIDE SCHOOL
OH... (LIGHT BULB MO-MENT!)
SO IMPOR-TANT...
INDEED, D-SENSEI HAD REFLECTED ON HIS WAYS!
RE-FLECT-ING!
SERI-OUSLY RE-FLECT-ING!

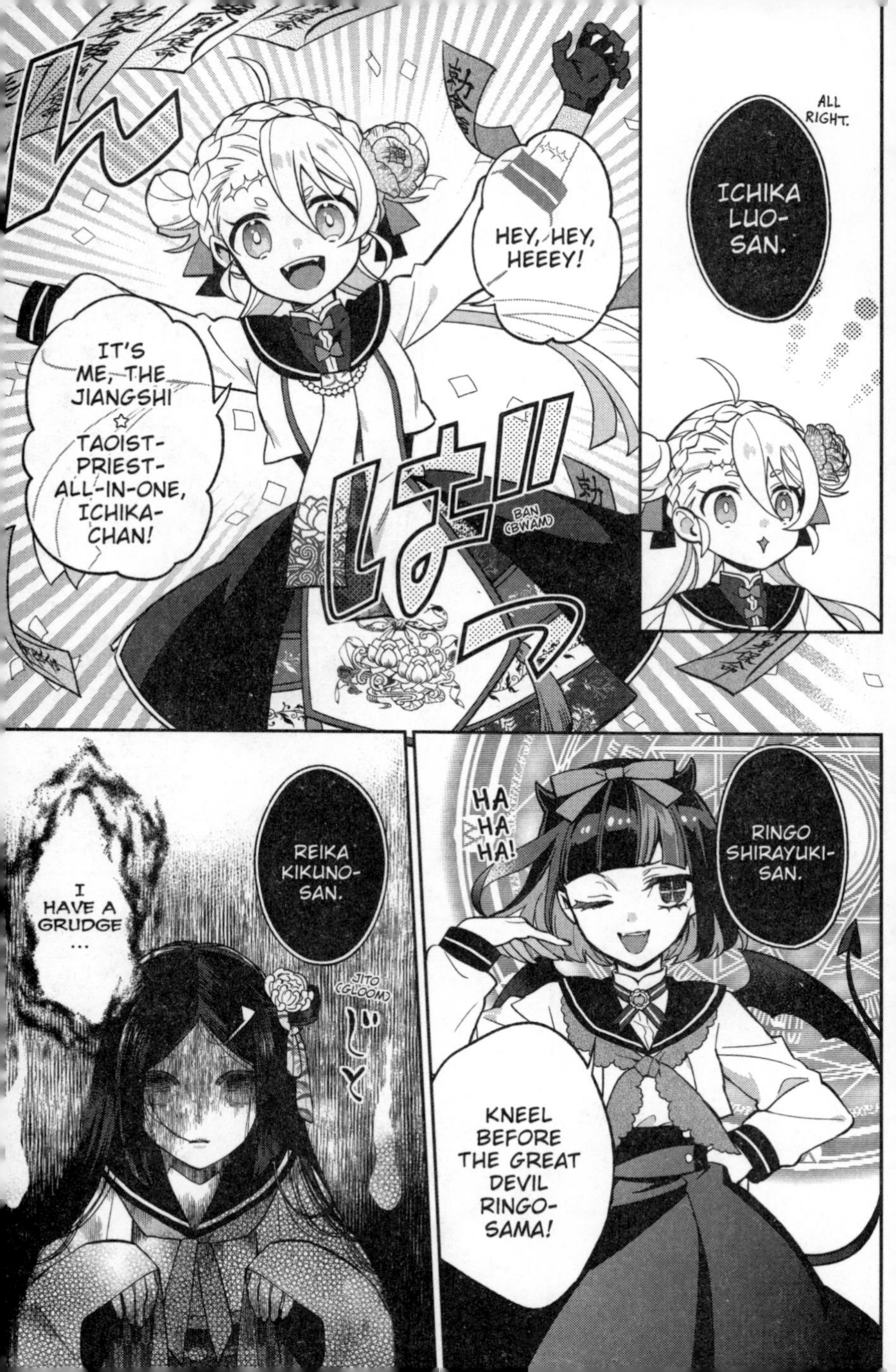
ALL RIGHT.
ICHIKA LUO-SAN.
HEY, HEY, HEEEY!
IT'S ME, THE JIANGSHI ☆ TAOIST-PRIEST-ALL-IN-ONE, ICHIKA-CHAN!
BAN (BWAM)
RINGO SHIRAYUKI-SAN.
HA HA HA!
KNEEL BEFORE THE GREAT DEVIL RINGO-SAMA!
REIKA KIKUNO-SAN.
I HAVE A GRUDGE ...
JITO (GLOOM)

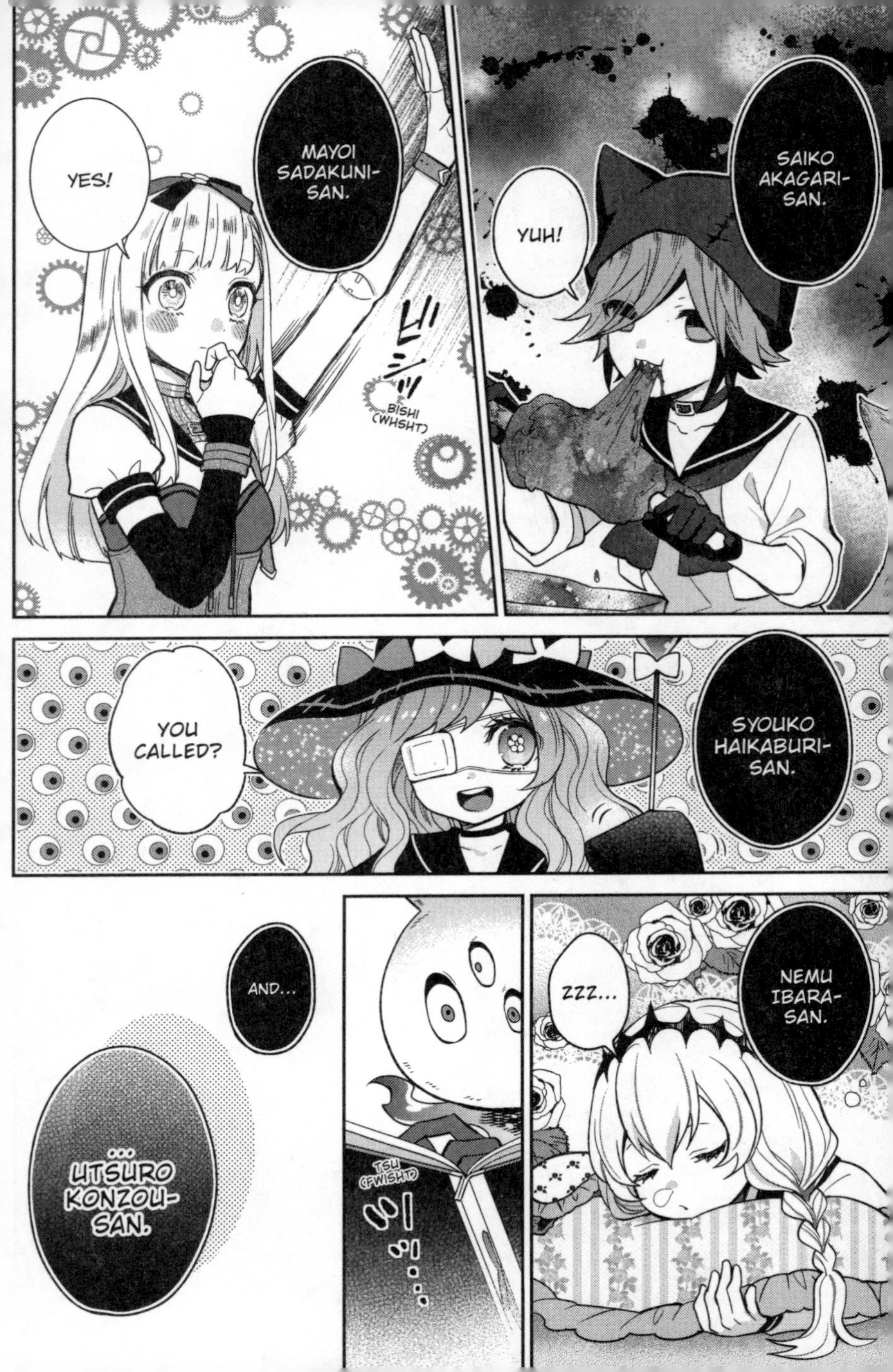
SAIKO AKAGARI-SAN.
YUH!
MAYOI SADAKUNI-SAN.
YES!
BISHI (WHSHT)
SYOUKO HAIKABURI-SAN.
YOU CALLED?
NEMU IBARA-SAN.
ZZZ...
TSU (FWISHT)
AND...
...UTSURO KONZOU-SAN.

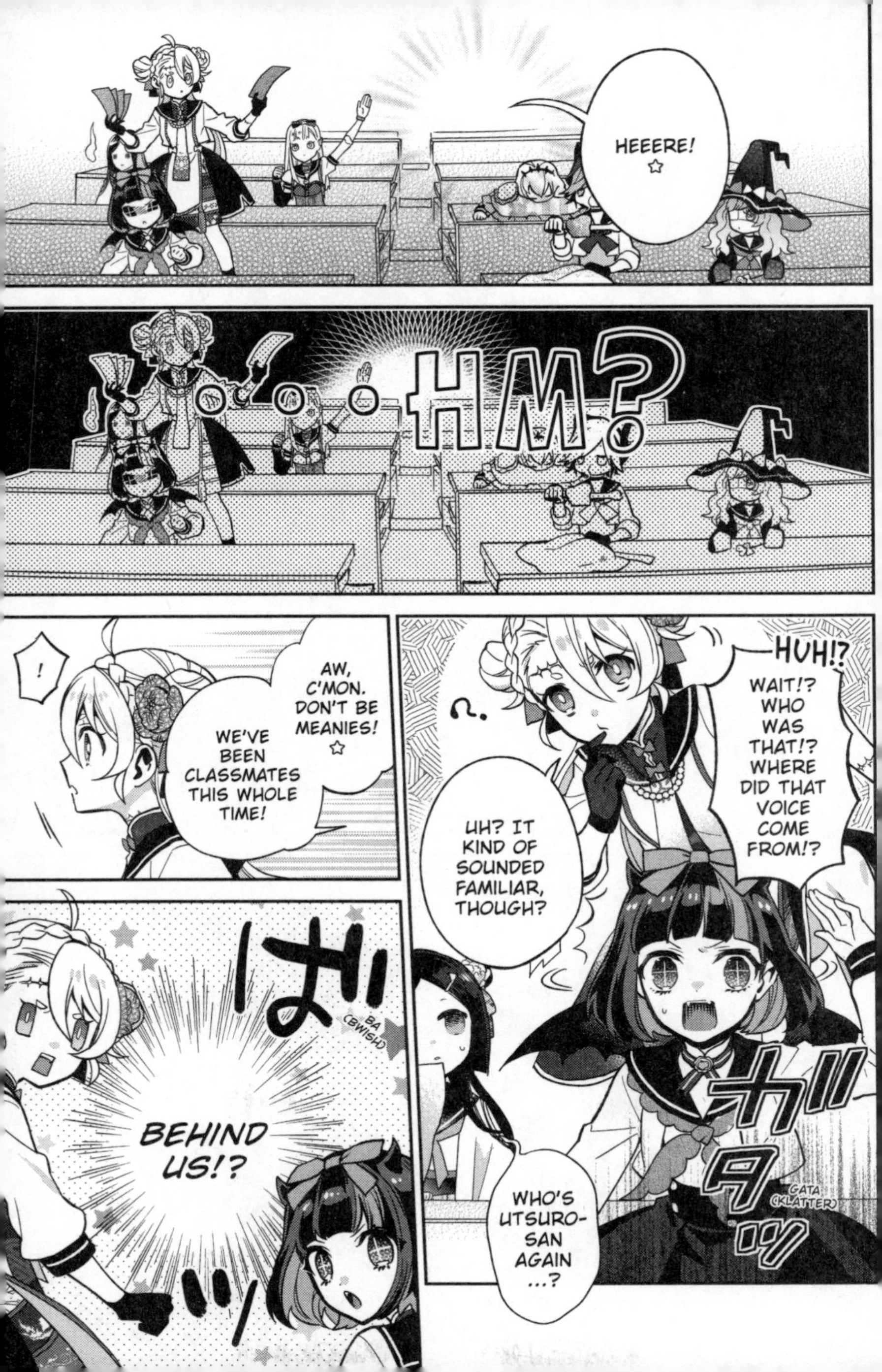
HEEERE! ☆
...HM?
—HUH!?
WAIT!? WHO WAS THAT!? WHERE DID THAT VOICE COME FROM!?
UH? IT KIND OF SOUNDED FAMILIAR, THOUGH?
GATA (KLATTER)
WHO'S UTSURO-SAN AGAIN ...?
!
AW, C'MON. DON'T BE MEANIES! ☆
WE'VE BEEN CLASSMATES THIS WHOLE TIME!
BA (BWISH)
BEHIND US!?

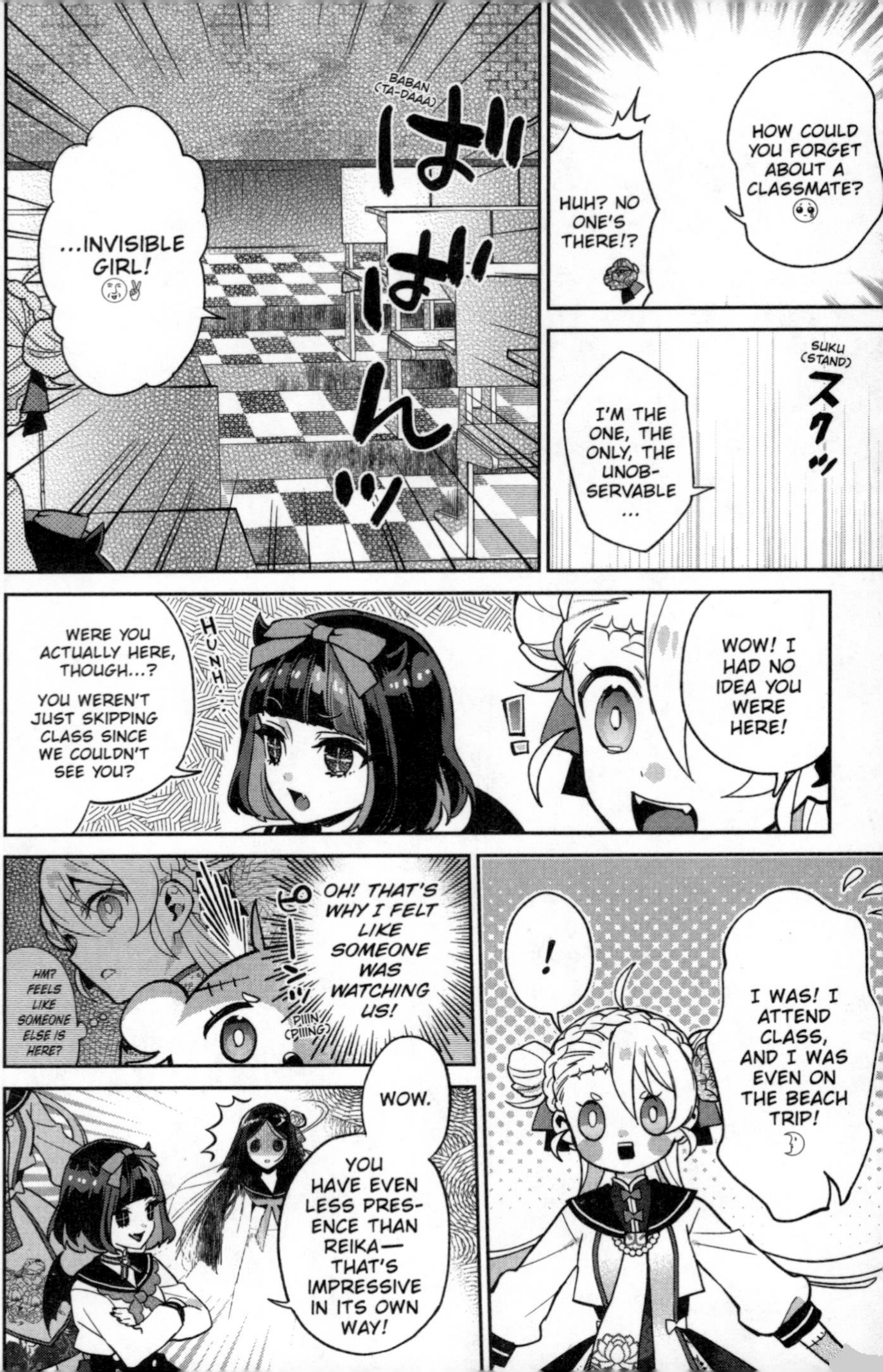
HOW COULD YOU FORGET ABOUT A CLASSMATE?
HUH? NO ONE'S THERE!?
SUKU (STAND)
スクッ
I'M THE ONE, THE ONLY, THE UNOB-SERVABLE ...
BABAN (TA-DAAA)
ばばんッ
...INVISIBLE GIRL!
WOW! I HAD NO IDEA YOU WERE HERE!
!
WERE YOU ACTUALLY HERE, THOUGH...?
YOU WEREN'T JUST SKIPPING CLASS SINCE WE COULDN'T SEE YOU?
HUNH...
I WAS! I ATTEND CLASS, AND I WAS EVEN ON THE BEACH TRIP!
!
OH! THAT'S WHY I FELT LIKE SOMEONE WAS WATCHING US!
ピーン
PIIIN (PIIING)
HM? FEELS LIKE SOMEONE ELSE IS HERE?
WOW.
YOU HAVE EVEN LESS PRES-ENCE THAN REIKA—THAT'S IMPRESSIVE IN ITS OWN WAY!

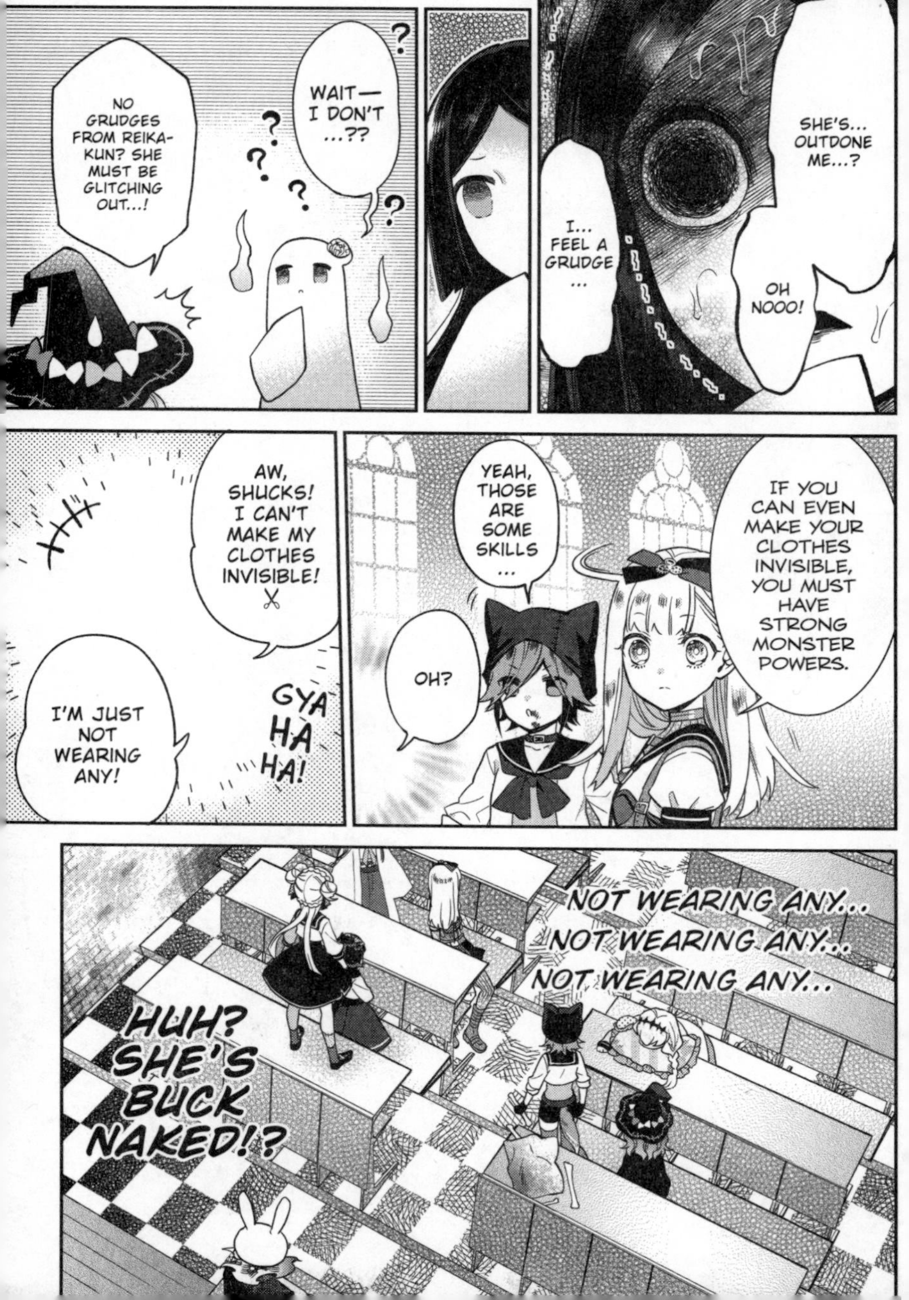
SHE'S... OUTDONE ME...?
OH NOOO!
I... FEEL A GRUDGE ...
WAIT— I DON'T ...??
NO GRUDGES FROM REIKA-KUN? SHE MUST BE GLITCHING OUT...!
IF YOU CAN EVEN MAKE YOUR CLOTHES INVISIBLE, YOU MUST HAVE STRONG MONSTER POWERS.
YEAH, THOSE ARE SOME SKILLS ...
OH?
AW, SHUCKS! I CAN'T MAKE MY CLOTHES INVISIBLE!
I'M JUST NOT WEARING ANY!
GYA HA HA HA!
NOT WEARING ANY...
NOT WEARING ANY...
NOT WEARING ANY...
HUH? SHE'S BUCK NAKED!?

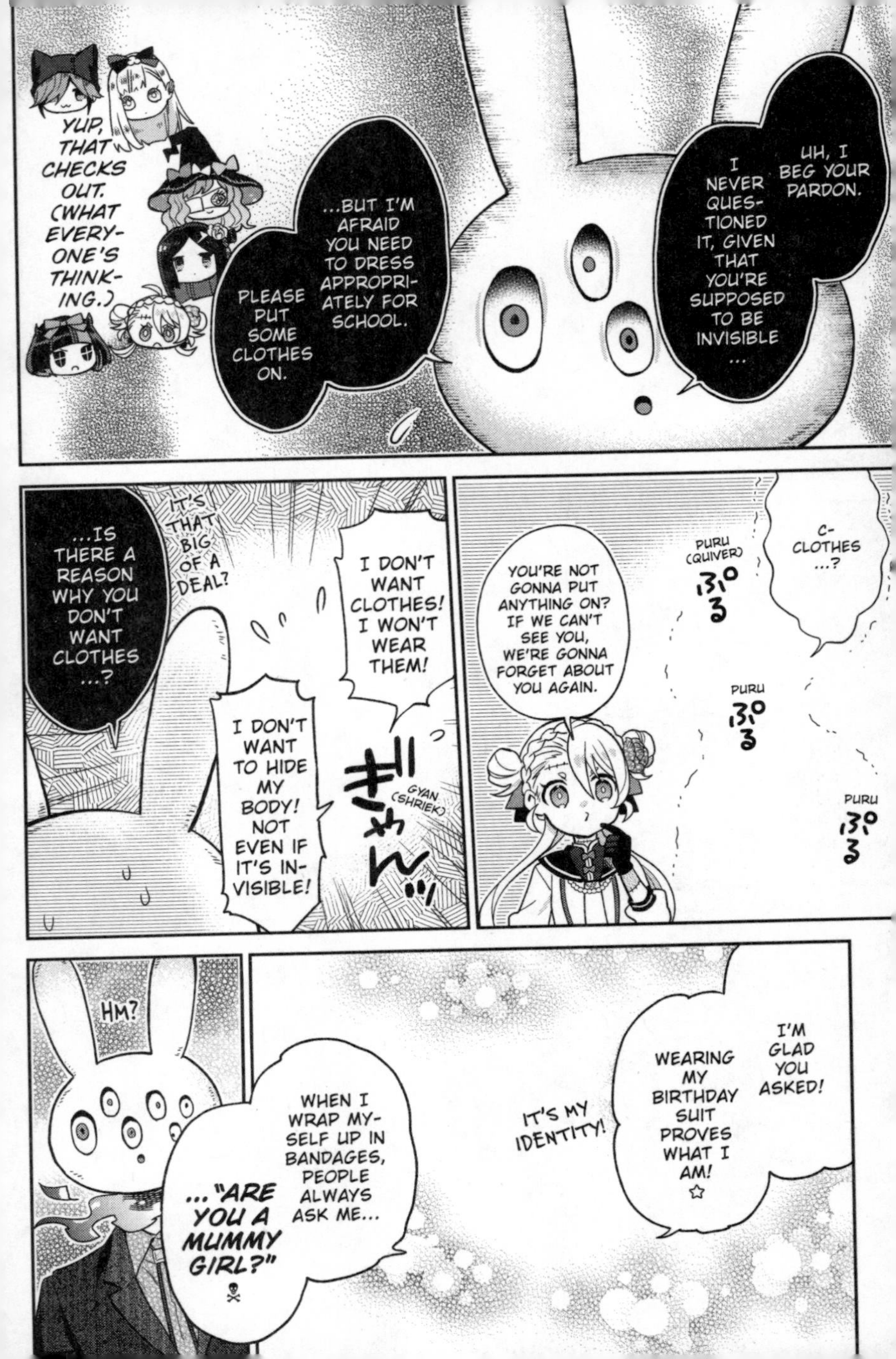
UH, I BEG YOUR PARDON.
I NEVER QUESTIONED IT, GIVEN THAT YOU'RE SUPPOSED TO BE INVISIBLE ...
...BUT I'M AFRAID YOU NEED TO DRESS APPROPRIATELY FOR SCHOOL.
PLEASE PUT SOME CLOTHES ON.
YUP, THAT CHECKS OUT. (WHAT EVERYONE'S THINKING.)
C-CLOTHES ...?
PURU (QUIVER) ぷる
YOU'RE NOT GONNA PUT ANYTHING ON? IF WE CAN'T SEE YOU, WE'RE GONNA FORGET ABOUT YOU AGAIN.
PURU ぷる
PURU ぷる
I DON'T WANT CLOTHES! I WON'T WEAR THEM!
I DON'T WANT TO HIDE MY BODY! NOT EVEN IF IT'S INVISIBLE!
ぎゃんッ
GYAN (SHRIEK)
IT'S THAT BIG OF A DEAL?
...IS THERE A REASON WHY YOU DON'T WANT CLOTHES ...?
I'M GLAD YOU ASKED!
WEARING MY BIRTHDAY SUIT PROVES WHAT I AM! ☆
IT'S MY IDENTITY!
WHEN I WRAP MYSELF UP IN BANDAGES, PEOPLE ALWAYS ASK ME...
..."ARE YOU A MUMMY GIRL?"
HM?

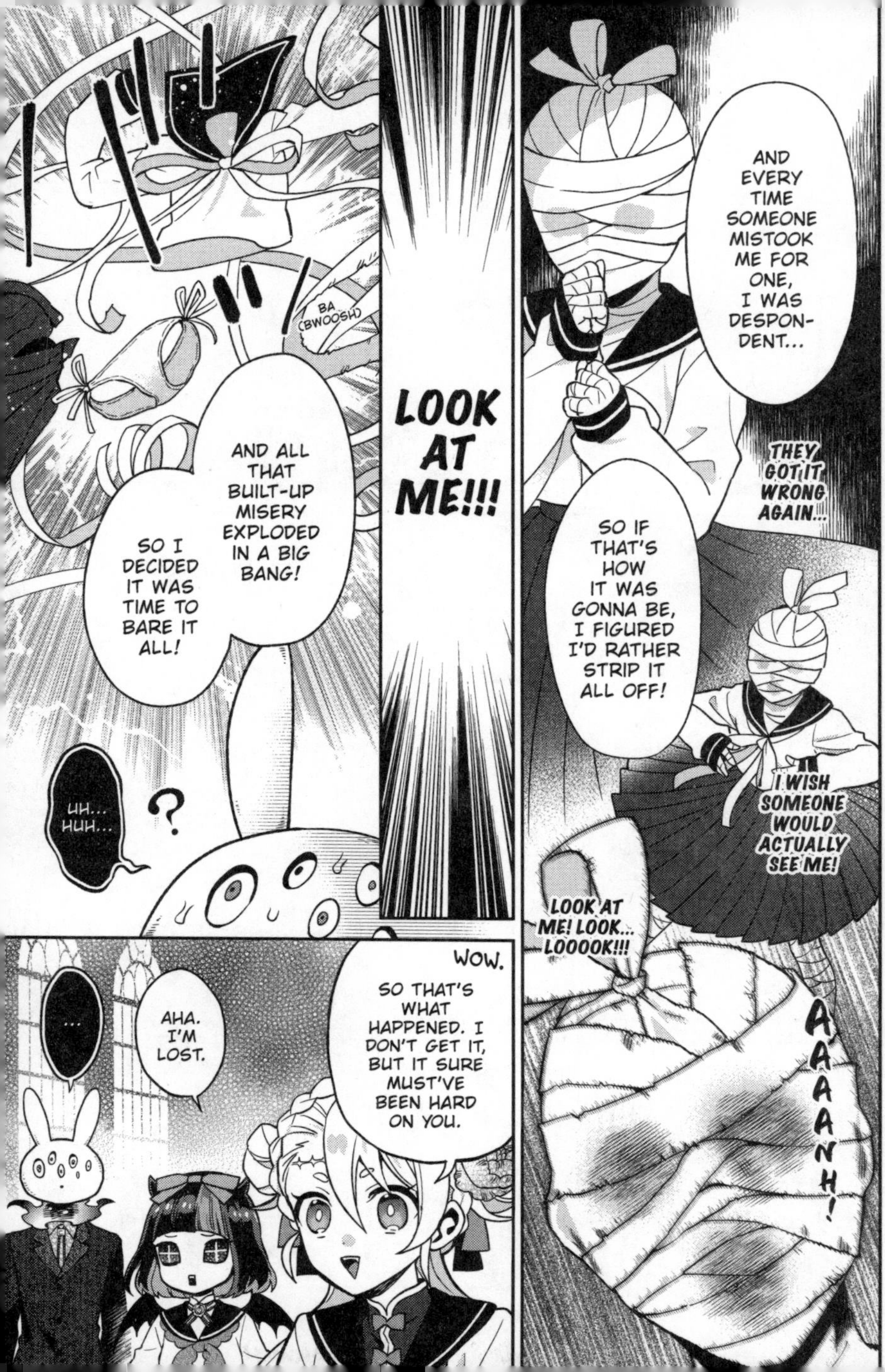
AND EVERY TIME SOMEONE MISTOOK ME FOR ONE, I WAS DESPONDENT...
THEY GOT IT WRONG AGAIN...
SO IF THAT'S HOW IT WAS GONNA BE, I FIGURED I'D RATHER STRIP IT ALL OFF!
I WISH SOMEONE WOULD ACTUALLY SEE ME!
LOOK AT ME! LOOK... LOOOOK!!!
AAAAANH!
LOOK AT ME!!!
AND ALL THAT BUILT-UP MISERY EXPLODED IN A BIG BANG!
SO I DECIDED IT WAS TIME TO BARE IT ALL!
BA (BWOOSH)
UH... HUH...
?
WOW.
SO THAT'S WHAT HAPPENED. I DON'T GET IT, BUT IT SURE MUST'VE BEEN HARD ON YOU.
AHA. I'M LOST.
...

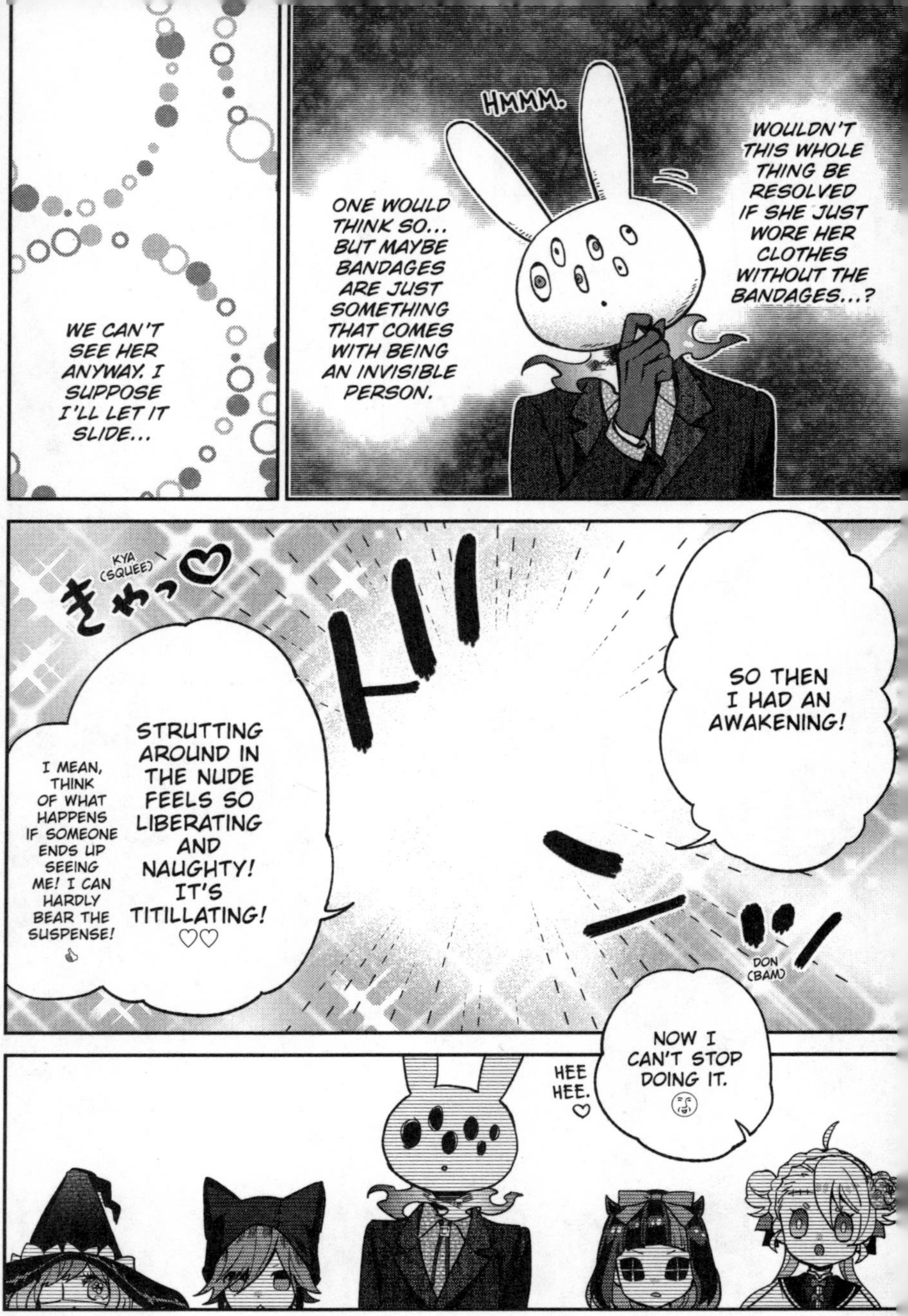
HMMM.
WOULDN'T THIS WHOLE THING BE RESOLVED IF SHE JUST WORE HER CLOTHES WITHOUT THE BANDAGES...?
ONE WOULD THINK SO... BUT MAYBE BANDAGES ARE JUST SOMETHING THAT COMES WITH BEING AN INVISIBLE PERSON.
WE CAN'T SEE HER ANYWAY. I SUPPOSE I'LL LET IT SLIDE...
SO THEN I HAD AN AWAKENING!
DON (BAM)
KYA (SQUEE)
STRUTTING AROUND IN THE NUDE FEELS SO LIBERATING AND NAUGHTY! IT'S TITILLATING! ♡♡
I MEAN, THINK OF WHAT HAPPENS IF SOMEONE ENDS UP SEEING ME! I CAN HARDLY BEAR THE SUSPENSE!
NOW I CAN'T STOP DOING IT.
HEE HEE. ♡

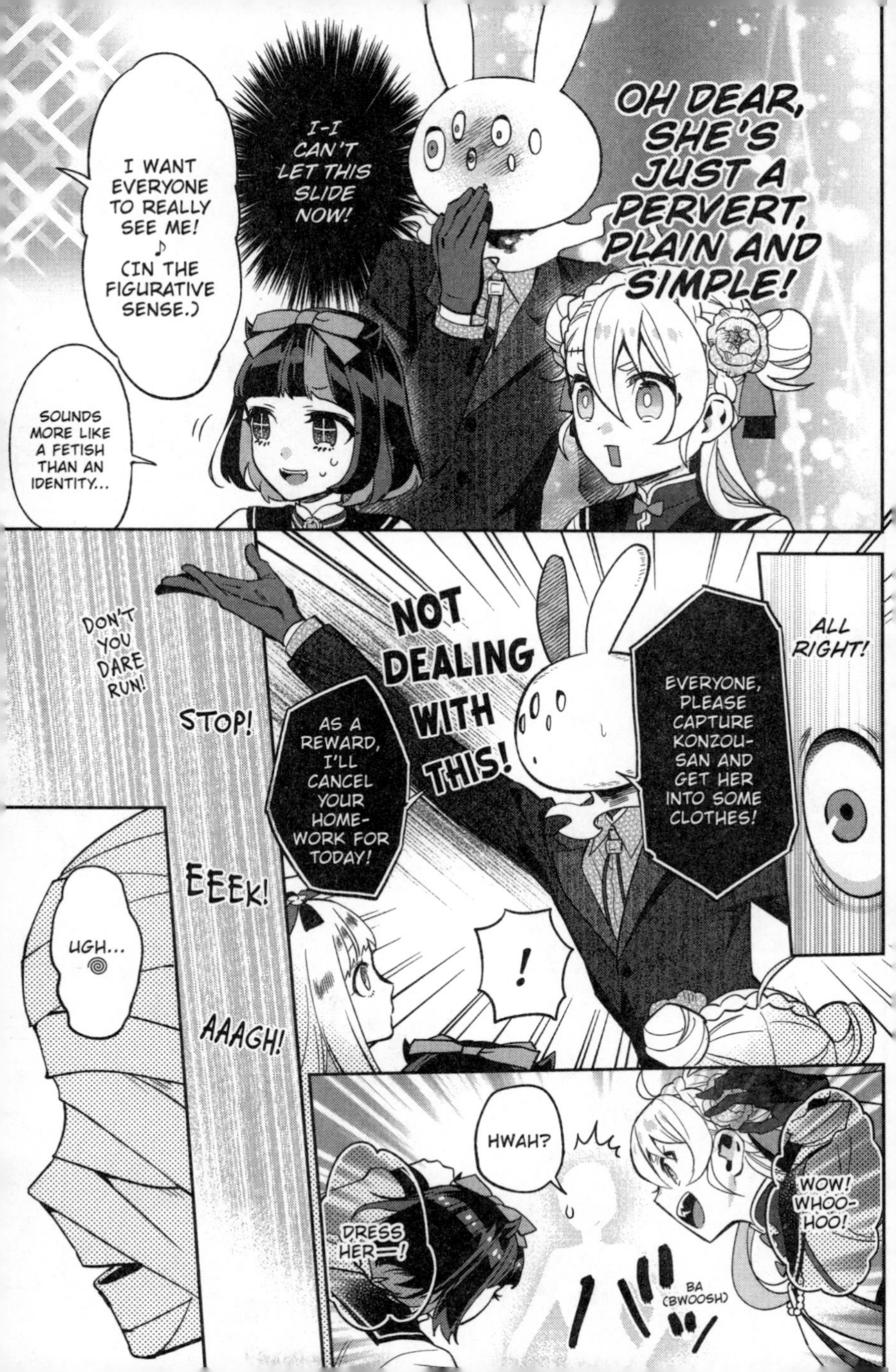
OH DEAR, SHE'S JUST A PERVERT, PLAIN AND SIMPLE!
I-I CAN'T LET THIS SLIDE NOW!
I WANT EVERYONE TO REALLY SEE ME! ♪
(IN THE FIGURATIVE SENSE.)
SOUNDS MORE LIKE A FETISH THAN AN IDENTITY...
ALL RIGHT!
EVERYONE, PLEASE CAPTURE KONZOU-SAN AND GET HER INTO SOME CLOTHES!
NOT DEALING WITH THIS!
AS A REWARD, I'LL CANCEL YOUR HOME-WORK FOR TODAY!
DON'T YOU DARE RUN!
STOP!
EEEK!
!
UGH...
AAAGH!
WOW! WHOO-HOO!
HWAH?
DRESS HER—!
BA (BWOOSH)

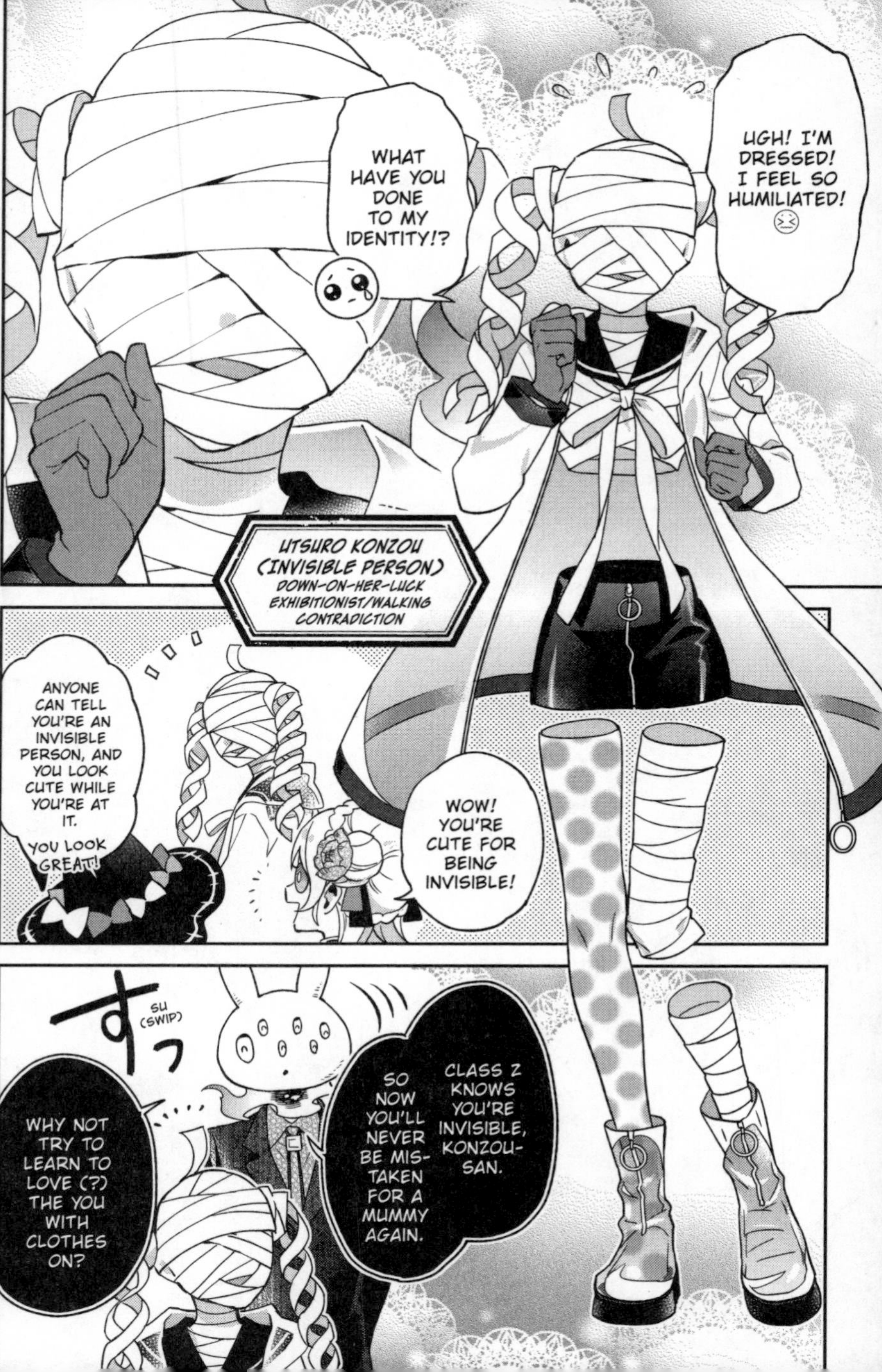
UGH! I'M DRESSED! I FEEL SO HUMILIATED!
WHAT HAVE YOU DONE TO MY IDENTITY!?
UTSURO KONZOU (INVISIBLE PERSON) DOWN-ON-HER-LUCK EXHIBITIONIST/WALKING CONTRADICTION
WOW! YOU'RE CUTE FOR BEING INVISIBLE!
ANYONE CAN TELL YOU'RE AN INVISIBLE PERSON, AND YOU LOOK CUTE WHILE YOU'RE AT IT.
YOU LOOK GREAT!
CLASS 2 KNOWS YOU'RE INVISIBLE, KONZOU-SAN.
SO NOW YOU'LL NEVER BE MIS-TAKEN FOR A MUMMY AGAIN.
すっ
SU (SWIP)
WHY NOT TRY TO LEARN TO LOVE (?) THE YOU WITH CLOTHES ON?

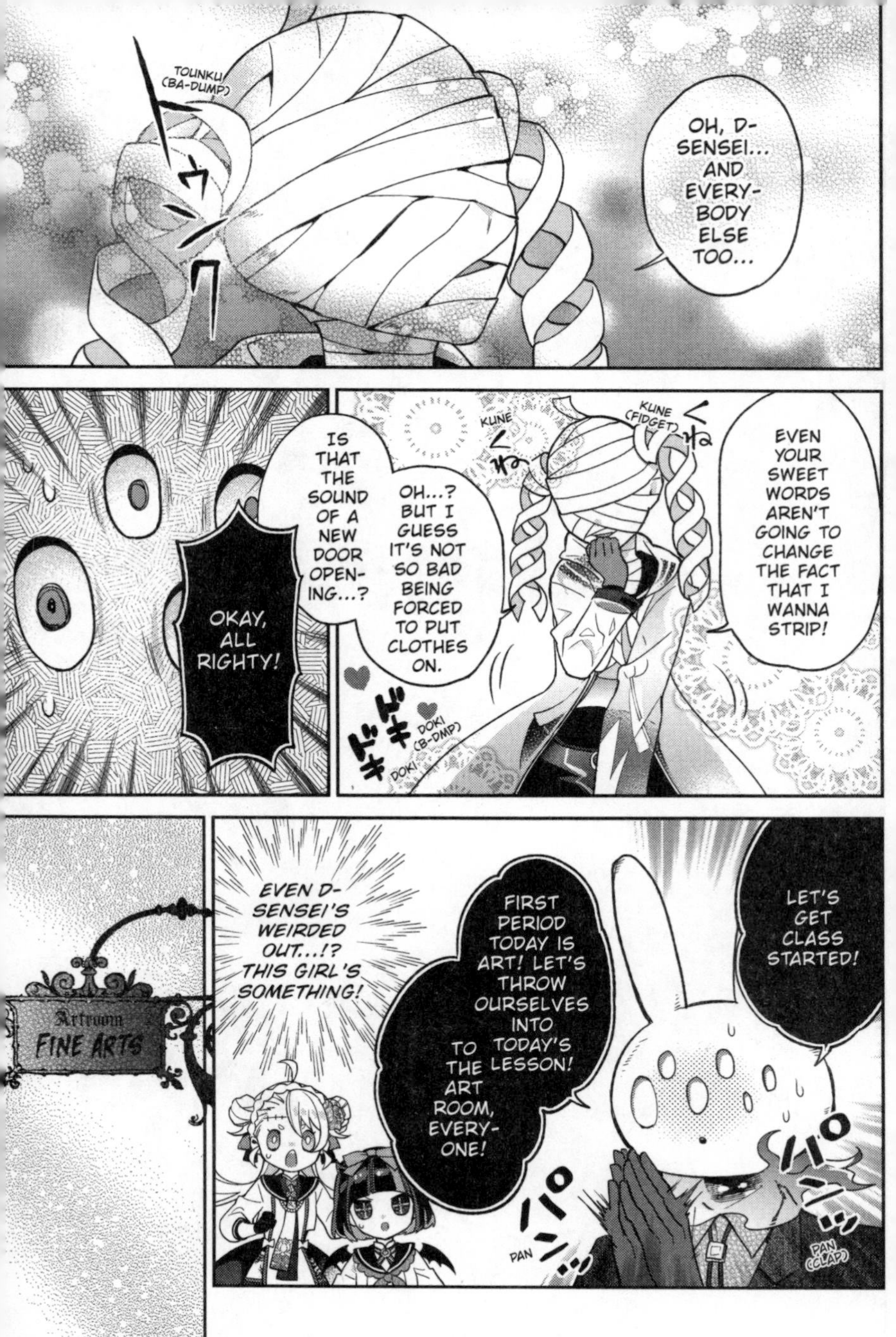
TOUNKU (BA-DUMP)
OH, D-SENSEI... AND EVERYBODY ELSE TOO...
EVEN YOUR SWEET WORDS AREN'T GOING TO CHANGE THE FACT THAT I WANNA STRIP!
KUNE (FIDGET)
KUNE
OH...? BUT I GUESS IT'S NOT SO BAD BEING FORCED TO PUT CLOTHES ON.
IS THAT THE SOUND OF A NEW DOOR OPENING...?
DOKI DOKI (B-DMP)
OKAY, ALL RIGHTY!
LET'S GET CLASS STARTED!
FIRST PERIOD TODAY IS ART! LET'S THROW OURSELVES INTO TODAY'S LESSON!
TO THE ART ROOM, EVERYONE!
PAN (CLAP)
PAN
EVEN D-SENSEI'S WEIRDED OUT...!? THIS GIRL'S SOMETHING!
Artroom
FINE ARTS

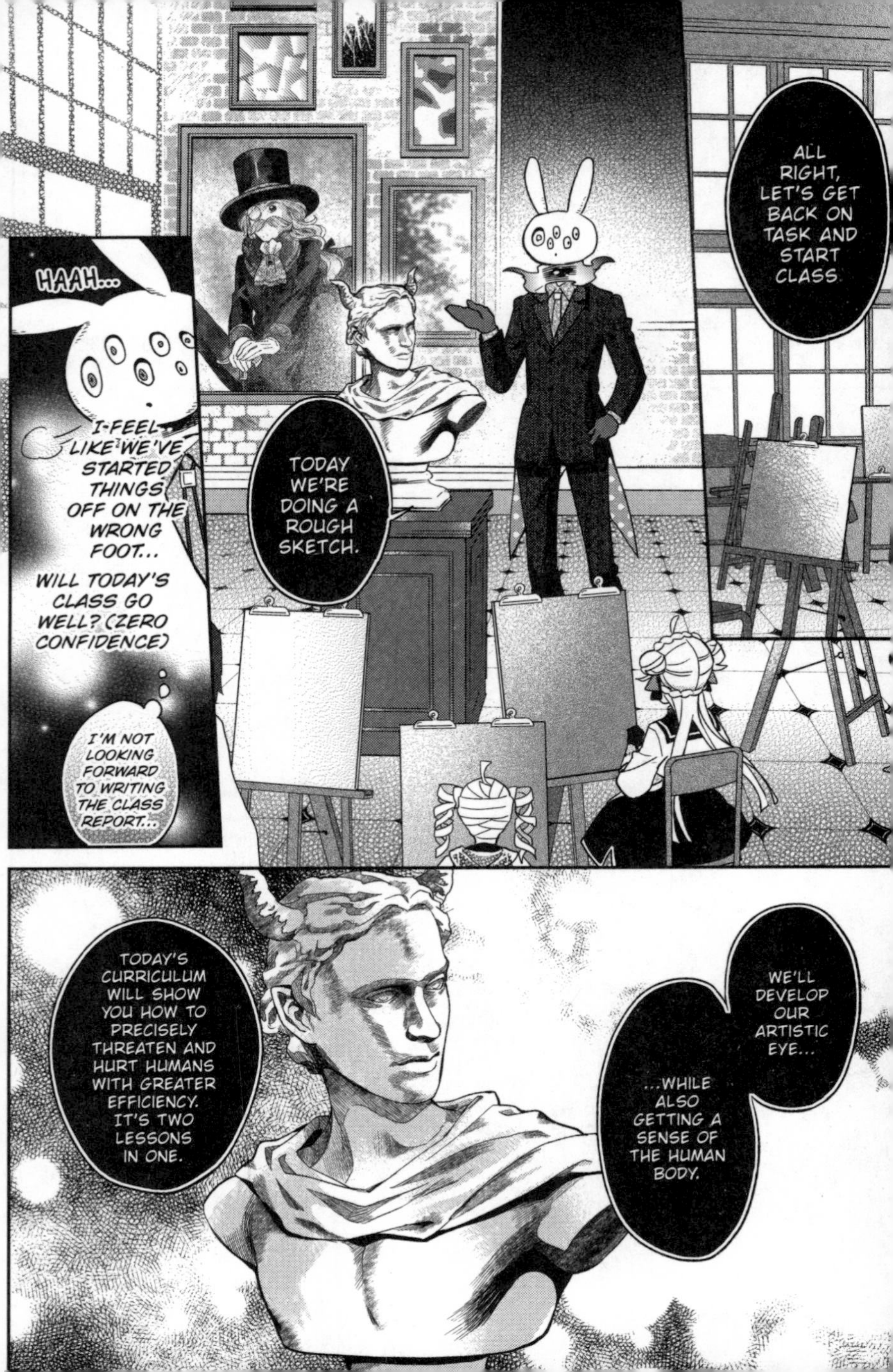
ALL RIGHT, LET'S GET BACK ON TASK AND START CLASS.
TODAY WE'RE DOING A ROUGH SKETCH.
HAAH...
I-FEEL LIKE WE'VE STARTED THINGS OFF ON THE WRONG FOOT...
WILL TODAY'S CLASS GO WELL? (ZERO CONFIDENCE)
I'M NOT LOOKING FORWARD TO WRITING THE CLASS REPORT...
TODAY'S CURRICULUM WILL SHOW YOU HOW TO PRECISELY THREATEN AND HURT HUMANS WITH GREATER EFFICIENCY. IT'S TWO LESSONS IN ONE.
WE'LL DEVELOP OUR ARTISTIC EYE...
...WHILE ALSO GETTING A SENSE OF THE HUMAN BODY.

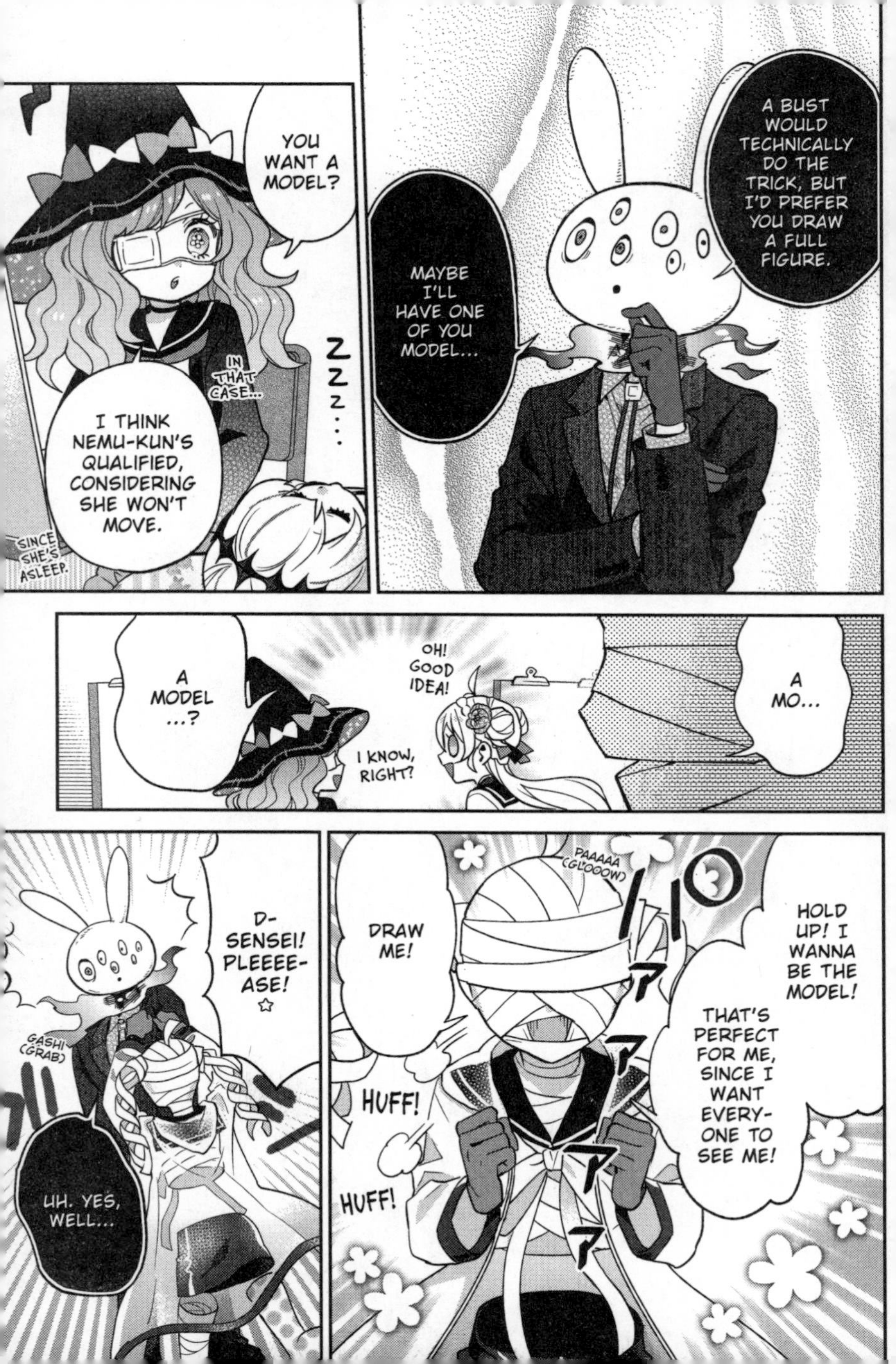
A BUST WOULD TECHNICALLY DO THE TRICK, BUT I'D PREFER YOU DRAW A FULL FIGURE.
MAYBE I'LL HAVE ONE OF YOU MODEL...
YOU WANT A MODEL?
ZZZ...
IN THAT CASE...
I THINK NEMU-KUN'S QUALIFIED, CONSIDERING SHE WON'T MOVE.
SINCE SHE'S ASLEEP.
A MO...
OH! GOOD IDEA!
I KNOW, RIGHT?
A MODEL ...?
PAAAAA (GLOOOW)
HOLD UP! I WANNA BE THE MODEL!
THAT'S PERFECT FOR ME, SINCE I WANT EVERY-ONE TO SEE ME!
DRAW ME!
HUFF!
HUFF!
D-SENSEI! PLEEEE-ASE! ☆
GASHI (GRAB)
UH. YES, WELL...

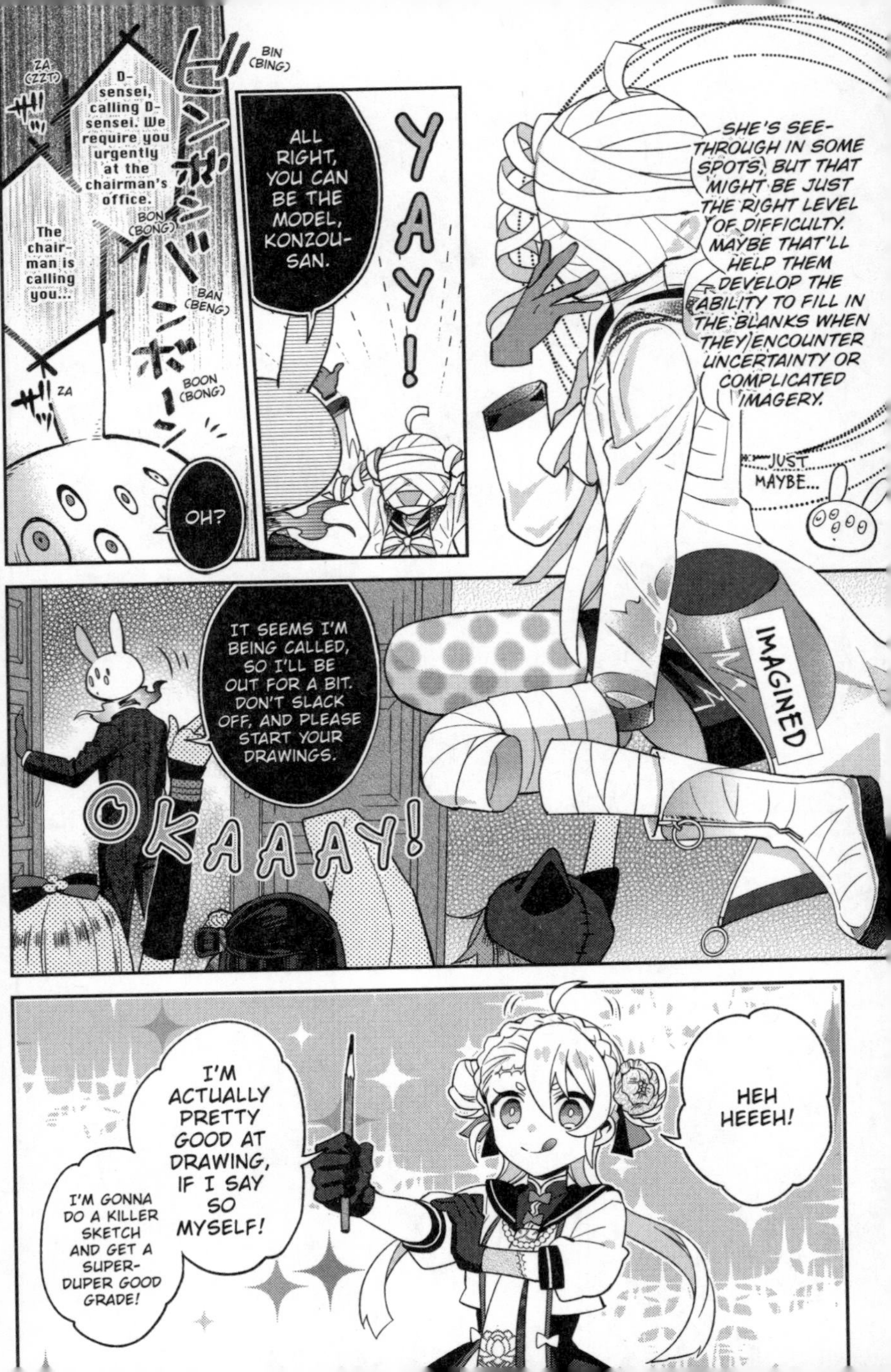
SHE'S SEE-THROUGH IN SOME SPOTS, BUT THAT MIGHT BE JUST THE RIGHT LEVEL OF DIFFICULTY. MAYBE THAT'LL HELP THEM DEVELOP THE ABILITY TO FILL IN THE BLANKS WHEN THEY ENCOUNTER UNCERTAINTY OR COMPLICATED IMAGERY.
...JUST MAYBE...
IMAGINED
ALL RIGHT, YOU CAN BE THE MODEL, KONZOU-SAN.
YAY!
OH?
BIN (BING)
BON (BONG)
BAN (BENG)
BOON (BONG)
ZA (ZZZT)
D-sensei, calling D-sensei. We require you urgently at the chairman's office.
The chair-man is calling you...
ZA
IT SEEMS I'M BEING CALLED, SO I'LL BE OUT FOR A BIT. DON'T SLACK OFF, AND PLEASE START YOUR DRAWINGS.
OKAAAY!
HEH HEEEH!
I'M ACTUALLY PRETTY GOOD AT DRAWING, IF I SAY SO MYSELF!
I'M GONNA DO A KILLER SKETCH AND GET A SUPER-DUPER GOOD GRADE!

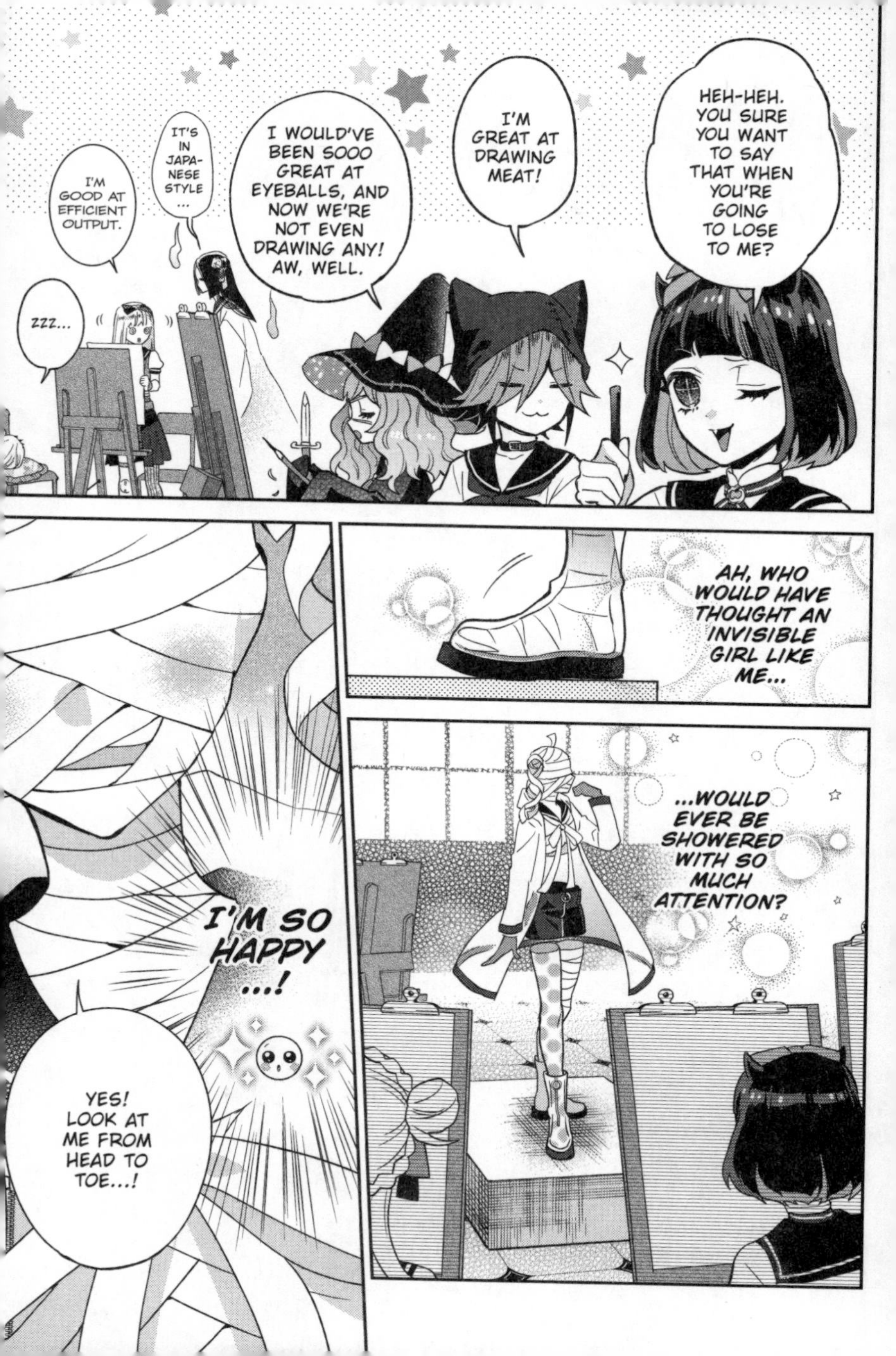
HEH-HEH. YOU SURE YOU WANT TO SAY THAT WHEN YOU'RE GOING TO LOSE TO ME?
I'M GREAT AT DRAWING MEAT!
I WOULD'VE BEEN SOOO GREAT AT EYEBALLS, AND NOW WE'RE NOT EVEN DRAWING ANY! AW, WELL.
IT'S IN JAPANESE STYLE...
I'M GOOD AT EFFICIENT OUTPUT.
ZZZ...
AH, WHO WOULD HAVE THOUGHT AN INVISIBLE GIRL LIKE ME...
...WOULD EVER BE SHOWERED WITH SO MUCH ATTENTION?
I'M SO HAPPY ...!
YES! LOOK AT ME FROM HEAD TO TOE...!

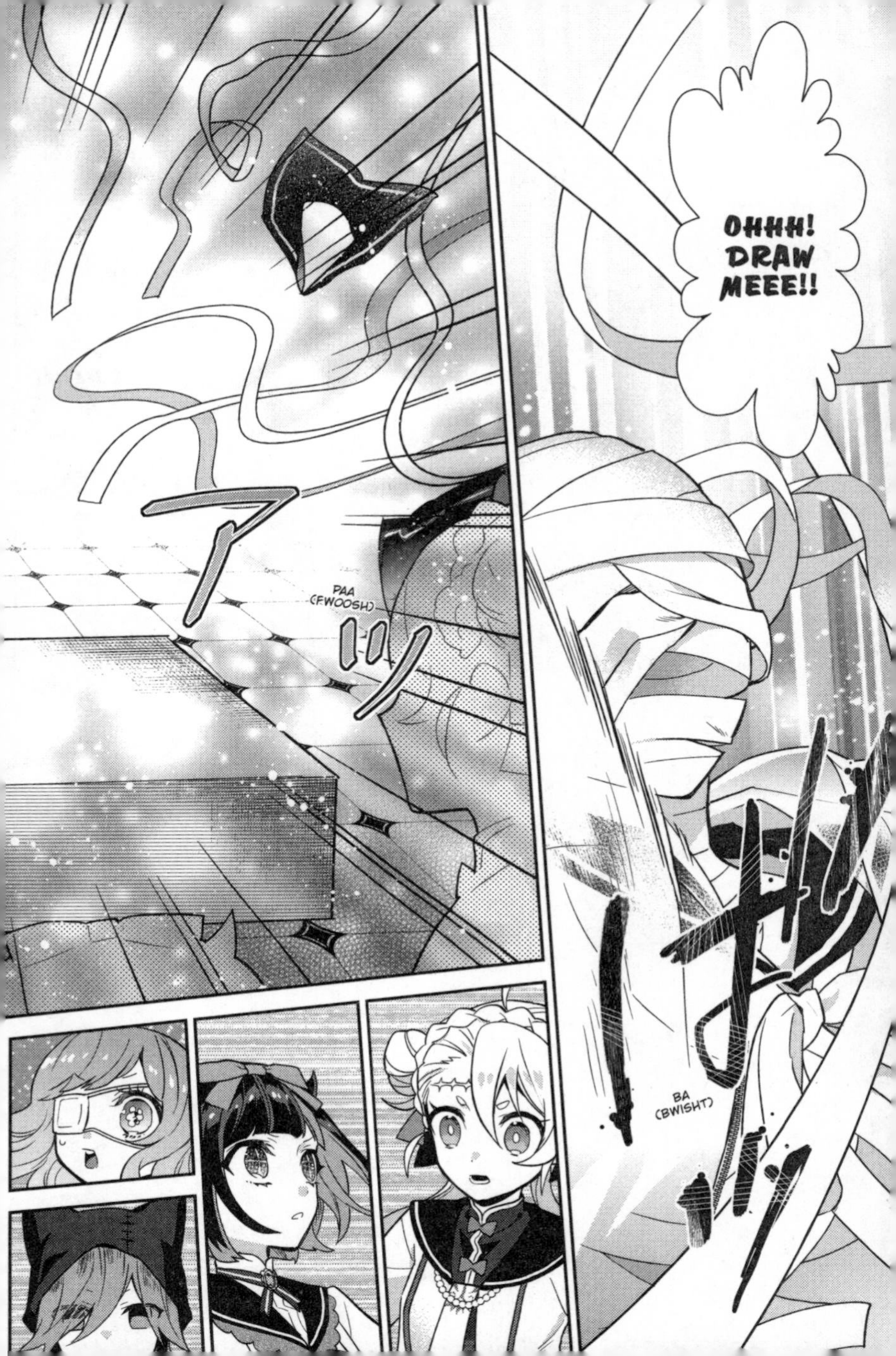
OHHH! DRAW MEEE!!
BA (BWISHT)
PAA (FWOOSH)

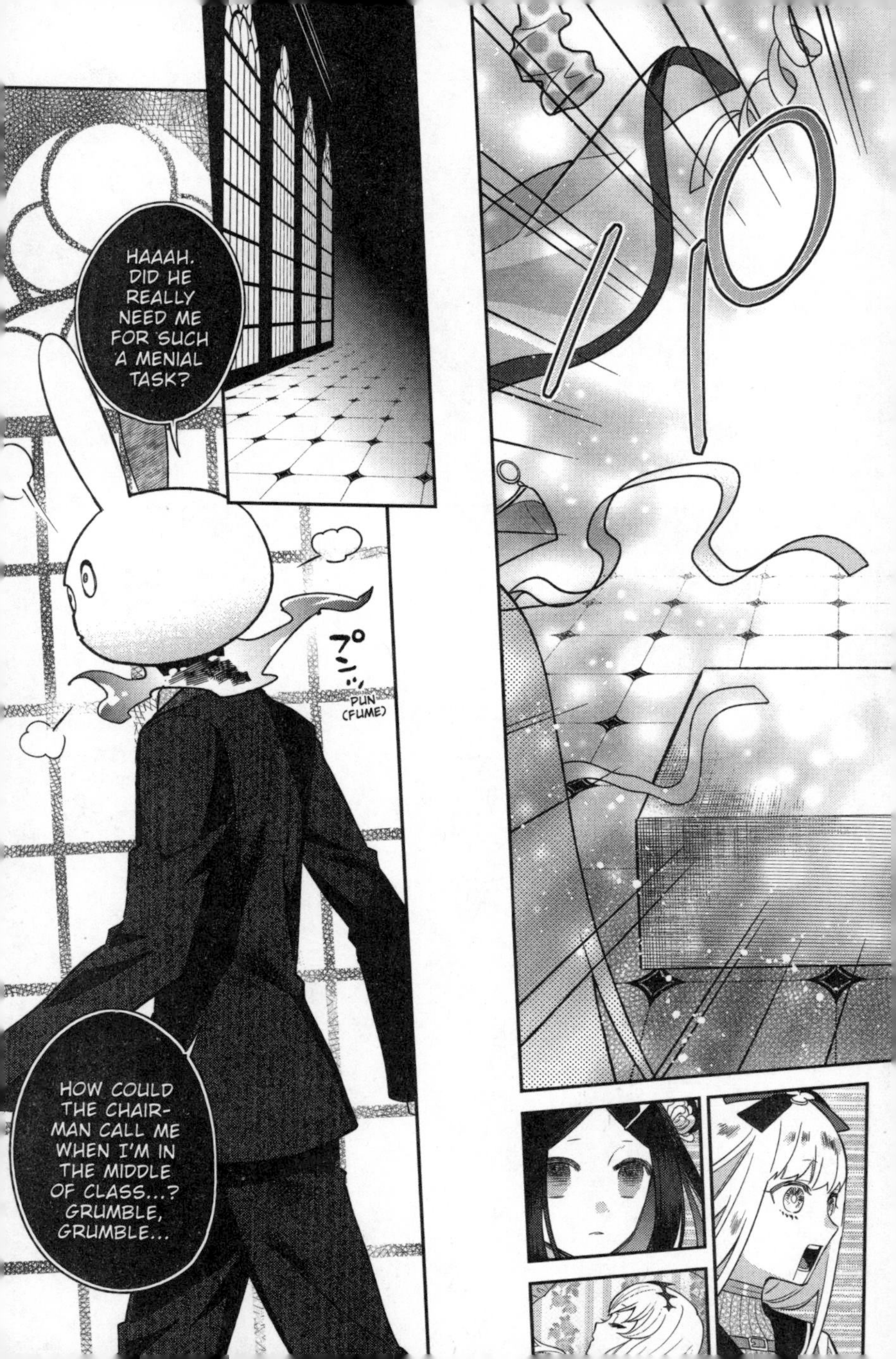
HAAAH. DID HE REALLY NEED ME FOR SUCH A MENIAL TASK?
プンッ
PUN (FUME)
HOW COULD THE CHAIR-MAN CALL ME WHEN I'M IN THE MIDDLE OF CLASS...? GRUMBLE, GRUMBLE...

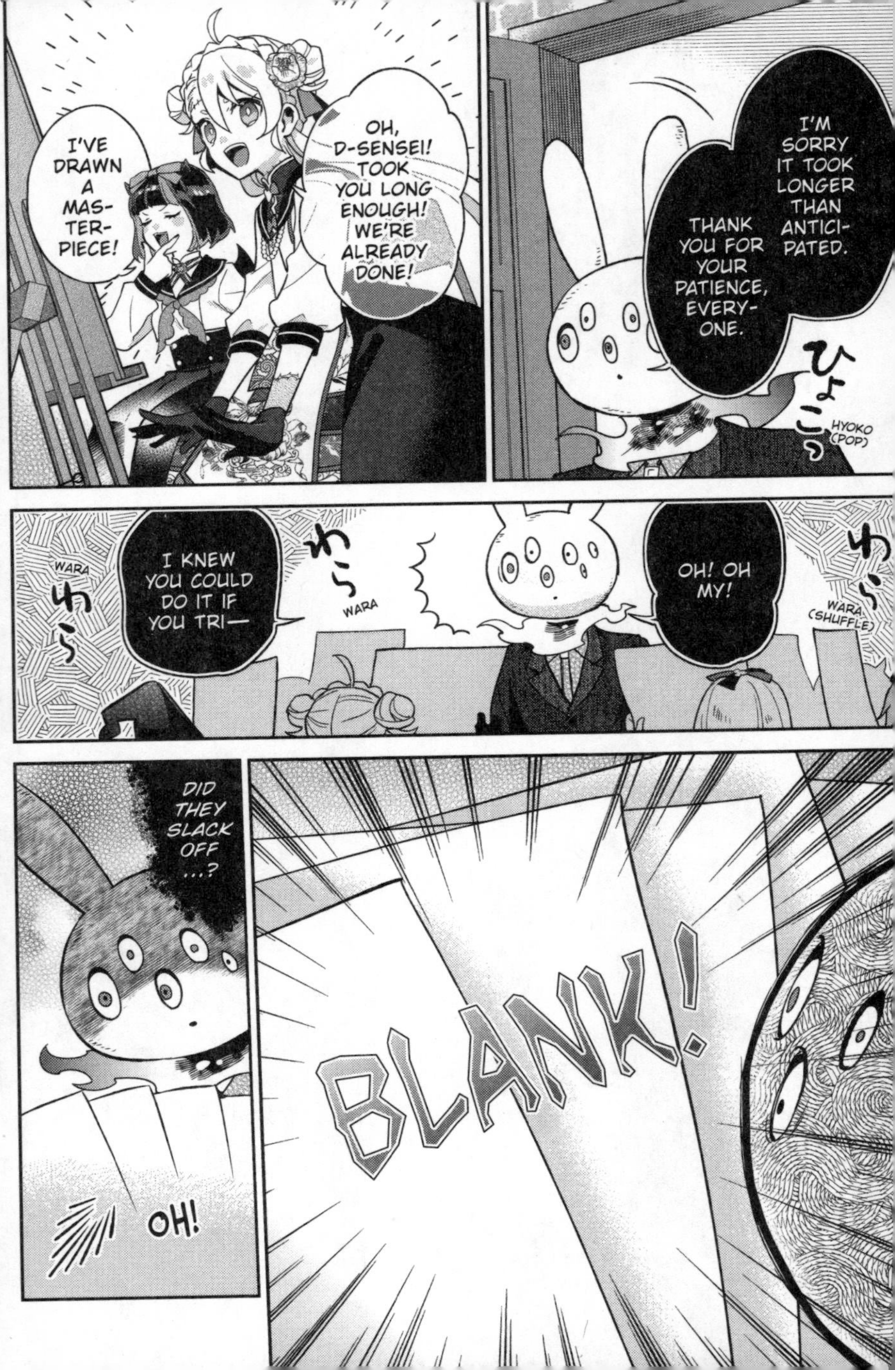
I'M SORRY IT TOOK LONGER THAN ANTICI-PATED.
THANK YOU FOR YOUR PATIENCE, EVERY-ONE.
ひょこっ
HYOKO (POP)
OH, D-SENSEI! TOOK YOU LONG ENOUGH! WE'RE ALREADY DONE!
I'VE DRAWN A MAS-TER-PIECE!
わら
WARA (SHUFFLE)
OH! OH MY!
わら
WARA
I KNEW YOU COULD DO IT IF YOU TRI—
わら
WARA
BLANK!
DID THEY SLACK OFF ...?
OH!

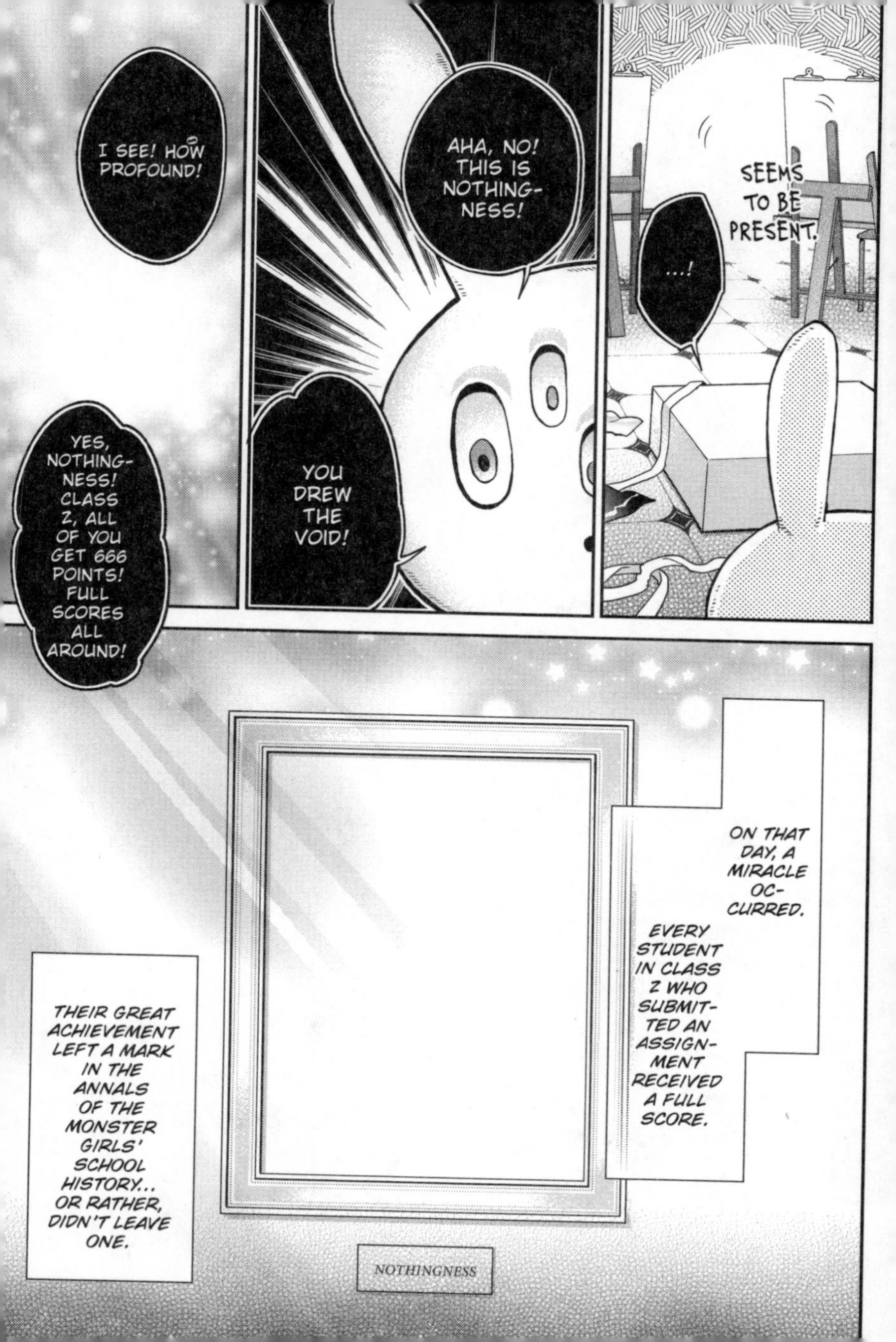
SEEMS TO BE PRESENT.
...!
AHA, NO! THIS IS NOTHINGNESS!
YOU DREW THE VOID!
I SEE! HOW PROFOUND!
YES, NOTHINGNESS! CLASS Z, ALL OF YOU GET 666 POINTS! FULL SCORES ALL AROUND!
ON THAT DAY, A MIRACLE OCCURRED.
EVERY STUDENT IN CLASS Z WHO SUBMITTED AN ASSIGNMENT RECEIVED A FULL SCORE.
NOTHINGNESS
THEIR GREAT ACHIEVEMENT LEFT A MARK IN THE ANNALS OF THE MONSTER GIRLS' SCHOOL HISTORY... OR RATHER, DIDN'T LEAVE ONE.

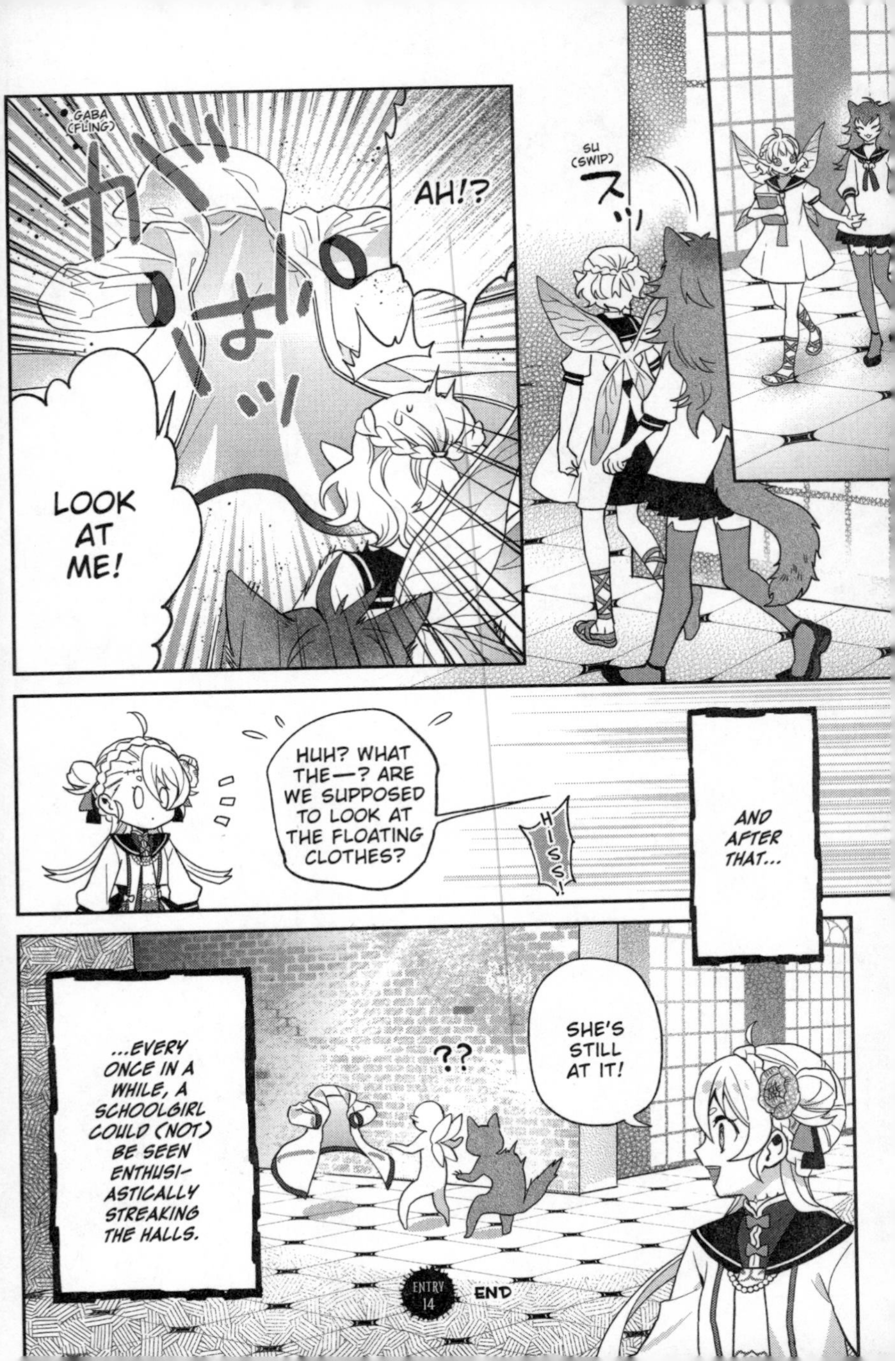
SU (SWIP)
ス
GABA (FLING)
AH!?
LOOK AT ME!
AND AFTER THAT...
HISS!
HUH? WHAT THE—? ARE WE SUPPOSED TO LOOK AT THE FLOATING CLOTHES?
SHE'S STILL AT IT!
??
...EVERY ONCE IN A WHILE, A SCHOOLGIRL COULD (NOT) BE SEEN ENTHUSI-ASTICALLY STREAKING THE HALLS.
ENTRY 14 END

Monster Girls' School

Class Report

Monster Year: 20020 Month: Slack Day: 49th | Homeroom Class Z | Teacher D | Teacher Species Dullahan

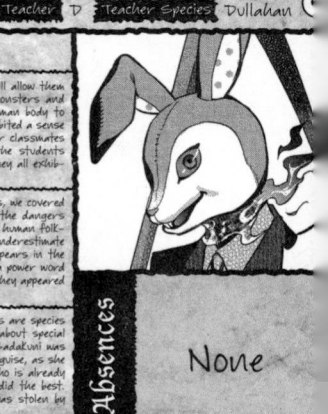

Classes and such

	Subject	Studied Material
1st Period	Art	They learned about sketching the monster body. This will allow them to cultivate the artistic sensibilities required of elite monsters and will also help them understand the workings of the human body to better subject it to pain. Konzou, who was the model, exhibited a sense of selflessness and generously posed fully nude for her classmates (which I did not see, since she's invisible). Although the students learned nothing about anatomy (since she's invisible), they all exhibited their latent artistic talents.
2nd Period	Theory of Trans-mogistry	In order to build upon their repertoire of scaring tactics, we covered transmogrifying of self and others, and they learned the dangers of inviting their teacher's wrath. I attempted to use the human folktale "Crackle Mountain" to drive home that they cannot underestimate the humans. However, it seems the power food that appears in the story—the granny stew—turned into something of a power word for them that stimulated their appetites for lunch, and they appeared to absorb nothing from the lesson.
3rd Period	Applied Trans-mogistry	We put theory into practice. But as none of the students are species that have transfiguration abilities, we instead learned about special effects makeup and techniques for disguising oneself. Sadakuni was several steps ahead of everyone else when it came to disguise, as she could exchange her body parts. But of course Kikuno, who is already see-through, and Konzou, who is entirely see-through, did the best. (In addition, it seems Sadakuni's replacement eyeball was stolen by a thief after class.)
4th Period	Monster World History	We learned about the dragon who accidentally turned the skin of a human (Siegfried) invincible after bleeding all over him. Using the dragon's bloodcurdling story as an example of what not to do, I tried to instill in my students that they should always fall backward when dying. This requires turning around before bleeding on one's opponent after being cut, which was of course too difficult. Instead of cutting their losses, the students themselves were cut up.
5th Period	Home Ec	We did a practical cooking exercise. In order to recover from the failure that was second and third period, I had them make and eat raccoon-dog soup—in other words, I wanted them to get a taste of failure. However, they seemed to have taken a liking to the raccoon dog's dialogue in "Crackle Mountain" and wouldn't stop taunting each other with the line, "You ate the granny stew! You ate the granny stew!" In the end, they never learned not to underestimate humans. I should have done this lesson during second period.
6th Period	X	X

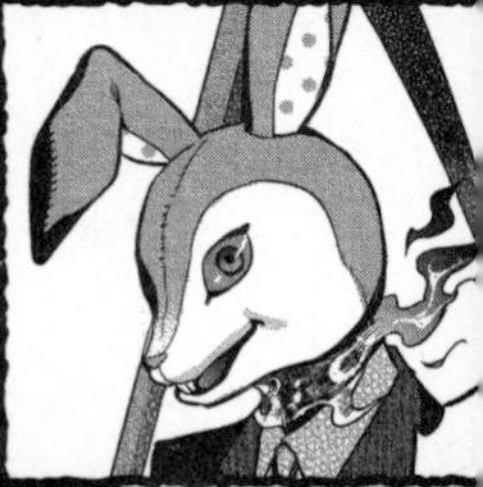

Absences	None
Tardies	None
Left Early	None
Permitted Absences	None

Special Mentions (Goals, worries, etc.)

I would like to ask that you please refrain from calling teachers away during important class time. However, it did help me today, as this saved me from seeing one of the students in the nude (though I wouldn't have been able to see her anyway).

Today's exemplary students

Name and affiliation	All
Method	
Reason	A new wind rises in the world of monster modern art

Photo evidence section

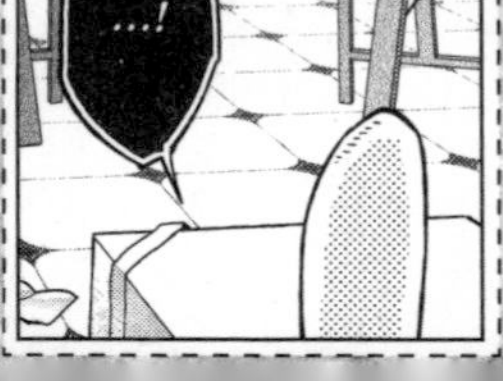
...!

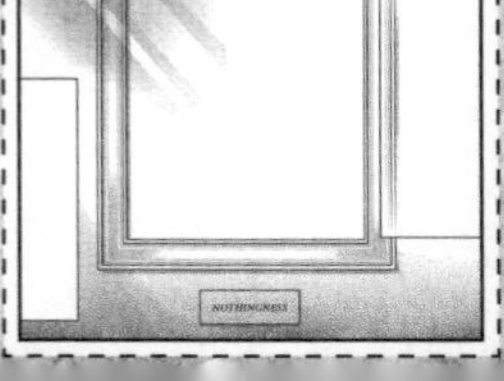
NOTHINGNESS

Supplemental Lesson Manga ENTRY 1

HAH—
HAH—
HAH
...
?
HAAA-CHOO!
べちょ
BECHO (SPLATCH)
びちょ
BICHO (SPLITCH)
SPIT!?
PUT ON SOME CLOTHES IF YOU'RE COLD!
DO I HAVE TO?

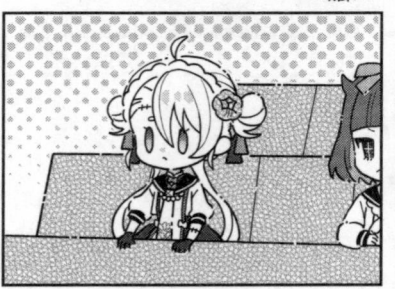

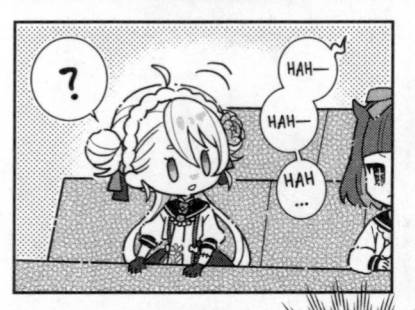

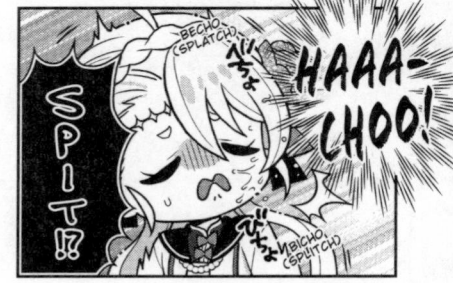

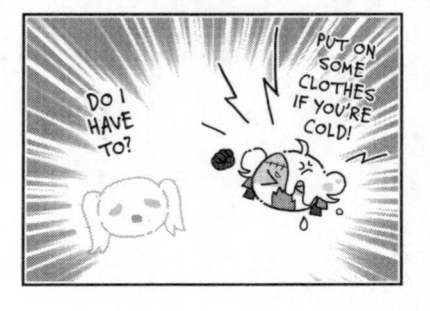

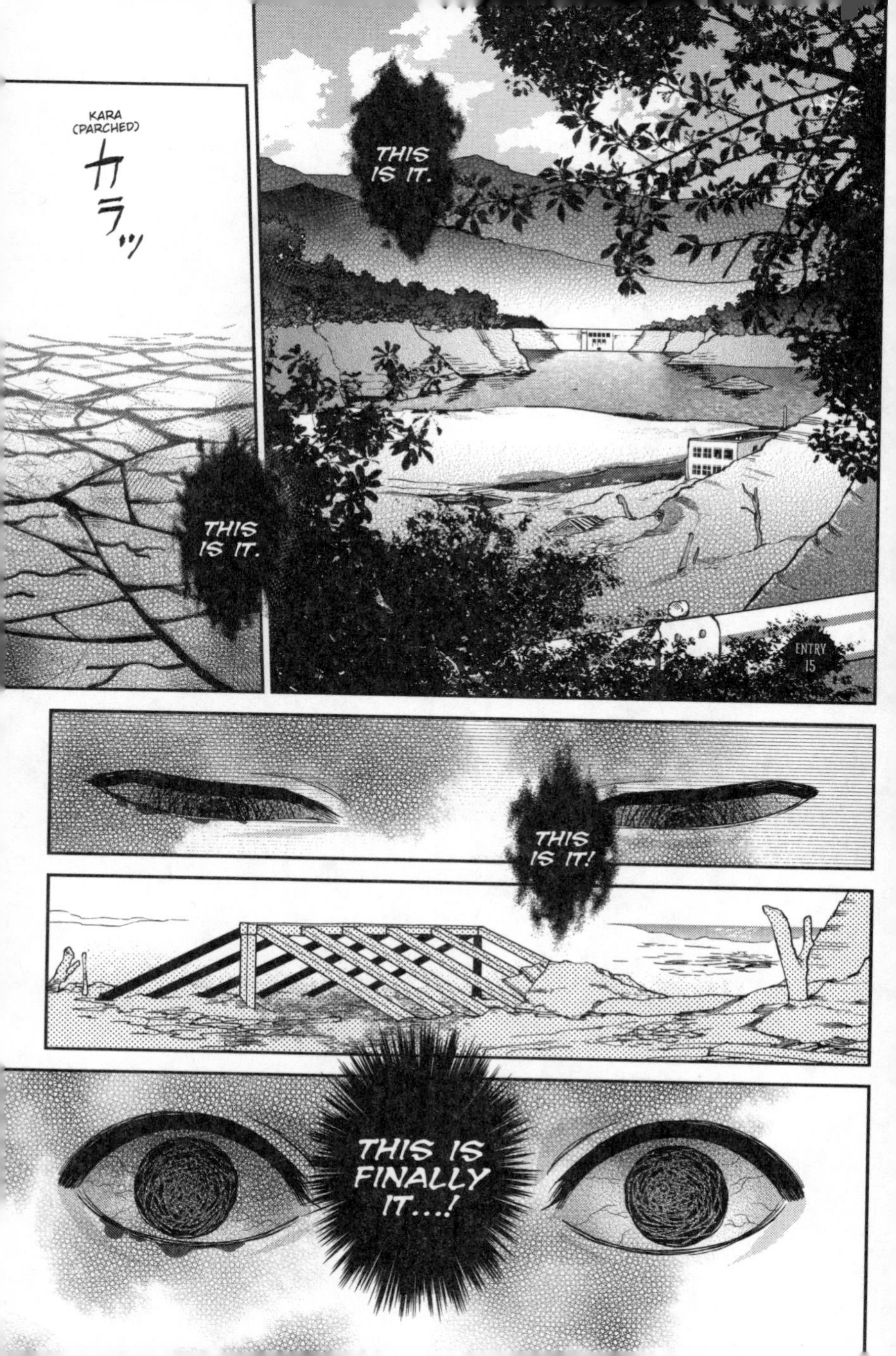
THIS IS IT.
ENTRY 15
KARA (PARCHED)
カラッ
THIS IS IT.
THIS IS IT!
THIS IS FINALLY IT...!

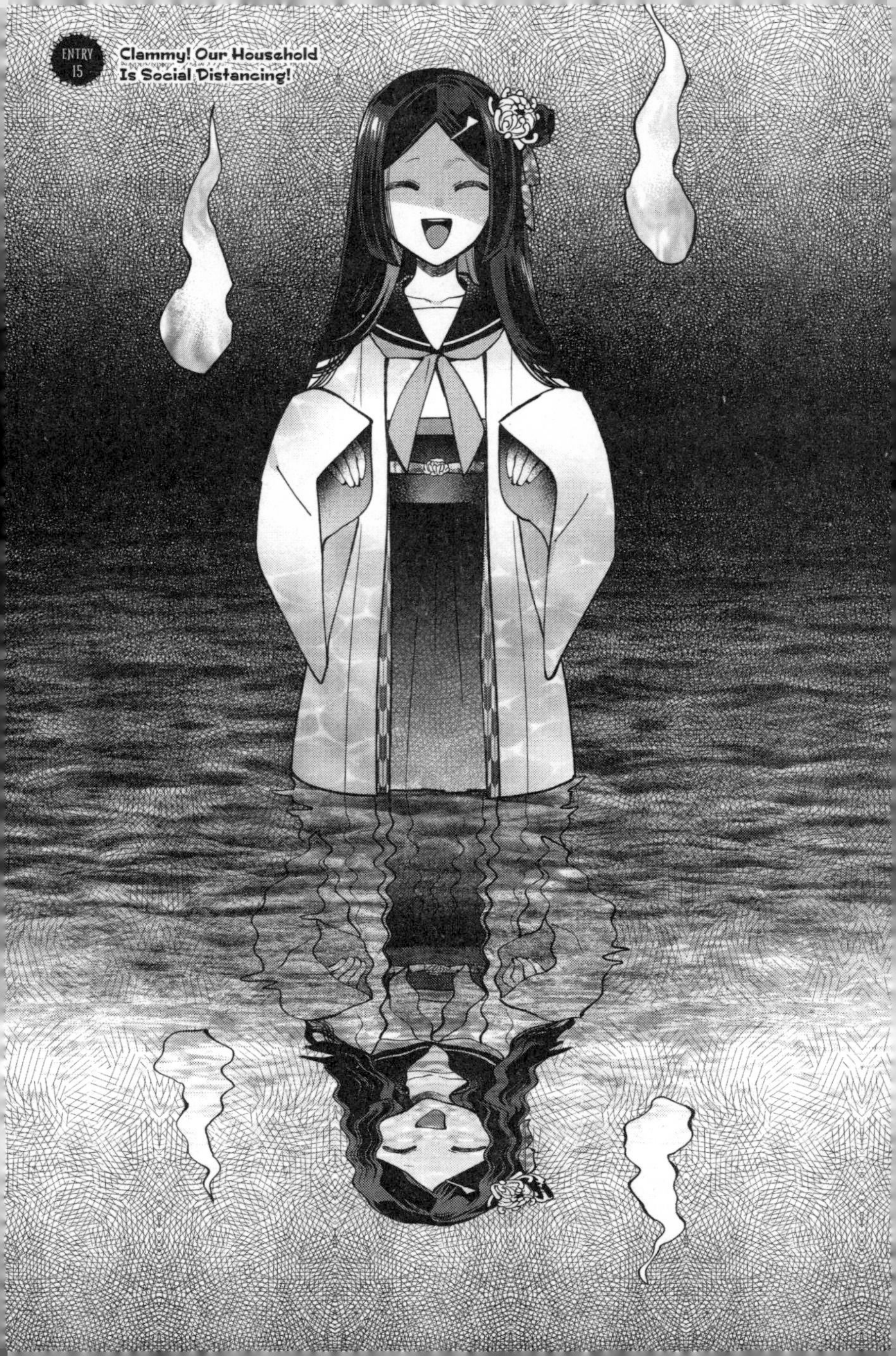
ENTRY 15
Clammy! Our Household Is Social Distancing!

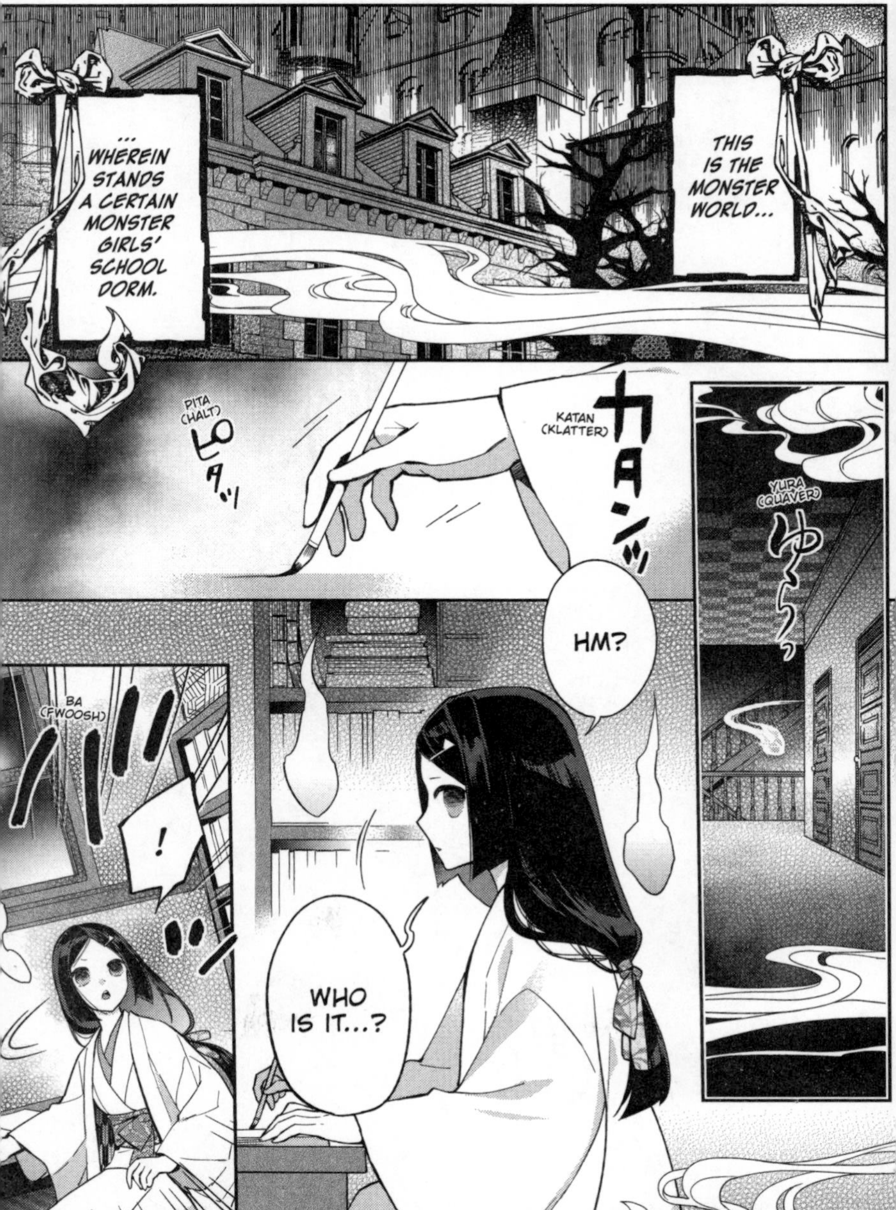
THIS IS THE MONSTER WORLD...
...WHEREIN STANDS A CERTAIN MONSTER GIRLS' SCHOOL DORM.
YURA (QUAVER)
KATAN (KLATTER)
PITA (HALT)
HM?
!
BA (FWOOSH)
WHO IS IT...?

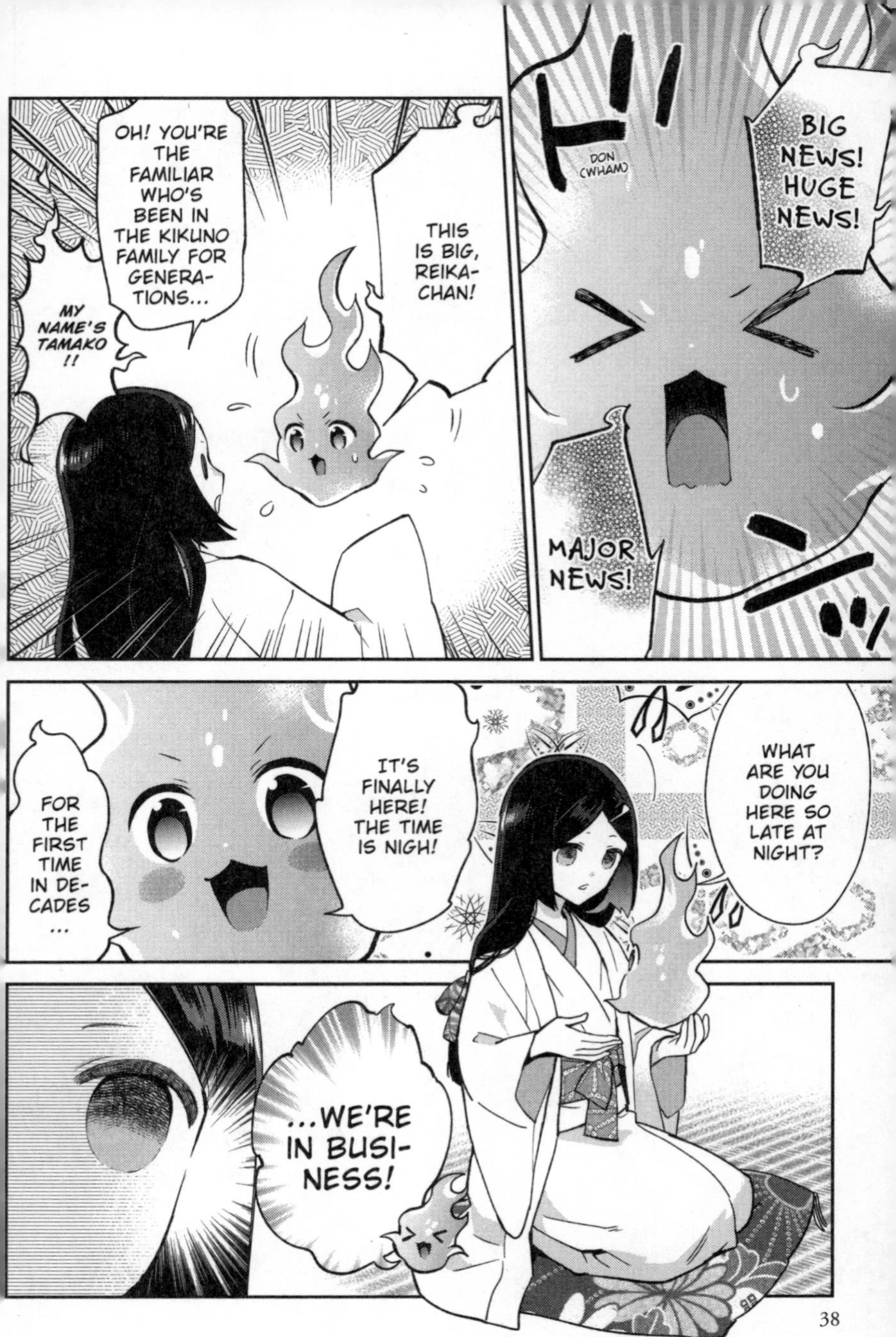
BIG NEWS! HUGE NEWS!
DON (WHAM)
MAJOR NEWS!
THIS IS BIG, REIKA-CHAN!
OH! YOU'RE THE FAMILIAR WHO'S BEEN IN THE KIKUNO FAMILY FOR GENERA-TIONS...
MY NAME'S TAMAKO!!
WHAT ARE YOU DOING HERE SO LATE AT NIGHT?
IT'S FINALLY HERE! THE TIME IS NIGH!
FOR THE FIRST TIME IN DE-CADES...
...WE'RE IN BUSI-NESS!

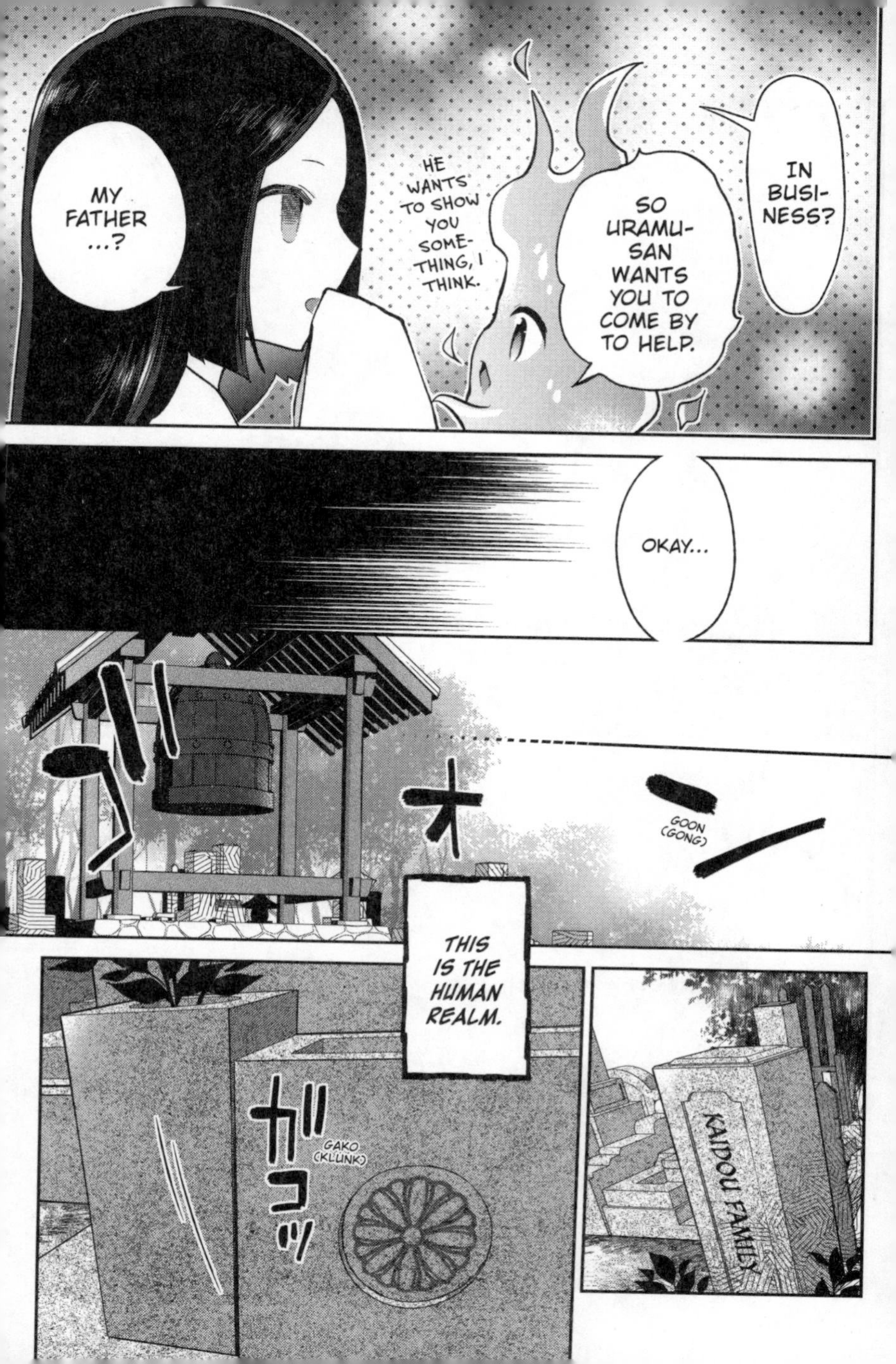
IN BUSI-NESS?
SO URAMU-SAN WANTS YOU TO COME BY TO HELP.
HE WANTS TO SHOW YOU SOME-THING, I THINK.
MY FATHER ...?
OKAY...
GOON (GONG)
THIS IS THE HUMAN REALM.
GAKO (KLUNK)
KAIDOU FAMILY

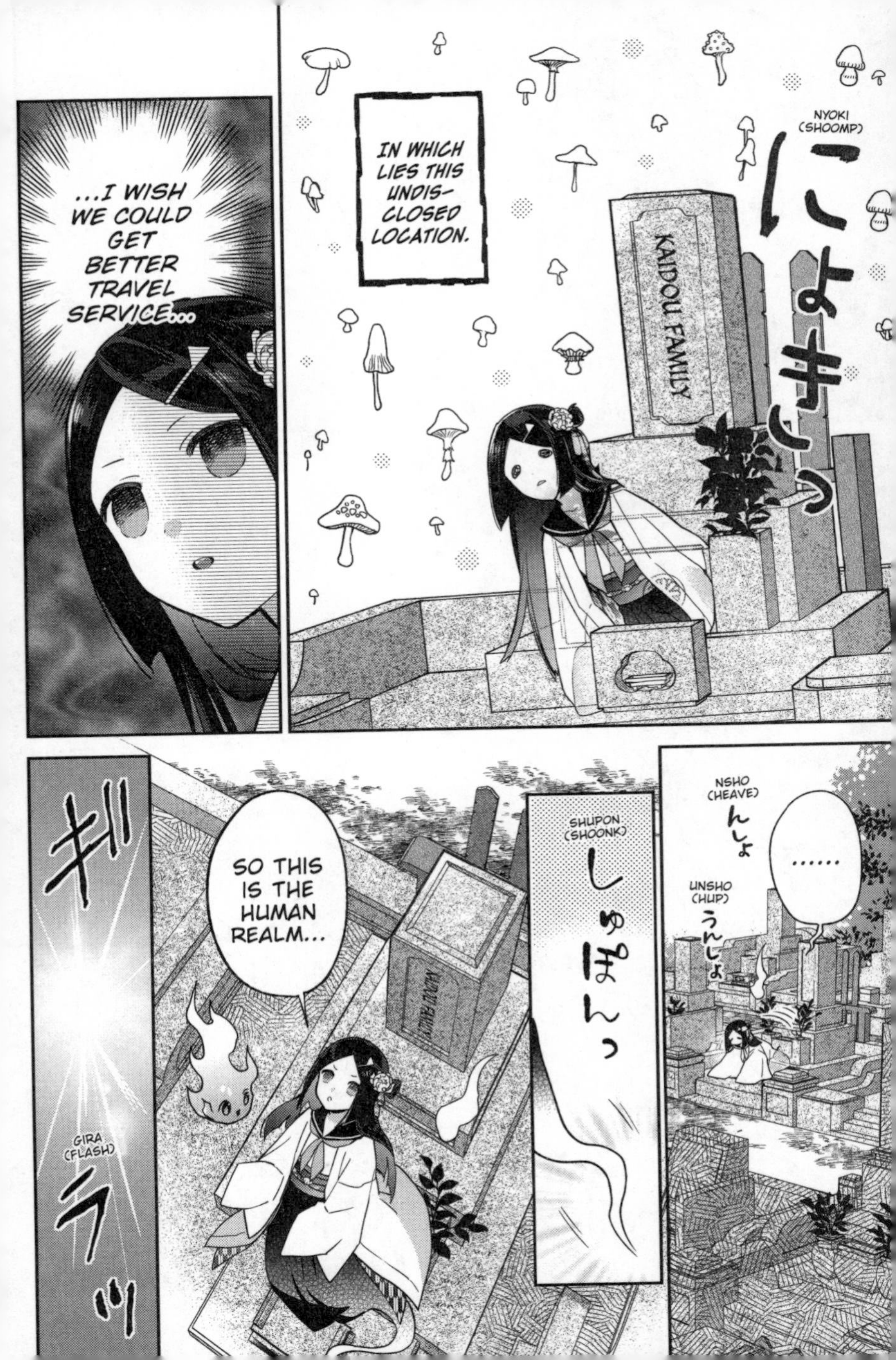
NYOKI (SHOOMP)
にょきっ
KAIDOU FAMILY
IN WHICH LIES THIS UNDIS-CLOSED LOCATION.
...I WISH WE COULD GET BETTER TRAVEL SERVICE...
......
NSHO (HEAVE)
んしょ
UNSHO (HUP)
うんしょ
SHUPON (SHOONK)
しゅぽんっ
SO THIS IS THE HUMAN REALM...
GIRA (FLASH)
ギラッ

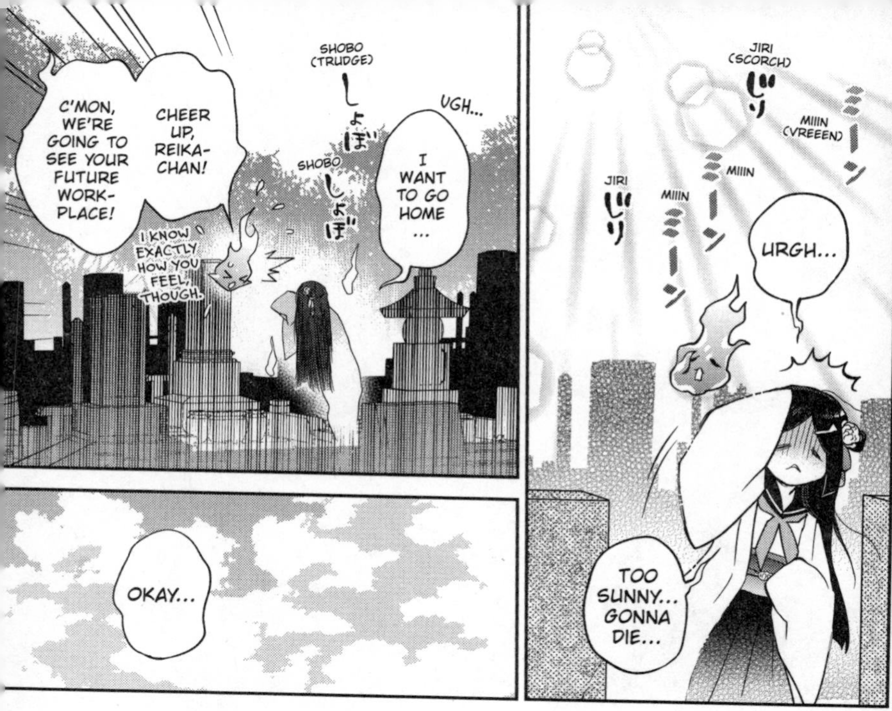
JIRI (SCORCH)
じり
MIIIN (VREEEN)
ミーン
MIIIN
ミーン
JIRI
じり
MIIIN
ミーン
URGH...
TOO SUNNY... GONNA DIE...
C'MON, WE'RE GOING TO SEE YOUR FUTURE WORK-PLACE!
CHEER UP, REIKA-CHAN!
I KNOW EXACTLY HOW YOU FEEL, THOUGH.
SHOBO (TRUDGE)
しょぼ
SHOBO
しょぼ
UGH...
I WANT TO GO HOME ...
OKAY...
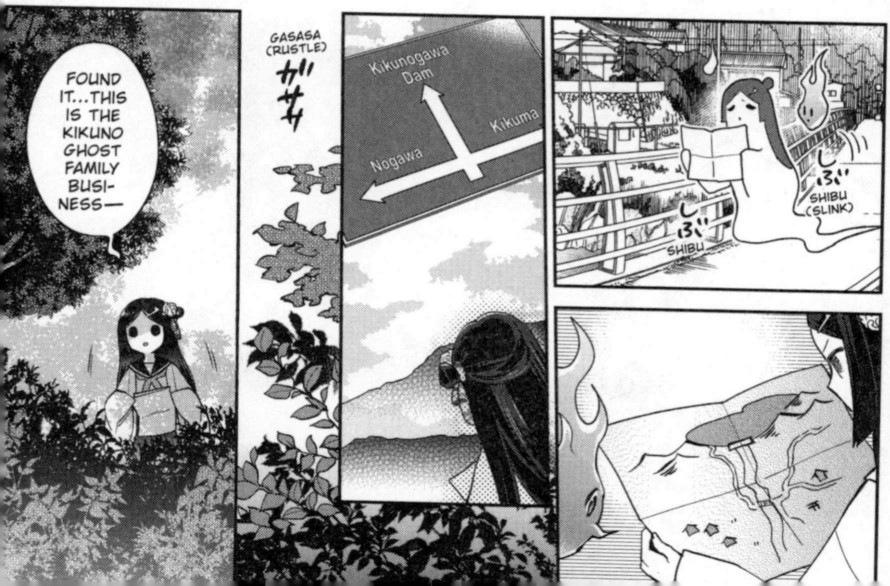
しぶ
SHIBU (SLINK)
しぶ
SHIBU
Kikunogawa Dam
Kikuma
Nogawa
GASASA (RUSTLE)
がサ
FOUND IT...THIS IS THE KIKUNO GHOST FAMILY BUSI-NESS—

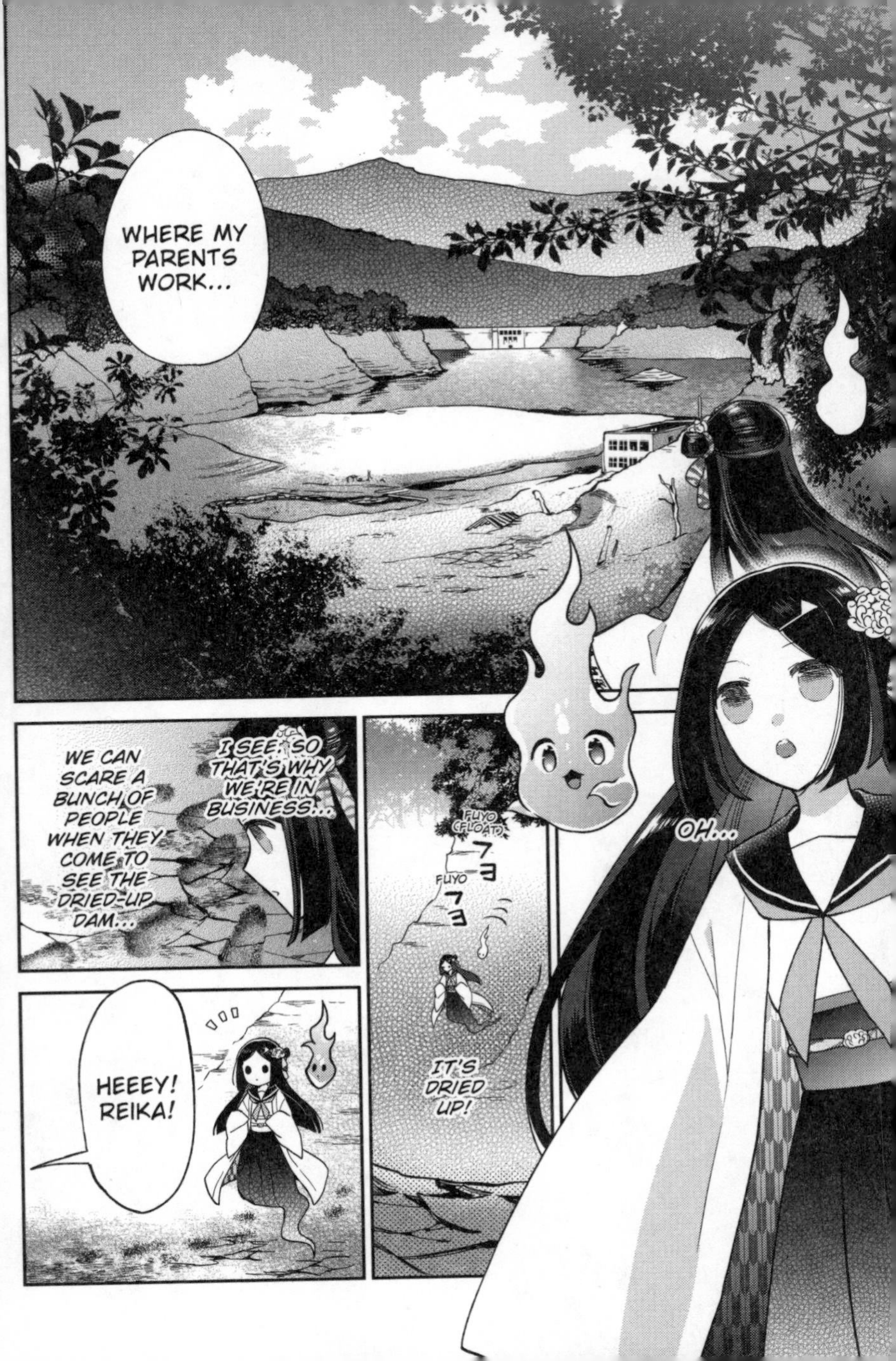
WHERE MY PARENTS WORK...
OH...
FUYO (FLOAT) フヨ
FUYO フヨ
IT'S DRIED UP!
I SEE. SO THAT'S WHY WE'RE IN BUSINESS...
WE CAN SCARE A BUNCH OF PEOPLE WHEN THEY COME TO SEE THE DRIED-UP DAM...
HEEEY! REIKA!

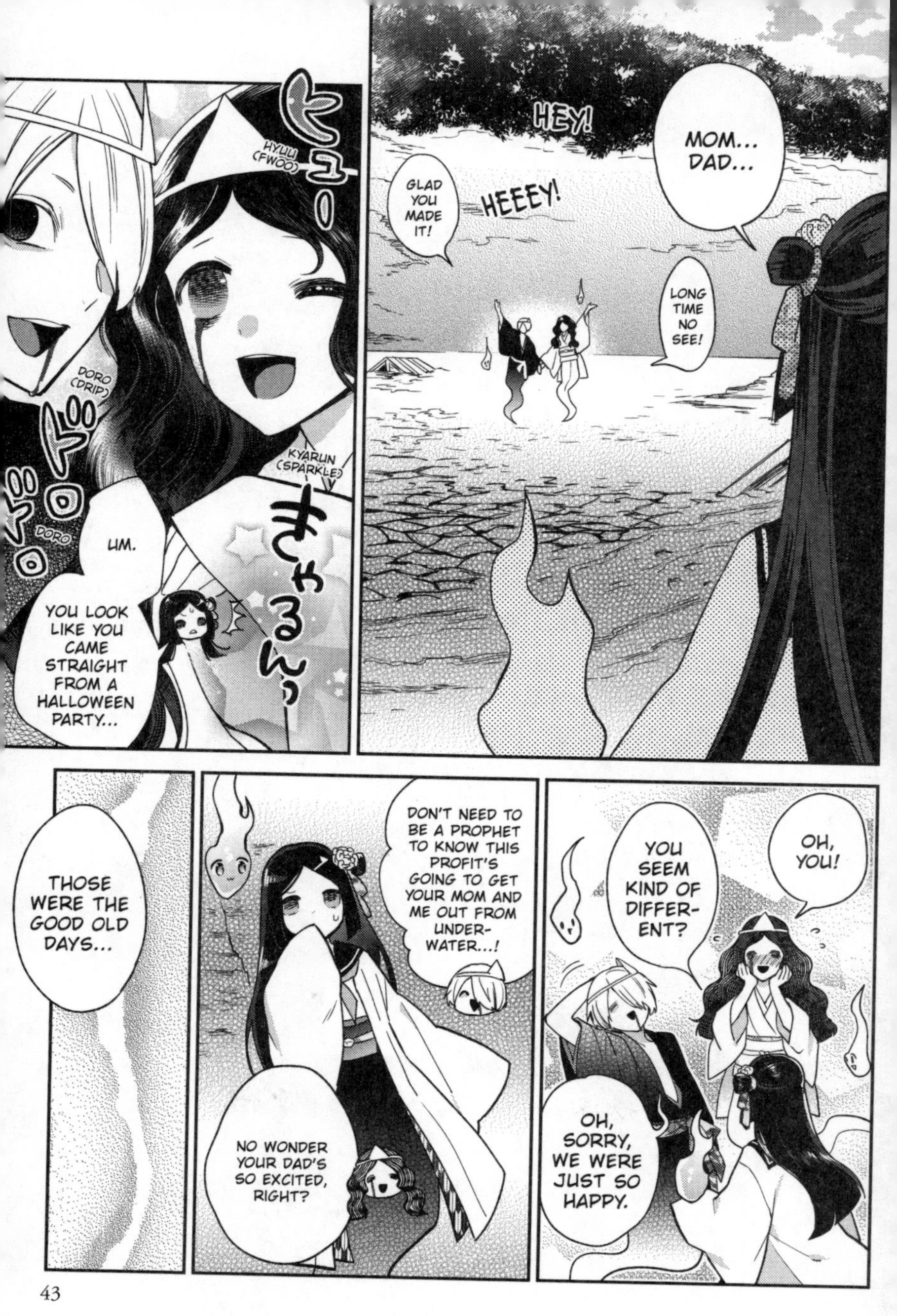
MOM... DAD...
HEY!
HEEEY!
GLAD YOU MADE IT!
LONG TIME NO SEE!
ヒュー
HYULI (FWOO)
ドロドロ
DORO (DRIP)
DORO
KYARUN (SPARKLE)
きゃるん
UM.
YOU LOOK LIKE YOU CAME STRAIGHT FROM A HALLOWEEN PARTY...
OH, YOU!
YOU SEEM KIND OF DIFFER-ENT?
OH, SORRY, WE WERE JUST SO HAPPY.
DON'T NEED TO BE A PROPHET TO KNOW THIS PROFIT'S GOING TO GET YOUR MOM AND ME OUT FROM UNDER-WATER...!
NO WONDER YOUR DAD'S SO EXCITED, RIGHT?
THOSE WERE THE GOOD OLD DAYS...

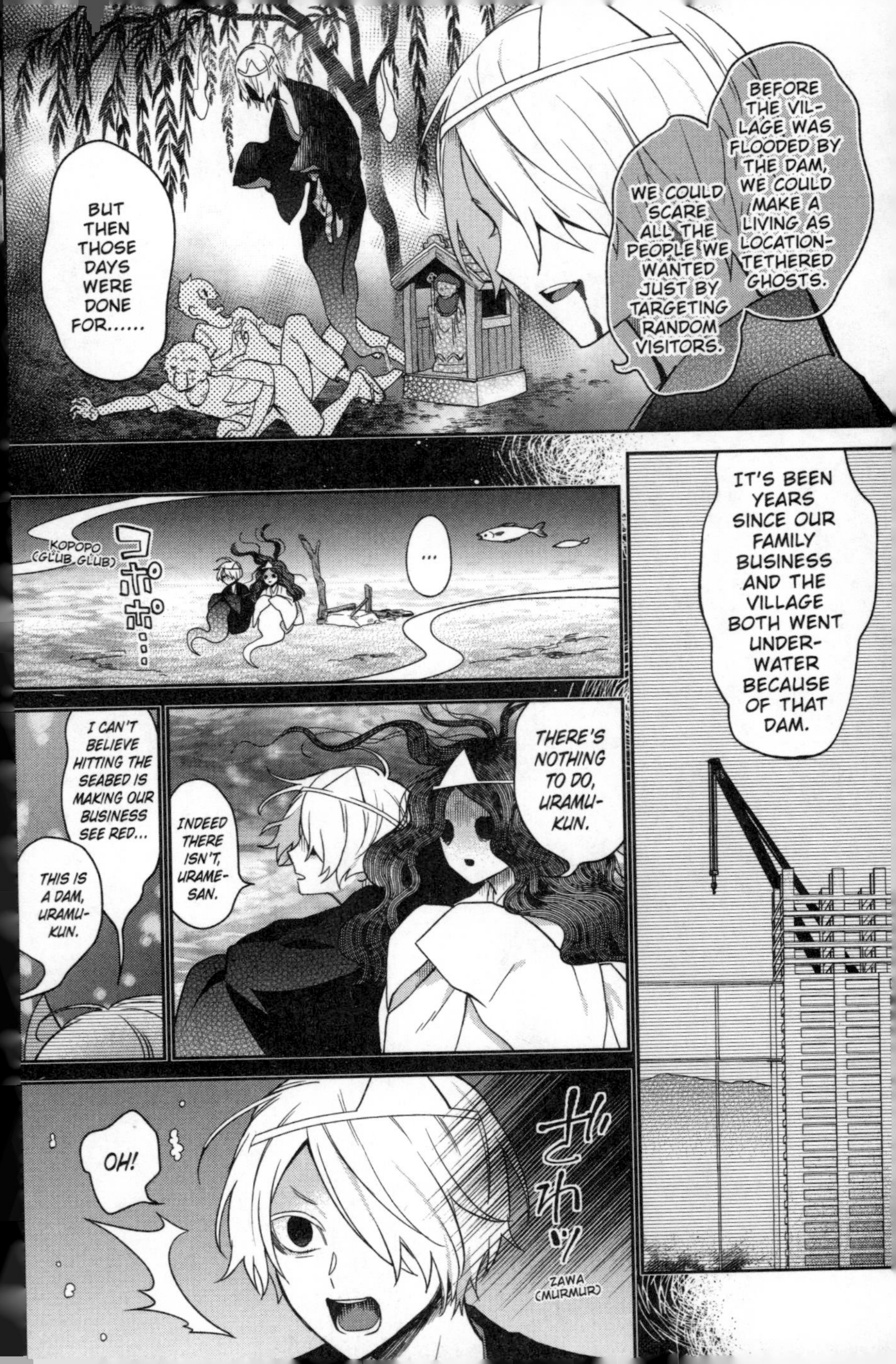
BEFORE THE VIL-LAGE WAS FLOODED BY THE DAM, WE COULD MAKE A LIVING AS LOCATION-TETHERED GHOSTS.
WE COULD SCARE ALL THE PEOPLE WE WANTED JUST BY TARGETING RANDOM VISITORS.
BUT THEN THOSE DAYS WERE DONE FOR......
IT'S BEEN YEARS SINCE OUR FAMILY BUSINESS AND THE VILLAGE BOTH WENT UNDER-WATER BECAUSE OF THAT DAM.
...
コポポ...
KOPOPO (GLUB GLUB)
THERE'S NOTHING TO DO, URAMU-KUN.
INDEED THERE ISN'T, URAME-SAN.
I CAN'T BELIEVE HITTING THE SEABED IS MAKING OUR BUSINESS SEE RED...
THIS IS A DAM, URAMU-KUN.
ざわッ
ZAWA (MURMUR)
OH!

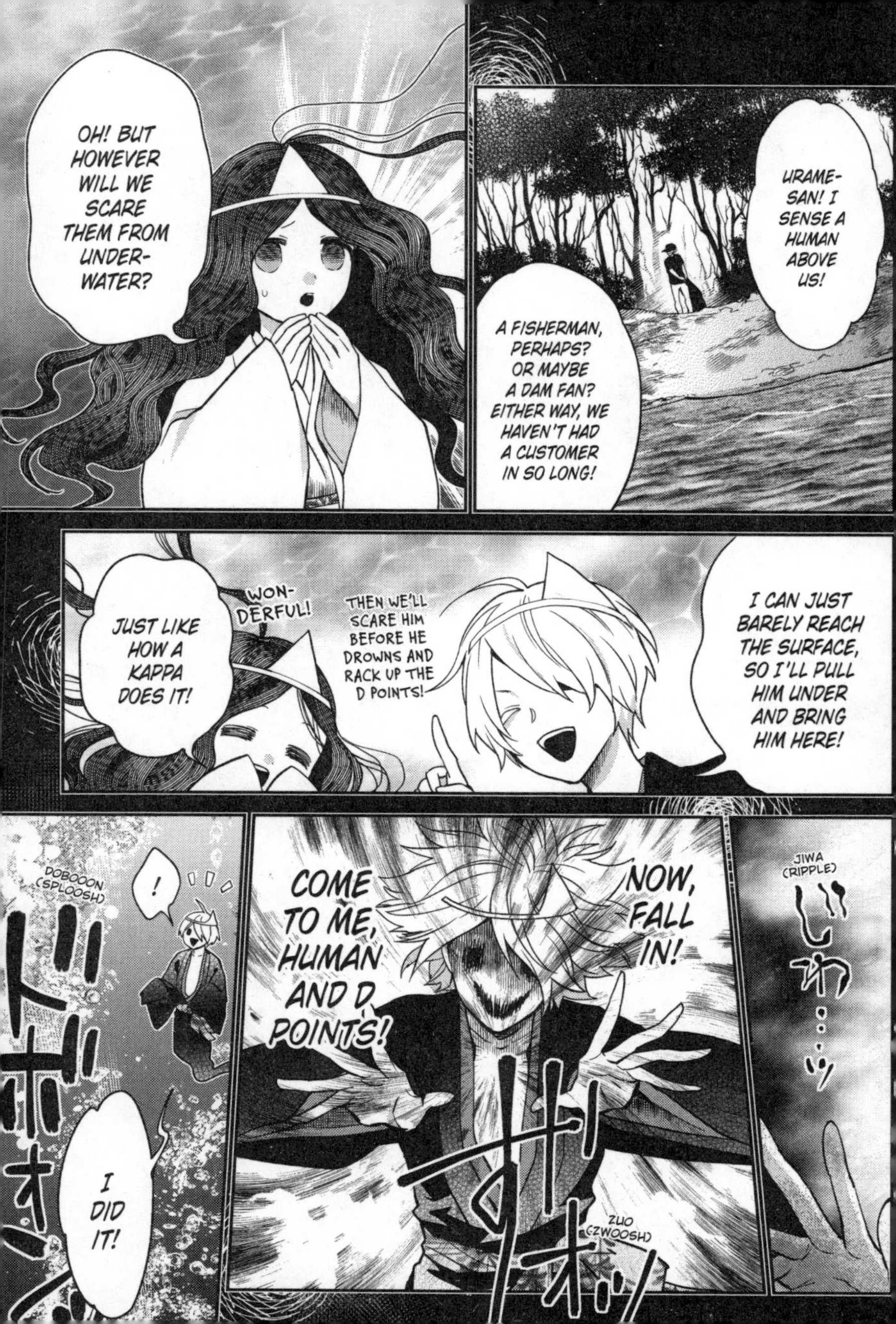
URAME-SAN! I SENSE A HUMAN ABOVE US!
A FISHERMAN, PERHAPS? OR MAYBE A DAM FAN? EITHER WAY, WE HAVEN'T HAD A CUSTOMER IN SO LONG!
OH! BUT HOWEVER WILL WE SCARE THEM FROM UNDER-WATER?
I CAN JUST BARELY REACH THE SURFACE, SO I'LL PULL HIM UNDER AND BRING HIM HERE!
THEN WE'LL SCARE HIM BEFORE HE DROWNS AND RACK UP THE D POINTS!
WON-DERFUL!
JUST LIKE HOW A KAPPA DOES IT!
JIWA (RIPPLE)
NOW, FALL IN!
COME TO ME, HUMAN AND D POINTS!
ZUO (ZWOOSH)
DOBOOON (SPLOOSH)
!
I DID IT!

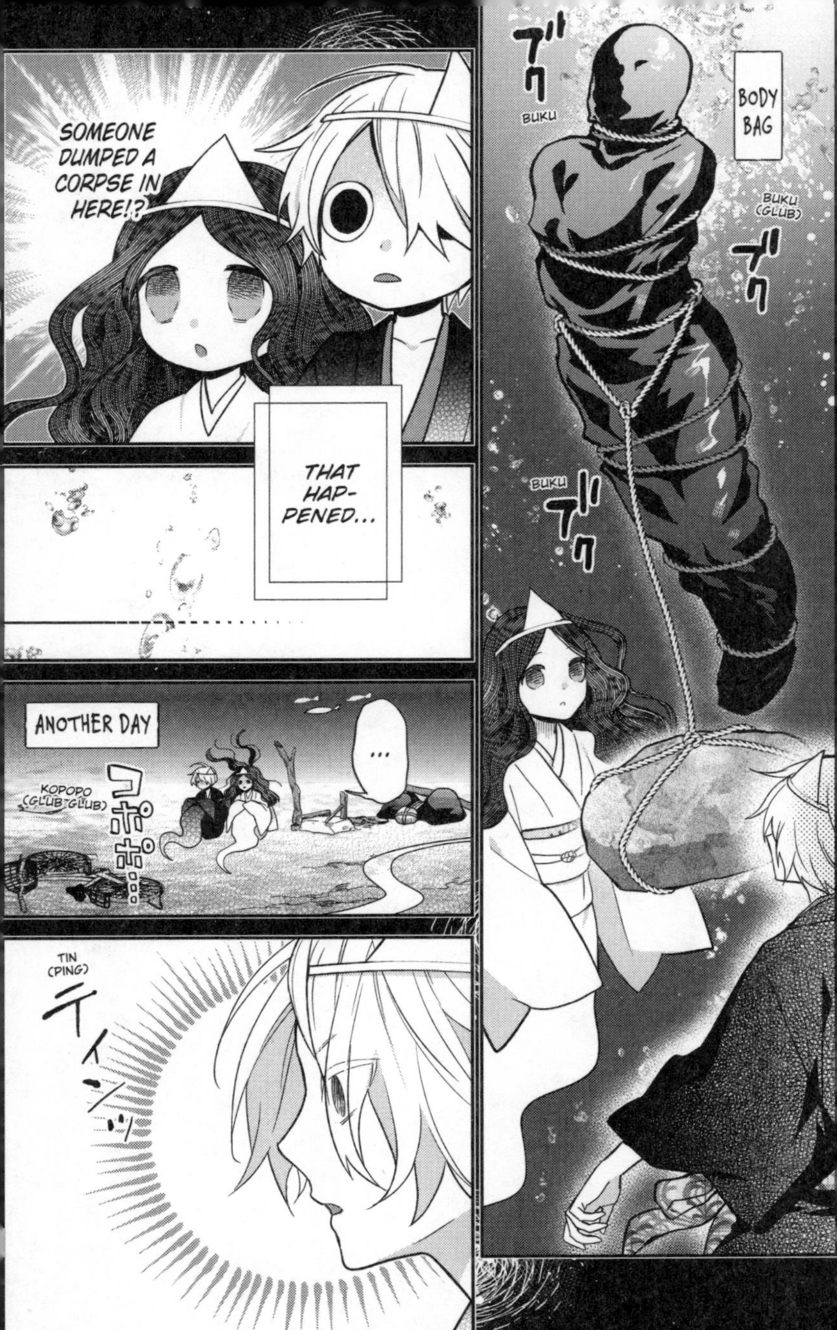
BODY BAG
ブク
BUKU
ブク
BUKU (GLUB)
ブク
BUKU
SOMEONE DUMPED A CORPSE IN HERE!?
THAT HAP-PENED...
ANOTHER DAY
...
コポポ...
KOPOPO (GLUB GLUB)
TIN (PING)

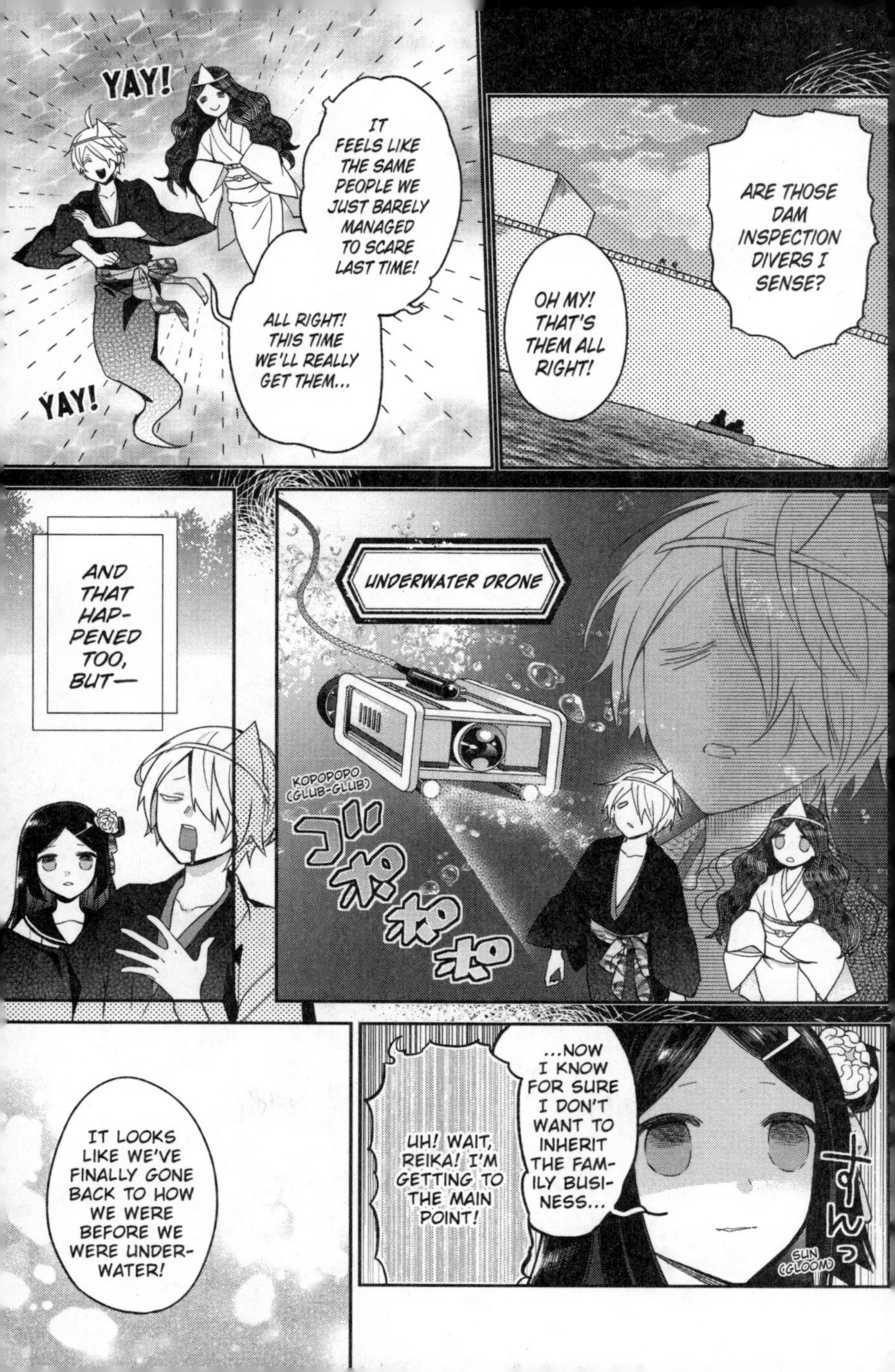
ARE THOSE DAM INSPECTION DIVERS I SENSE?
OH MY! THAT'S THEM ALL RIGHT!
YAY!
IT FEELS LIKE THE SAME PEOPLE WE JUST BARELY MANAGED TO SCARE LAST TIME!
ALL RIGHT! THIS TIME WE'LL REALLY GET THEM...
YAY!
UNDERWATER DRONE
KOPOPOPO (GLUB-GLUB)
ゴポポポ
AND THAT HAP-PENED TOO, BUT—
...NOW I KNOW FOR SURE I DON'T WANT TO INHERIT THE FAM-ILY BUSI-NESS...
すんっ
SUN (GLOOM)
UH! WAIT, REIKA! I'M GETTING TO THE MAIN POINT!
IT LOOKS LIKE WE'VE FINALLY GONE BACK TO HOW WE WERE BEFORE WE WERE UNDER-WATER!

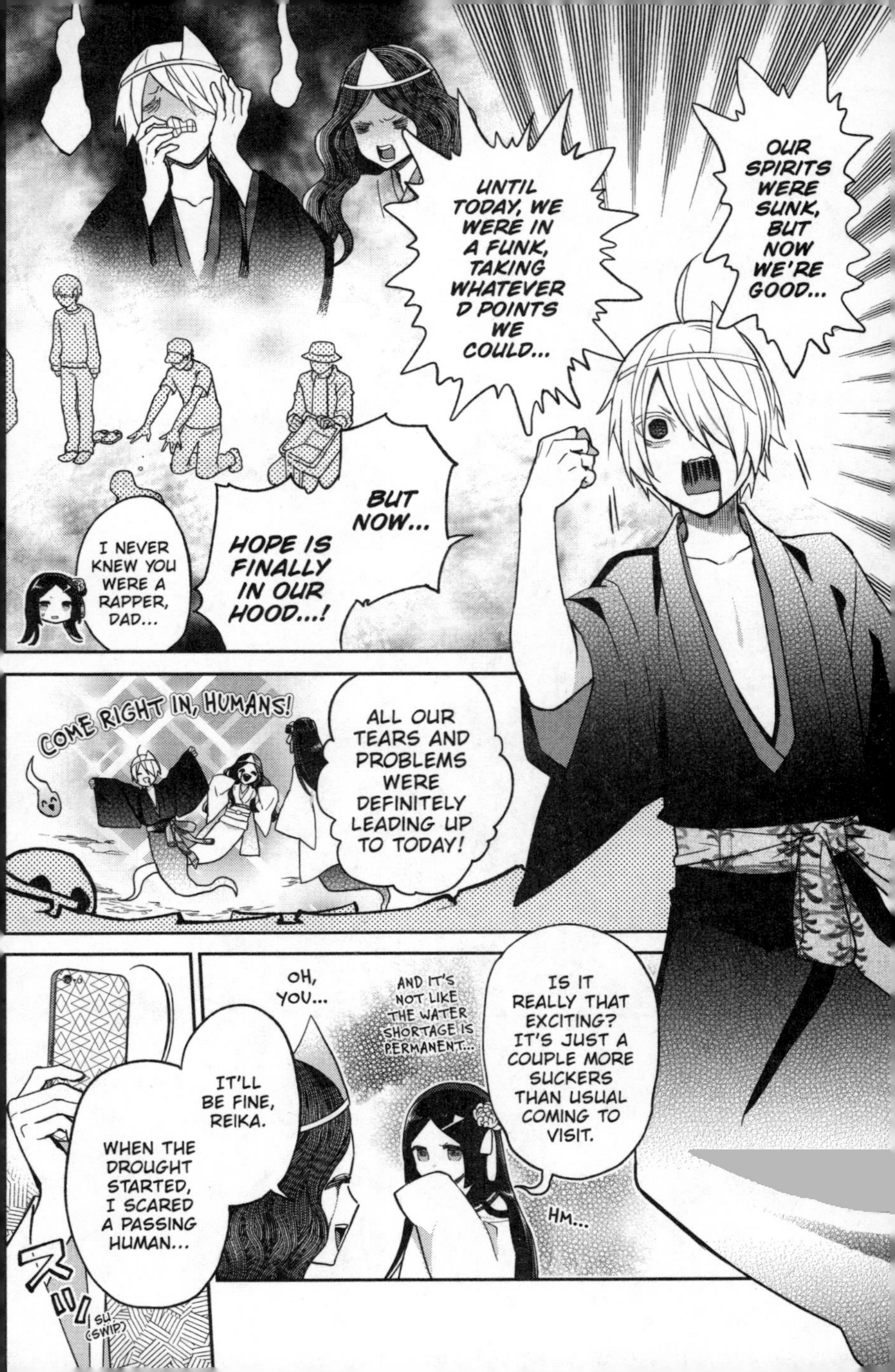
OUR SPIRITS WERE SUNK, BUT NOW WE'RE GOOD...
UNTIL TODAY, WE WERE IN A FUNK, TAKING WHATEVER D POINTS WE COULD...
BUT NOW...
HOPE IS FINALLY IN OUR HOOD...!
I NEVER KNEW YOU WERE A RAPPER, DAD...
ALL OUR TEARS AND PROBLEMS WERE DEFINITELY LEADING UP TO TODAY!
COME RIGHT IN, HUMANS!
IS IT REALLY THAT EXCITING? IT'S JUST A COUPLE MORE SUCKERS THAN USUAL COMING TO VISIT.
HM...
AND IT'S NOT LIKE THE WATER SHORTAGE IS PERMANENT...
OH, YOU...
IT'LL BE FINE, REIKA.
WHEN THE DROUGHT STARTED, I SCARED A PASSING HUMAN...
SU (SWIP)

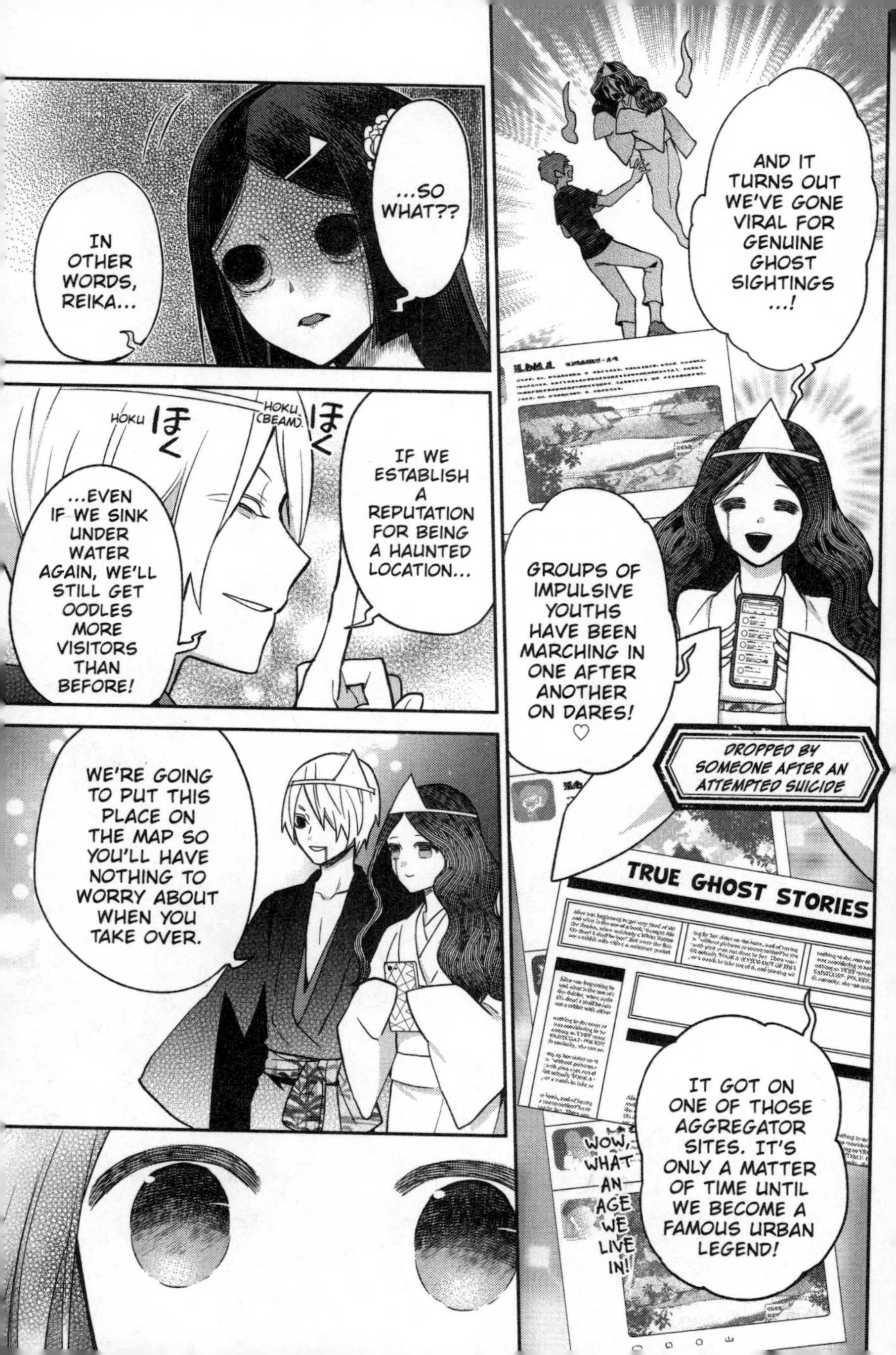
AND IT TURNS OUT WE'VE GONE VIRAL FOR GENUINE GHOST SIGHTINGS ...!
GROUPS OF IMPULSIVE YOUTHS HAVE BEEN MARCHING IN ONE AFTER ANOTHER ON DARES! ♡
DROPPED BY SOMEONE AFTER AN ATTEMPTED SUICIDE
TRUE GHOST STORIES
IT GOT ON ONE OF THOSE AGGREGATOR SITES. IT'S ONLY A MATTER OF TIME UNTIL WE BECOME A FAMOUS URBAN LEGEND!
WOW, WHAT AN AGE WE LIVE IN!
...SO WHAT??
IN OTHER WORDS, REIKA...
IF WE ESTABLISH A REPUTATION FOR BEING A HAUNTED LOCATION...
ほく
HOKU (BEAM)
ほく
HOKU
...EVEN IF WE SINK UNDER WATER AGAIN, WE'LL STILL GET OODLES MORE VISITORS THAN BEFORE!
WE'RE GOING TO PUT THIS PLACE ON THE MAP SO YOU'LL HAVE NOTHING TO WORRY ABOUT WHEN YOU TAKE OVER.

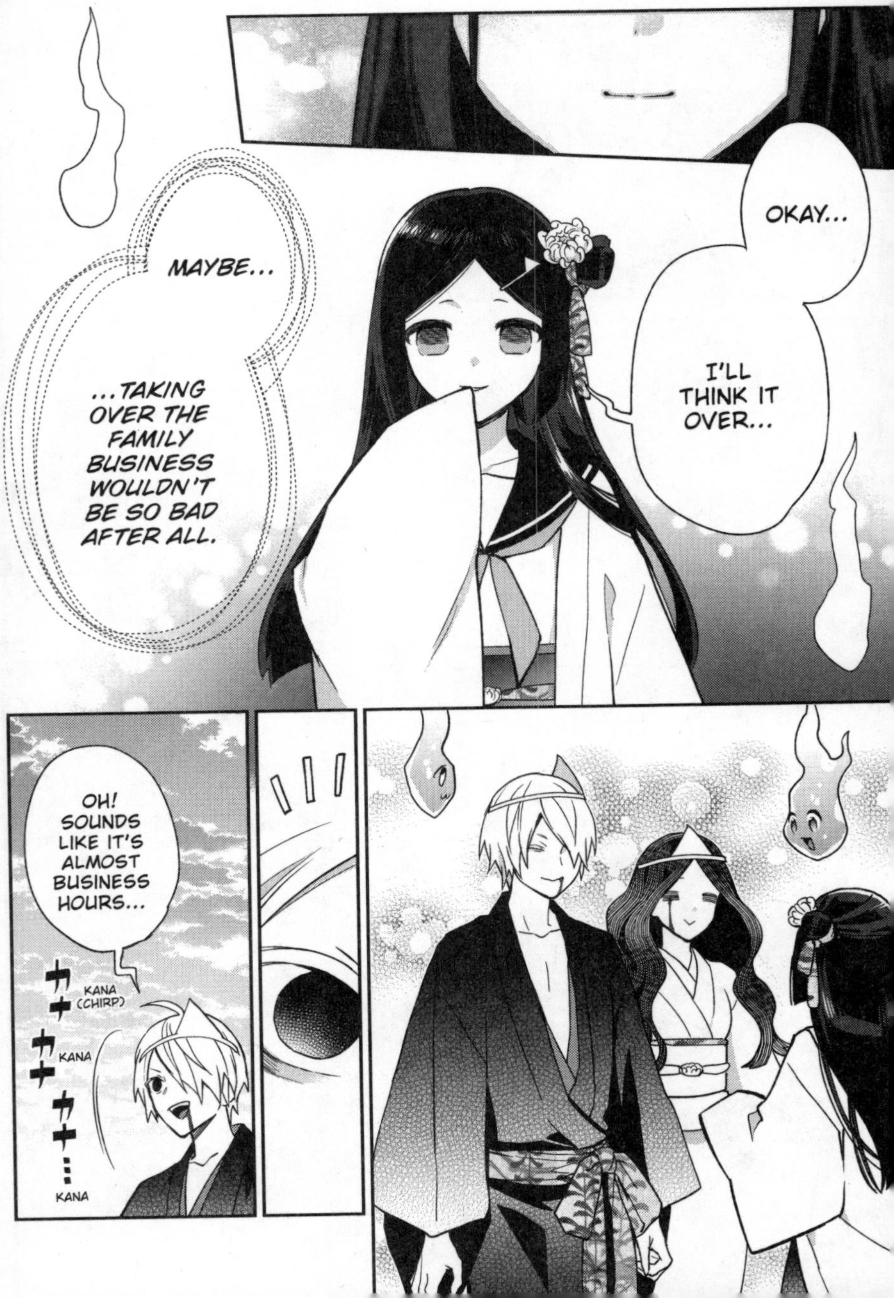
OKAY...
I'LL THINK IT OVER...
MAYBE...
...TAKING OVER THE FAMILY BUSINESS WOULDN'T BE SO BAD AFTER ALL.
OH! SOUNDS LIKE IT'S ALMOST BUSINESS HOURS...
カナ KANA (CHIRP)
カナ KANA
カナ... KANA

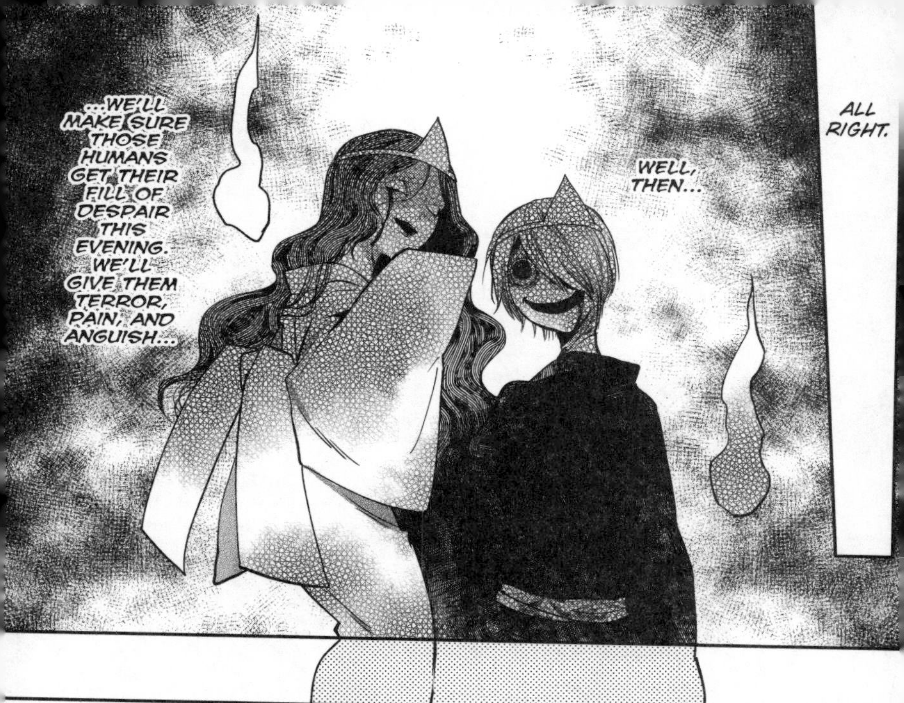
ALL RIGHT.
WELL, THEN...
...WE'LL MAKE SURE THOSE HUMANS GET THEIR FILL OF DESPAIR THIS EVENING. WE'LL GIVE THEM TERROR, PAIN, AND ANGUISH...
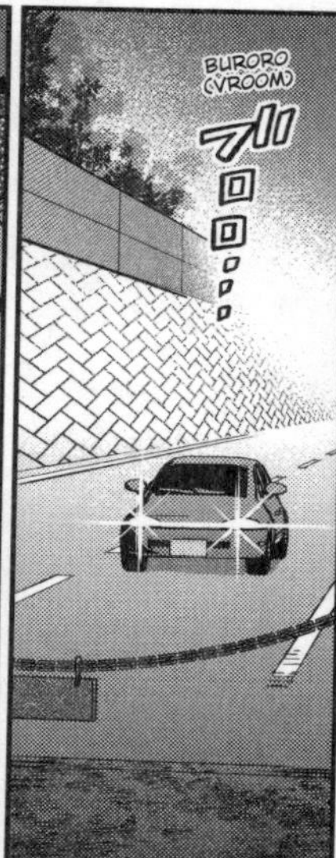
BURORO (VROOM)
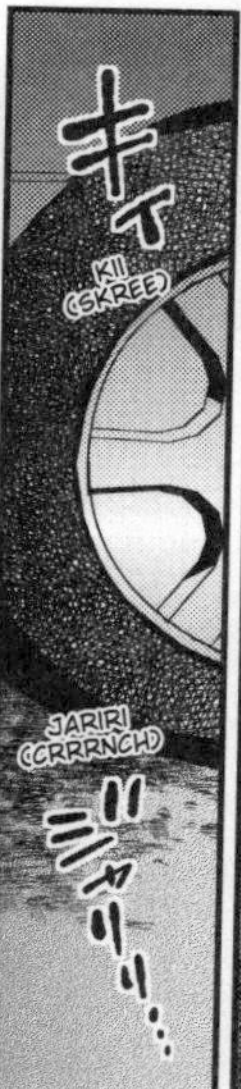
KII (SKREE)
JARIRI (CRRRNCH)
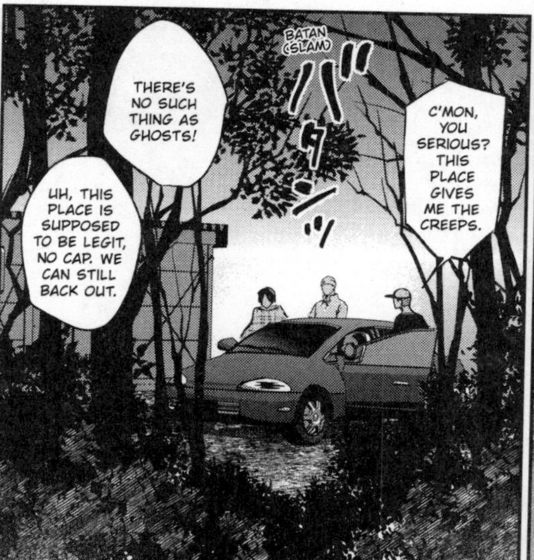
BATAN (SLAM)
C'MON, YOU SERIOUS? THIS PLACE GIVES ME THE CREEPS.
THERE'S NO SUCH THING AS GHOSTS!
UH, THIS PLACE IS SUPPOSED TO BE LEGIT, NO CAP. WE CAN STILL BACK OUT.

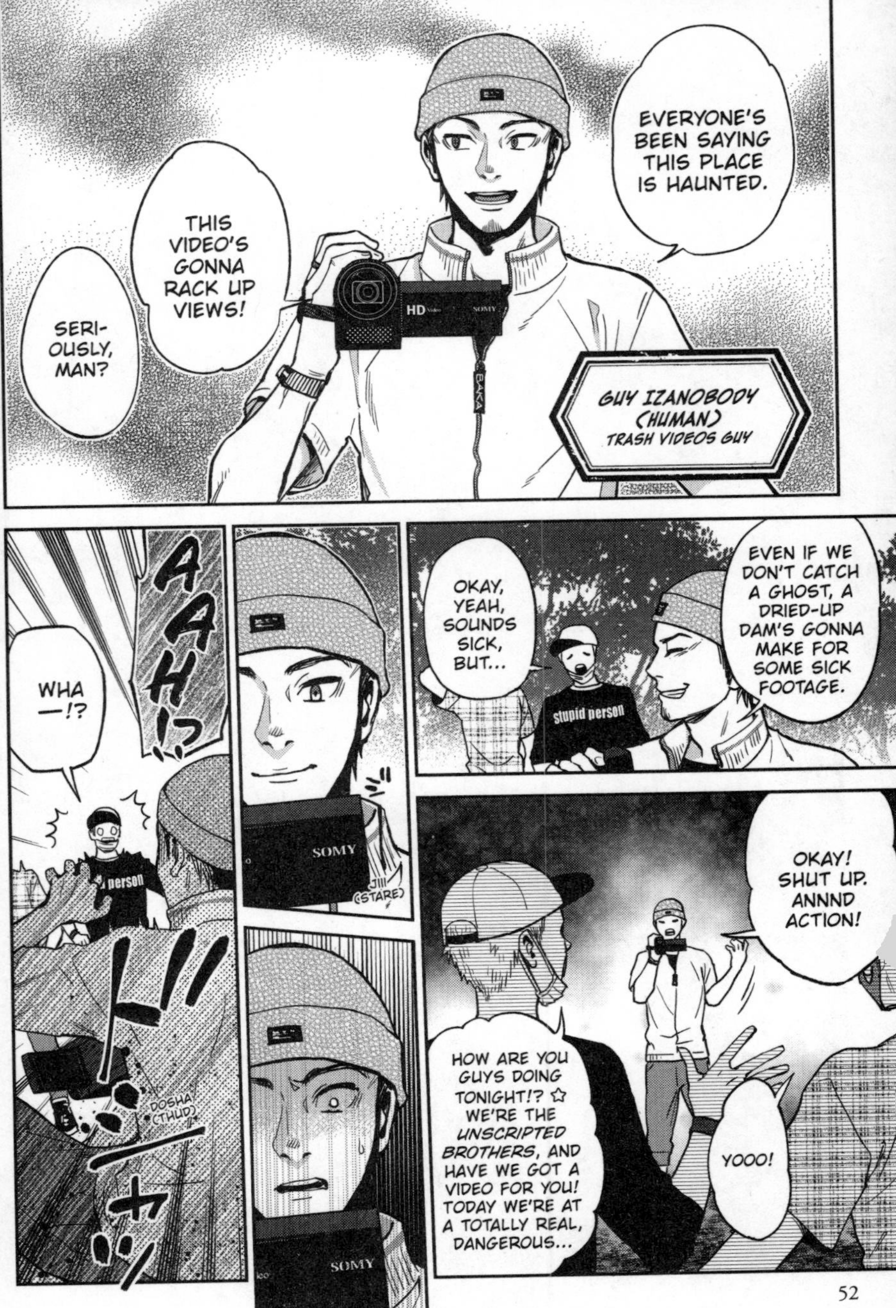
EVERYONE'S BEEN SAYING THIS PLACE IS HAUNTED.
THIS VIDEO'S GONNA RACK UP VIEWS!
SERI-OUSLY, MAN?
GUY IZANOBODY (HUMAN) TRASH VIDEOS GUY
EVEN IF WE DON'T CATCH A GHOST, A DRIED-UP DAM'S GONNA MAKE FOR SOME SICK FOOTAGE.
OKAY, YEAH, SOUNDS SICK, BUT...
Stupid person
JIII (STARE)
OKAY! SHUT UP. ANNND ACTION!
HOW ARE YOU GUYS DOING TONIGHT!? ☆ WE'RE THE UNSCRIPTED BROTHERS, AND HAVE WE GOT A VIDEO FOR YOU! TODAY WE'RE AT A TOTALLY REAL, DANGEROUS...
YOOO!
AAAH!?
WHA —!?
DOSHA (THUD)

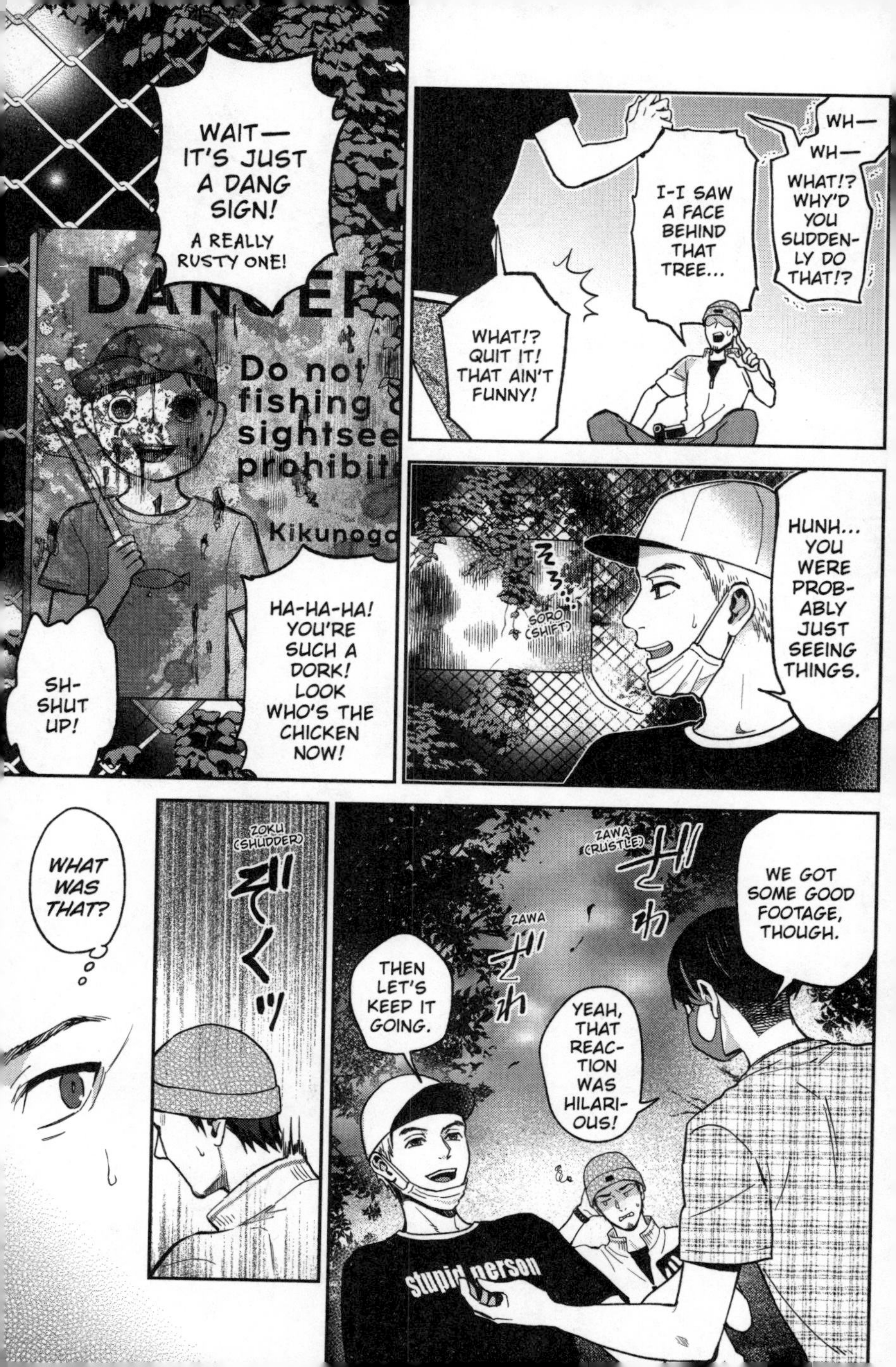
WH—
WH—
WHAT!? WHY'D YOU SUDDEN-LY DO THAT!?
I-I SAW A FACE BEHIND THAT TREE...
WHAT!? QUIT IT! THAT AIN'T FUNNY!
HUNH... YOU WERE PROB-ABLY JUST SEEING THINGS.
そろ…
SORO (SHIFT)
WAIT— IT'S JUST A DANG SIGN!
A REALLY RUSTY ONE!
DANGER
Do not fishing sightsee prohibit
Kikunoga
HA-HA-HA! YOU'RE SUCH A DORK! LOOK WHO'S THE CHICKEN NOW!
SH-SHUT UP!
WE GOT SOME GOOD FOOTAGE, THOUGH.
ざわ
ZAWA (RUSTLE)
ざわ
ZAWA
YEAH, THAT REAC-TION WAS HILARI-OUS!
THEN LET'S KEEP IT GOING.
stupid person
ぞくッ
ZOKU (SHUDDER)
WHAT WAS THAT?

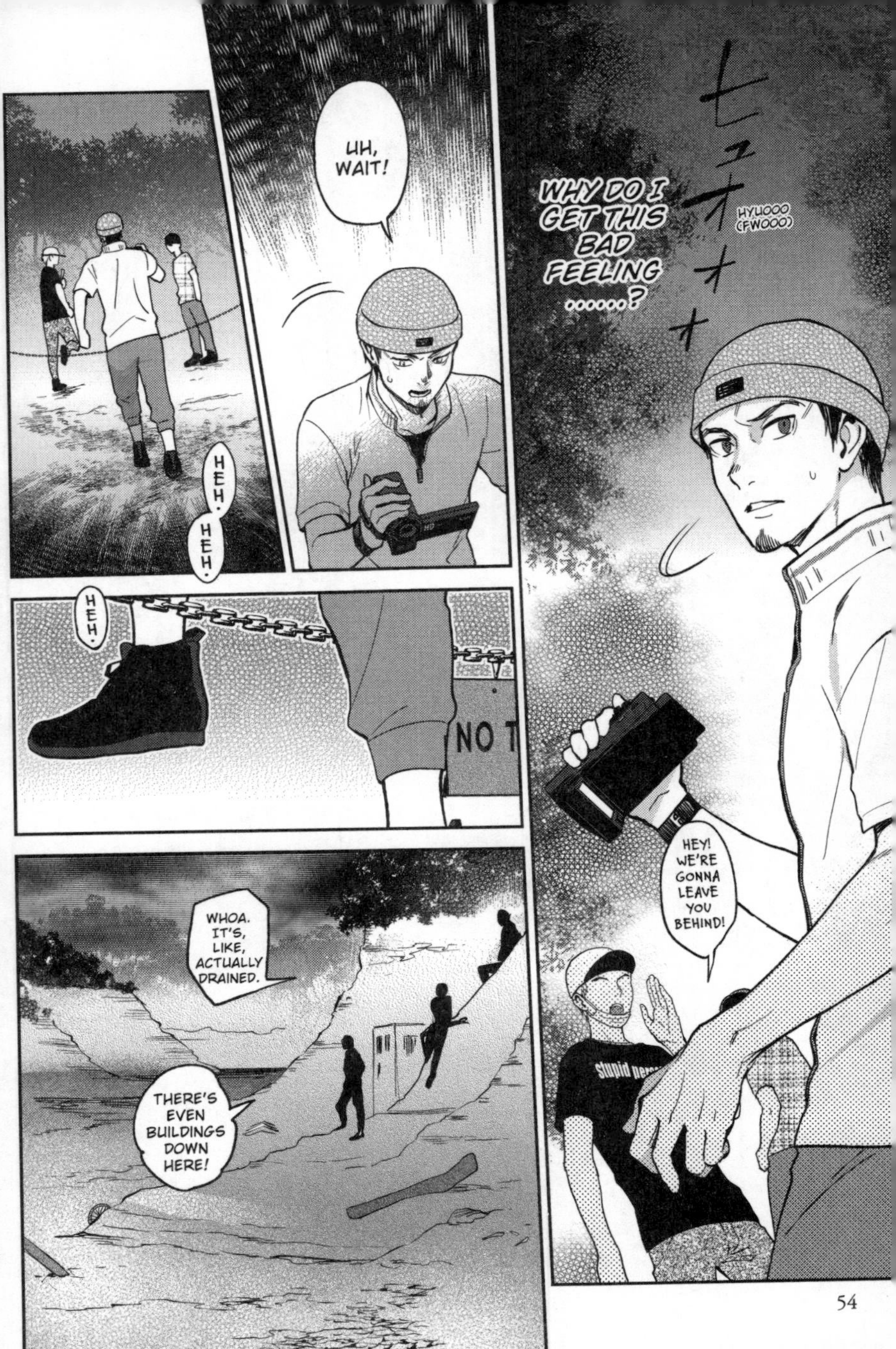
WHY DO I GET THIS BAD FEELING ....?
HYUOOO (FWOOO)
HEY! WE'RE GONNA LEAVE YOU BEHIND!
UH, WAIT!
HEH. HEH.
HEH.
NO T
WHOA. IT'S, LIKE, ACTUALLY DRAINED.
THERE'S EVEN BUILDINGS DOWN HERE!

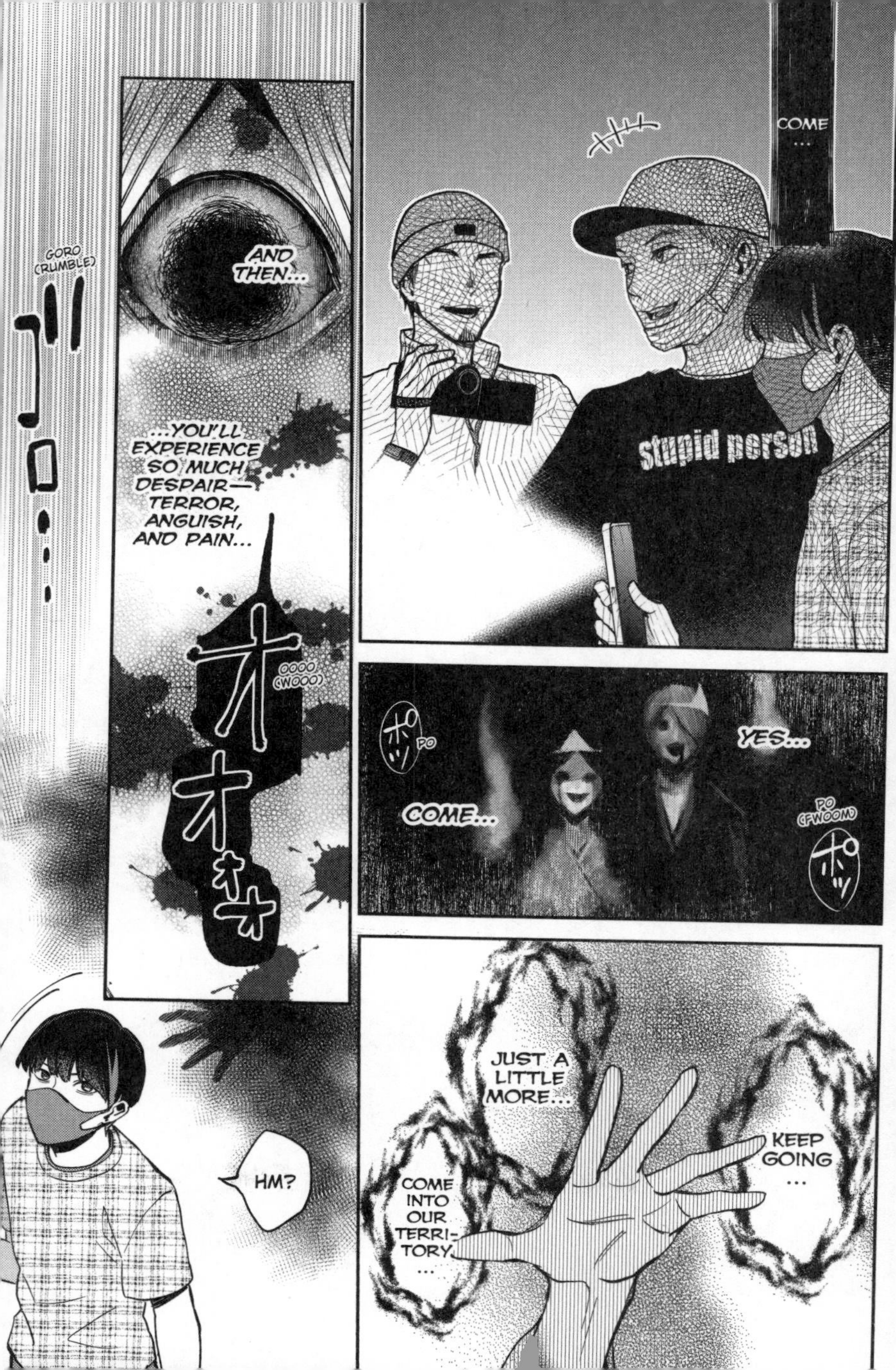
COME...
stupid person
YES...
PO
COME...
PO (FWOOM)
KEEP GOING...
JUST A LITTLE MORE...
COME INTO OUR TERRI-TORY...
GORO (RUMBLE)
AND THEN...
...YOU'LL EXPERIENCE SO MUCH DESPAIR—TERROR, ANGUISH, AND PAIN...
OOOO (WOOO)
HM?

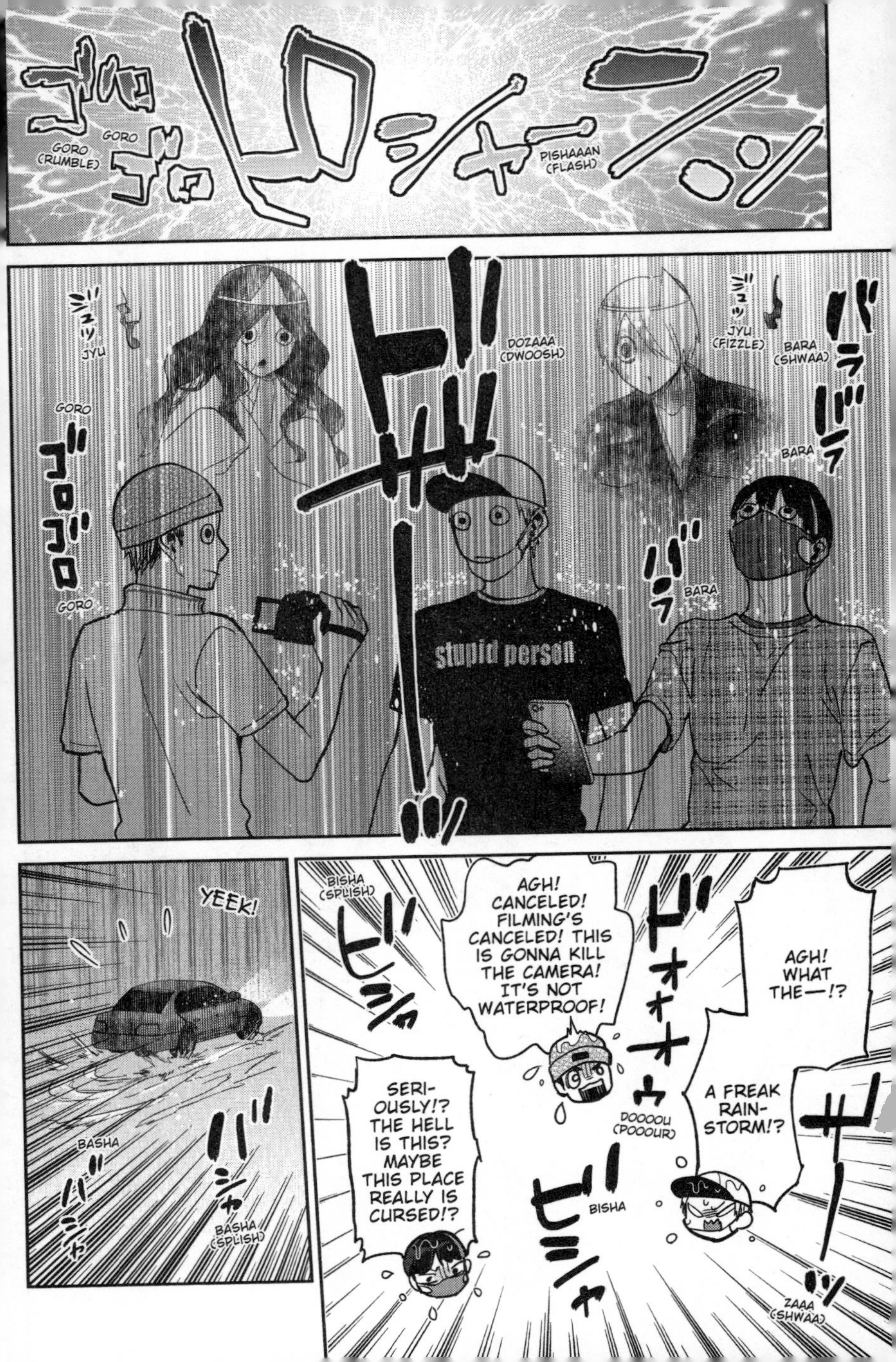
GORO GORO (RUMBLE)
PISHAAAN (FLASH)
BARA (SHWAA)
BARA
BARA
JYU (FIZZLE)
DOZAAA (DWOOSH)
JYU
GORO
GORO
BISHA (SPLISH)
AGH! CANCELED! FILMING'S CANCELED! THIS IS GONNA KILL THE CAMERA! IT'S NOT WATERPROOF!
AGH! WHAT THE—!?
A FREAK RAIN-STORM!?
DOOOOU (POOOUR)
SERI-OUSLY!? THE HELL IS THIS? MAYBE THIS PLACE REALLY IS CURSED!?
BISHA
ZAAA (SHWAA)
YEEK!
BASHA
BASHA (SPLISH)

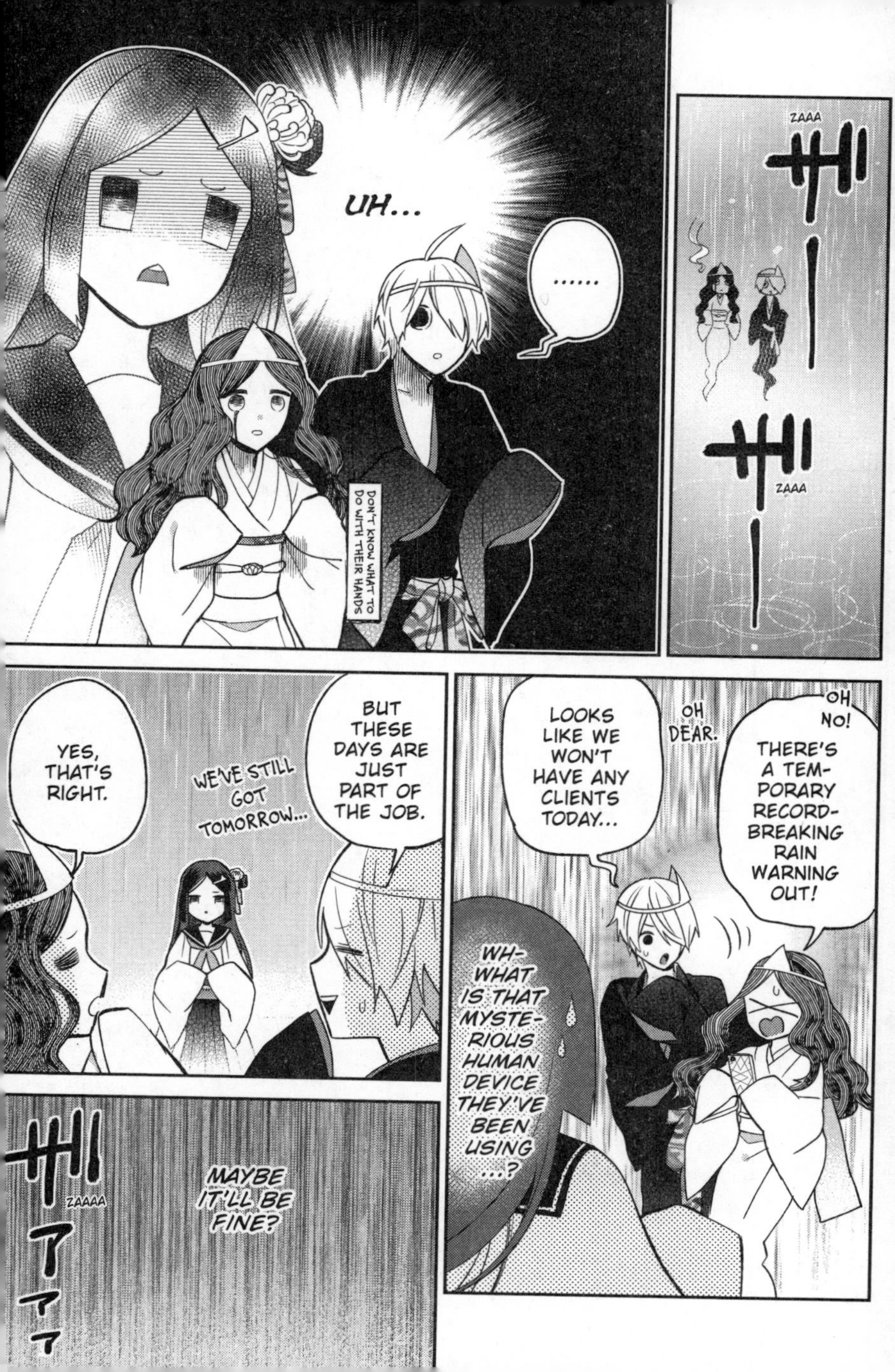
ZAAA
ザー
ZAAA
ザー
UH...
......
DON'T KNOW WHAT TO DO WITH THEIR HANDS
OH NO!
THERE'S A TEMPORARY RECORD-BREAKING RAIN WARNING OUT!
OH DEAR.
LOOKS LIKE WE WON'T HAVE ANY CLIENTS TODAY...
WH-WHAT IS THAT MYSTERIOUS HUMAN DEVICE THEY'VE BEEN USING...?
BUT THESE DAYS ARE JUST PART OF THE JOB.
WE'VE STILL GOT TOMORROW...
YES, THAT'S RIGHT.
ZAAAA
ザアア
MAYBE IT'LL BE FINE?

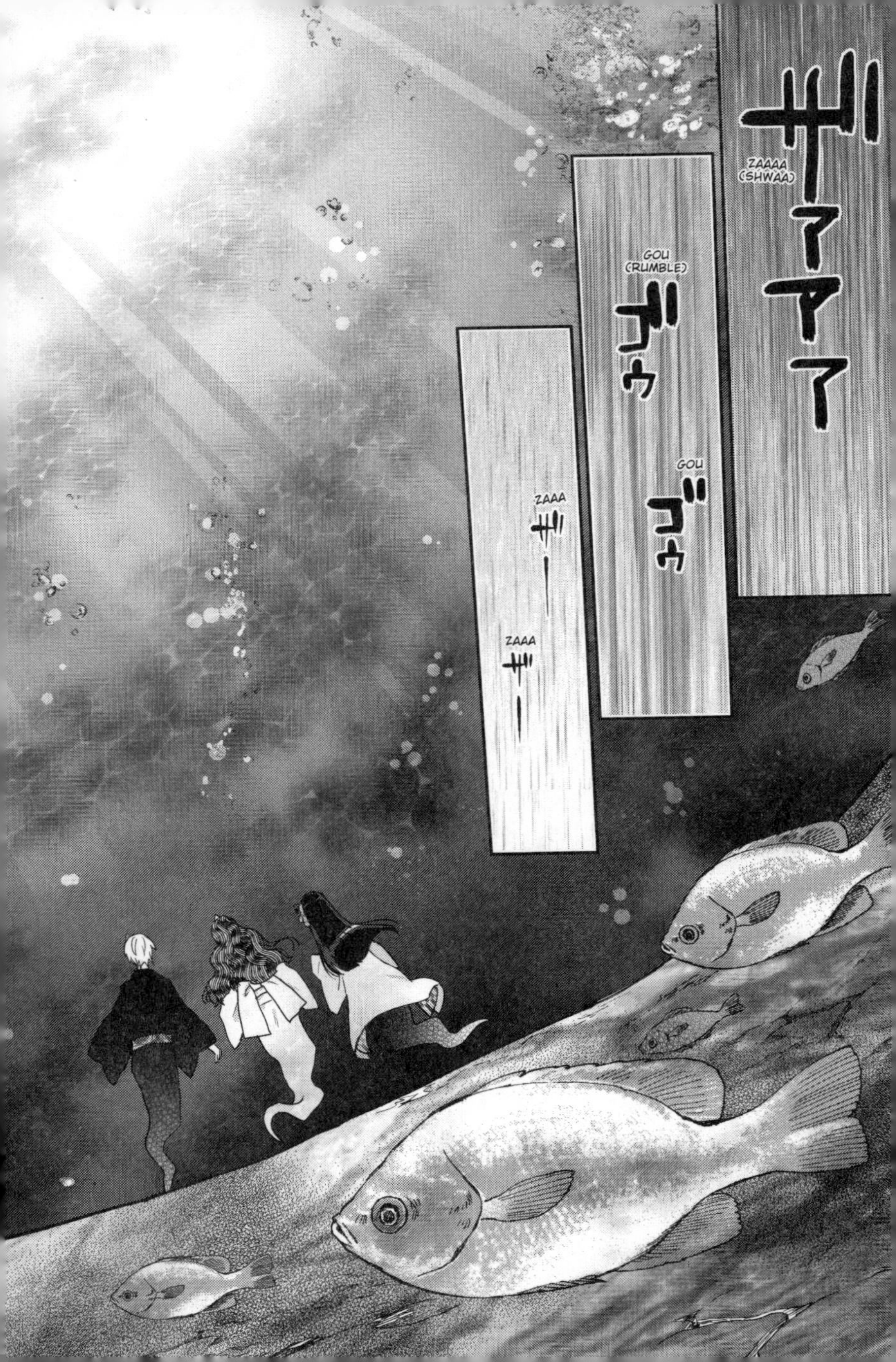
ザァアア
ZAAAA (SHWAA)
ゴウ
GOU (RUMBLE)
ゴウ
GOU
ザー
ZAAA
ザー
ZAAA

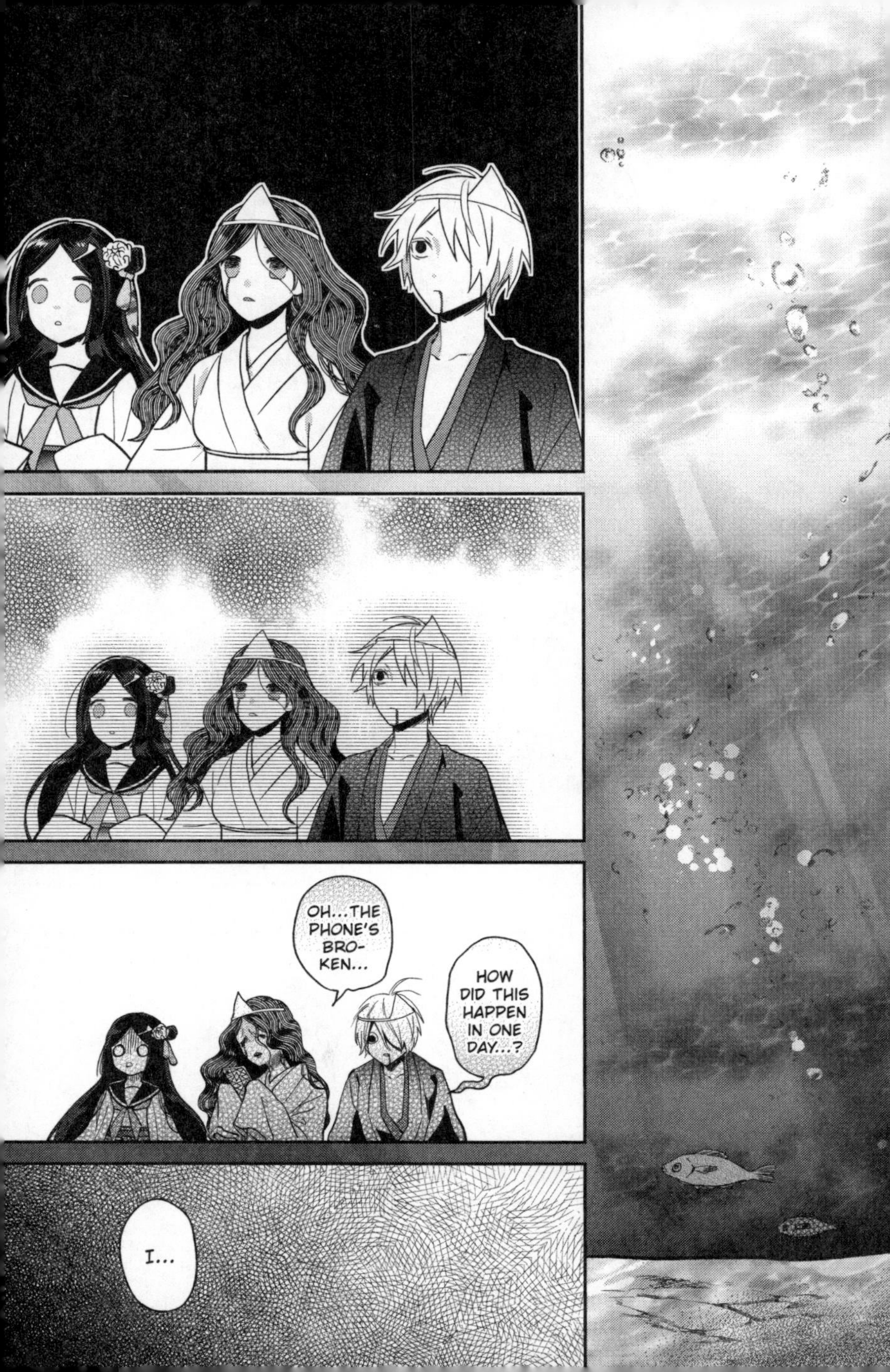
OH...THE PHONE'S BROKEN...
HOW DID THIS HAPPEN IN ONE DAY...?
I...

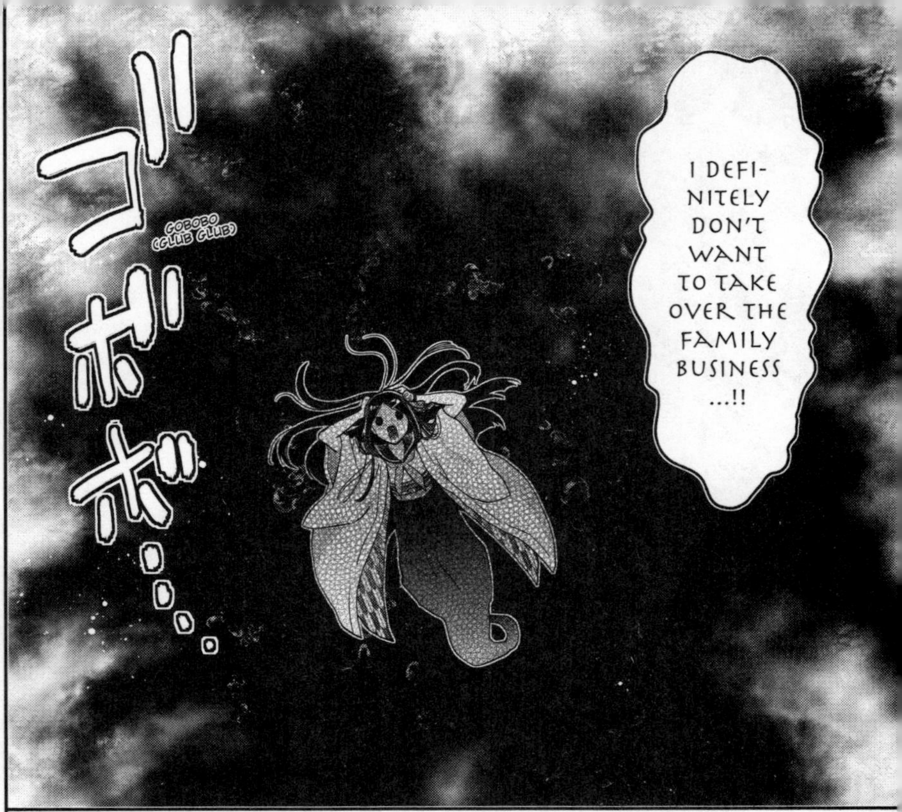
I DEFI-
NITELY
DON'T
WANT
TO TAKE
OVER THE
FAMILY
BUSINESS
...!!
GOBOBO
(GLUB GLUB)
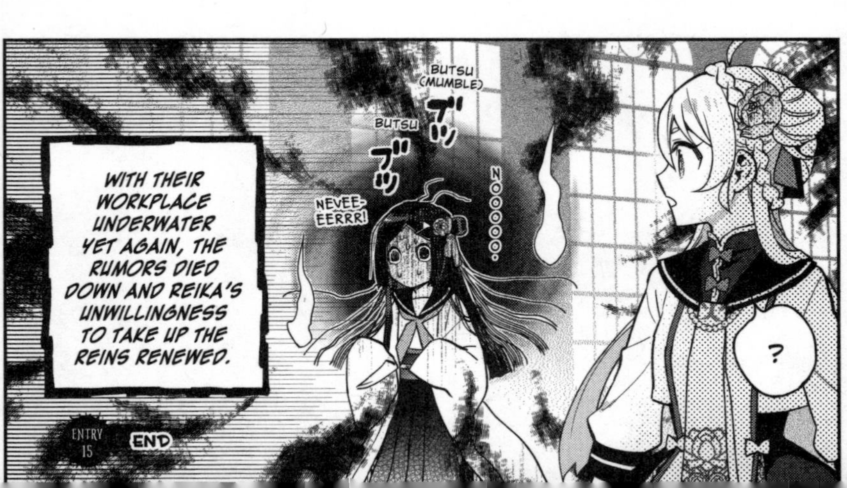
?
BUTSU
(MUMBLE)
BUTSU
NOOOOOO.
NEVEE-
EERRR!
WITH THEIR WORKPLACE UNDERWATER YET AGAIN, THE RUMORS DIED DOWN AND REIKA'S UNWILLINGNESS TO TAKE UP THE REINS RENEWED.
ENTRY 15 END

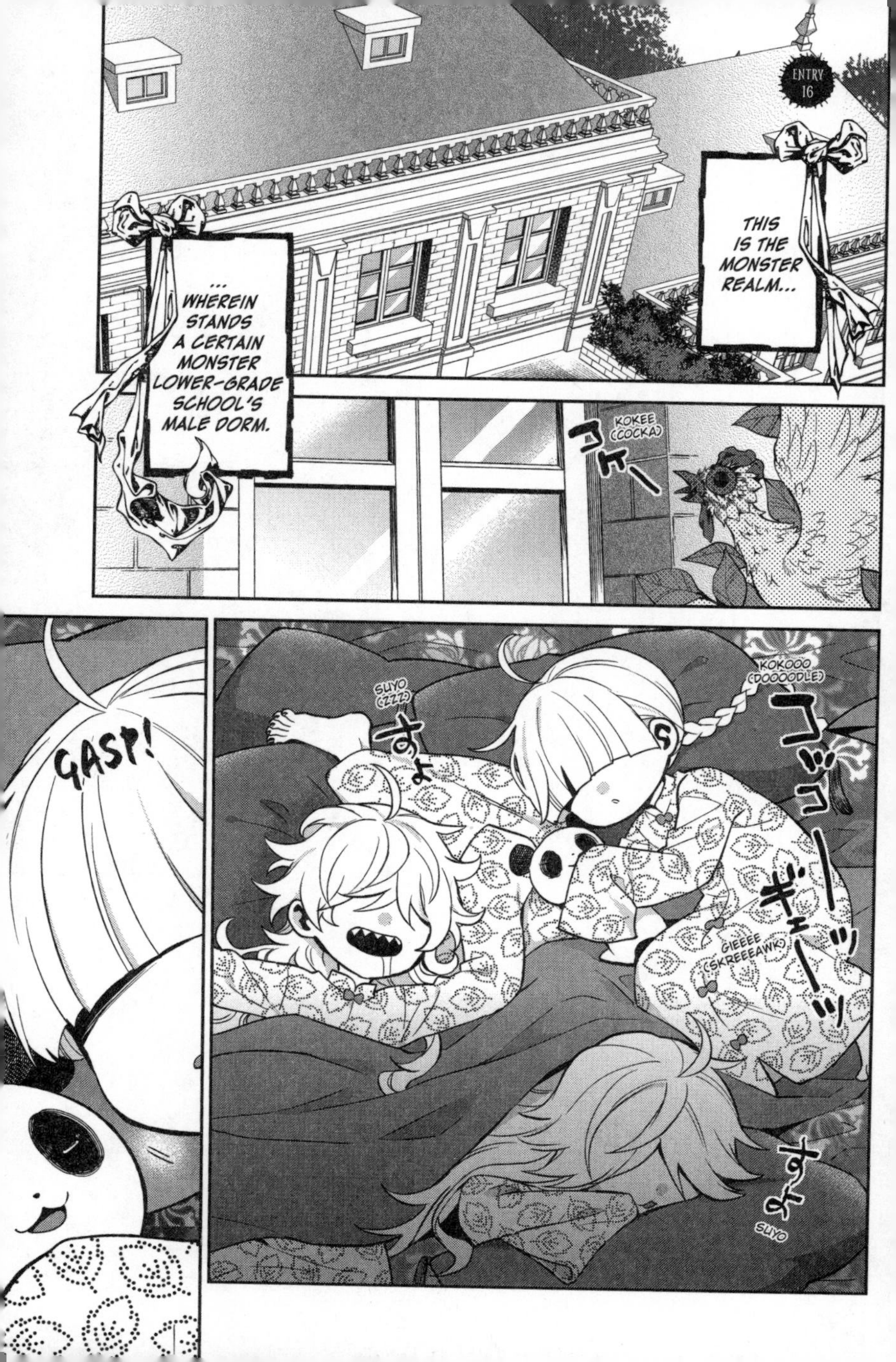
ENTRY 16
THIS IS THE MONSTER REALM...
...WHEREIN STANDS A CERTAIN MONSTER LOWER-GRADE SCHOOL'S MALE DORM.
KOKEE (COCKA)
コケー
KOKOOO (DOOOODLE)
コッコー
GIEEEE (SKREEEAWK)
ギェーッ
SUYO (ZZZ)
すよ
SUYO
すよ
GASP!

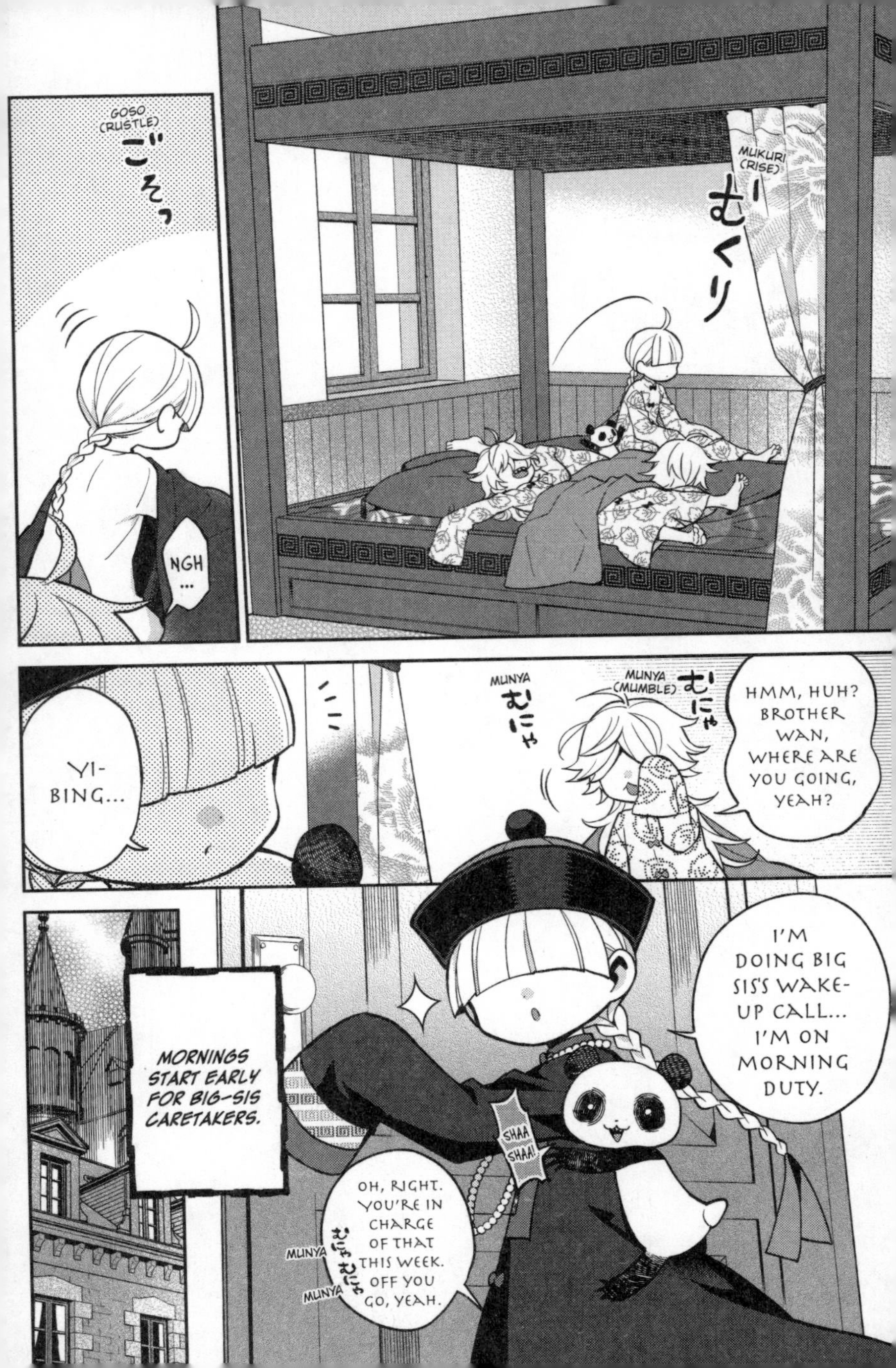
むくり
MUKURI (RISE)
ごそっ
GOSO (RUSTLE)
NGH...
むにゃ
MUNYA (MUMBLE)
HMM, HUH? BROTHER WAN, WHERE ARE YOU GOING, YEAH?
むにゃ
MUNYA
YI-BING...
I'M DOING BIG SIS'S WAKE-UP CALL... I'M ON MORNING DUTY.
MORNINGS START EARLY FOR BIG-SIS CARETAKERS.
SHAA SHAA!
OH, RIGHT. YOU'RE IN CHARGE OF THAT THIS WEEK. OFF YOU GO, YEAH.
むにゃ むにゃ
MUNYA MUNYA

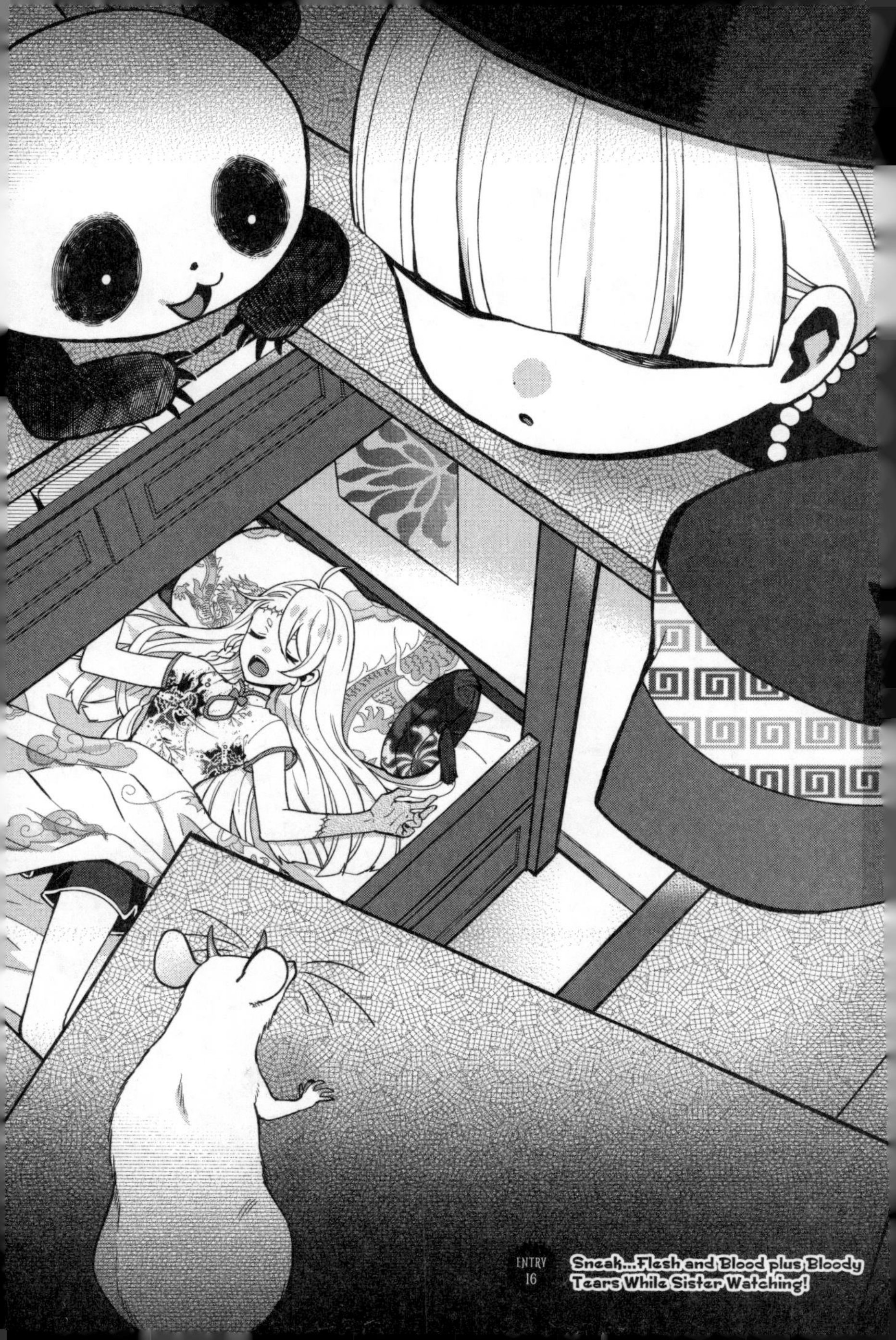
ENTRY 16
Sneak...Flesh and Blood plus Bloody Tears While Sister Watching!

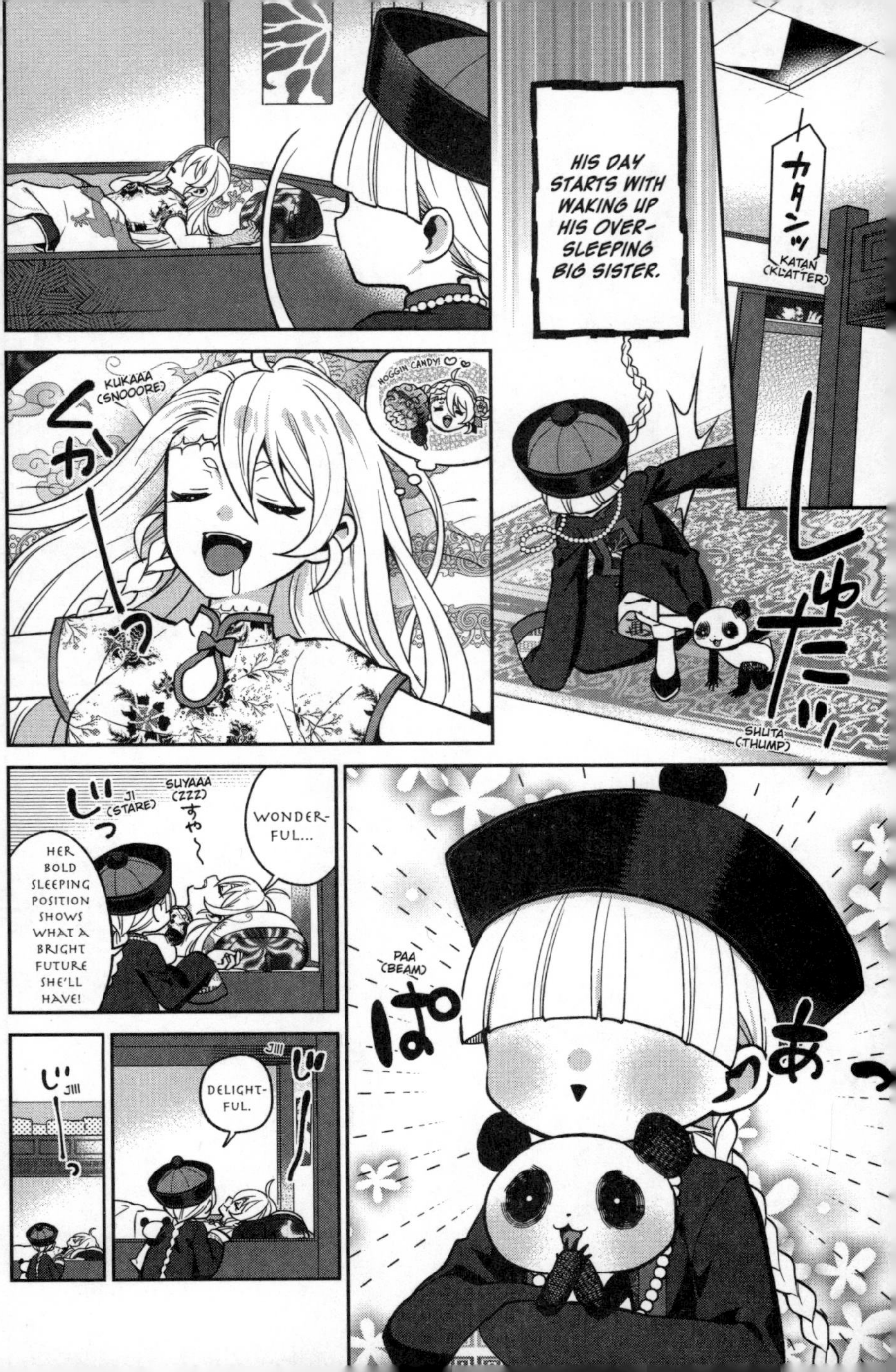
HIS DAY STARTS WITH WAKING UP HIS OVER-SLEEPING BIG SISTER.
カタンッ
KATAN (KLATTER)
しゅたっ
SHUTA (THUMP)
くかーっ
KUKAAA (SNOOORE)
NOGGIN CANDY!
ぱあっ
PAA (BEAM)
じっ
JI (STARE)
すや〜
SUYAAA (ZZZ)
WONDER-FUL...
HER BOLD SLEEPING POSITION SHOWS WHAT A BRIGHT FUTURE SHE'LL HAVE!
じーっ
JIII
DELIGHT-FUL.
じーっ
JIII

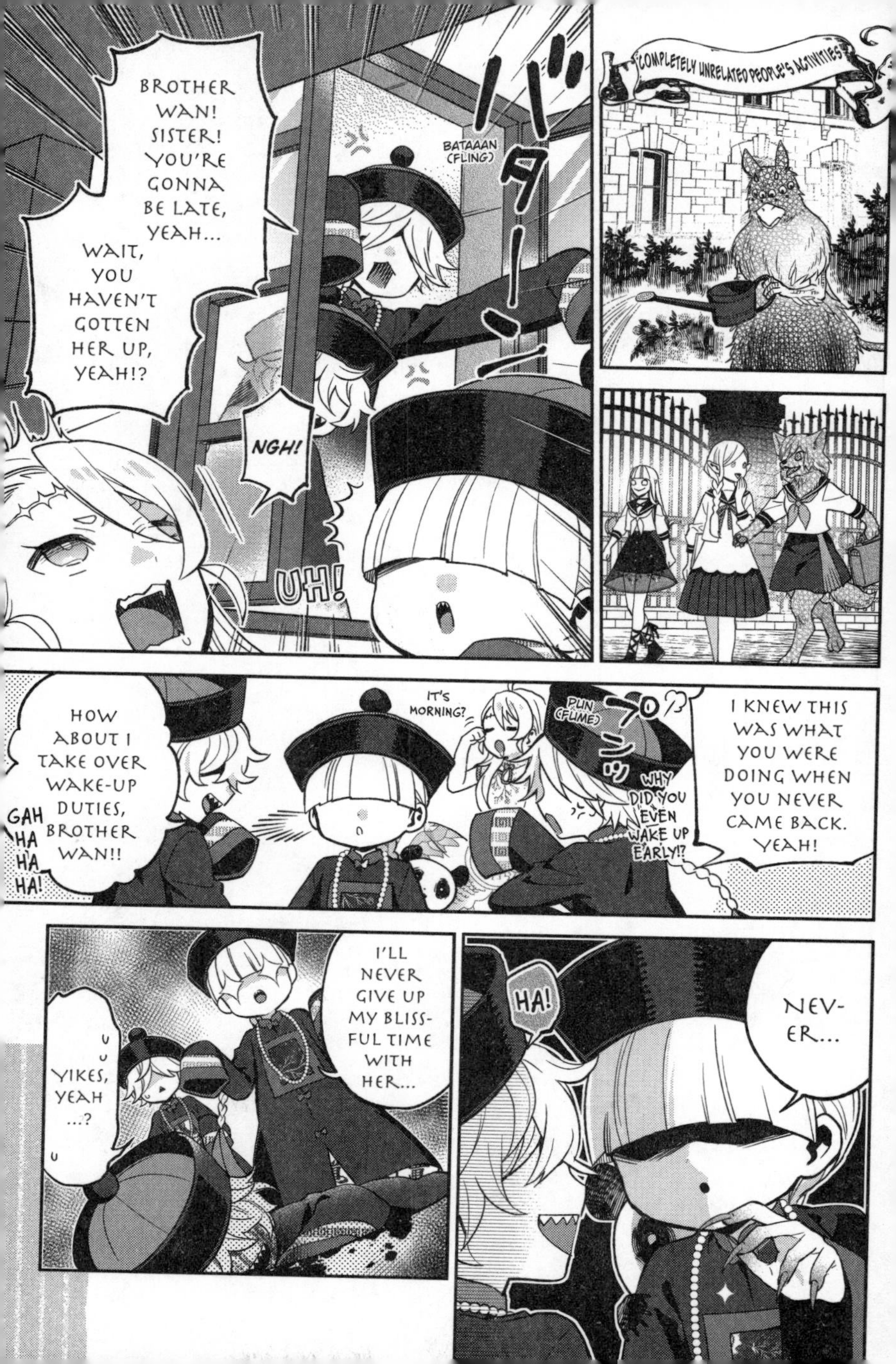
COMPLETELY UNRELATED PEOPLE'S ACTIVITIES
BATAAAN (FLING)
BROTHER WAN! SISTER! YOU'RE GONNA BE LATE, YEAH...
WAIT, YOU HAVEN'T GOTTEN HER UP, YEAH!?
NGH!
UH!
I KNEW THIS WAS WHAT YOU WERE DOING WHEN YOU NEVER CAME BACK. YEAH!
PUN (FUME)
WHY DID YOU EVEN WAKE UP EARLY!?
IT'S MORNING?
HOW ABOUT I TAKE OVER WAKE-UP DUTIES, BROTHER WAN!!
GAH HA HA HA!
NEV-ER...
HA!
I'LL NEVER GIVE UP MY BLISS-FUL TIME WITH HER...
YIKES, YEAH ...?

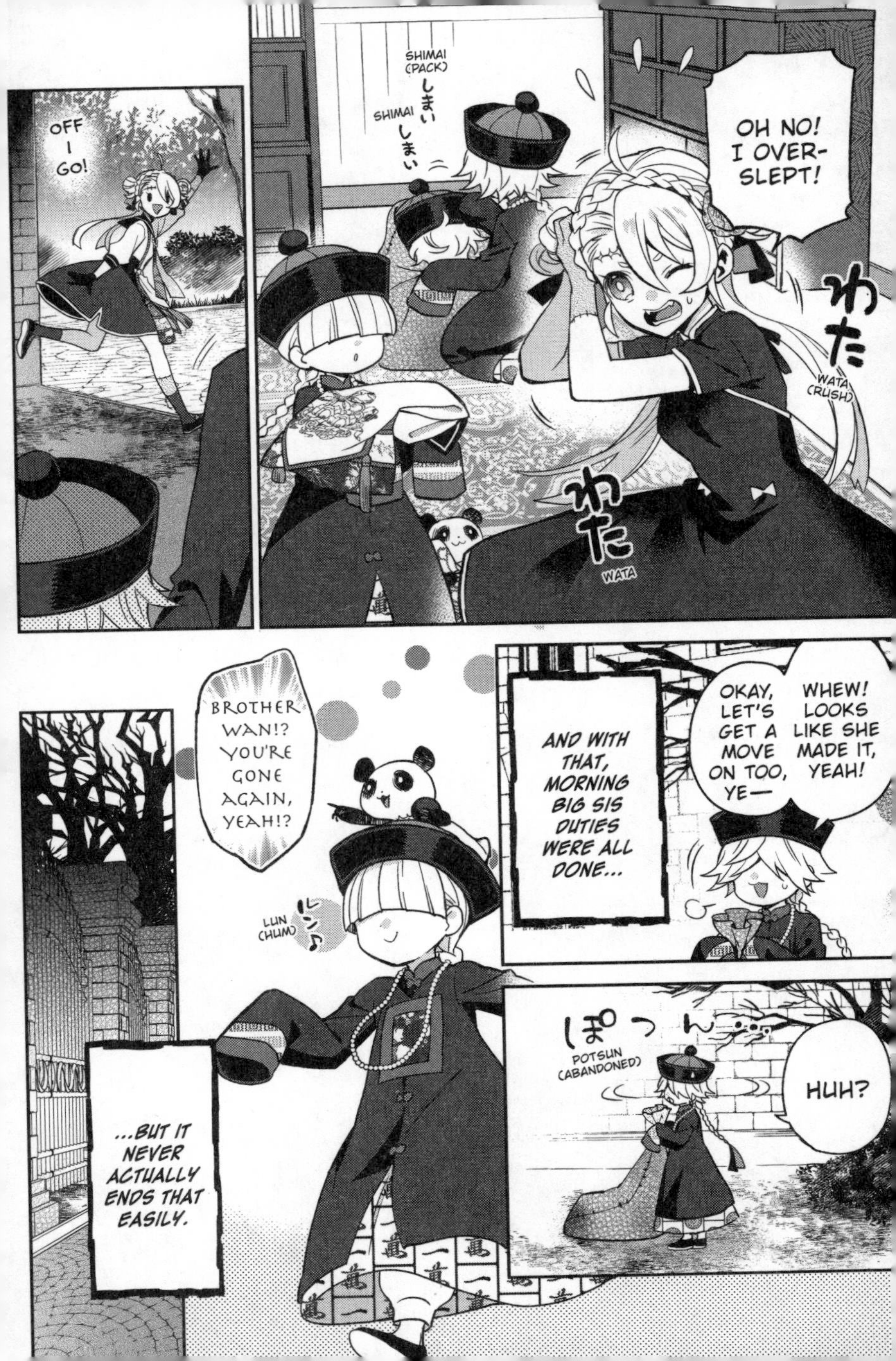
OH NO! I OVER-SLEPT!
わた
WATA (RUSH)
わた
WATA
しまい しまい
SHIMAI (PACK)
SHIMAI
OFF I GO!
WHEW! LOOKS LIKE SHE MADE IT, YEAH!
OKAY, LET'S GET A MOVE ON TOO, YE—
AND WITH THAT, MORNING BIG SIS DUTIES WERE ALL DONE...
BROTHER WAN!? YOU'RE GONE AGAIN, YEAH!?
ルン♪
LUN (CHUM)
ぽつん
POTSUN (ABANDONED)
HUH?
...BUT IT NEVER ACTUALLY ENDS THAT EASILY.

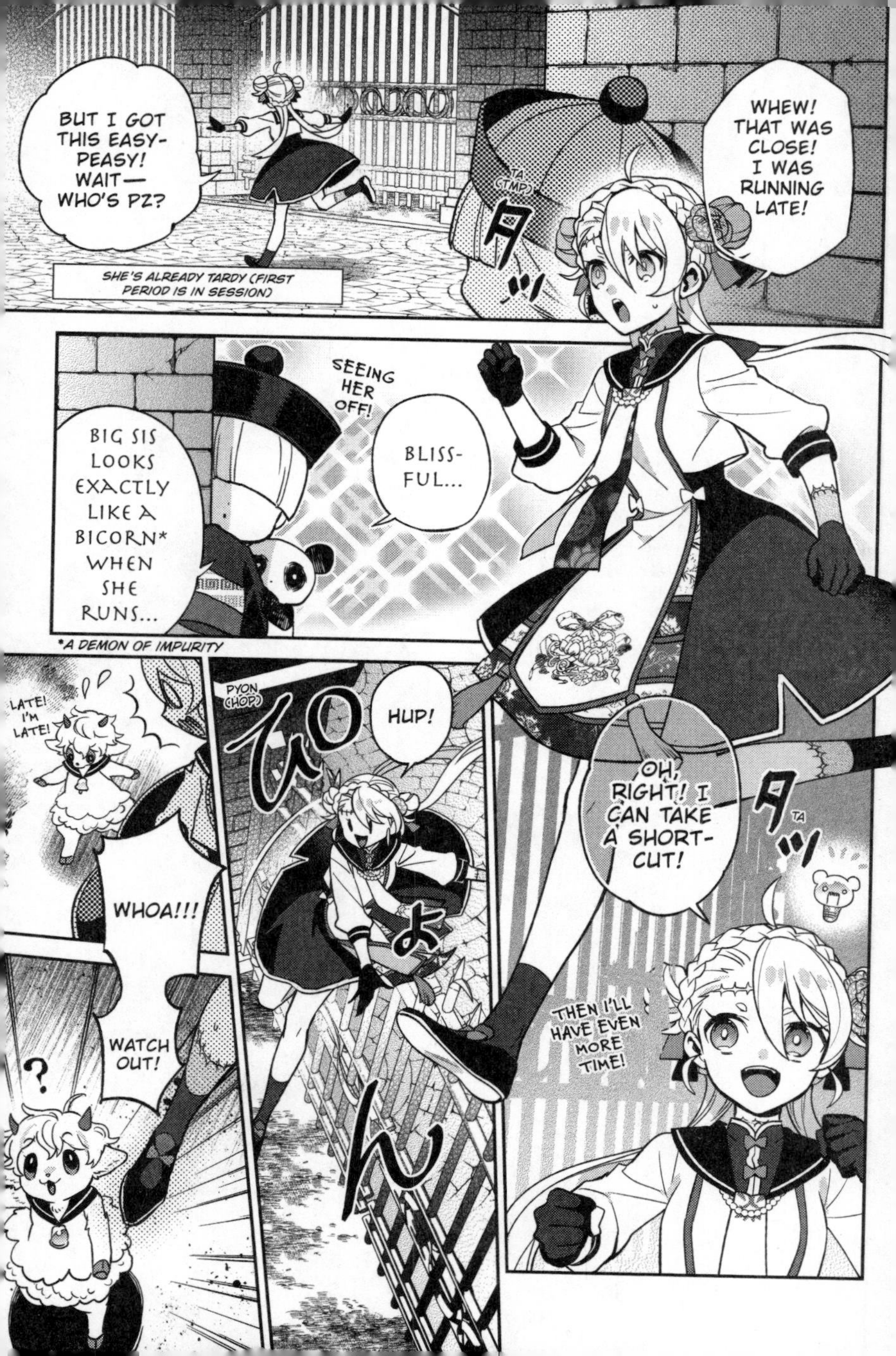
WHEW! THAT WAS CLOSE! I WAS RUNNING LATE!
TA (TMP)
BUT I GOT THIS EASY-PEASY! WAIT— WHO'S PZ?
SHE'S ALREADY TARDY (FIRST PERIOD IS IN SESSION)
SEEING HER OFF!
BLISS-FUL...
BIG SIS LOOKS EXACTLY LIKE A BICORN* WHEN SHE RUNS...
*A DEMON OF IMPURITY
OH, RIGHT! I CAN TAKE A SHORT-CUT!
TA
THEN I'LL HAVE EVEN MORE TIME!
PYON (HOP)
HUP!
LATE! I'M LATE!
WHOA!!!
WATCH OUT!
?

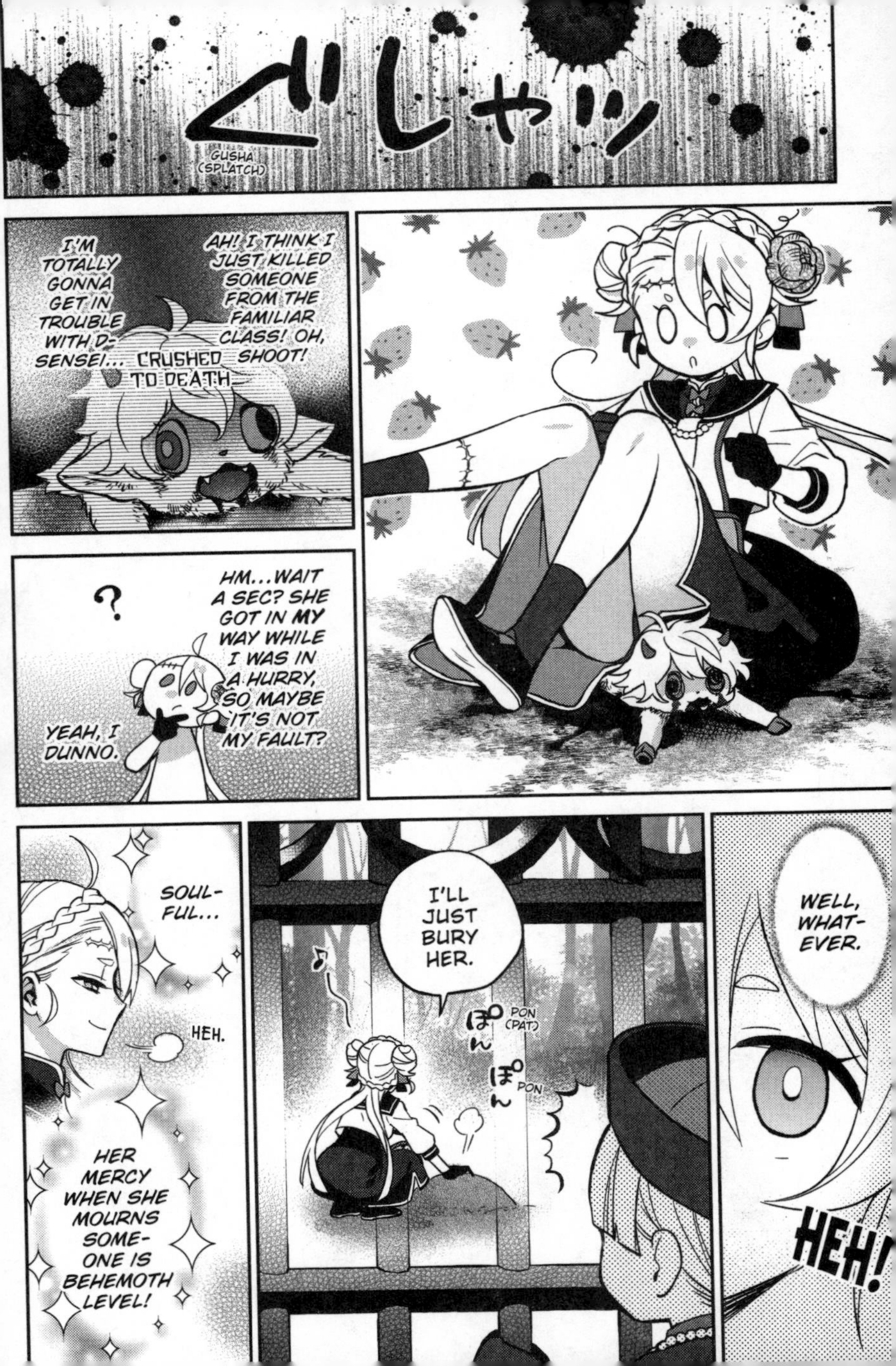
ぐしゃッ
GUSHA (SPLATCH)
AH! I THINK I JUST KILLED SOMEONE FROM THE FAMILIAR CLASS! OH, SHOOT!
I'M TOTALLY GONNA GET IN TROUBLE WITH D-SENSEI...
CRUSHED TO DEATH
HM...WAIT A SEC? SHE GOT IN MY WAY WHILE I WAS IN A HURRY, SO MAYBE IT'S NOT MY FAULT?
?
YEAH, I DUNNO.
WELL, WHAT-EVER.
HEH!
I'LL JUST BURY HER.
ぽん PON (PAT)
ぽん PON
SOUL-FUL...
HEH.
HER MERCY WHEN SHE MOURNS SOME-ONE IS BEHEMOTH LEVEL!

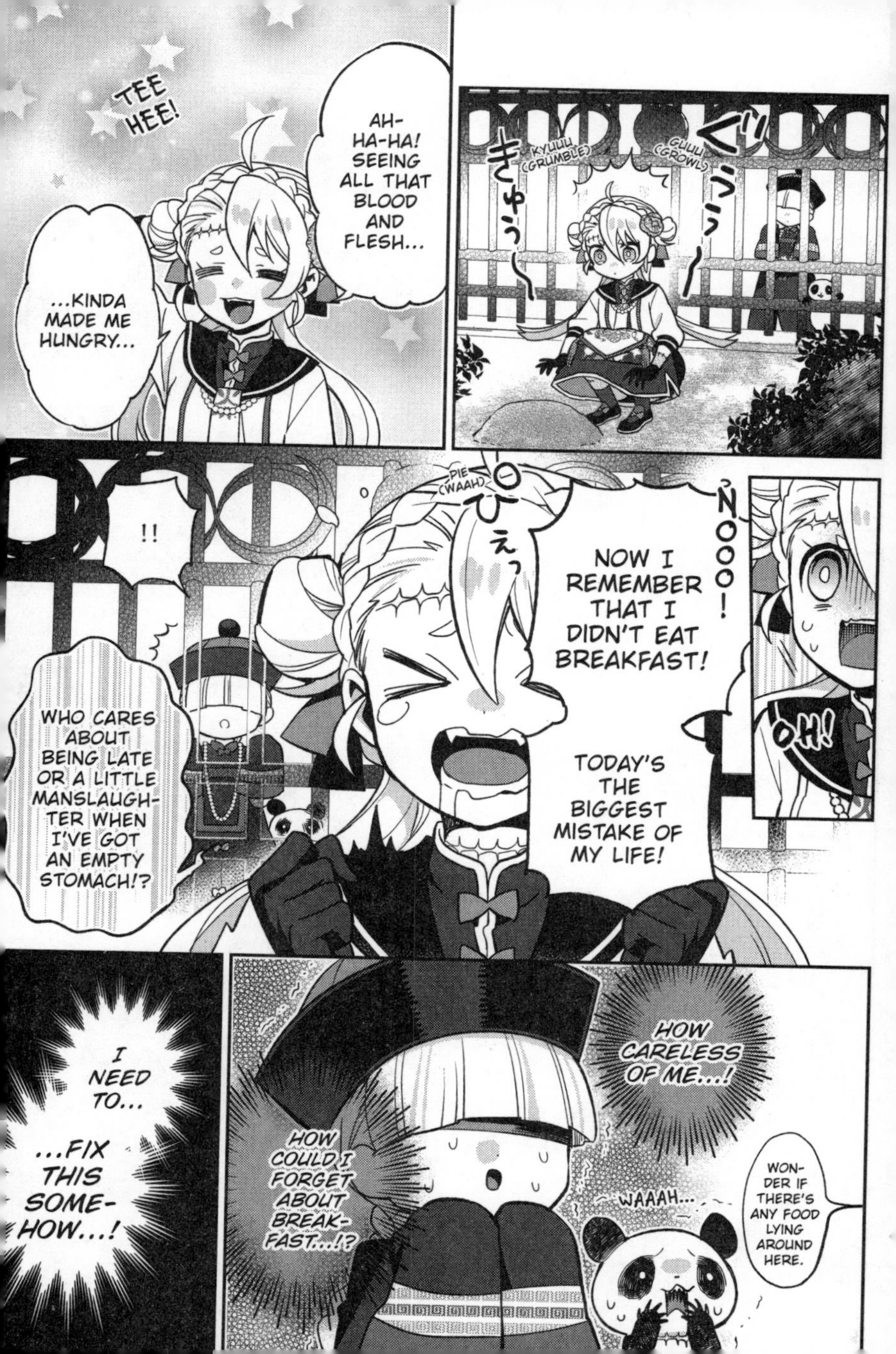
KYUUU (GRUMBLE)
GUUU (GROWL)
AH-HA-HA! SEEING ALL THAT BLOOD AND FLESH...
...KINDA MADE ME HUNGRY...
TEE HEE!
OH!
NOOOO!
NOW I REMEMBER THAT I DIDN'T EAT BREAKFAST!
TODAY'S THE BIGGEST MISTAKE OF MY LIFE!
PIE (WAAH)
!!
WHO CARES ABOUT BEING LATE OR A LITTLE MANSLAUGHTER WHEN I'VE GOT AN EMPTY STOMACH!?
HOW CARELESS OF ME...!
HOW COULD I FORGET ABOUT BREAKFAST...!?
WAAAH...
WONDER IF THERE'S ANY FOOD LYING AROUND HERE.
I NEED TO...
...FIX THIS SOMEHOW...!

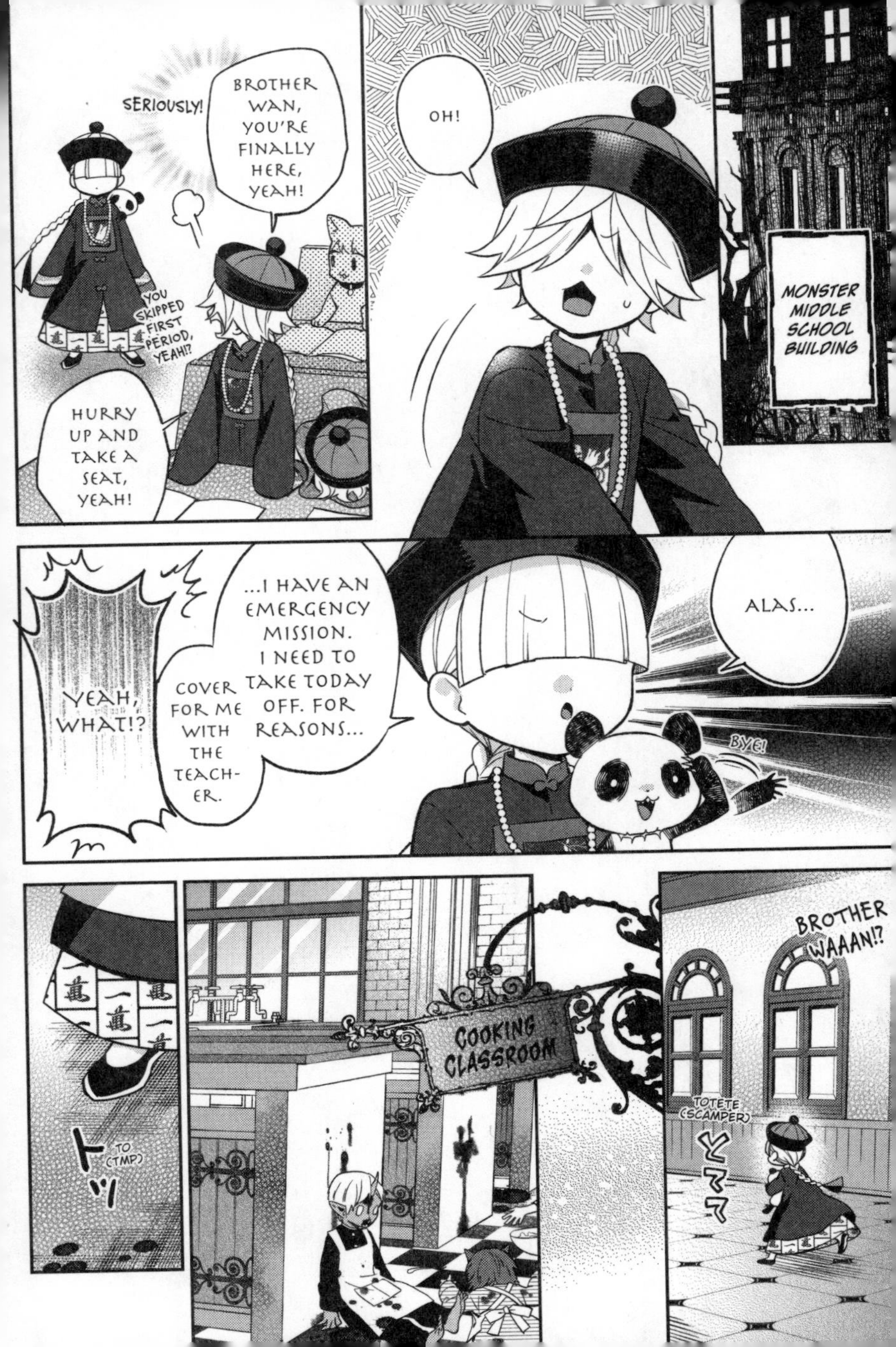
MONSTER MIDDLE SCHOOL BUILDING
OH!
BROTHER WAN, YOU'RE FINALLY HERE, YEAH!
SERIOUSLY!
YOU SKIPPED FIRST PERIOD, YEAH!?
HURRY UP AND TAKE A SEAT, YEAH!
ALAS...
BYE!
...I HAVE AN EMERGENCY MISSION. I NEED TO TAKE TODAY OFF. FOR REASONS...
COVER FOR ME WITH THE TEACH-ER.
YEAH, WHAT!?
BROTHER WAAAN!?
TOTETE (SCAMPER)
COOKING CLASSROOM
TO (TMP)

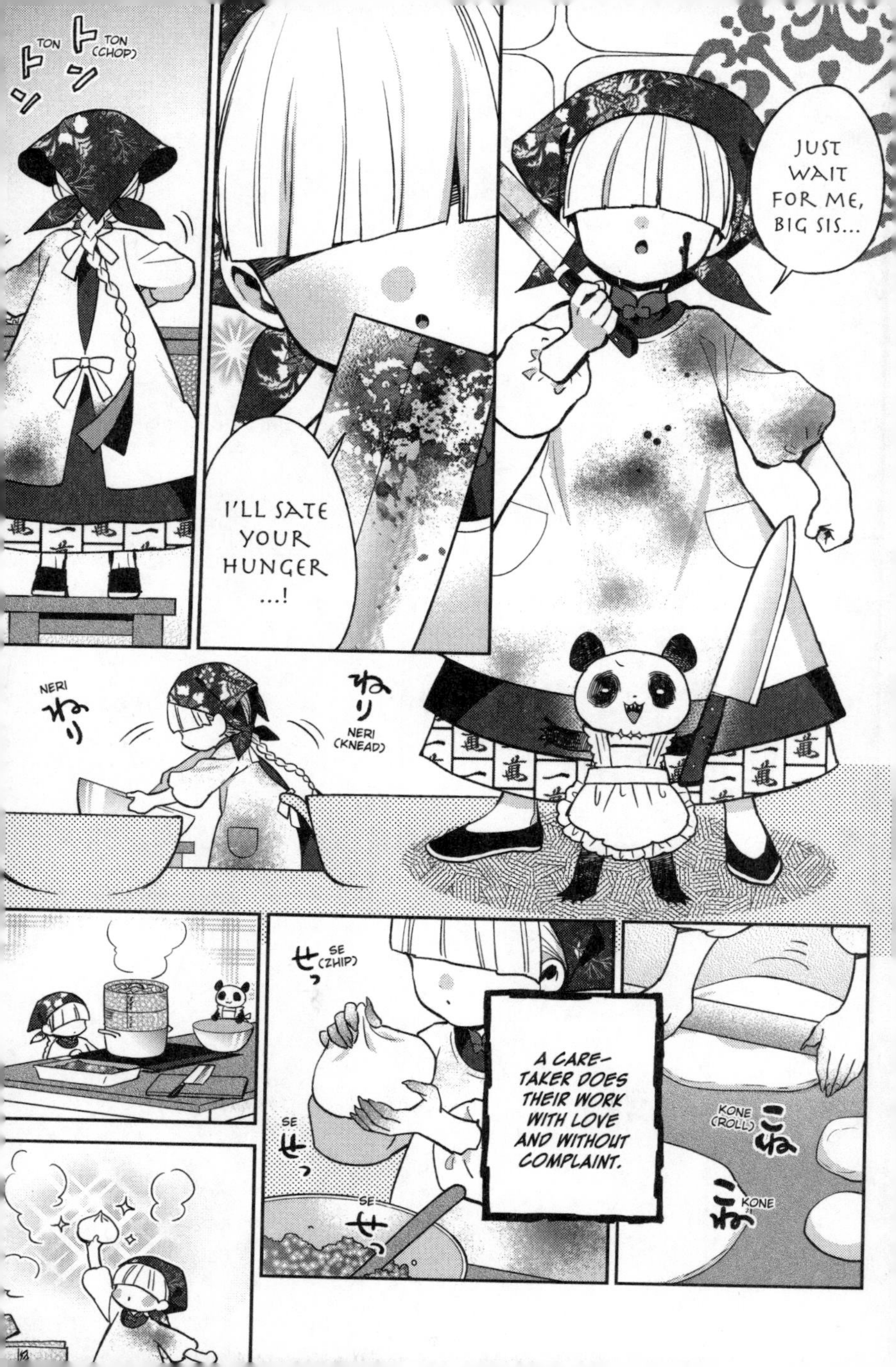
JUST WAIT FOR ME, BIG SIS...
I'LL SATE YOUR HUNGER ...!
TON TON (CHOP)
ねり NERI (KNEAD)
NERI ねり
こね KONE (ROLL)
こね KONE
A CARE-TAKER DOES THEIR WORK WITH LOVE AND WITHOUT COMPLAINT.
せっ SE
せっ SE
せっ SE (ZHIP)

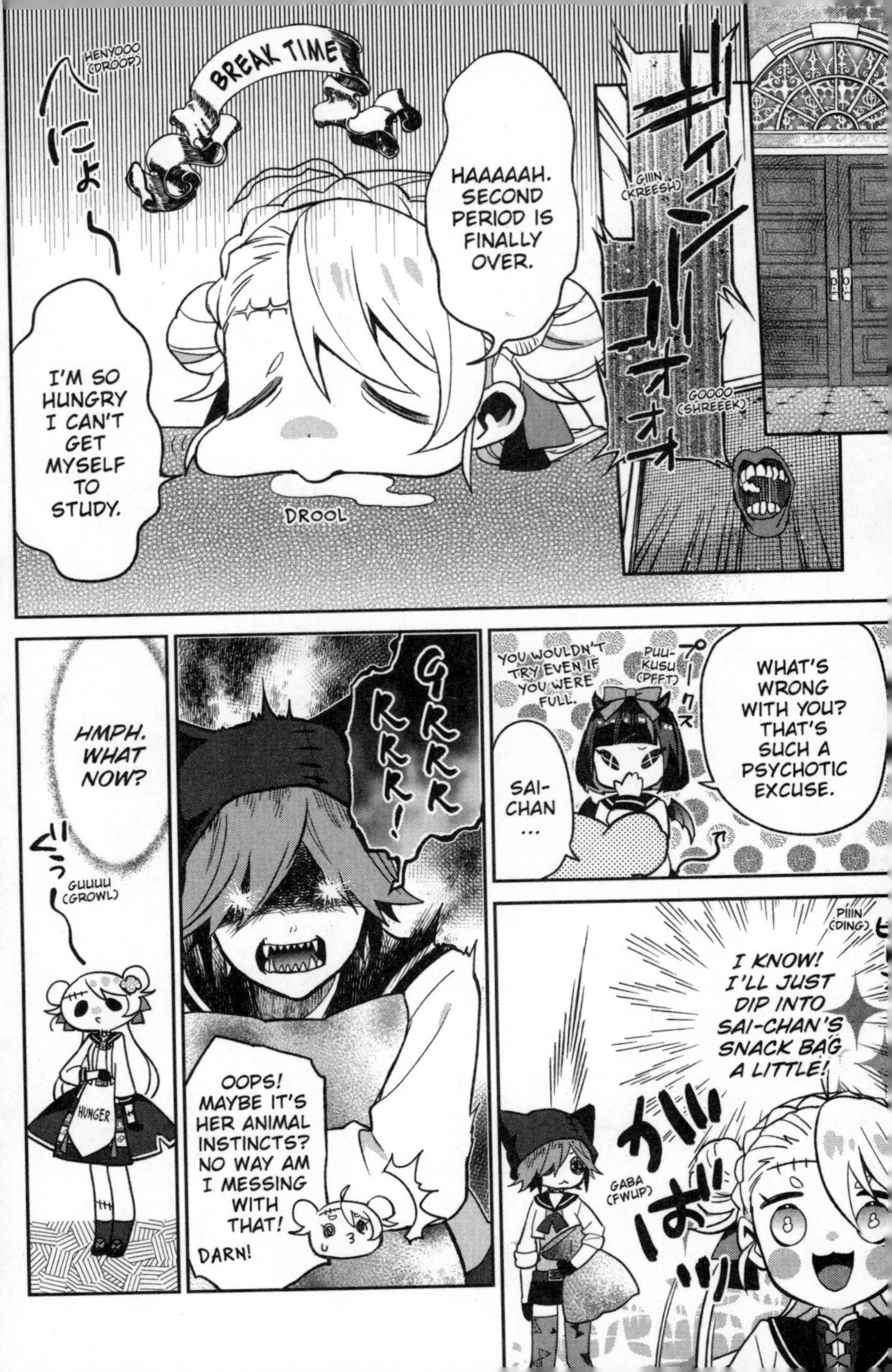
GIIIN (KREESH)
GOOOO (SHREEEK)
HAAAAAH. SECOND PERIOD IS FINALLY OVER.
BREAK TIME
HENYOOO (DROOP)
I'M SO HUNGRY I CAN'T GET MYSELF TO STUDY.
DROOL
WHAT'S WRONG WITH YOU? THAT'S SUCH A PSYCHOTIC EXCUSE.
PUU-KUSU (PFFT)
YOU WOULDN'T TRY EVEN IF YOU WERE FULL.
SAI-CHAN...
PIIIN (DING)
I KNOW! I'LL JUST DIP INTO SAI-CHAN'S SNACK BAG A LITTLE!
GABA (FWUP)
GRRRR RRRR!
OOPS! MAYBE IT'S HER ANIMAL INSTINCTS? NO WAY AM I MESSING WITH THAT!
DARN!
HMPH. WHAT NOW?
GUUUU (GROWL)
HUNGER

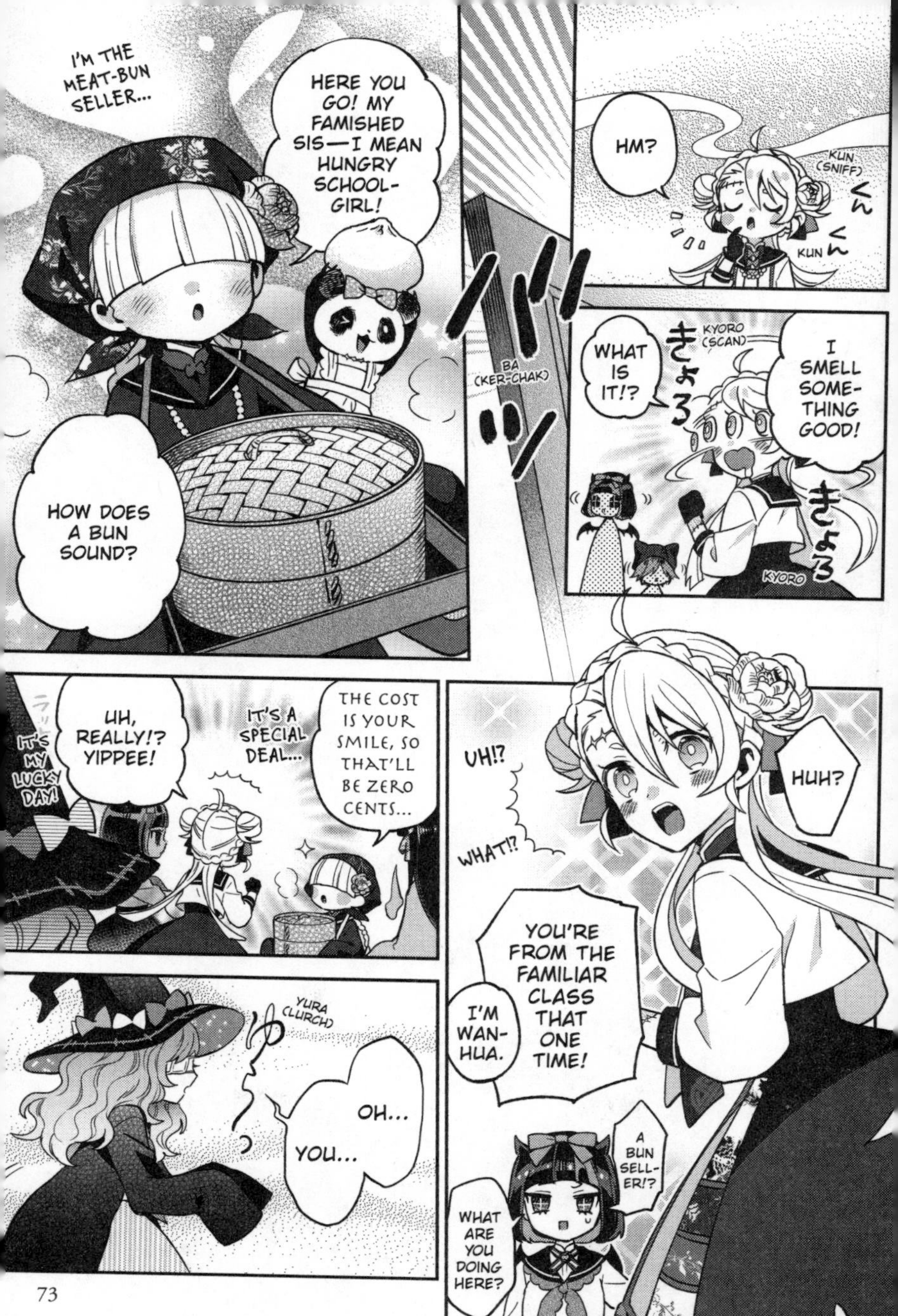
HM?
KUN (SNIFF)
くん
くん
KUN
I SMELL SOME-THING GOOD!
KYORO (SCAN)
きょろ
WHAT IS IT!?
きょろ
KYORO
BA (KER-CHAK)
I'M THE MEAT-BUN SELLER...
HERE YOU GO! MY FAMISHED SIS—I MEAN HUNGRY SCHOOL-GIRL!
HOW DOES A BUN SOUND?
HUH?
UH!?
WHAT!?
YOU'RE FROM THE FAMILIAR CLASS THAT ONE TIME!
I'M WAN-HUA.
A BUN SELL-ER!?
WHAT ARE YOU DOING HERE?
THE COST IS YOUR SMILE, SO THAT'LL BE ZERO CENTS...
IT'S A SPECIAL DEAL...
UH, REALLY!? YIPPEE!
IT'S MY LUCKY DAY!
YURA (LURCH)
OH...
YOU...

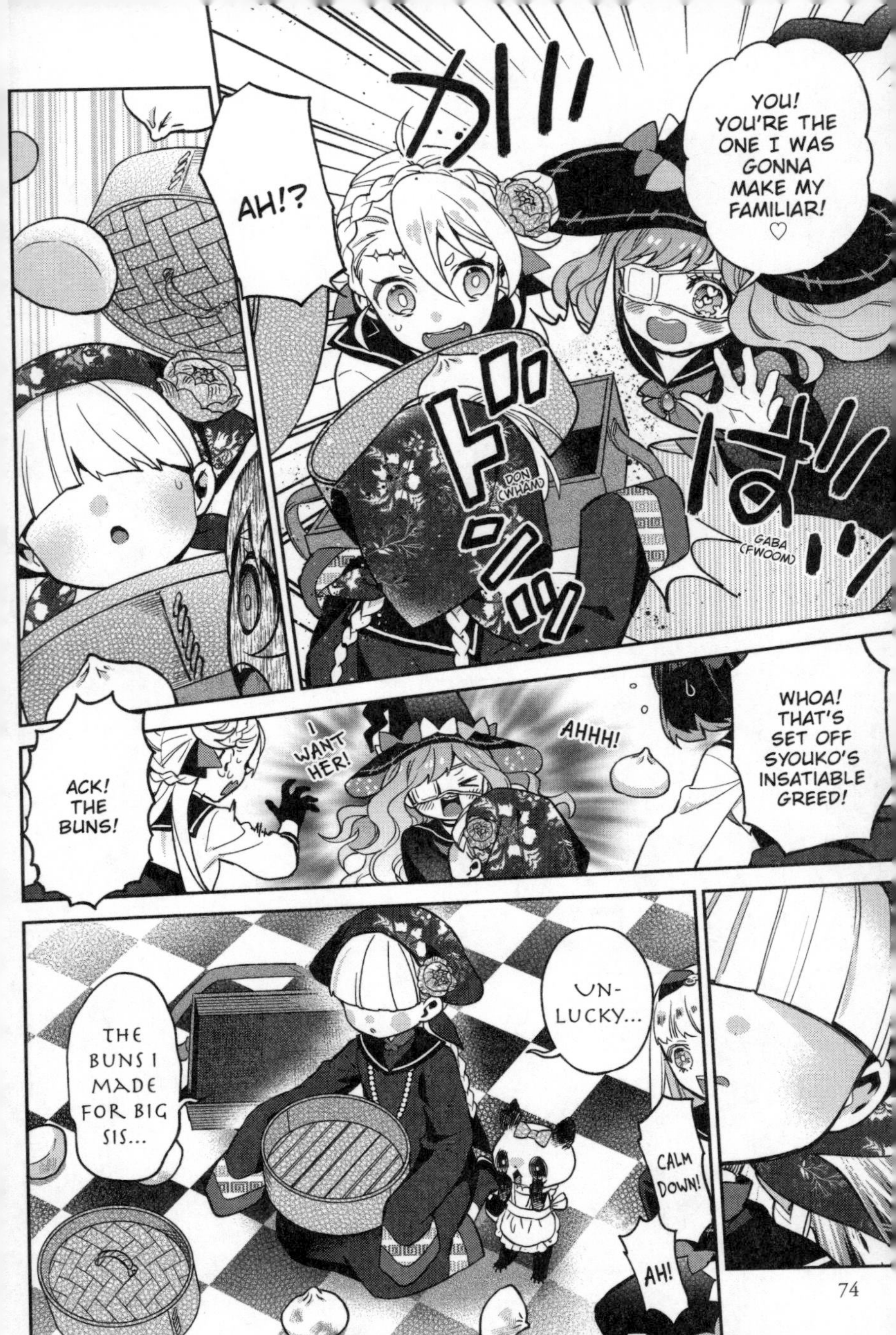
YOU! YOU'RE THE ONE I WAS GONNA MAKE MY FAMILIAR! ♡
AH!?
GABA (FWOOM)
DON (WHAM)
WHOA! THAT'S SET OFF SYOUKO'S INSATIABLE GREED!
AHHH!
I WANT HER!
ACK! THE BUNS!
UN-LUCKY...
THE BUNS I MADE FOR BIG SIS...
CALM DOWN!
AH!

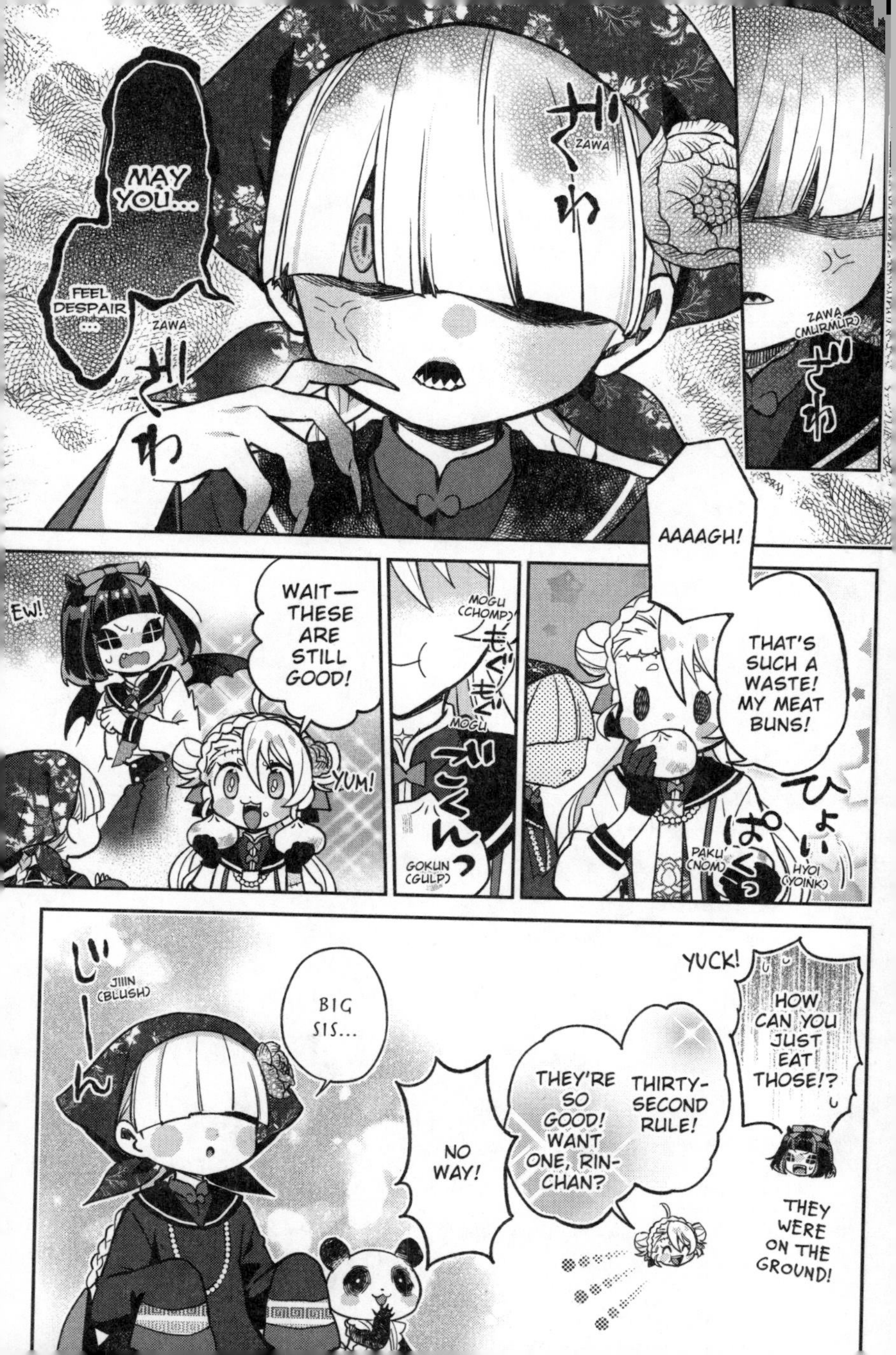
ZAWA (MURMUR)
ZAWA
MAY YOU...
FEEL DESPAIR...
ZAWA
AAAAGH!
THAT'S SUCH A WASTE! MY MEAT BUNS!
HYOI (YOINK)
PAKU (NOM)
MOGU (CHOMP)
MOGU
GOKUN (GULP)
WAIT— THESE ARE STILL GOOD!
YUM!
EW!
YUCK!
HOW CAN YOU JUST EAT THOSE!?
THEY WERE ON THE GROUND!
THIRTY-SECOND RULE!
THEY'RE SO GOOD! WANT ONE, RIN-CHAN?
NO WAY!
BIG SIS...
JIIIN (BLUSH)

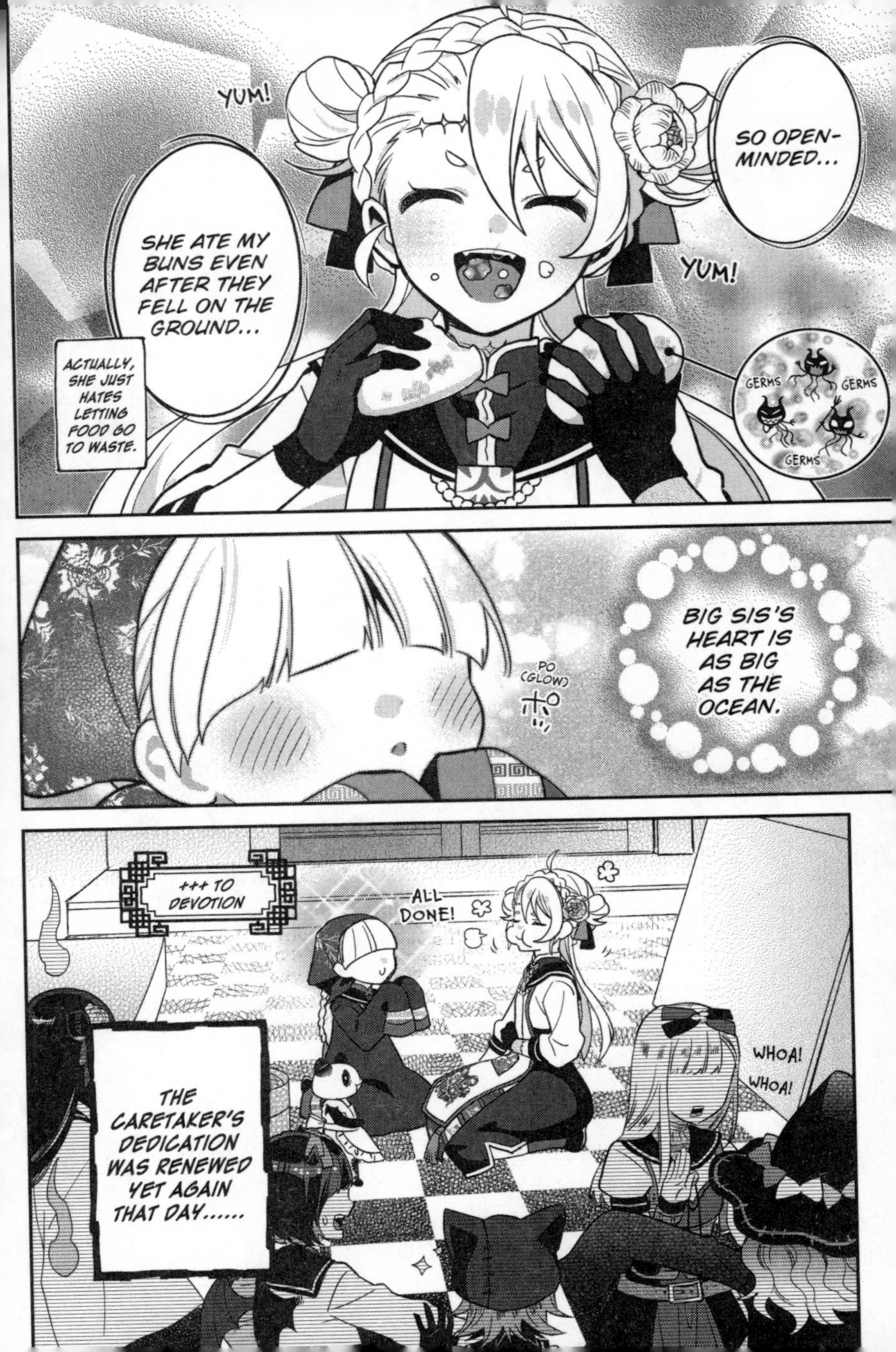
SO OPEN-MINDED...
YUM!
YUM!
SHE ATE MY BUNS EVEN AFTER THEY FELL ON THE GROUND...
ACTUALLY, SHE JUST HATES LETTING FOOD GO TO WASTE.
GERMS
GERMS
GERMS
BIG SIS'S HEART IS AS BIG AS THE OCEAN.
PO (GLOW)
+++ TO DEVOTION
ALL DONE!
WHOA!
WHOA!
THE CARETAKER'S DEDICATION WAS RENEWED YET AGAIN THAT DAY......

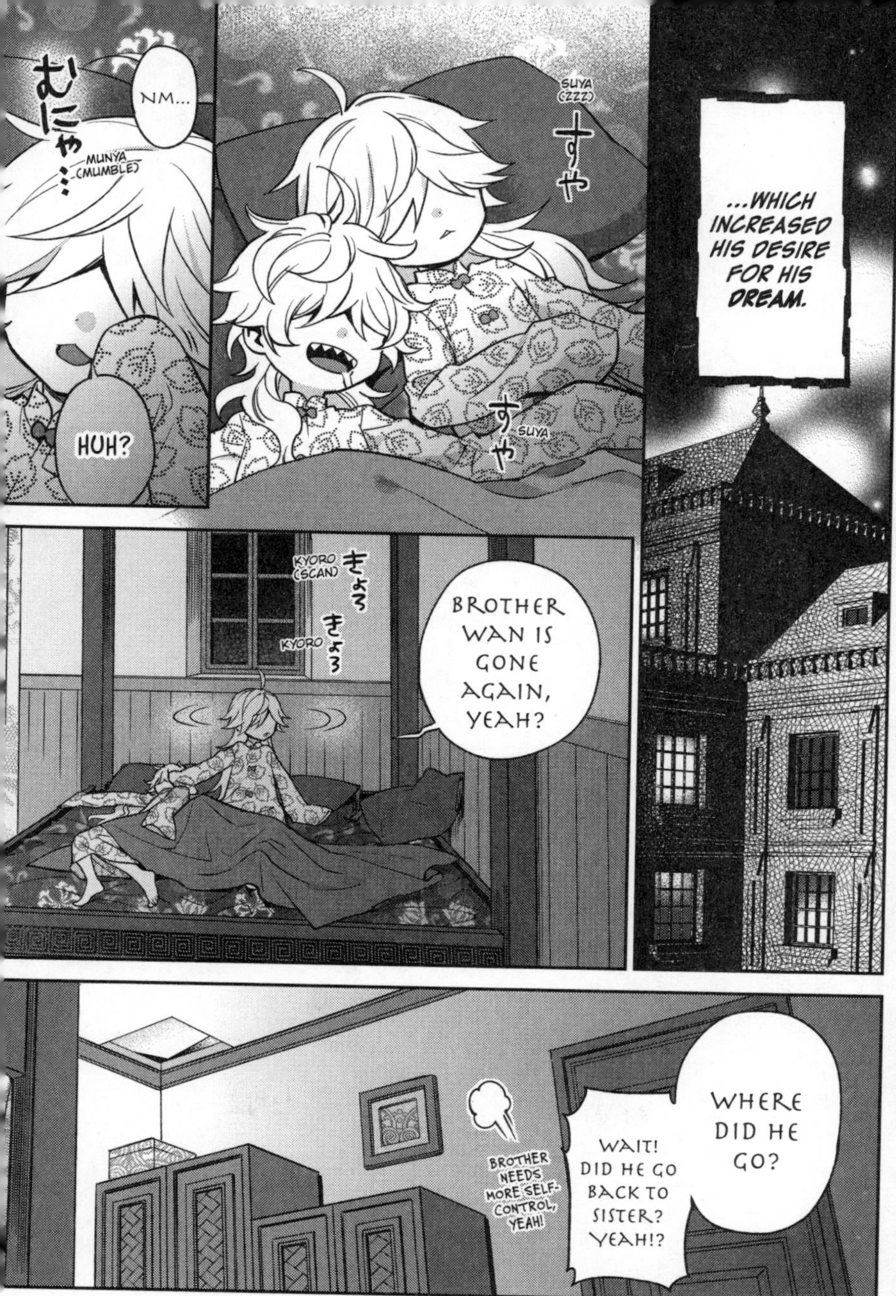
...WHICH INCREASED HIS DESIRE FOR HIS DREAM.
すや
SUYA (ZZZ)
すや
SUYA
NM...
むにゃ…
MUNYA (MUMBLE)
HUH?
BROTHER WAN IS GONE AGAIN, YEAH?
きょろ
KYORO (SCAN)
きょろ
KYORO
WHERE DID HE GO?
WAIT! DID HE GO BACK TO SISTER? YEAH!?
BROTHER NEEDS MORE SELF-CONTROL, YEAH!

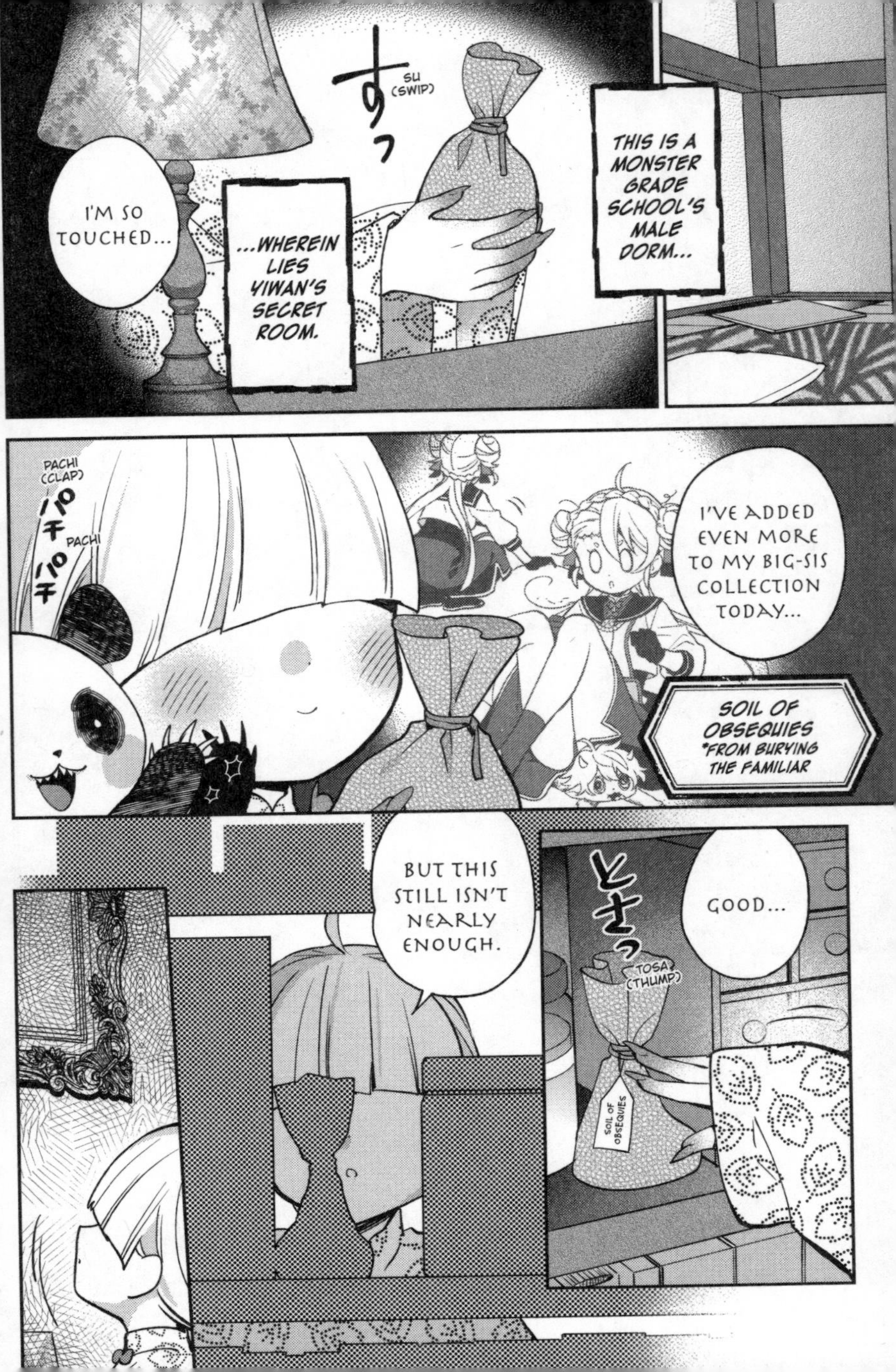
THIS IS A MONSTER GRADE SCHOOL'S MALE DORM...
SU (SWIP)
...WHEREIN LIES YIWAN'S SECRET ROOM.
I'M SO TOUCHED...
I'VE ADDED EVEN MORE TO MY BIG-SIS COLLECTION TODAY...
PACHI (CLAP) PACHI
SOIL OF OBSEQUIES *FROM BURYING THE FAMILIAR
GOOD...
TOSA (THUMP)
SOIL OF OBSEQUIES
BUT THIS STILL ISN'T NEARLY ENOUGH.

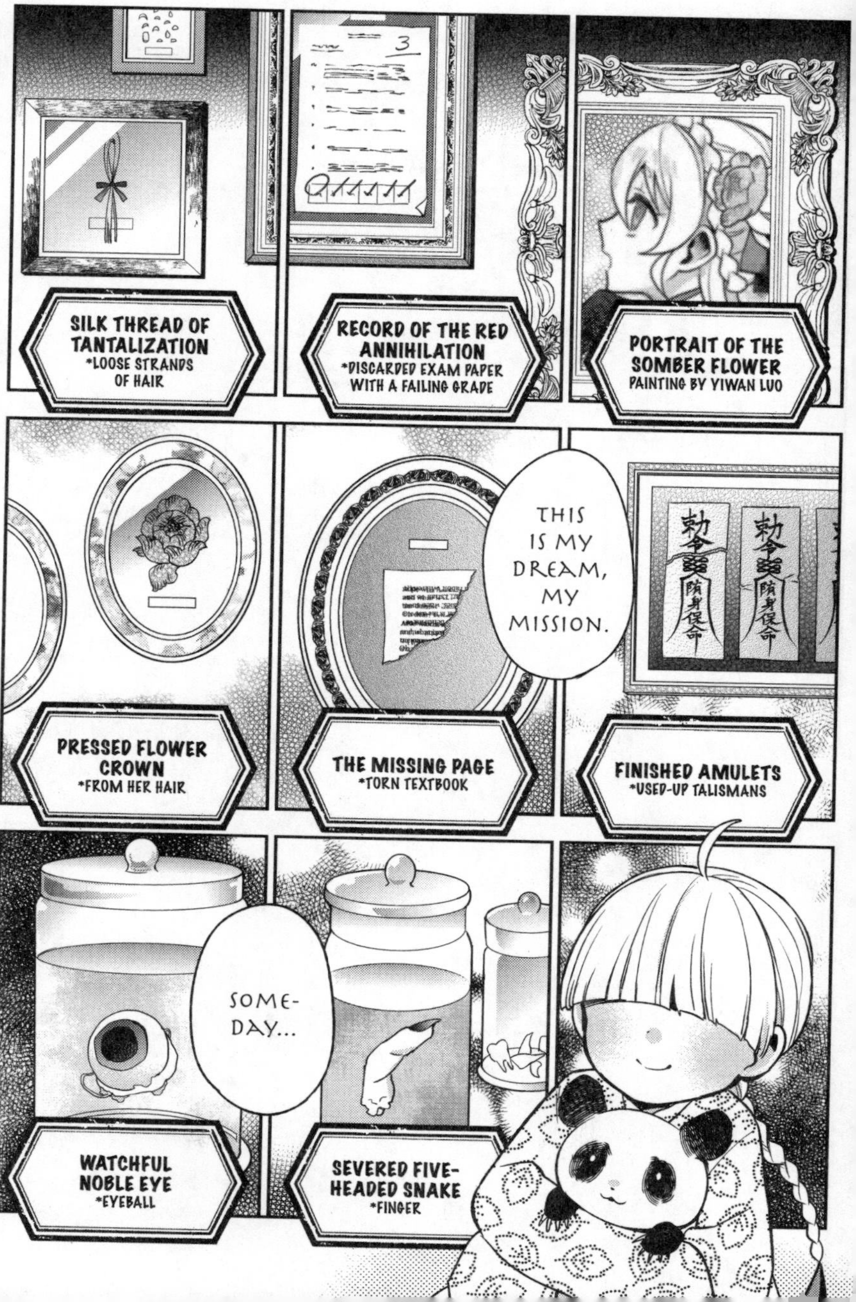
PORTRAIT OF THE SOMBER FLOWER
PAINTING BY YIWAN LUO
RECORD OF THE RED ANNIHILATION
*DISCARDED EXAM PAPER WITH A FAILING GRADE
SILK THREAD OF TANTALIZATION
*LOOSE STRANDS OF HAIR
勅令隨身保命
FINISHED AMULETS
*USED-UP TALISMANS
THIS IS MY DREAM, MY MISSION.
THE MISSING PAGE
*TORN TEXTBOOK
PRESSED FLOWER CROWN
*FROM HER HAIR
SEVERED FIVE-HEADED SNAKE
*FINGER
SOME-DAY...
WATCHFUL NOBLE EYE
*EYEBALL

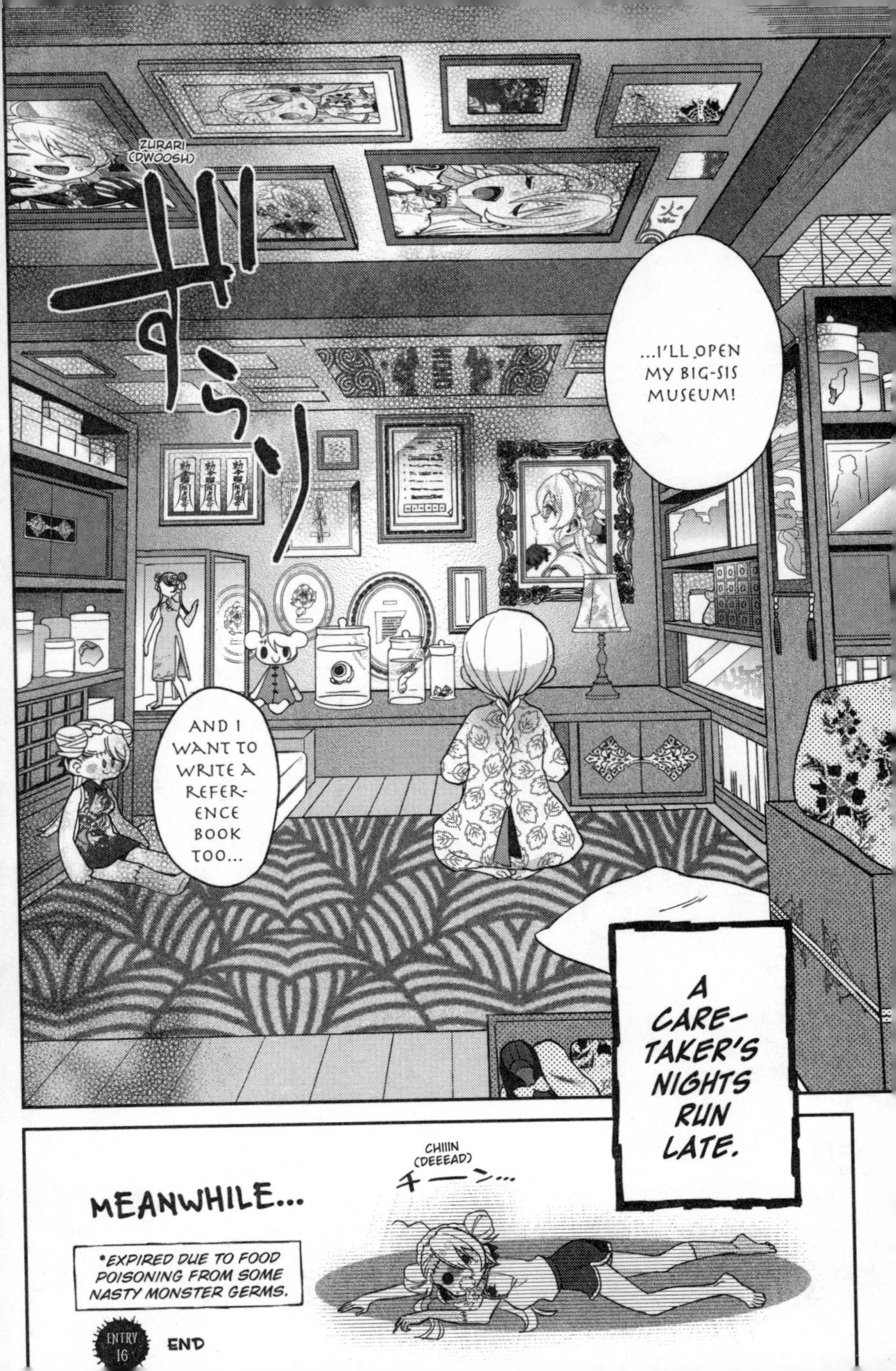
...I'LL OPEN MY BIG-SIS MUSEUM!
ZURARI (DWOOSH)
ずらーり
AND I WANT TO WRITE A REFERENCE BOOK TOO...
A CARETAKER'S NIGHTS RUN LATE.
CHIIN (DEEEAD)
チーン...
MEANWHILE...
*EXPIRED DUE TO FOOD POISONING FROM SOME NASTY MONSTER GERMS.
ENTRY 16
END

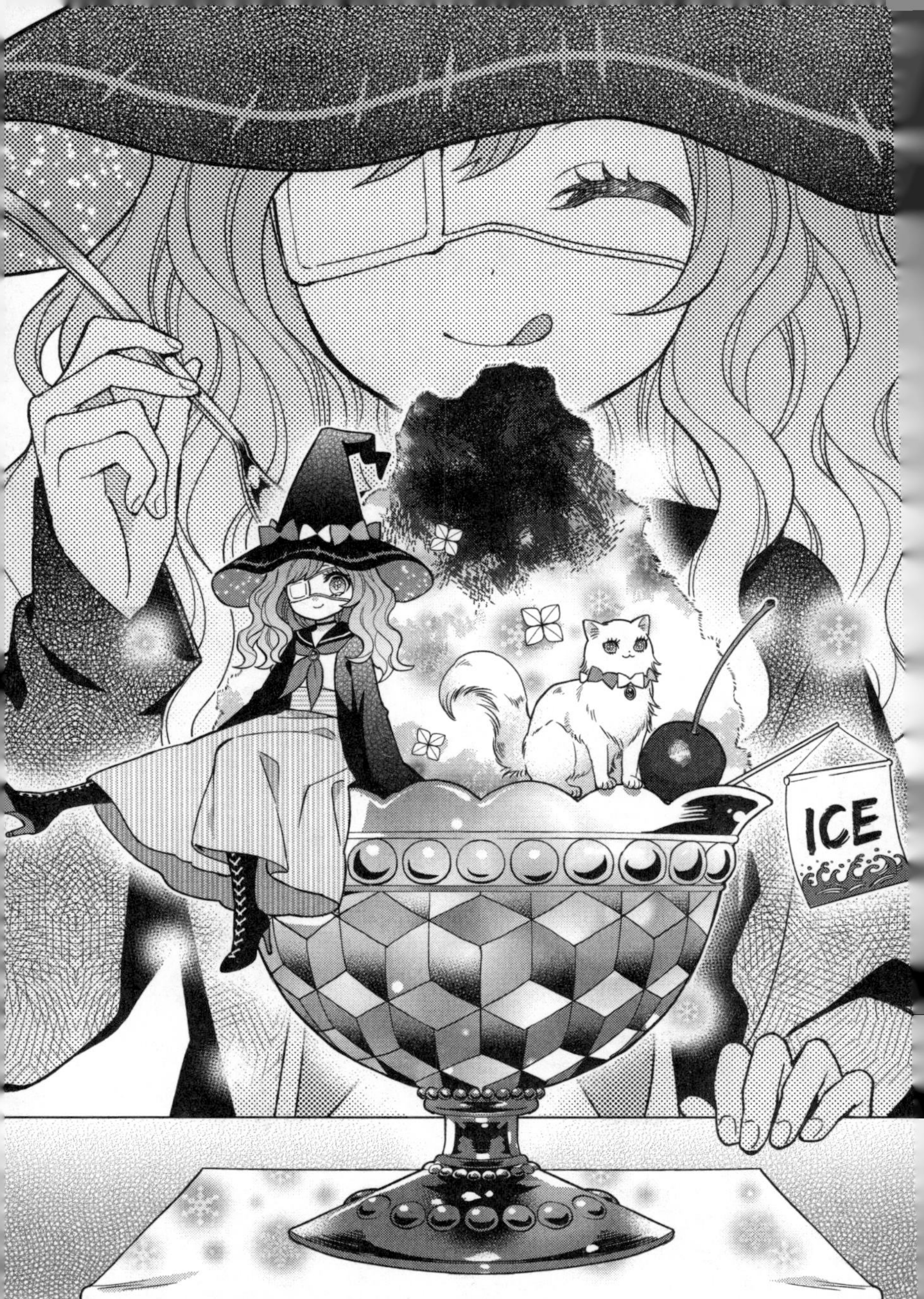
ICE

ENTRY 17

Sliiip...Tonight I'm Coming for Your BLANK!

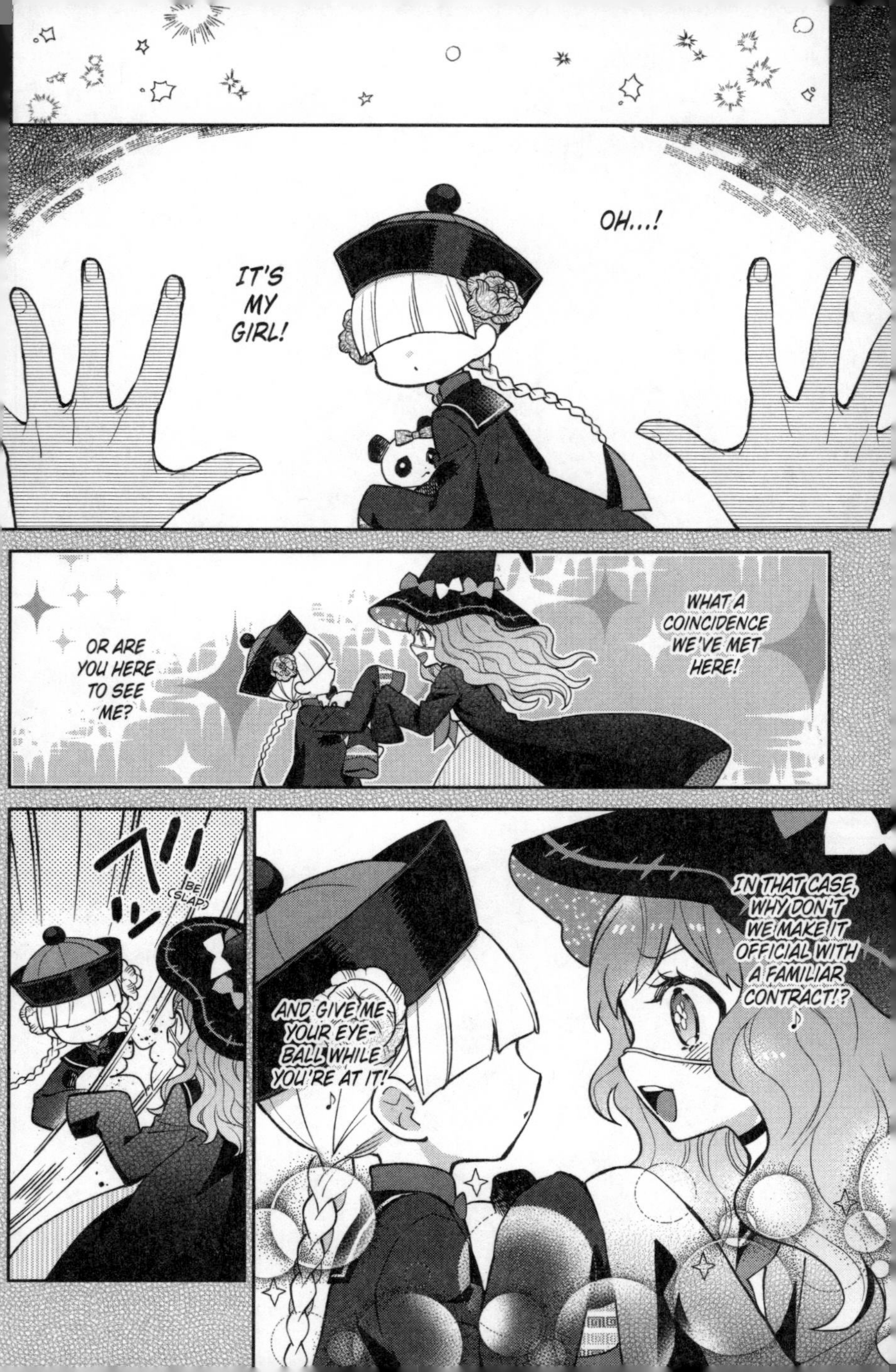
OH...!
IT'S MY GIRL!
WHAT A COINCIDENCE WE'VE MET HERE!
OR ARE YOU HERE TO SEE ME?
IN THAT CASE, WHY DON'T WE MAKE IT OFFICIAL WITH A FAMILIAR CONTRACT!? ♪
AND GIVE ME YOUR EYE-BALL WHILE YOU'RE AT IT! ♪
BE (SLAP)

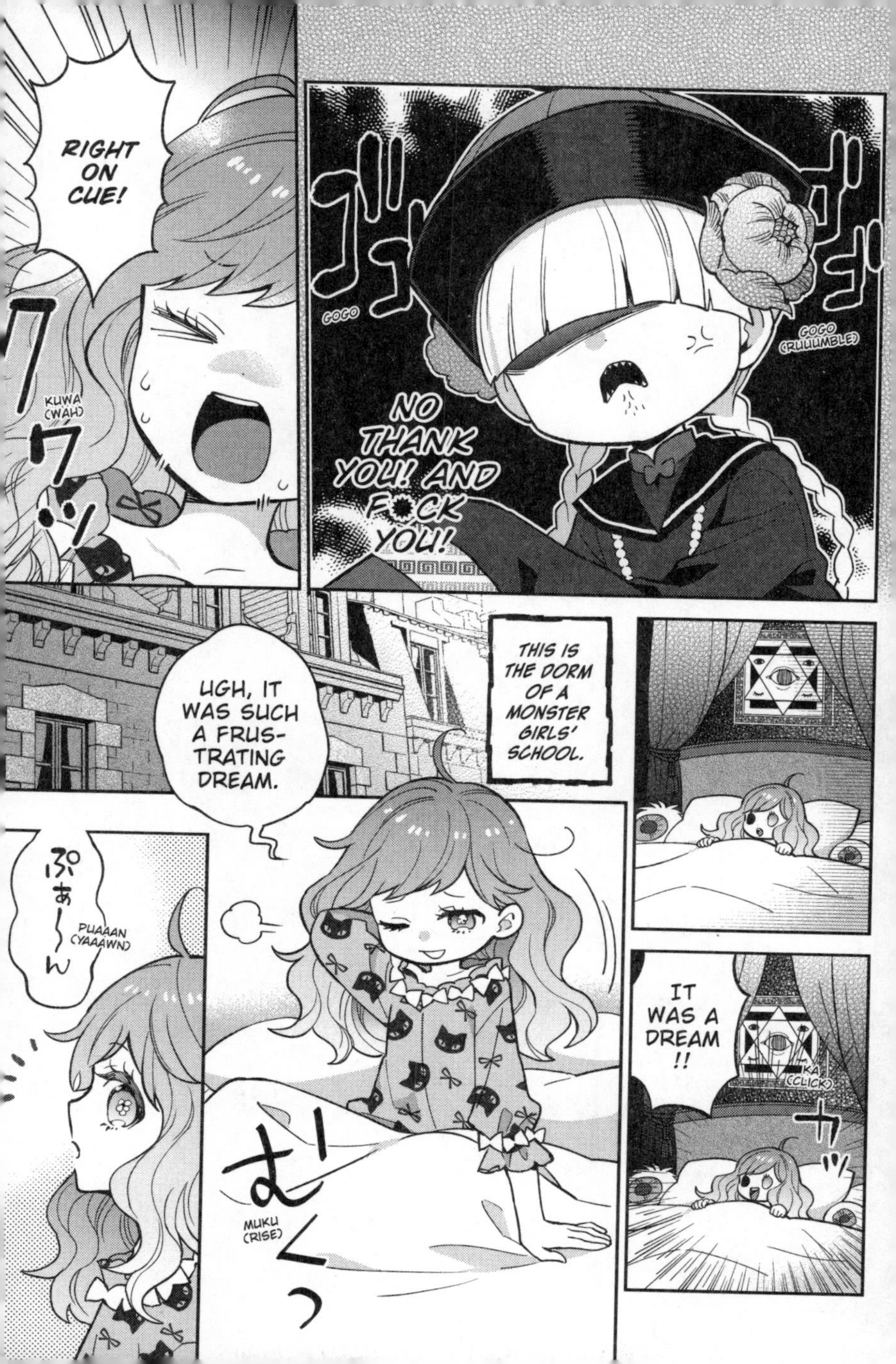
GOGO
GOGO (RUUUMBLE)
NO THANK YOU! AND F●CK YOU!
RIGHT ON CUE!
KUWA (WAH)
THIS IS THE DORM OF A MONSTER GIRLS' SCHOOL.
UGH, IT WAS SUCH A FRUS-TRATING DREAM.
IT WAS A DREAM !!
KA (CLICK)
MUKU (RISE)
ぷあ～ん
PUAAAN (YAAAWN)

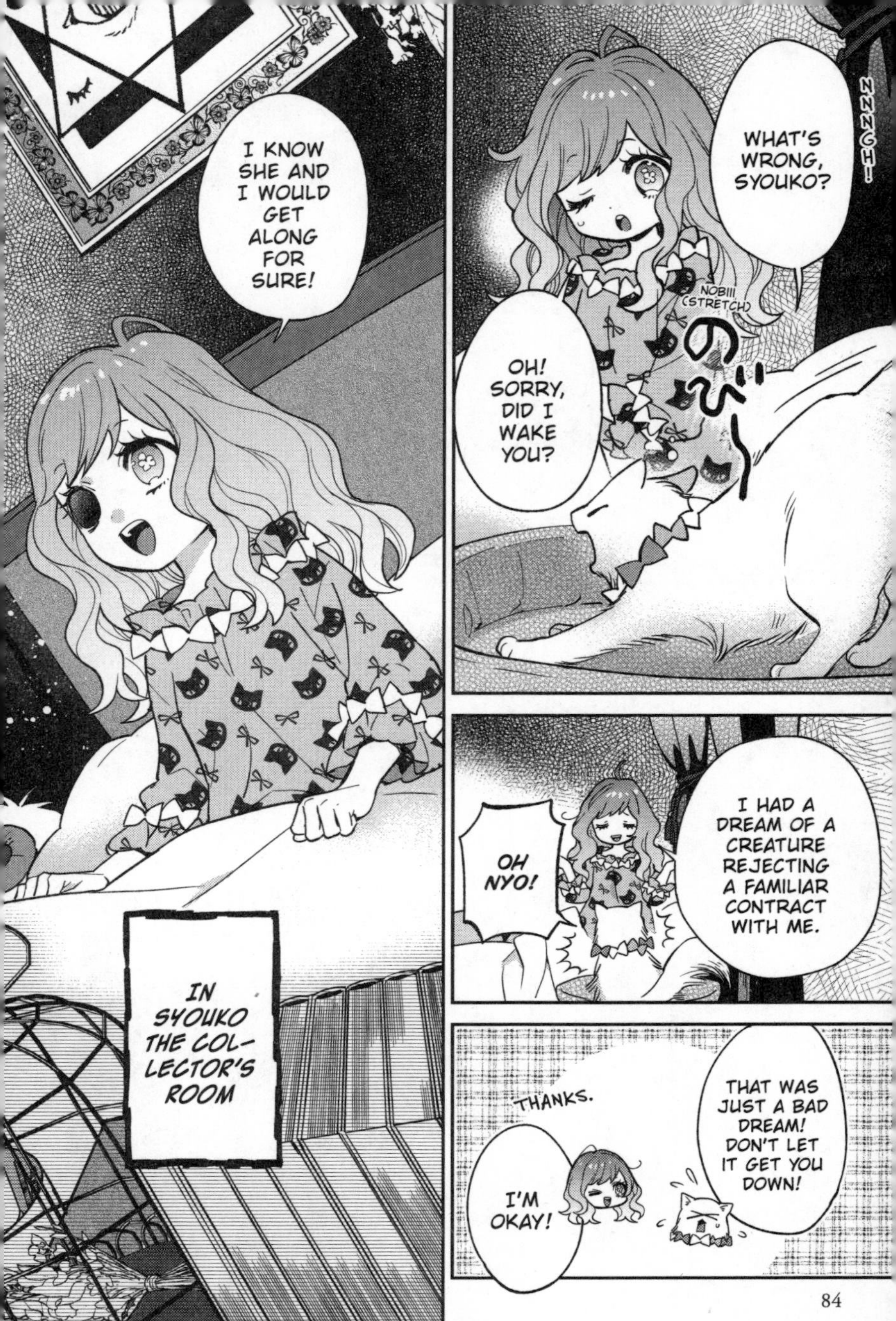
NNNNGH!
WHAT'S WRONG, SYOUKO?
NOBIII (STRETCH)
のび
OH! SORRY, DID I WAKE YOU?
I HAD A DREAM OF A CREATURE REJECTING A FAMILIAR CONTRACT WITH ME.
OH NYO!
THAT WAS JUST A BAD DREAM! DON'T LET IT GET YOU DOWN!
THANKS.
I'M OKAY!
I KNOW SHE AND I WOULD GET ALONG FOR SURE!
IN SYOUKO THE COLLECTOR'S ROOM

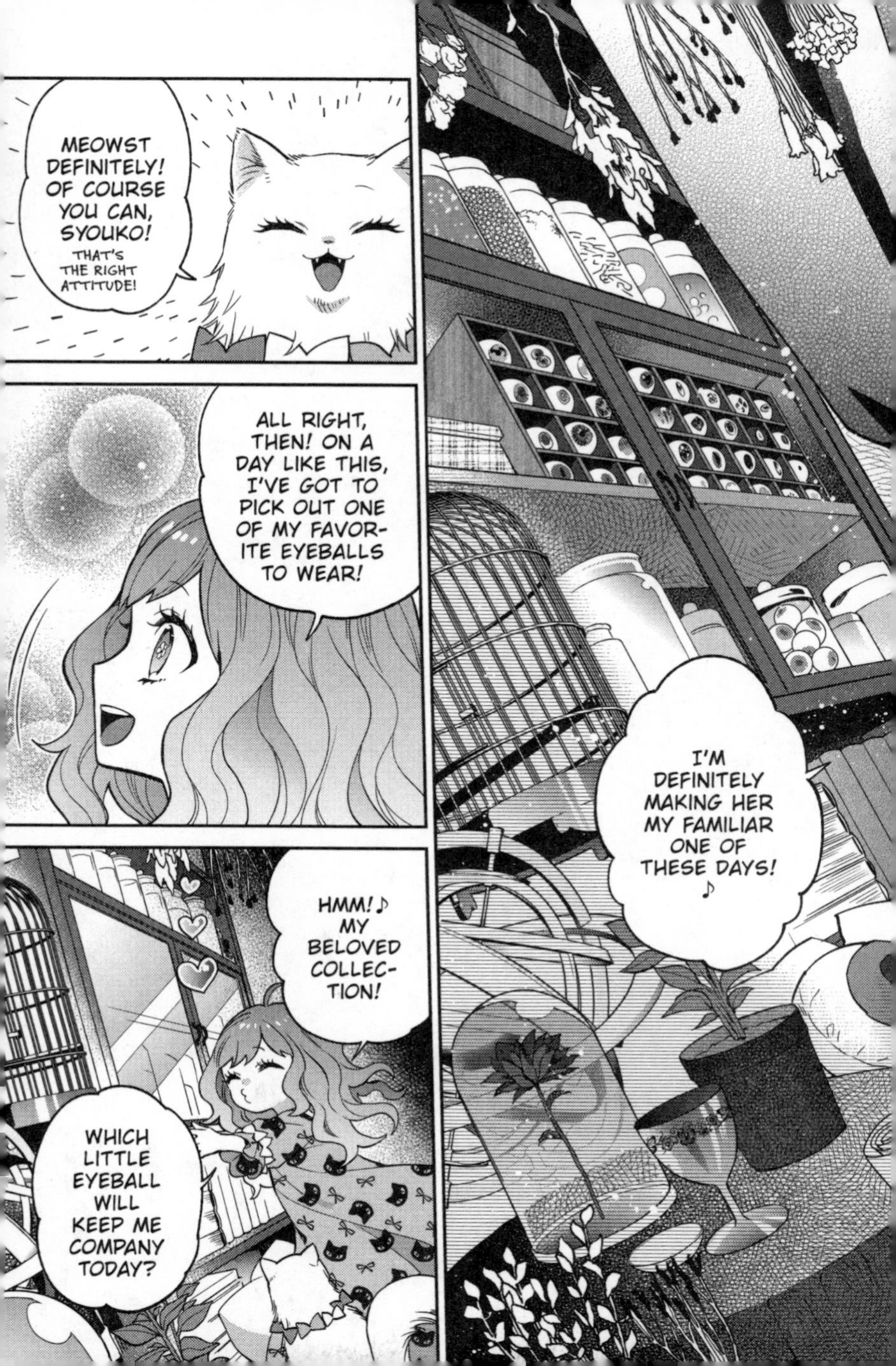
I'M DEFINITELY MAKING HER MY FAMILIAR ONE OF THESE DAYS! ♪
MEOWST DEFINITELY! OF COURSE YOU CAN, SYOUKO!
THAT'S THE RIGHT ATTITUDE!
ALL RIGHT, THEN! ON A DAY LIKE THIS, I'VE GOT TO PICK OUT ONE OF MY FAVOR-ITE EYEBALLS TO WEAR!
HMM!♪ MY BELOVED COLLEC-TION!
WHICH LITTLE EYEBALL WILL KEEP ME COMPANY TODAY?

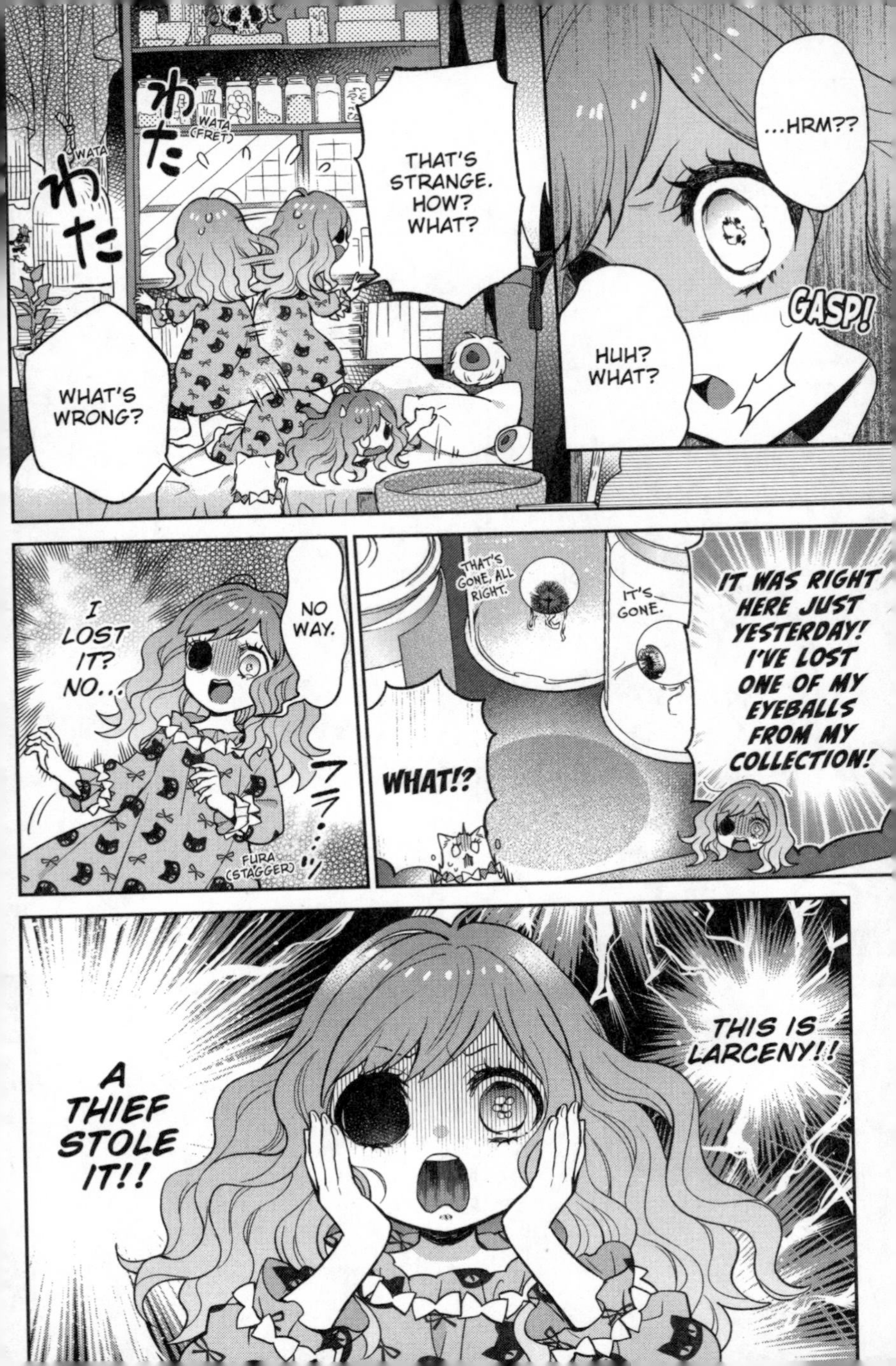
...HRM??
GASP!
HUH? WHAT?
THAT'S STRANGE. HOW? WHAT?
わた
WATA (FRET)
わた
WATA
WHAT'S WRONG?
IT WAS RIGHT HERE JUST YESTERDAY! I'VE LOST ONE OF MY EYEBALLS FROM MY COLLECTION!
IT'S GONE.
THAT'S GONE, ALL RIGHT.
WHAT!?
NO WAY.
I LOST IT? NO...
FURA (STAGGER)
THIS IS LARCENY!!
A THIEF STOLE IT!!

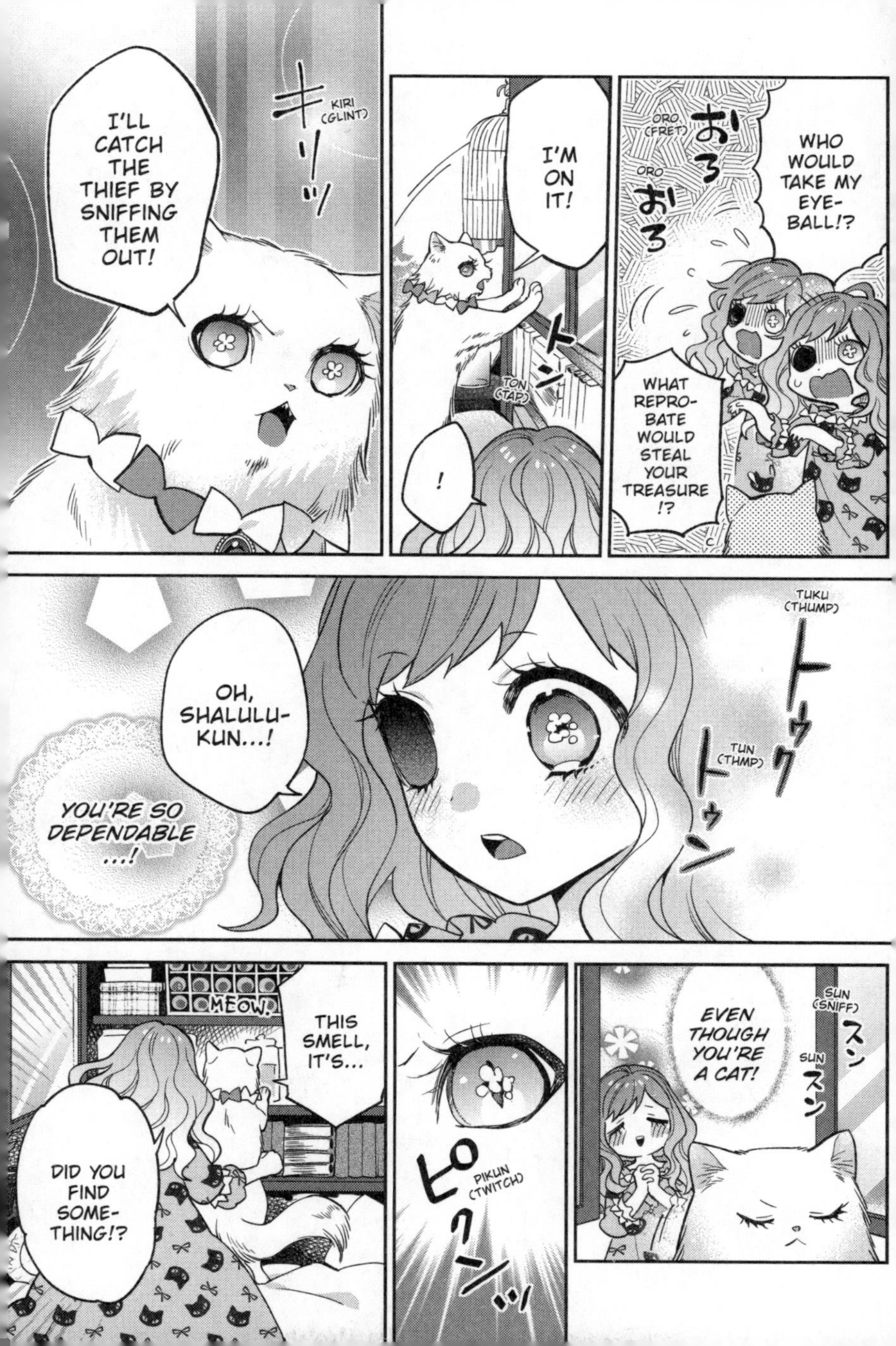
WHO WOULD TAKE MY EYE-BALL!?
ORO (FRET)
ORO
WHAT REPRO-BATE WOULD STEAL YOUR TREASURE !?
I'M ON IT!
TON (TAP)
!
KIRI (GLINT)
I'LL CATCH THE THIEF BY SNIFFING THEM OUT!
TUKU (THUMP)
TUN (THMP)
OH, SHALULU-KUN...!
YOU'RE SO DEPENDABLE ...!
SUN (SNIFF)
SUN
EVEN THOUGH YOU'RE A CAT!
PIKUN (TWITCH)
THIS SMELL, IT'S...
MEOW.
DID YOU FIND SOME-THING!?

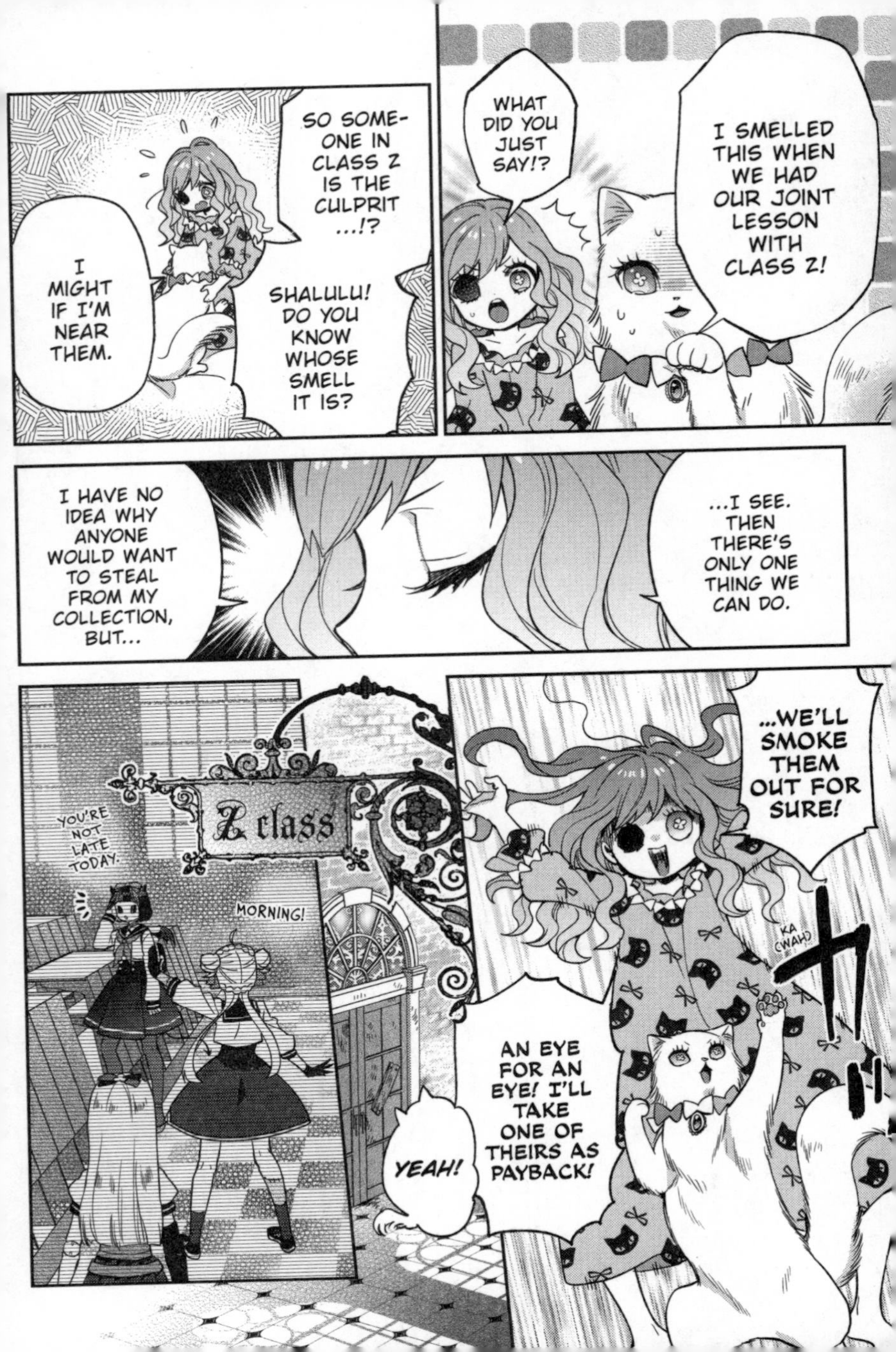
I SMELLED THIS WHEN WE HAD OUR JOINT LESSON WITH CLASS Z!
WHAT DID YOU JUST SAY!?
SO SOME-ONE IN CLASS Z IS THE CULPRIT ...!?
SHALULU! DO YOU KNOW WHOSE SMELL IT IS?
I MIGHT IF I'M NEAR THEM.
...I SEE. THEN THERE'S ONLY ONE THING WE CAN DO.
I HAVE NO IDEA WHY ANYONE WOULD WANT TO STEAL FROM MY COLLECTION, BUT...
...WE'LL SMOKE THEM OUT FOR SURE!
KA (WAH)
AN EYE FOR AN EYE! I'LL TAKE ONE OF THEIRS AS PAYBACK!
YEAH!
Z class
YOU'RE NOT LATE TODAY.
MORNING!

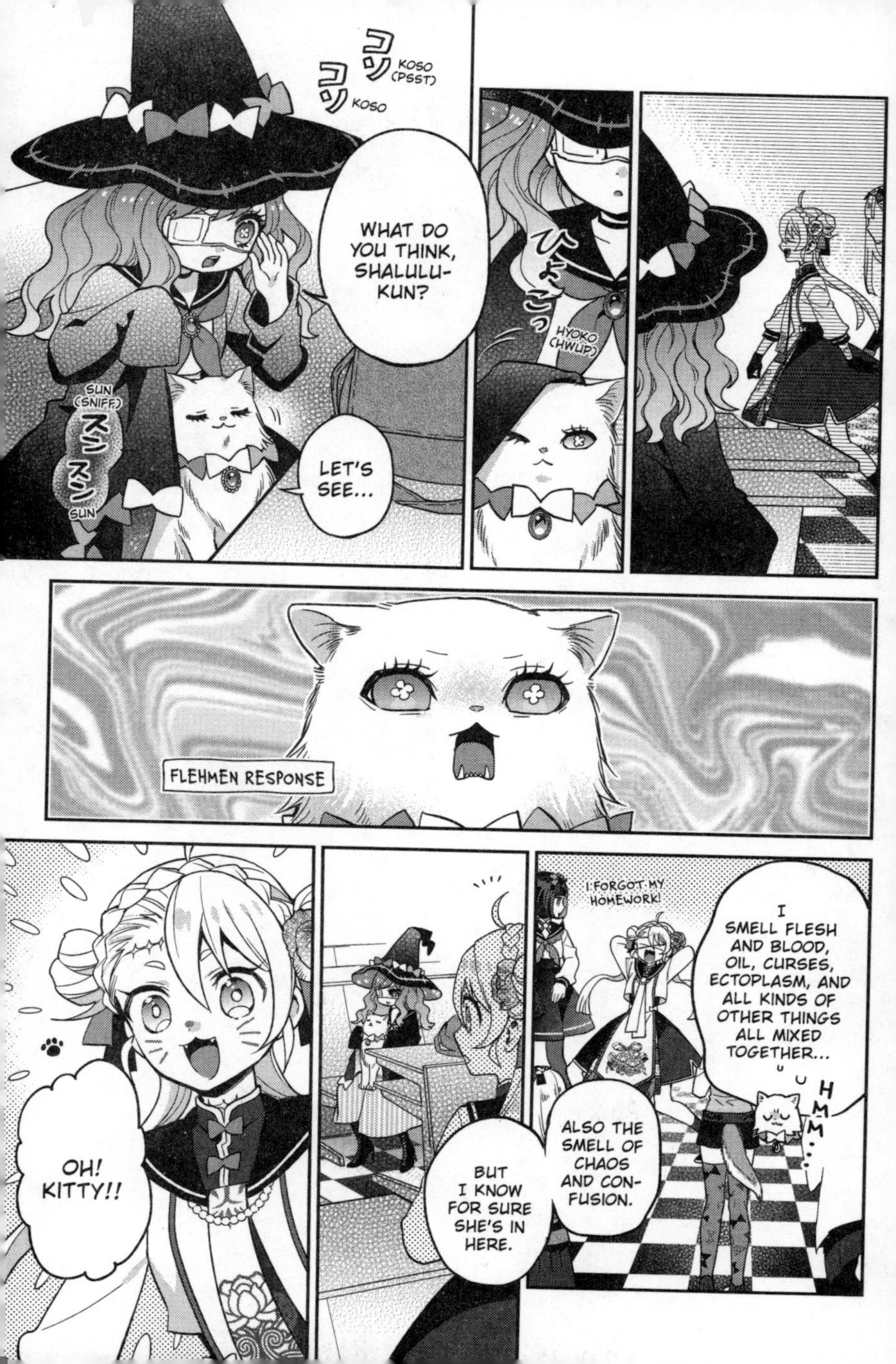
HYOKO (HWUP)
KOSO (PSST)
KOSO
WHAT DO YOU THINK, SHALULU-KUN?
SUN (SNIFF)
SUN
LET'S SEE...
FLEHMEN RESPONSE
I FORGOT MY HOMEWORK!
I SMELL FLESH AND BLOOD, OIL, CURSES, ECTOPLASM, AND ALL KINDS OF OTHER THINGS ALL MIXED TOGETHER...
HMM...
ALSO THE SMELL OF CHAOS AND CON-FUSION.
BUT I KNOW FOR SURE SHE'S IN HERE.
OH! KITTY!!

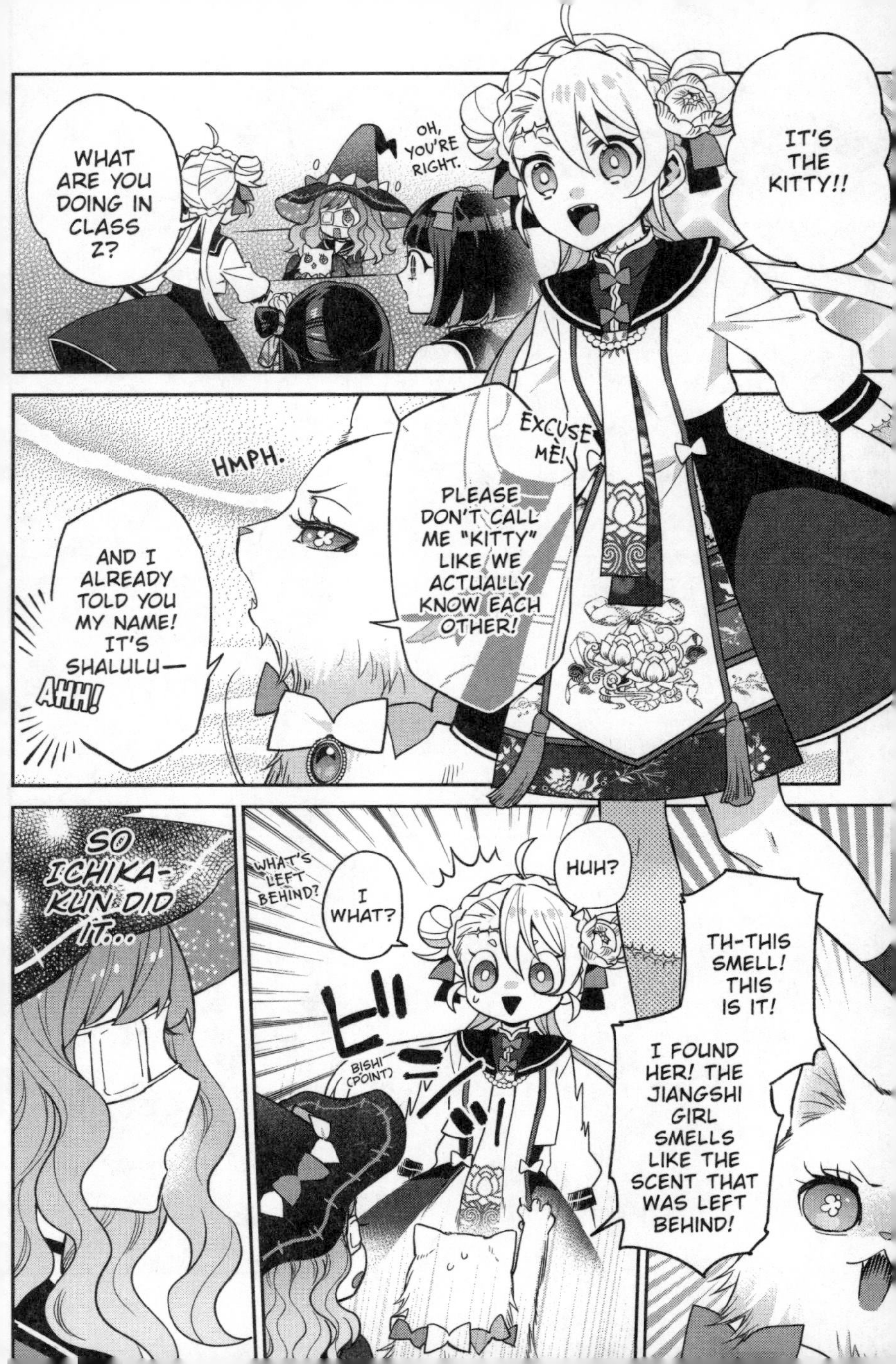
IT'S THE KITTY!!
OH, YOU'RE RIGHT.
WHAT ARE YOU DOING IN CLASS Z?
EXCUSE ME!
PLEASE DON'T CALL ME "KITTY" LIKE WE ACTUALLY KNOW EACH OTHER!
HMPH.
AND I ALREADY TOLD YOU MY NAME! IT'S SHALULU—
AHH!
TH-THIS SMELL! THIS IS IT!
HUH?
I FOUND HER! THE JIANGSHI GIRL SMELLS LIKE THE SCENT THAT WAS LEFT BEHIND!
I WHAT?
WHAT'S LEFT BEHIND?
BISHI (POINT)
SO ICHIKA-KUN DID IT...

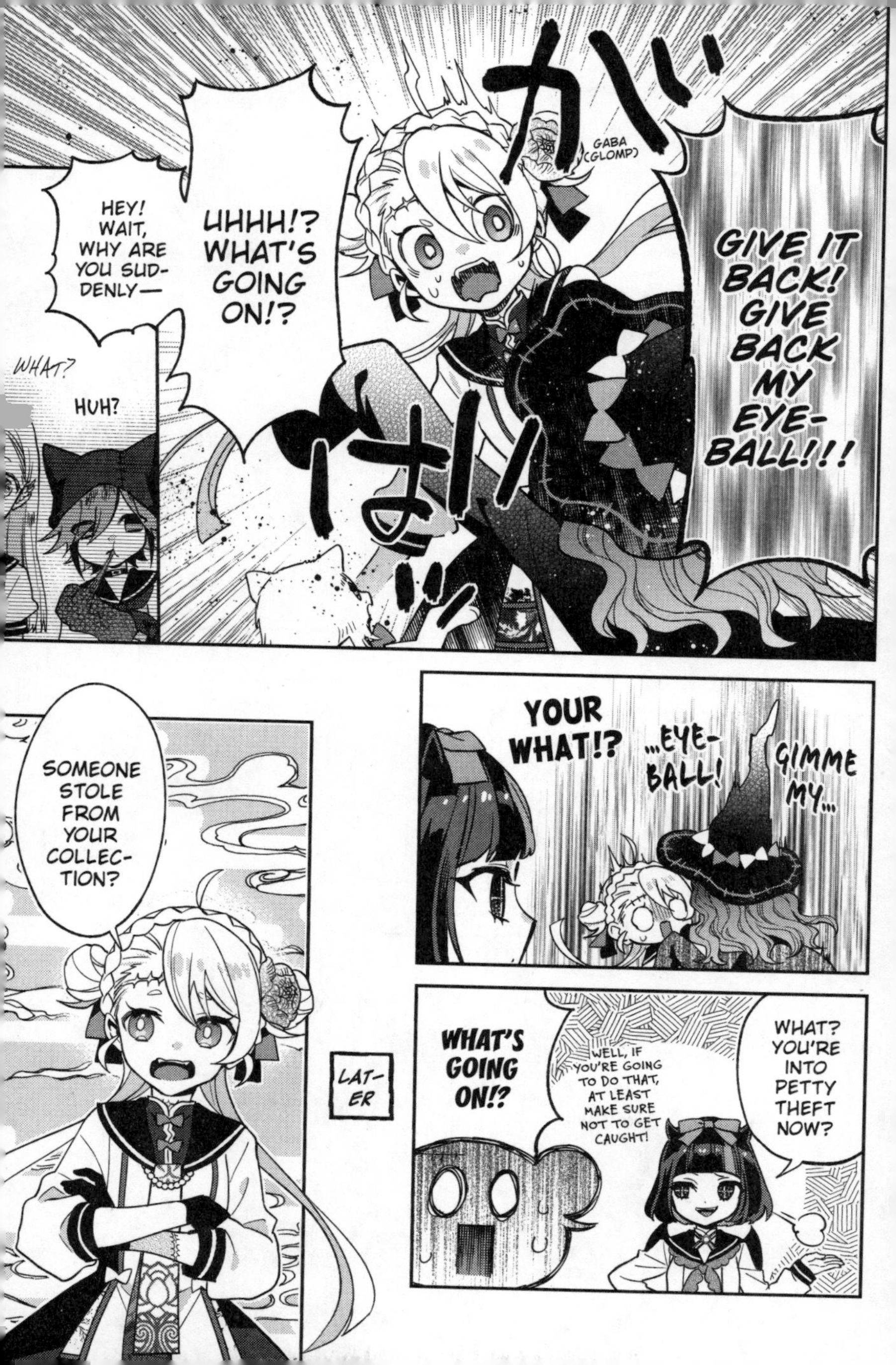
GABA (GLOMP)
GIVE IT BACK! GIVE BACK MY EYE-BALL!!!
UHHH!? WHAT'S GOING ON!?
HEY! WAIT, WHY ARE YOU SUD-DENLY—
WHAT?
HUH?
GIMME MY...
...EYE-BALL!
YOUR WHAT!?
SOMEONE STOLE FROM YOUR COLLEC-TION?
WHAT? YOU'RE INTO PETTY THEFT NOW?
WELL, IF YOU'RE GOING TO DO THAT, AT LEAST MAKE SURE NOT TO GET CAUGHT!
WHAT'S GOING ON!?
LAT-ER

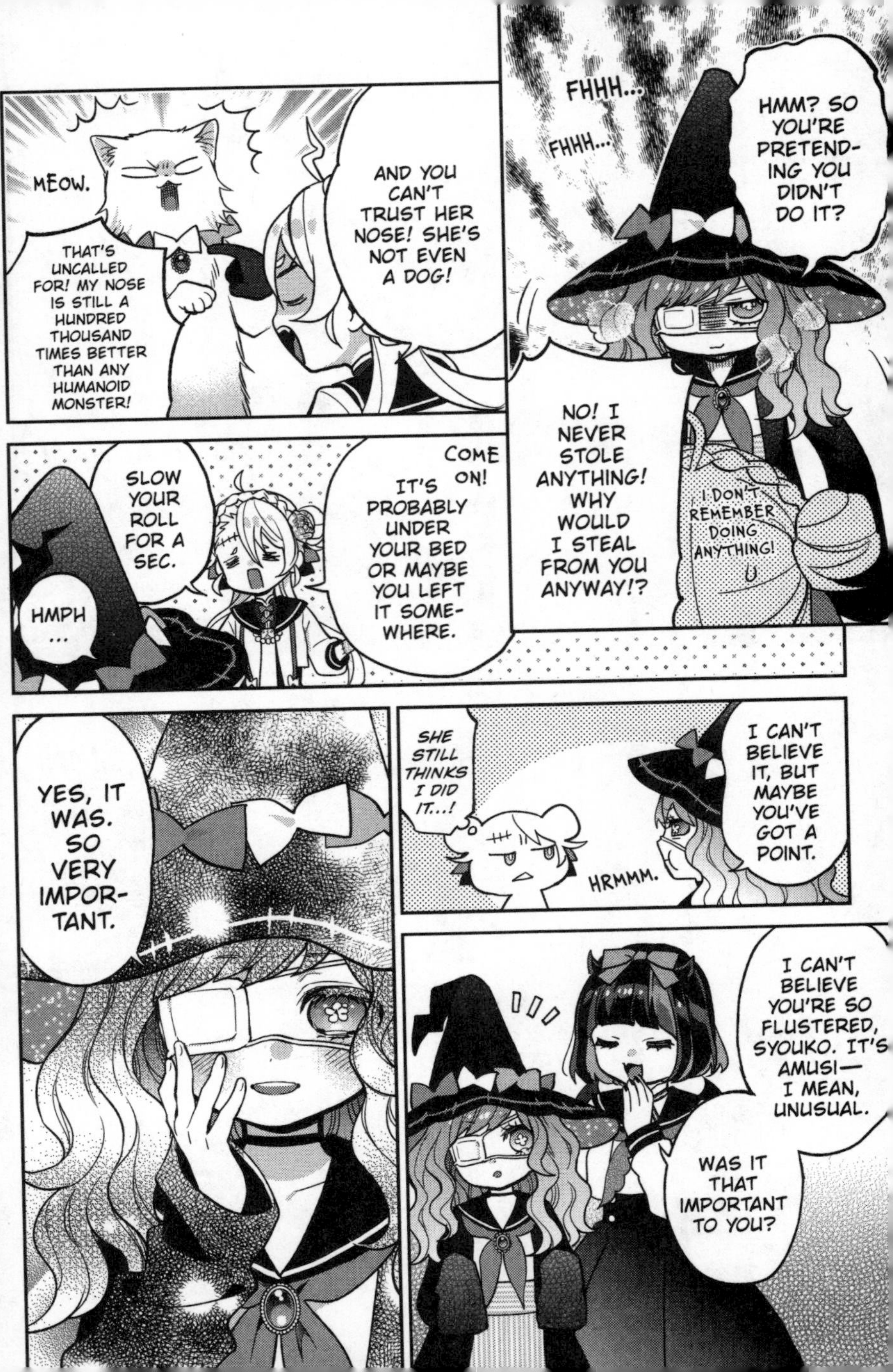
HMM? SO YOU'RE PRETEND-ING YOU DIDN'T DO IT?
FHHH...
FHHH...
NO! I NEVER STOLE ANYTHING! WHY WOULD I STEAL FROM YOU ANYWAY!?
I DON'T REMEMBER DOING ANYTHING!
AND YOU CAN'T TRUST HER NOSE! SHE'S NOT EVEN A DOG!
MEOW.
THAT'S UNCALLED FOR! MY NOSE IS STILL A HUNDRED THOUSAND TIMES BETTER THAN ANY HUMANOID MONSTER!
COME ON!
IT'S PROBABLY UNDER YOUR BED OR MAYBE YOU LEFT IT SOME-WHERE.
SLOW YOUR ROLL FOR A SEC.
HMPH ...
I CAN'T BELIEVE IT, BUT MAYBE YOU'VE GOT A POINT.
HRMMM.
SHE STILL THINKS I DID IT...!
I CAN'T BELIEVE YOU'RE SO FLUSTERED, SYOUKO. IT'S AMUSI— I MEAN, UNUSUAL.
WAS IT THAT IMPORTANT TO YOU?
YES, IT WAS. SO VERY IMPOR-TANT.

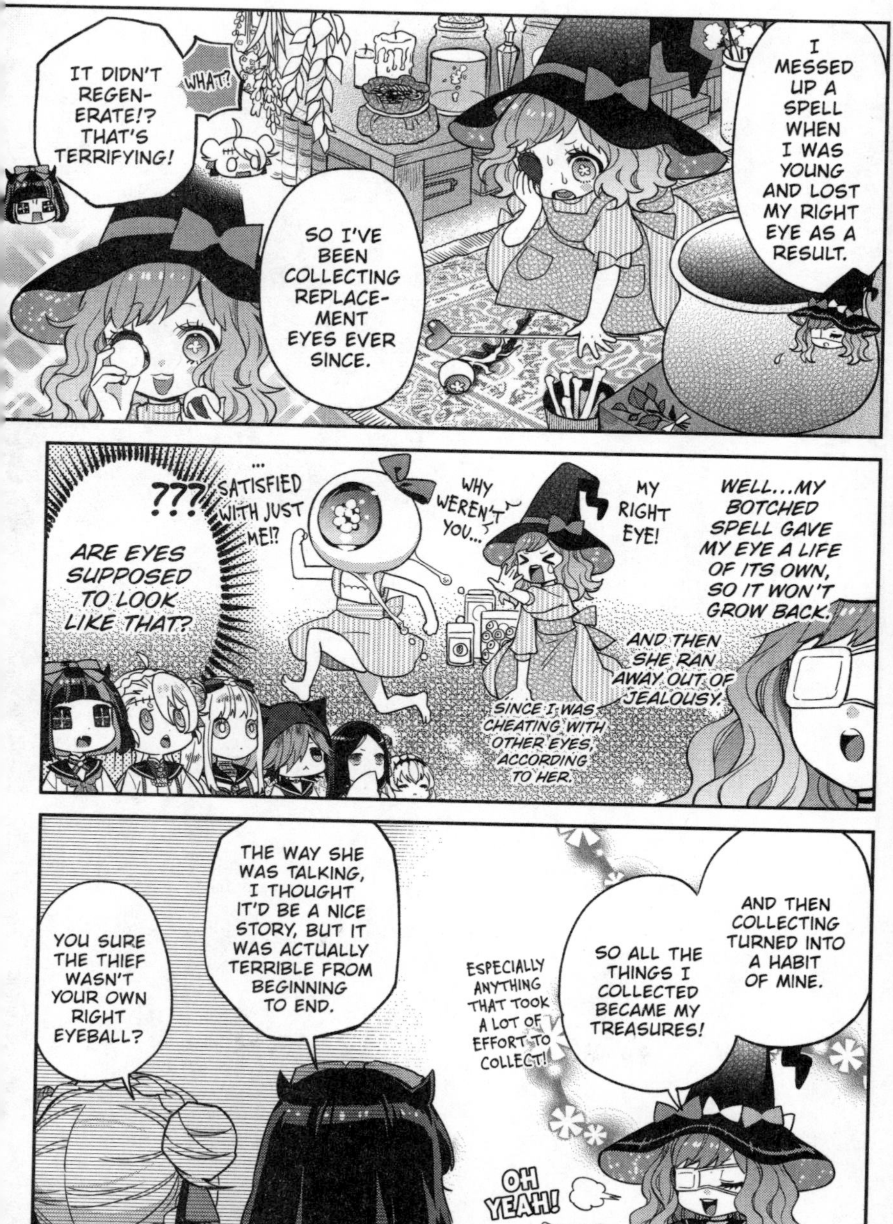
I MESSED UP A SPELL WHEN I WAS YOUNG AND LOST MY RIGHT EYE AS A RESULT.
SO I'VE BEEN COLLECTING REPLACE-MENT EYES EVER SINCE.
IT DIDN'T REGEN-ERATE!? THAT'S TERRIFYING!
WHAT?
WELL...MY BOTCHED SPELL GAVE MY EYE A LIFE OF ITS OWN, SO IT WON'T GROW BACK.
AND THEN SHE RAN AWAY OUT OF JEALOUSY.
SINCE I WAS CHEATING WITH OTHER EYES, ACCORDING TO HER.
MY RIGHT EYE!
WHY WEREN'T YOU...
...SATISFIED WITH JUST ME!?
???
ARE EYES SUPPOSED TO LOOK LIKE THAT?
AND THEN COLLECTING TURNED INTO A HABIT OF MINE.
SO ALL THE THINGS I COLLECTED BECAME MY TREASURES!
ESPECIALLY ANYTHING THAT TOOK A LOT OF EFFORT TO COLLECT!
OH YEAH!
THE WAY SHE WAS TALKING, I THOUGHT IT'D BE A NICE STORY, BUT IT WAS ACTUALLY TERRIBLE FROM BEGINNING TO END.
YOU SURE THE THIEF WASN'T YOUR OWN RIGHT EYEBALL?

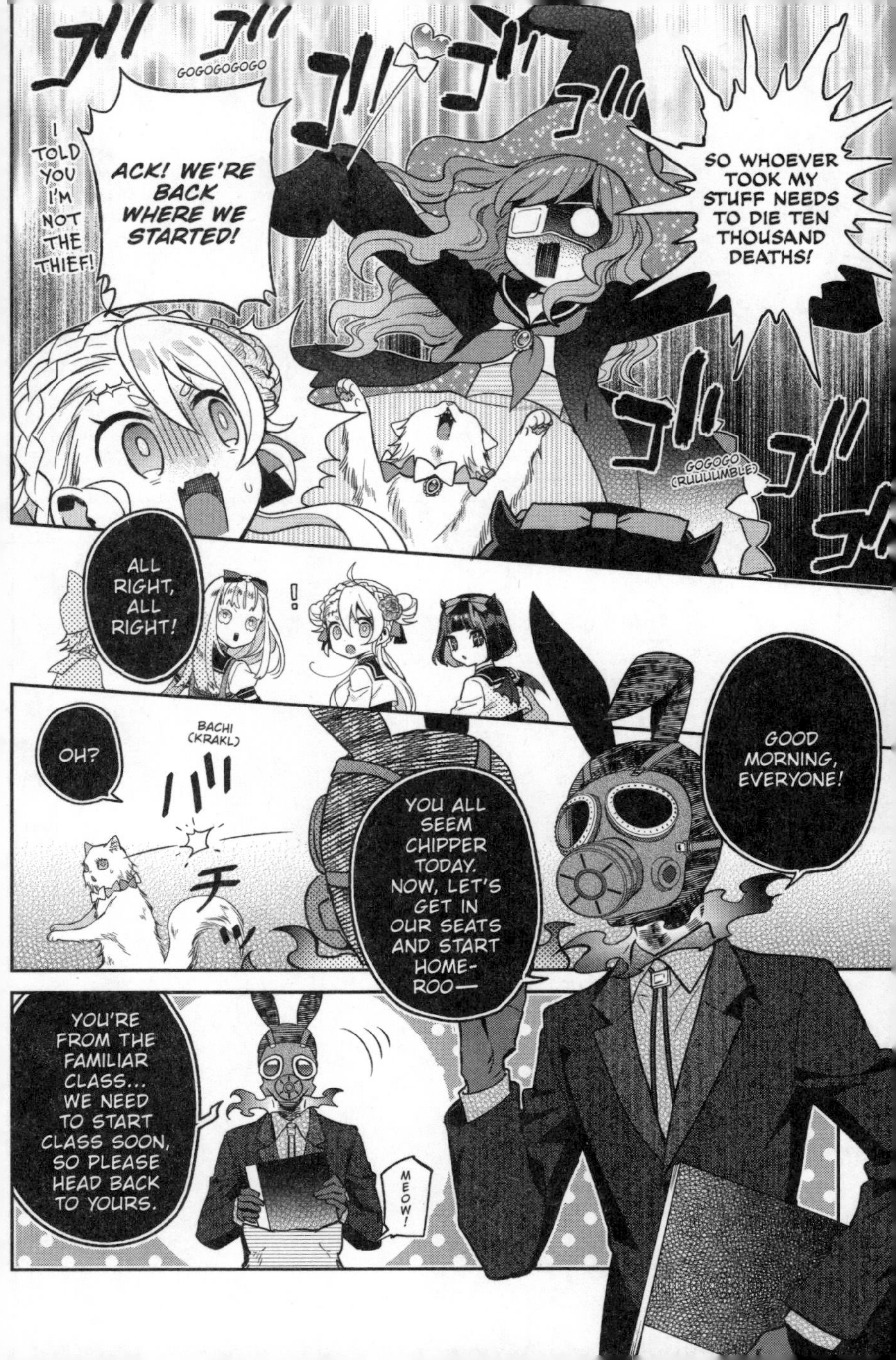
GOGOGOGOGO
SO WHOEVER TOOK MY STUFF NEEDS TO DIE TEN THOUSAND DEATHS!
ACK! WE'RE BACK WHERE WE STARTED!
I TOLD YOU I'M NOT THE THIEF!
GOGOGO (RUUUUMBLE)
ALL RIGHT, ALL RIGHT!
!
GOOD MORNING, EVERYONE!
YOU ALL SEEM CHIPPER TODAY. NOW, LET'S GET IN OUR SEATS AND START HOME-ROO—
BACHI (KRAKL)
OH?
YOU'RE FROM THE FAMILIAR CLASS... WE NEED TO START CLASS SOON, SO PLEASE HEAD BACK TO YOURS.
MEOW!

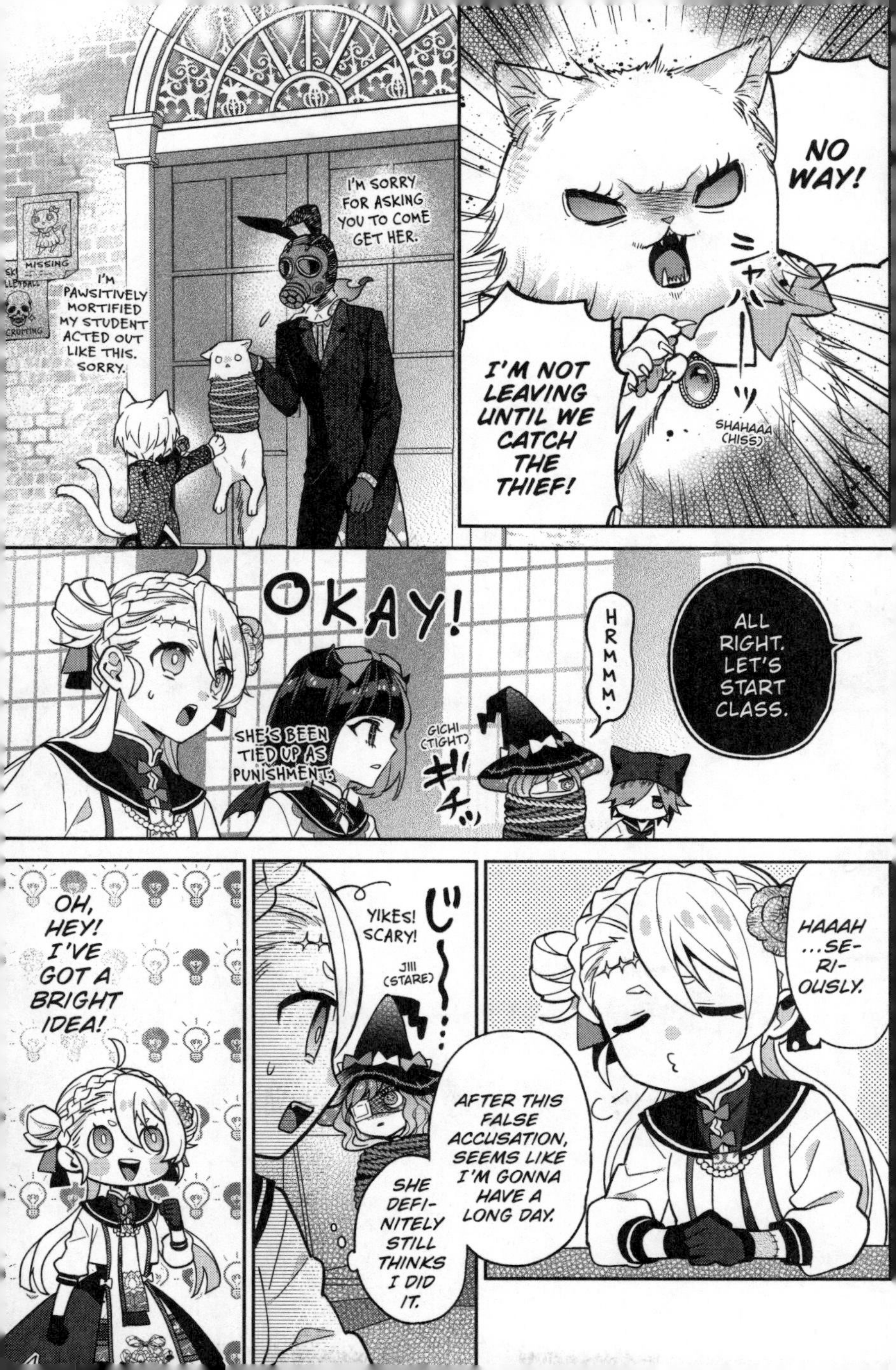
NO WAY!
ニャ
I'M NOT LEAVING UNTIL WE CATCH THE THIEF!
SHAHAAA (HISS)
I'M SORRY FOR ASKING YOU TO COME GET HER.
I'M PAWSITIVELY MORTIFIED MY STUDENT ACTED OUT LIKE THIS. SORRY.
MISSING
ALL RIGHT. LET'S START CLASS.
HRMMM.
GICHI (TIGHT)
OKAY!
SHE'S BEEN TIED UP AS PUNISHMENT.
HAAAH ...SE-RI-OUSLY.
AFTER THIS FALSE ACCUSATION, SEEMS LIKE I'M GONNA HAVE A LONG DAY.
YIKES! SCARY!
JIII (STARE)
SHE DEFI-NITELY STILL THINKS I DID IT.
OH, HEY! I'VE GOT A BRIGHT IDEA!

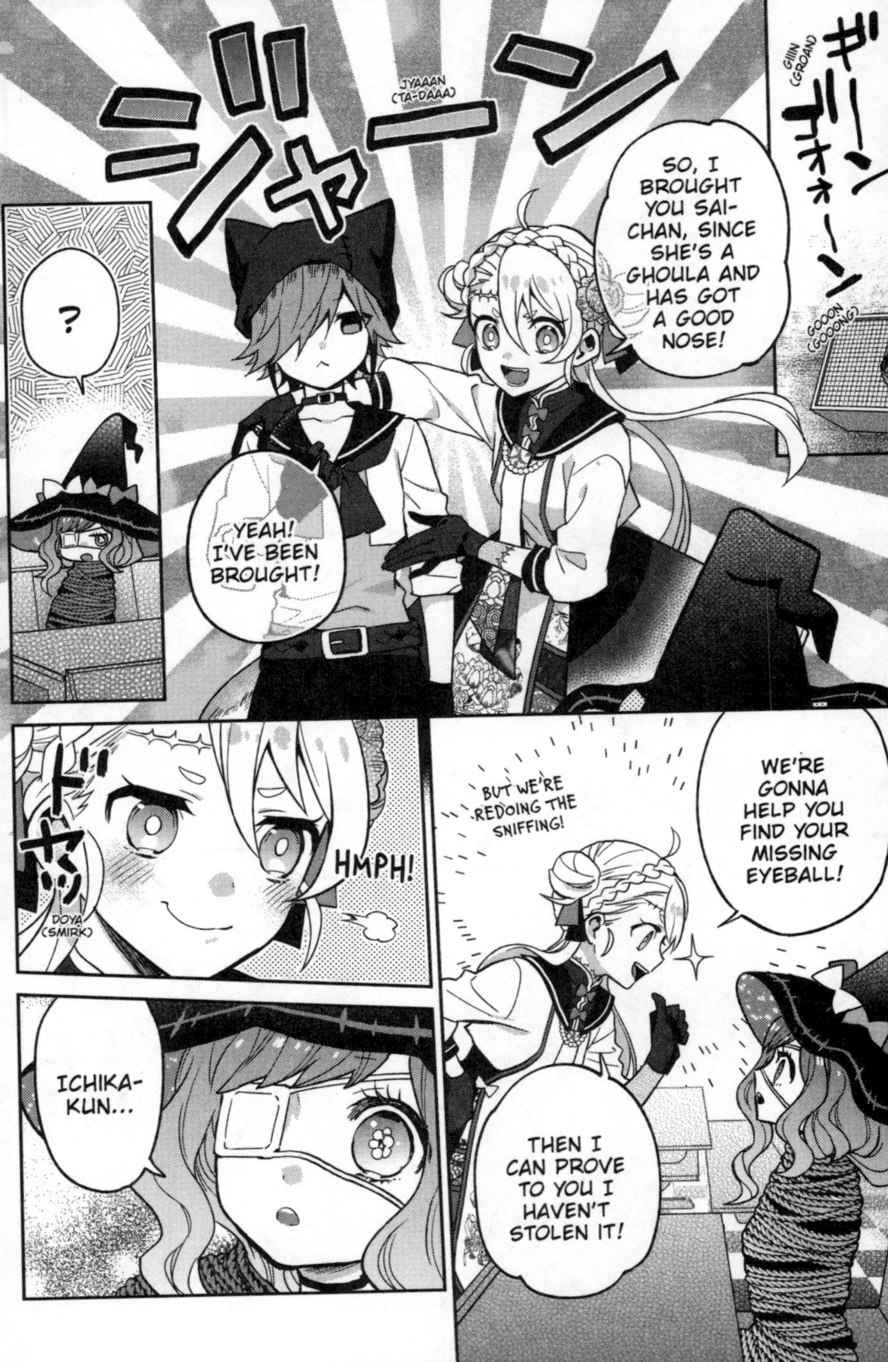
ギーン
GIIIN (GROAN)
ゴオォーン
GOOON (GOOONG)
SO, I BROUGHT YOU SAI-CHAN, SINCE SHE'S A GHOULA AND HAS GOT A GOOD NOSE!
ジャーン
JYAAAN (TA-DAAA)
YEAH! I'VE BEEN BROUGHT!
?
WE'RE GONNA HELP YOU FIND YOUR MISSING EYEBALL!
BUT WE'RE REDOING THE SNIFFING!
THEN I CAN PROVE TO YOU I HAVEN'T STOLEN IT!
ドヤッ
DOYA (SMIRK)
HMPH!
ICHIKA-KUN...

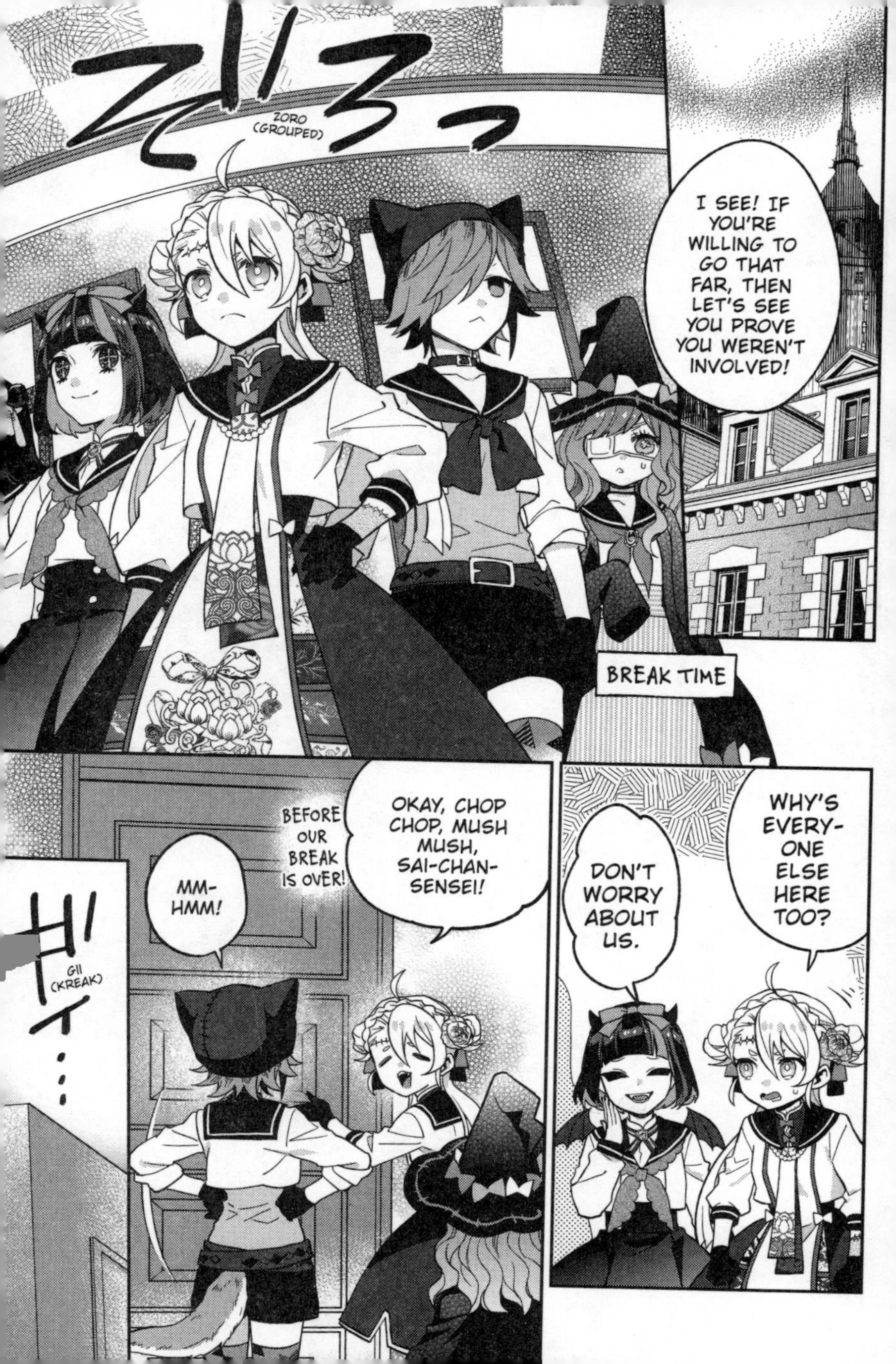
ZORO (GROUPED)
I SEE! IF YOU'RE WILLING TO GO THAT FAR, THEN LET'S SEE YOU PROVE YOU WEREN'T INVOLVED!
BREAK TIME
WHY'S EVERY-ONE ELSE HERE TOO?
DON'T WORRY ABOUT US.
OKAY, CHOP CHOP, MUSH MUSH, SAI-CHAN-SENSEI!
BEFORE OUR BREAK IS OVER!
MM-HMM!
GII (KREAK)
...

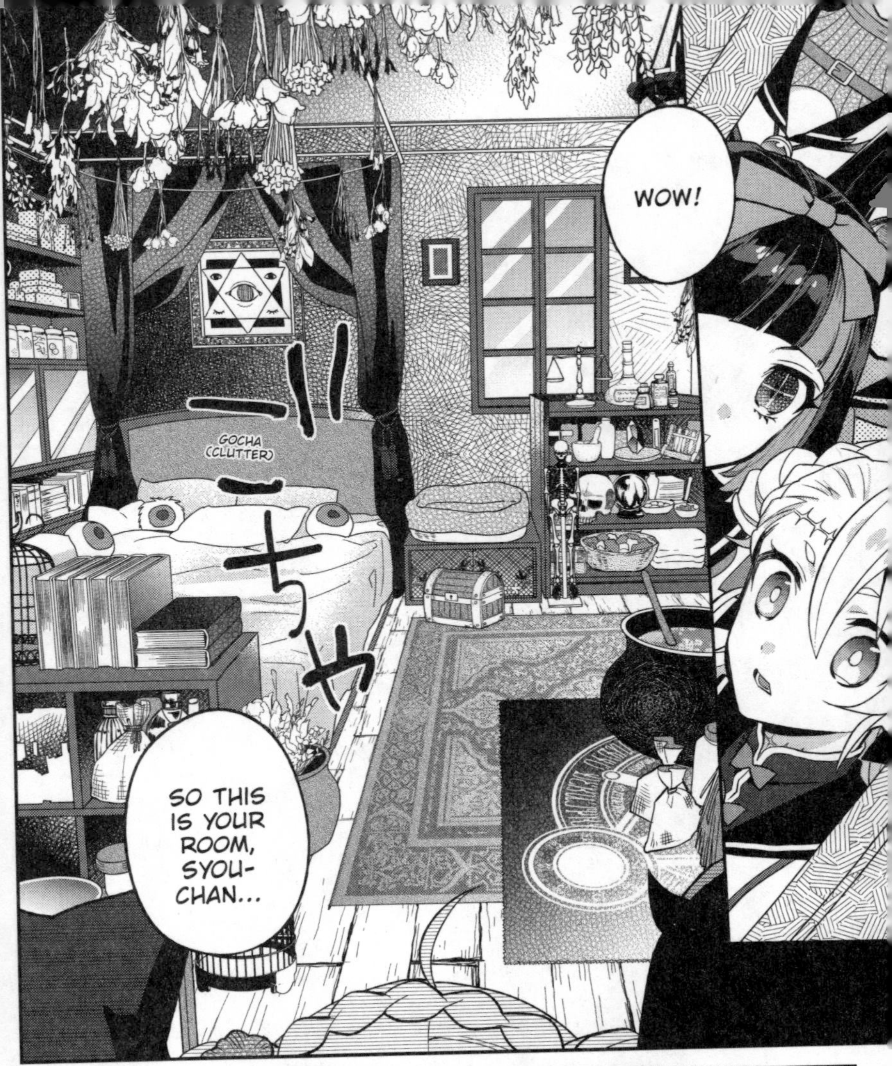
WOW!
GOCHA (CLUTTER)
SO THIS IS YOUR ROOM, SYOU-CHAN...
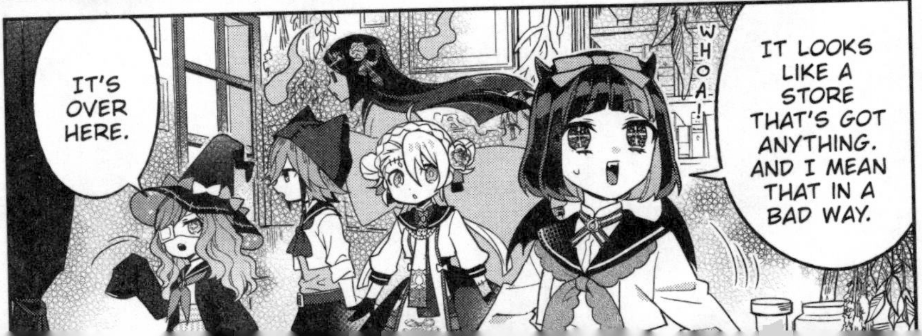
IT LOOKS LIKE A STORE THAT'S GOT ANYTHING. AND I MEAN THAT IN A BAD WAY.
WHOA-!
IT'S OVER HERE.

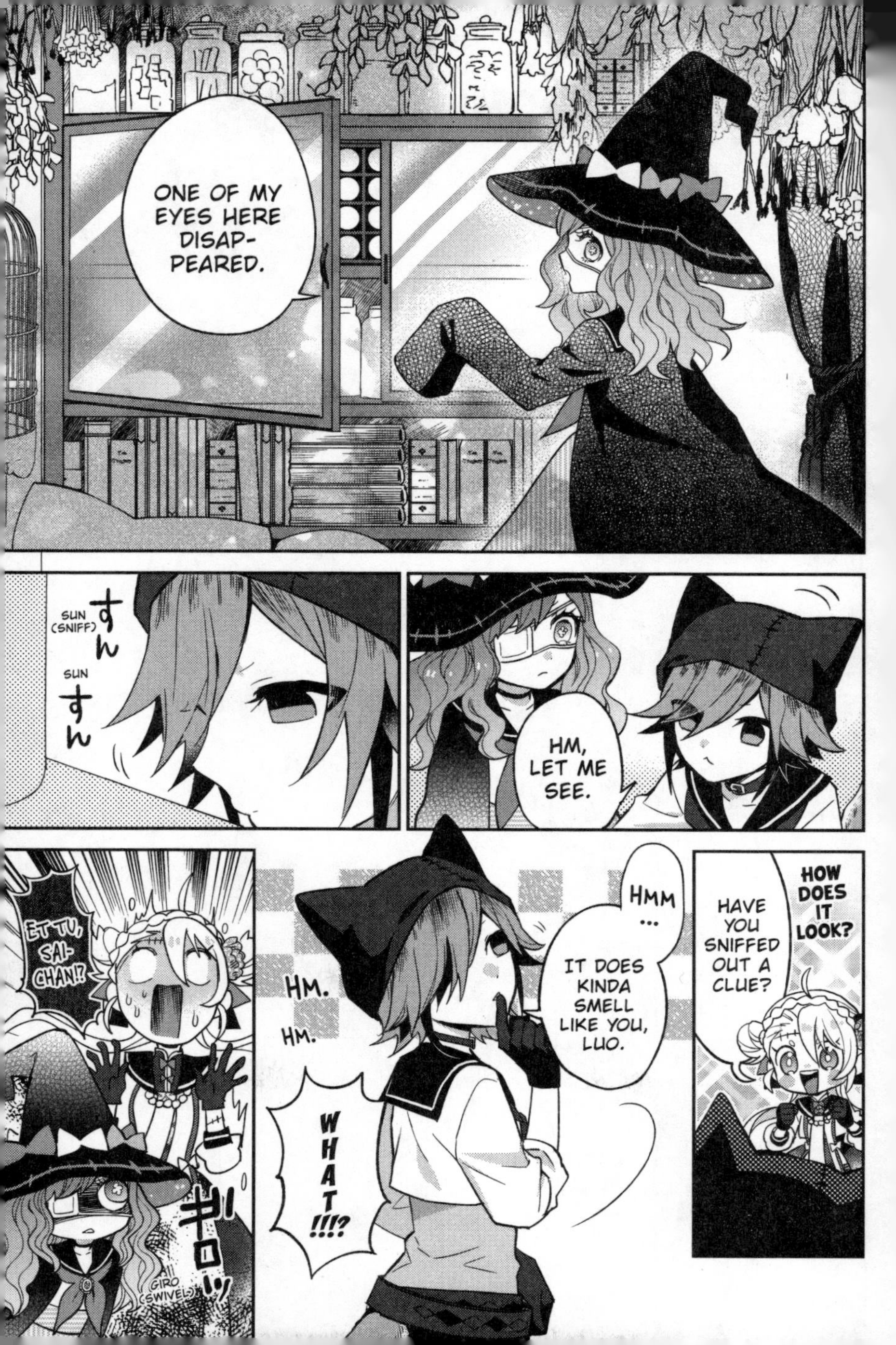
ONE OF MY EYES HERE DISAP-PEARED.
HM, LET ME SEE.
SUN (SNIFF) すん
SUN すん
HOW DOES IT LOOK?
HAVE YOU SNIFFED OUT A CLUE?
HMM ...
IT DOES KINDA SMELL LIKE YOU, LUO.
HM.
HM.
WHAT!!!?
ET TU, SAI-CHAN!?
ギロッ
GIRO (SWIVEL)

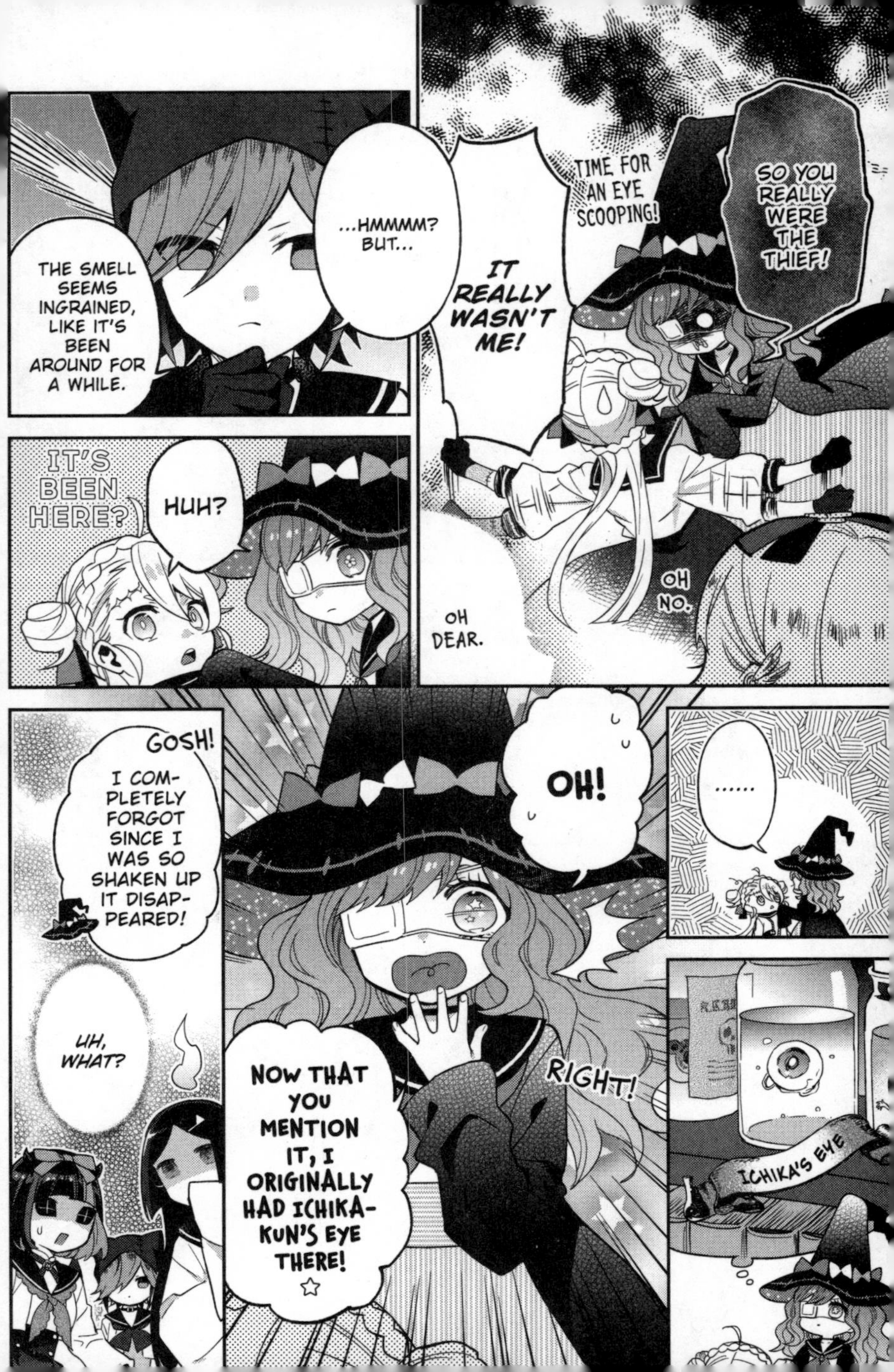
SO YOU REALLY WERE THE THIEF!
TIME FOR AN EYE SCOOPING!
IT REALLY WASN'T ME!
OH NO.
OH DEAR.
...HMMMM? BUT...
THE SMELL SEEMS INGRAINED, LIKE IT'S BEEN AROUND FOR A WHILE.
HUH?
IT'S BEEN HERE?
......
ICHIKA'S EYE
OH!
RIGHT!
NOW THAT YOU MENTION IT, I ORIGINALLY HAD ICHIKA-KUN'S EYE THERE! ☆
GOSH! I COMPLETELY FORGOT SINCE I WAS SO SHAKEN UP IT DISAPPEARED!
UH, WHAT?

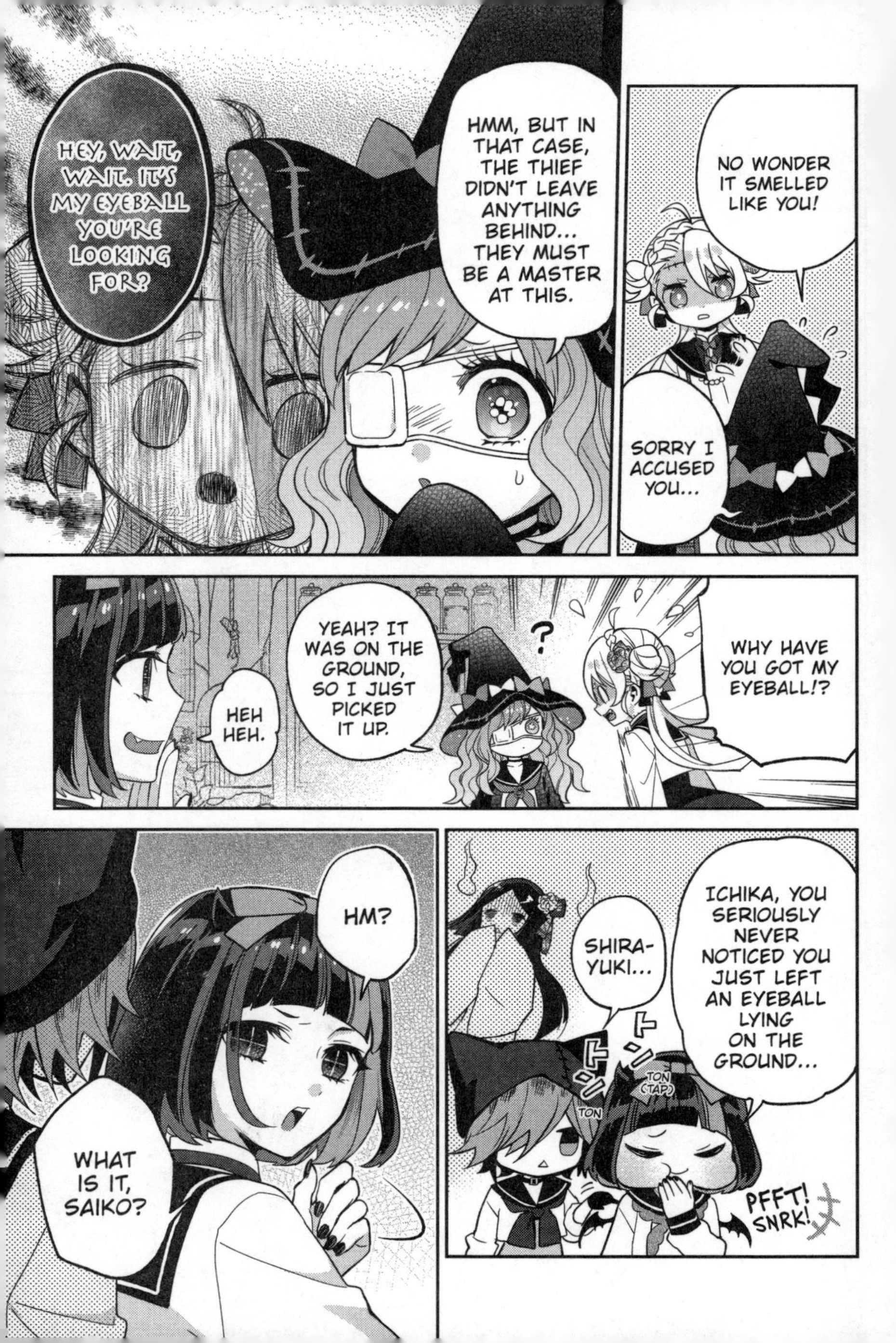
NO WONDER IT SMELLED LIKE YOU!
SORRY I ACCUSED YOU...
HMM, BUT IN THAT CASE, THE THIEF DIDN'T LEAVE ANYTHING BEHIND... THEY MUST BE A MASTER AT THIS.
HEY, WAIT, WAIT. IT'S MY EYEBALL YOU'RE LOOKING FOR?
WHY HAVE YOU GOT MY EYEBALL!?
?
YEAH? IT WAS ON THE GROUND, SO I JUST PICKED IT UP.
HEH HEH.
ICHIKA, YOU SERIOUSLY NEVER NOTICED YOU JUST LEFT AN EYEBALL LYING ON THE GROUND...
SHIRA-YUKI...
TON (TAP)
TON
PFFT! SNRK!
HM?
WHAT IS IT, SAIKO?

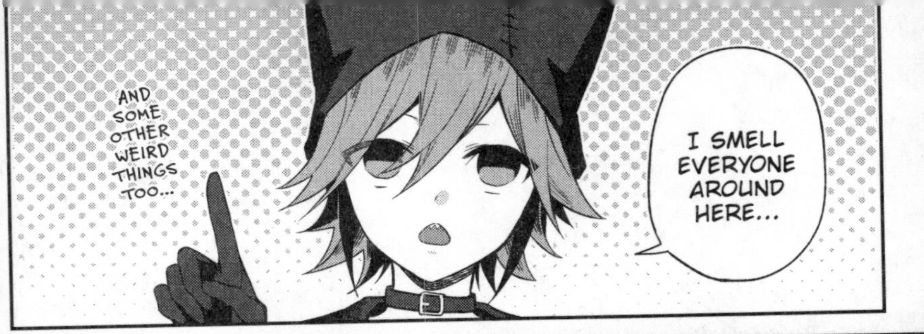
I SMELL EVERYONE AROUND HERE...
AND SOME OTHER WEIRD THINGS TOO...

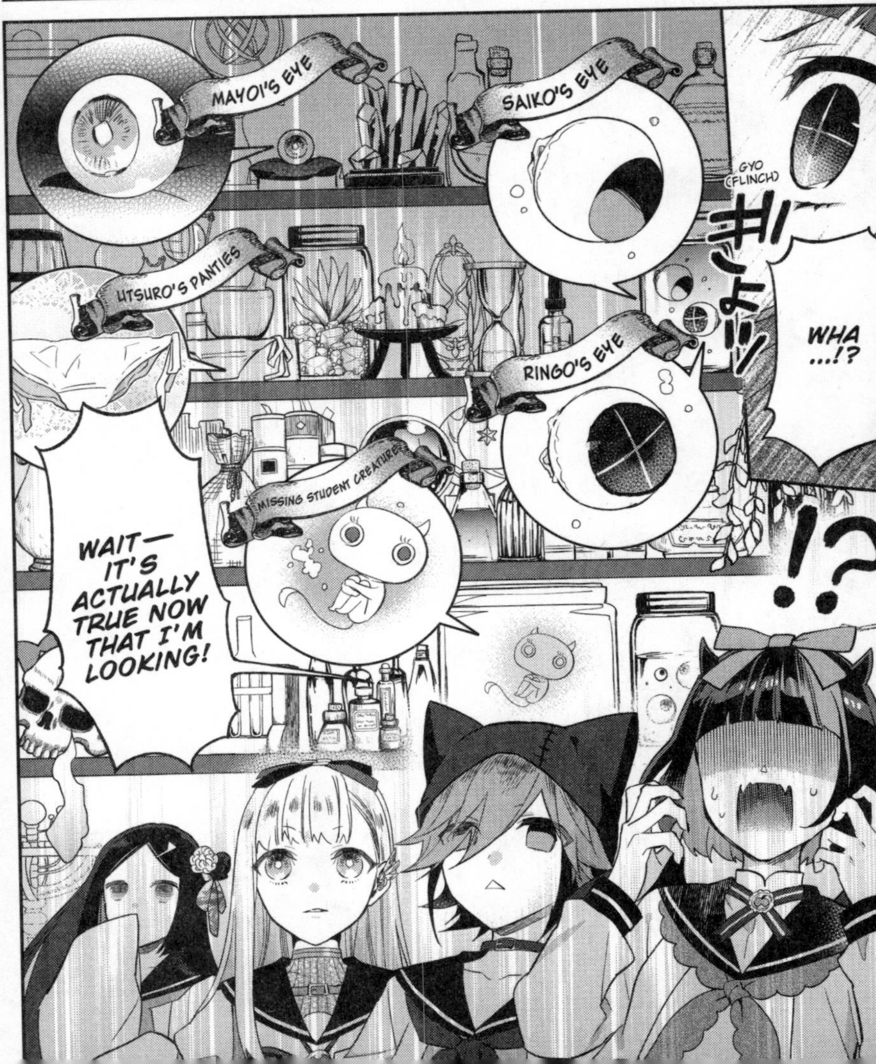
WHA ...!?
ぎょッ
GYO (FLINCH)
!?
SAIKO'S EYE
MAYOI'S EYE
RINGO'S EYE
UTSURO'S PANTIES
MISSING STUDENT CREATURE
WAIT— IT'S ACTUALLY TRUE NOW THAT I'M LOOKING!

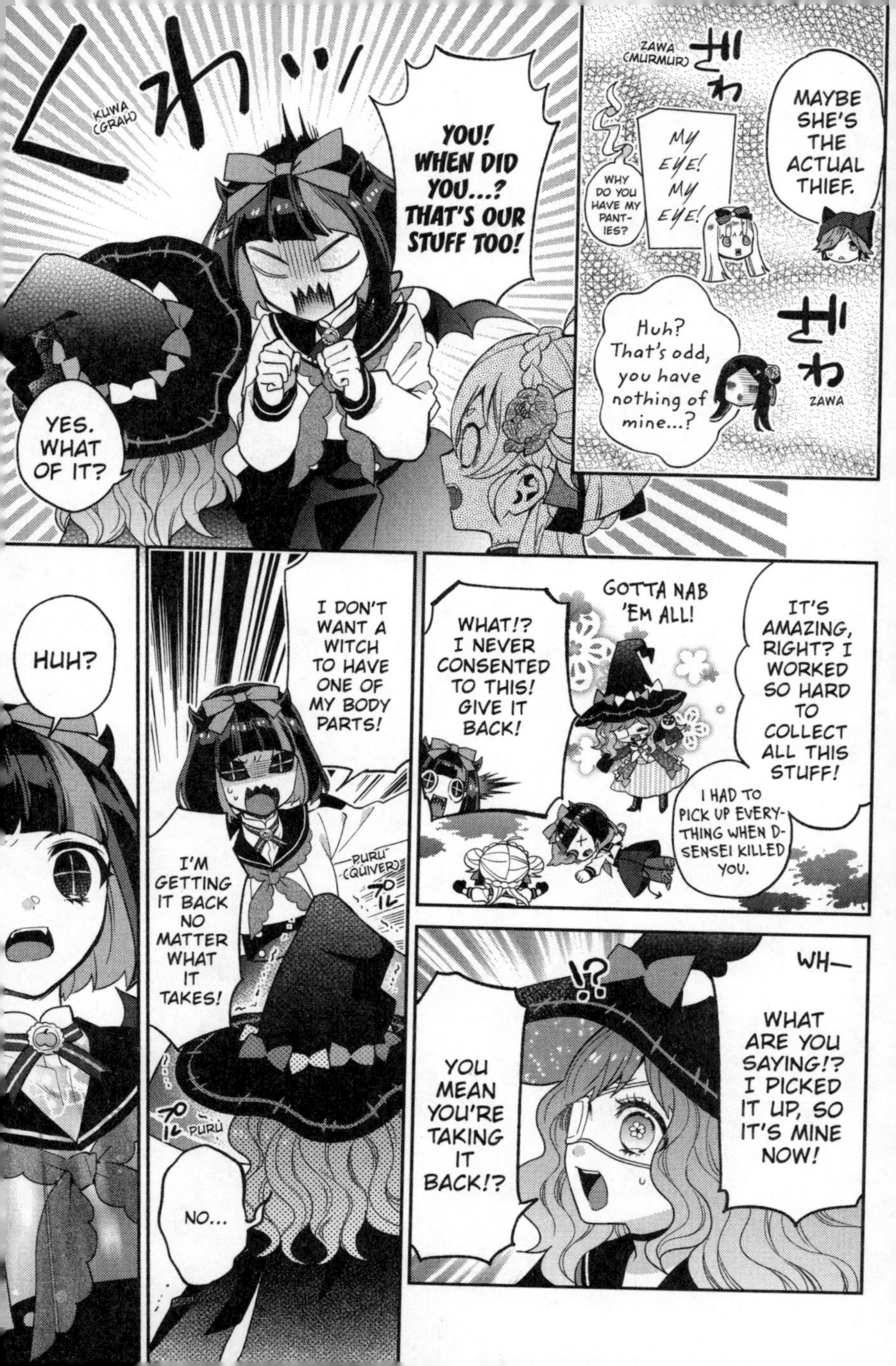
MAYBE SHE'S THE ACTUAL THIEF.
ZAWA (MURMUR)
MY EYE! MY EYE!
WHY DO YOU HAVE MY PANT-IES?
Huh? That's odd, you have nothing of mine...?
ZAWA
KUWA (GRAH)
YOU! WHEN DID YOU...? THAT'S OUR STUFF TOO!
YES. WHAT OF IT?
IT'S AMAZING, RIGHT? I WORKED SO HARD TO COLLECT ALL THIS STUFF!
GOTTA NAB 'EM ALL!
WHAT!? I NEVER CONSENTED TO THIS! GIVE IT BACK!
I HAD TO PICK UP EVERY-THING WHEN D-SENSEI KILLED YOU.
WH—
WHAT ARE YOU SAYING!? I PICKED IT UP, SO IT'S MINE NOW!
YOU MEAN YOU'RE TAKING IT BACK!?
I DON'T WANT A WITCH TO HAVE ONE OF MY BODY PARTS!
I'M GETTING IT BACK NO MATTER WHAT IT TAKES!
PURU (QUIVER)
PURU
NO...
HUH?

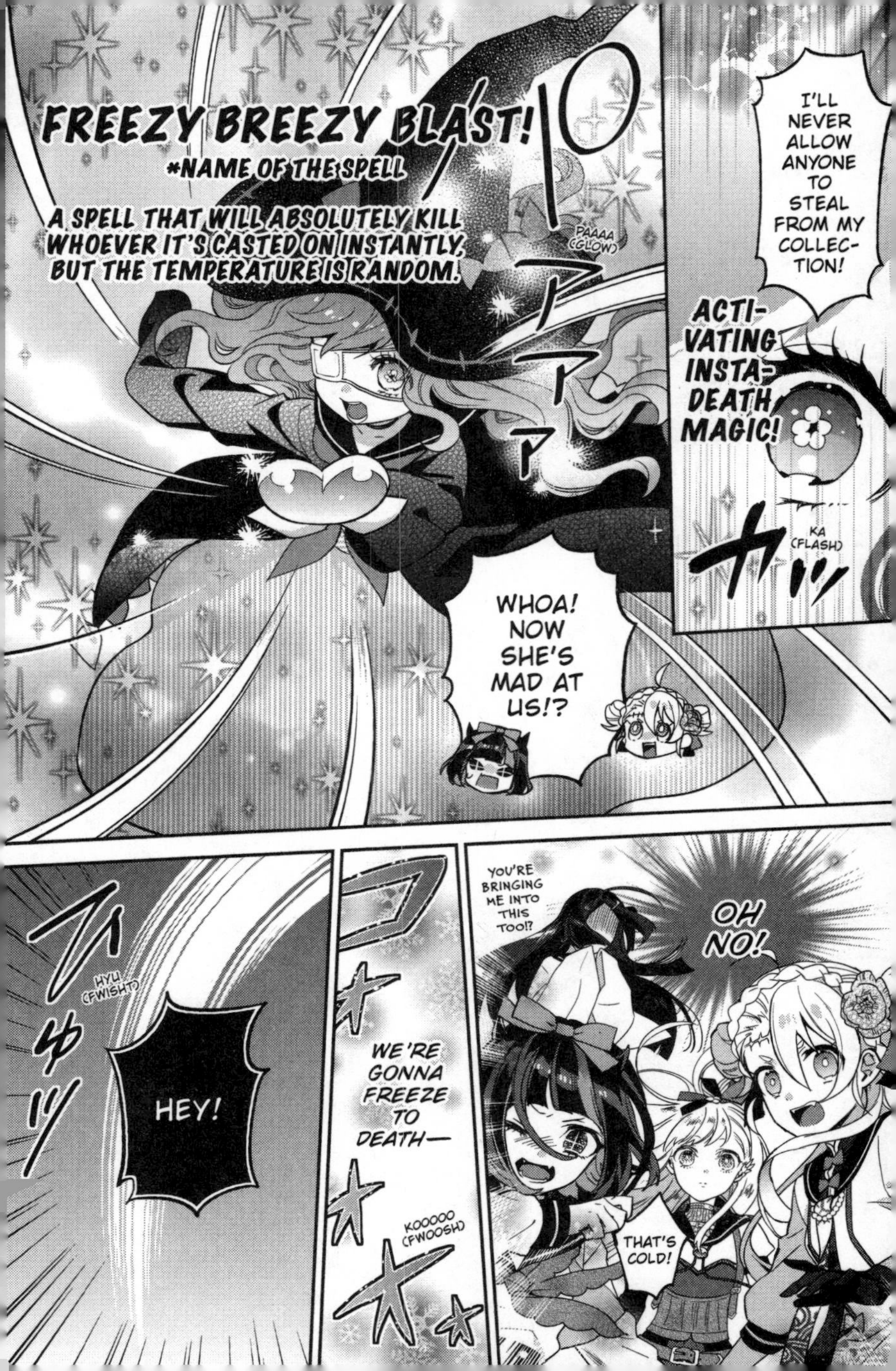
I'LL NEVER ALLOW ANYONE TO STEAL FROM MY COLLECTION!
ACTIVATING INSTA-DEATH MAGIC!
KA (FLASH)
FREEZY BREEZY BLAST!
*NAME OF THE SPELL
A SPELL THAT WILL ABSOLUTELY KILL WHOEVER IT'S CASTED ON INSTANTLY, BUT THE TEMPERATURE IS RANDOM.
PAAAA (GLOW)
WHOA! NOW SHE'S MAD AT US!?
OH NO!
YOU'RE BRINGING ME INTO THIS TOO!?
THAT'S COLD!
WE'RE GONNA FREEZE TO DEATH—
KOOOOO (FWOOSH)
HYU (FWISHT)
HEY!

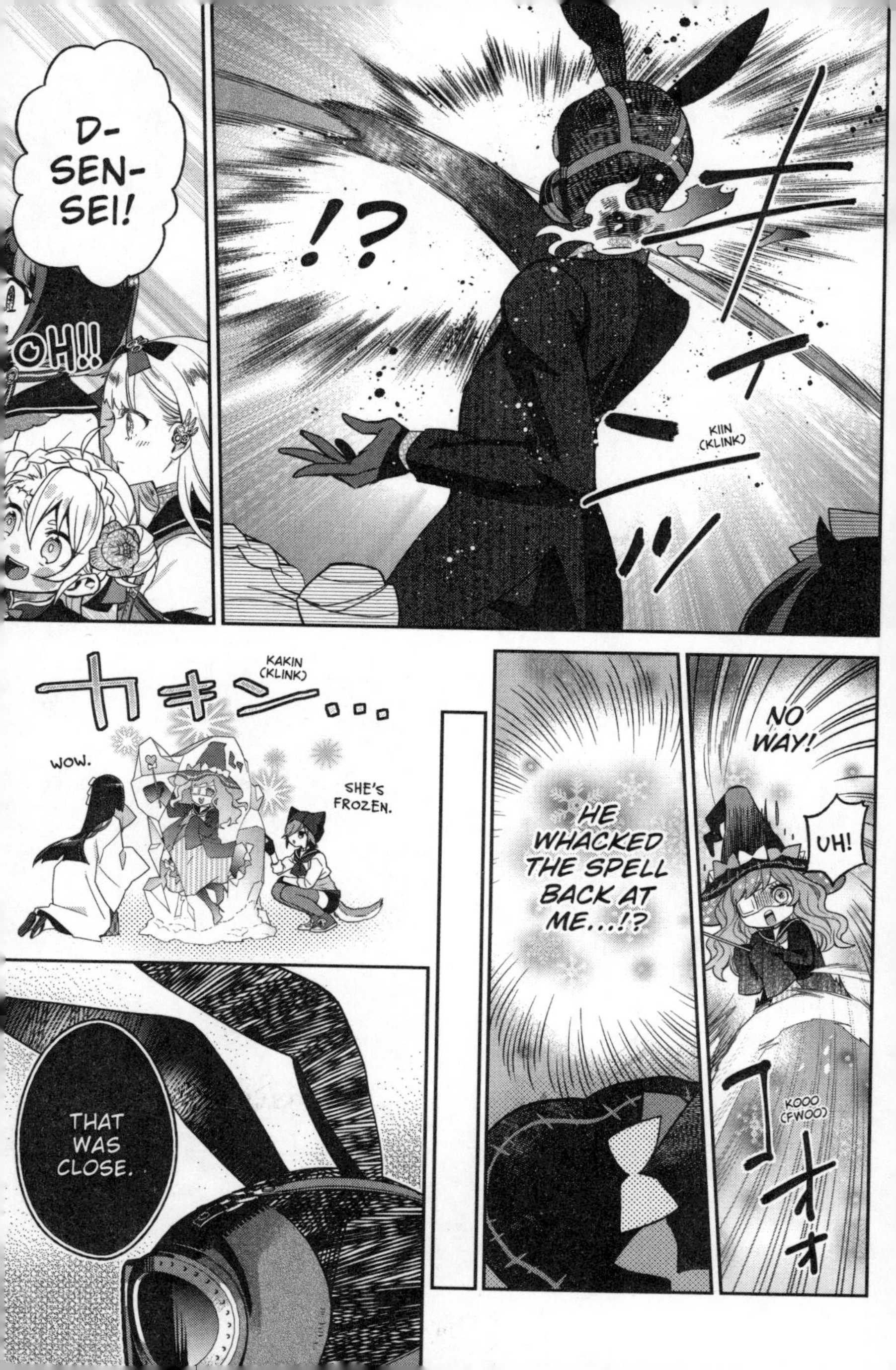
KIIN (KLINK)
!?
OH!!
D-SEN-SEI!
NO WAY!
UH!
KOOO (FWOO)
HE WHACKED THE SPELL BACK AT ME...!?
KAKIN (KLINK)
WOW.
SHE'S FROZEN.
THAT WAS CLOSE.

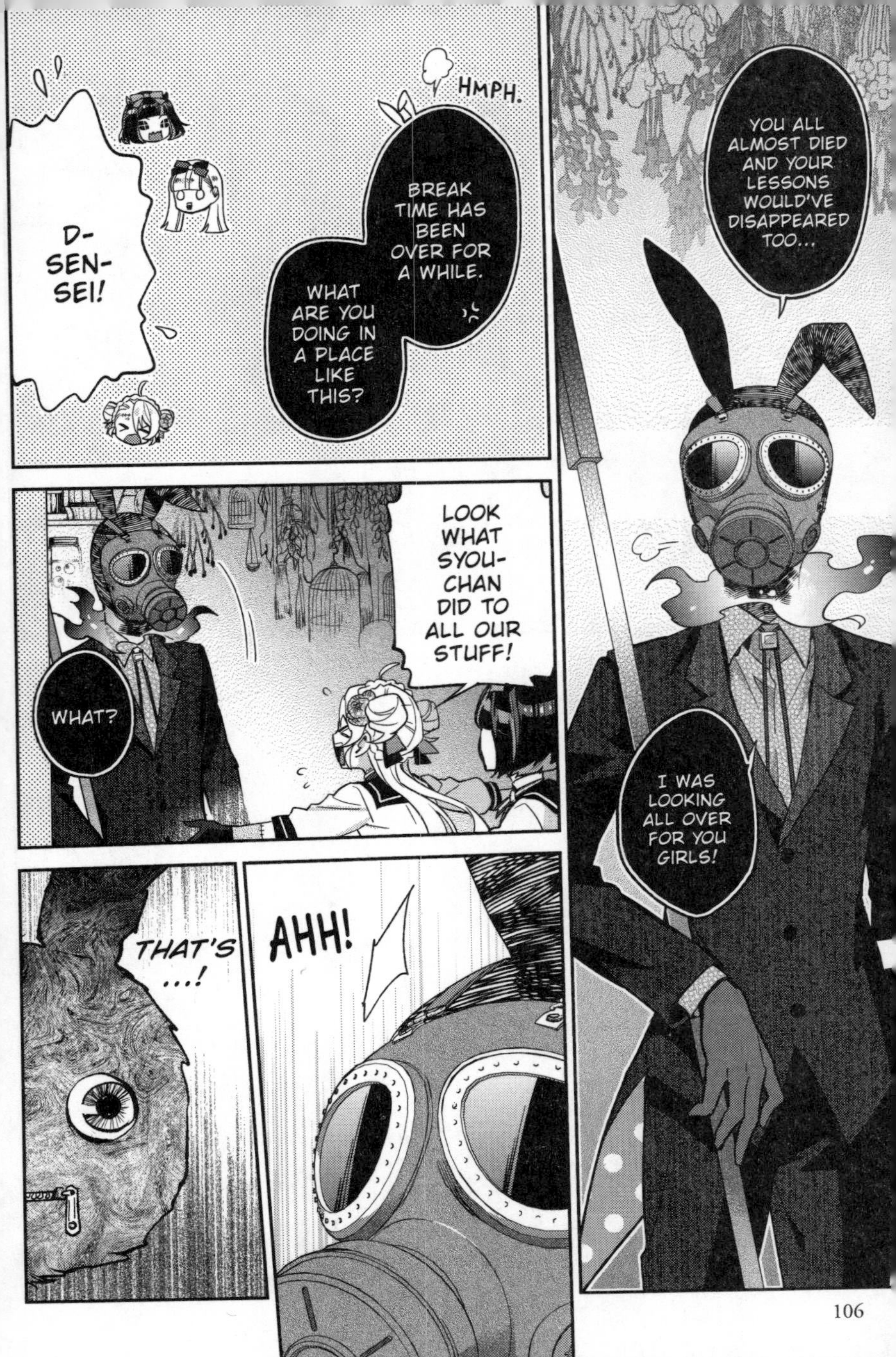
YOU ALL ALMOST DIED AND YOUR LESSONS WOULD'VE DISAPPEARED TOO...
I WAS LOOKING ALL OVER FOR YOU GIRLS!
HMPH.
BREAK TIME HAS BEEN OVER FOR A WHILE.
WHAT ARE YOU DOING IN A PLACE LIKE THIS?
D-SEN-SEI!
LOOK WHAT SYOU-CHAN DID TO ALL OUR STUFF!
WHAT?
AHH!
THAT'S ...!

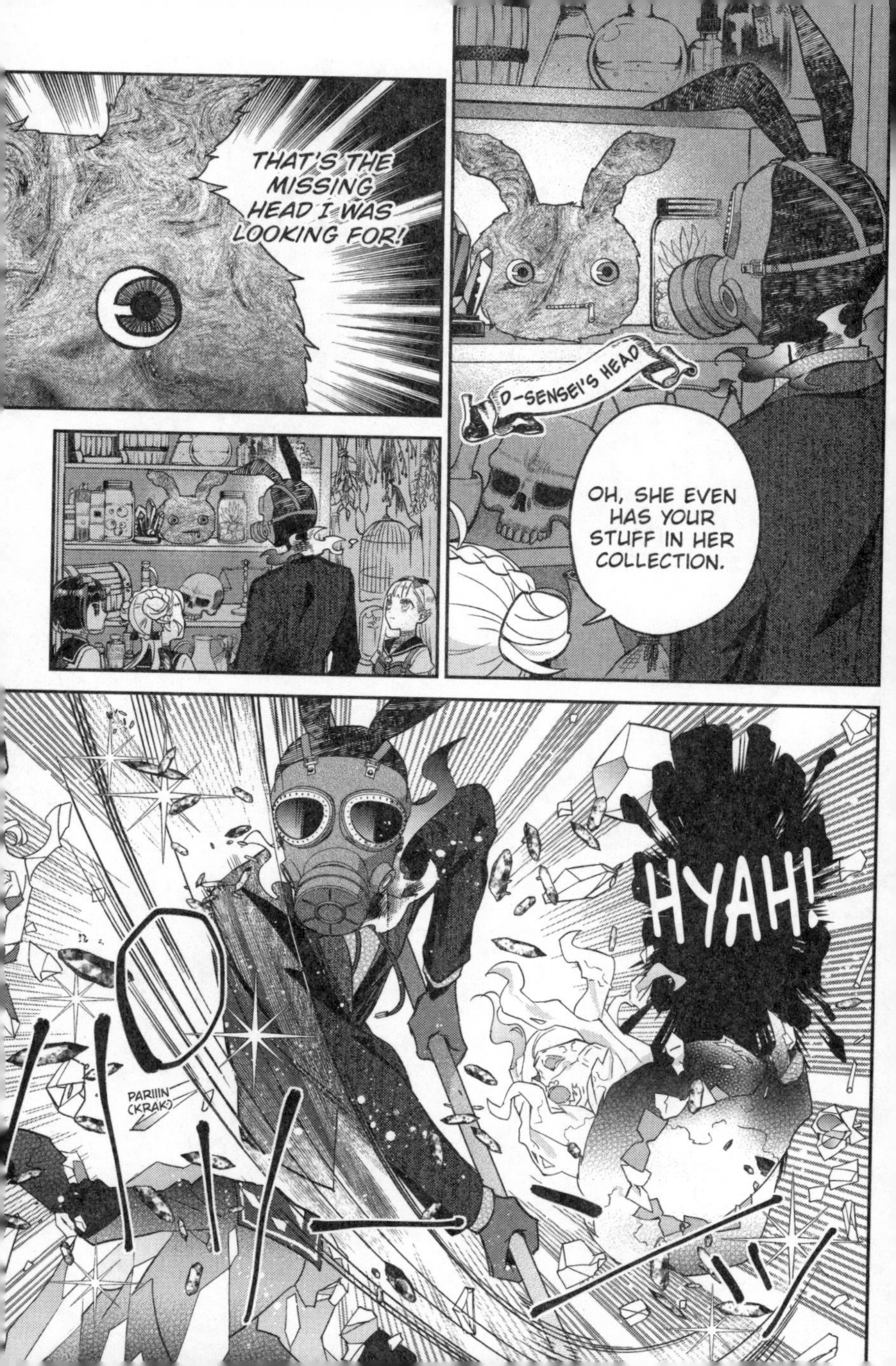
D-SENSEI'S HEAD
OH, SHE EVEN HAS YOUR STUFF IN HER COLLECTION.
THAT'S THE MISSING HEAD I WAS LOOKING FOR!
HYAH!
PARIIIN (KRAK)

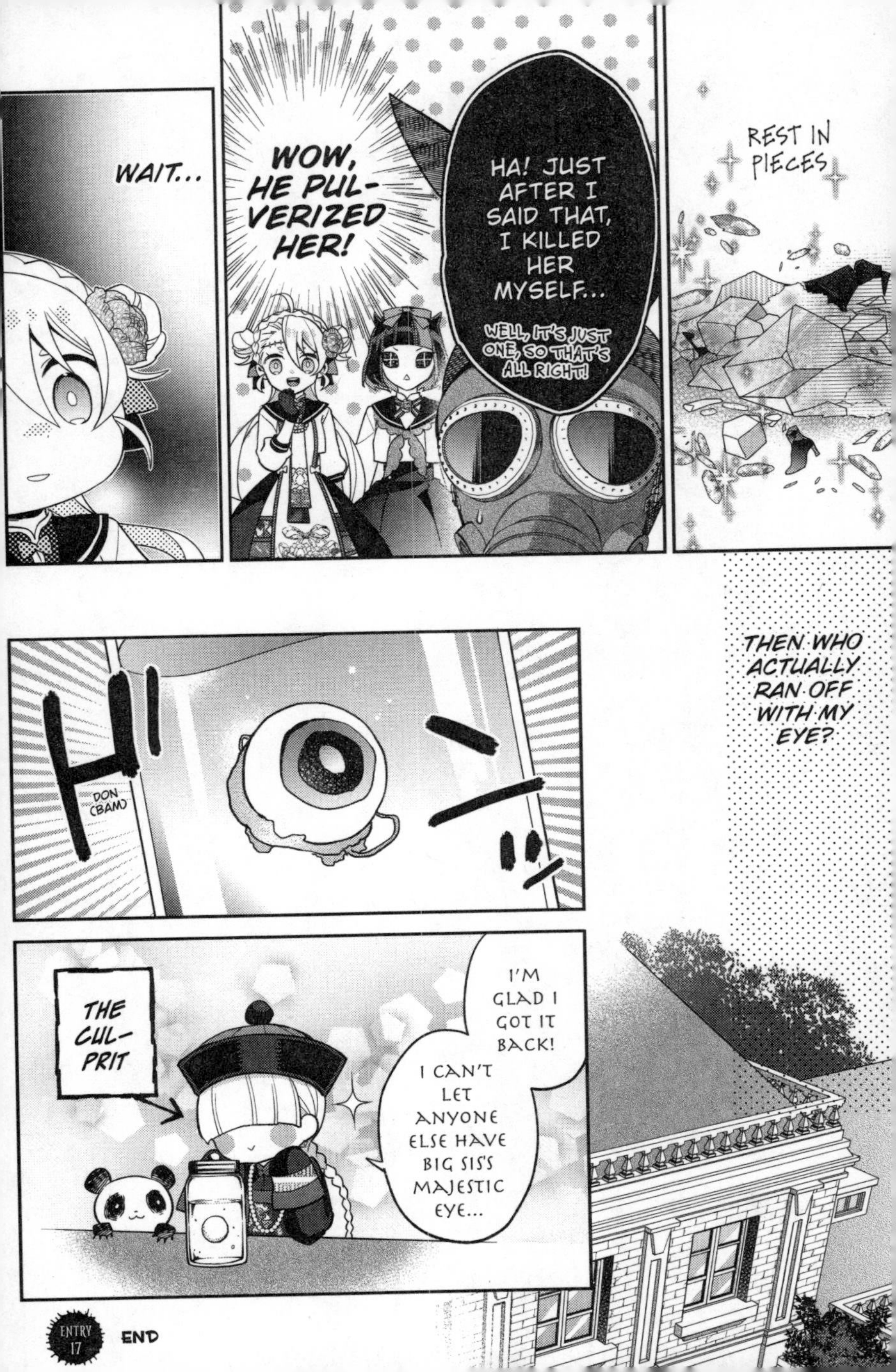
REST IN PIECES
HA! JUST AFTER I SAID THAT, I KILLED HER MYSELF...
WELL, IT'S JUST ONE, SO THAT'S ALL RIGHT!
WOW, HE PUL-VERIZED HER!
WAIT...
THEN WHO ACTUALLY RAN OFF WITH MY EYE?
HI
DON (BAM)
THE CUL-PRIT
I'M GLAD I GOT IT BACK!
I CAN'T LET ANYONE ELSE HAVE BIG SIS'S MAJESTIC EYE...
ENTRY 17
END

Monster Girls' School

Class Report

Monster Year: 20020 Month: Wrath Day: 124th **Homeroom** Class Z **Teacher** D **Teacher Species** Dullahan

Classes and such

	Subject	Studied Material
1st Period	Chimera Language	We learned the cockatrice's language, which is thought to be one of the hardest languages in the monster realm. The language is a mix of chicken, dragon, and snake, as well as toad, which is the language of its parent. It came to be the way it is over a long period of time. Naturally, Class Z has no hope of ever gleaning any understanding of it even if the world turns upside down. Their heads all exploded. (This foreshadowed Sadakuni's head exploding.)
2nd Period	Monster History	I borrowed some valuable documents from the HaiKaburi family, and we learned of the frequent injustices that occurred during the monster middle ages when witch judges made unfair rulings. This is better known as the "witch trials." Today, suspicious judgments during trials, bad sports calls, and fixed games are still referred to as witch trials, and this term also originated from the middle age witch trials. Once the students learned this little piece of trivia, they spared no time using it to verbally abuse HaiKaburi.
3rd Period	Home Ec	At this time, the Monstrum Girls High School had a fire drill. Normally, each year Class Z unanimously picks the staff room to be the origin of the hypothetical fire for the drill. While taste testing the cooking, Akagari and Shirayuki started an argument about the amount appropriate for a tasting -> Shirayuki used fire magic -> the cooking oil ignited -> I had Sadakuni go to put out the flames, since she couldn't be burned, but in an unlucky turn of events, she had an oil leak and also caught on fire -> Sadakuni's head exploded, blasting off around the classroom and spreading the flames... this was the scenario we came up with for the fire drill. (Though the original was a more ambiguous idea where Class Z simply wasn't careful around flames.) This fire drill exceeded the original scenario's expectations and I believe led to the enactment of a spectacular disaster drill.
4th Period	Special School Closure	Better left unsaid.
5th Period		
6th Period		

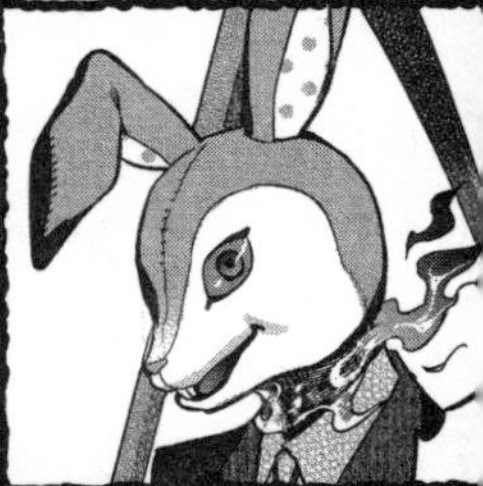

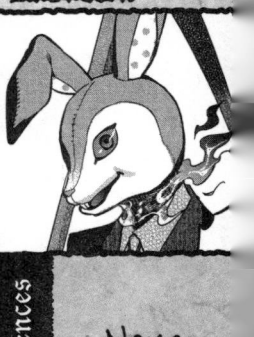

Absences	Tardies	Left Early	Permitted Absences
None	None	HaiKaburi	None

Special Mentions (Goals, worries, etc.)

Theft is one of the three great virtues in the monster realm. As it seems many natural thieves keep coming from my class, perhaps this means a bonus and revised budget is in store for us?

This week's executed students

Name and affiliation	Method	Reason
HaiKaburi (Witch)	Crushed ice	Theft and lacking self-awareness

Photo evidence section

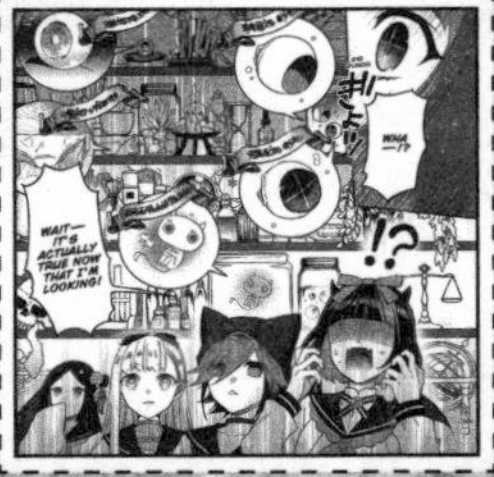
WHA—!?
WAIT— IT'S ACTUALLY TRUE NOW THAT I'M LOOKING!
!?

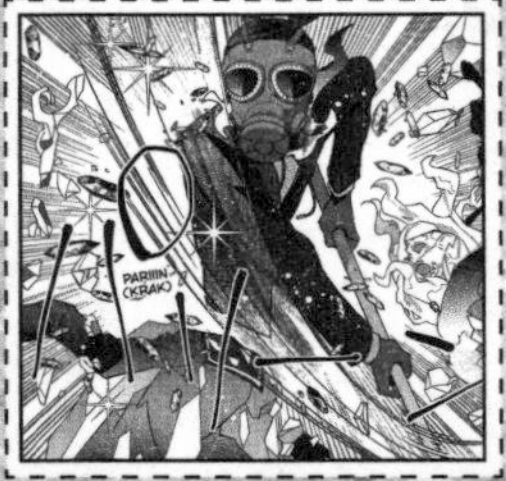
PARIIN (KRAK)

WHERE WILL
TOMORROW
TAKE ME?

STILL ON
THE RUN

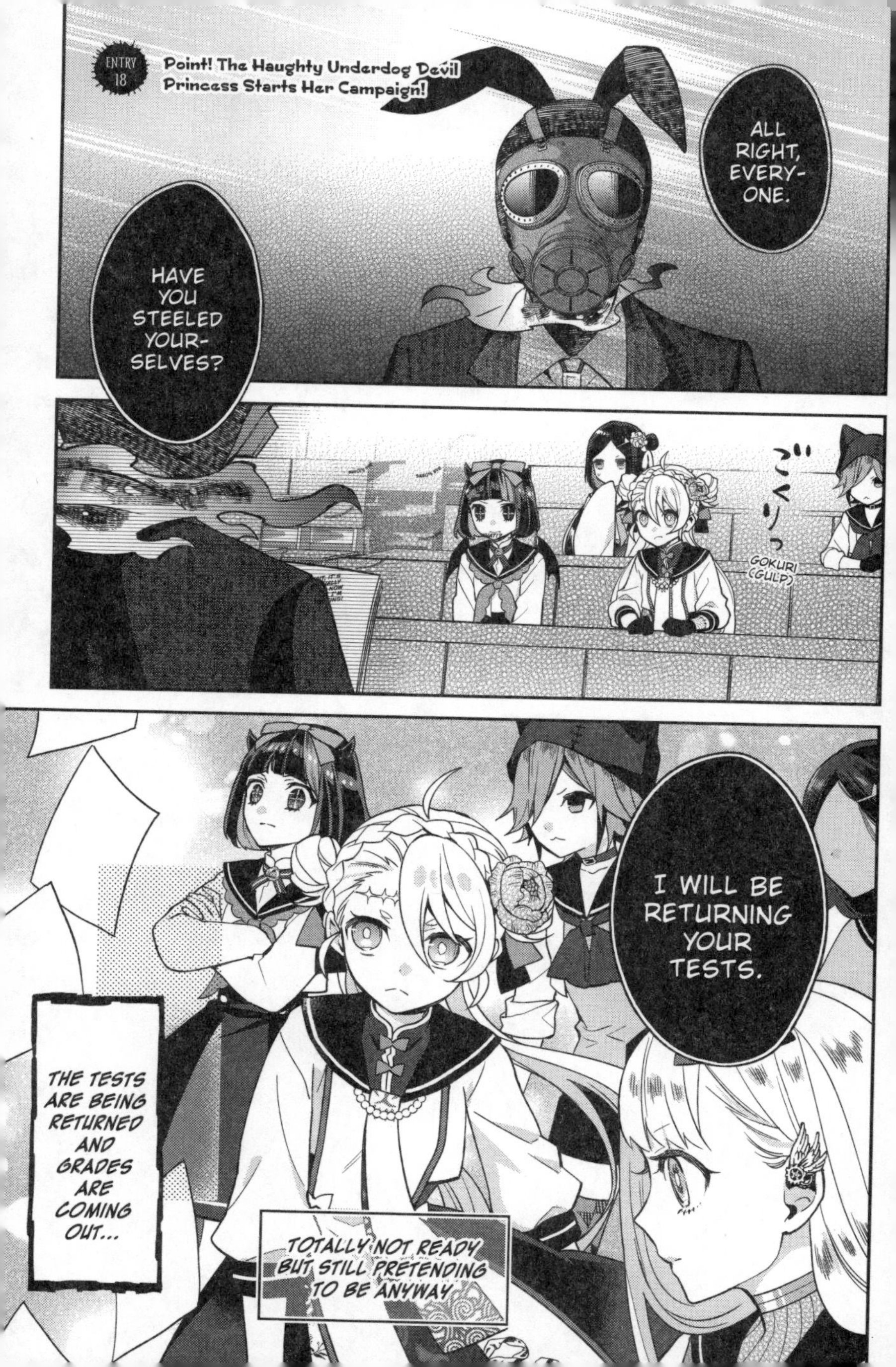
ENTRY 18
Point! The Haughty Underdog Devil Princess Starts Her Campaign!
ALL RIGHT, EVERY-ONE.
HAVE YOU STEELED YOUR-SELVES?
ごくりっ
GOKURI (GULP)
I WILL BE RETURNING YOUR TESTS.
THE TESTS ARE BEING RETURNED AND GRADES ARE COMING OUT...
TOTALLY NOT READY BUT STILL PRETENDING TO BE ANYWAY

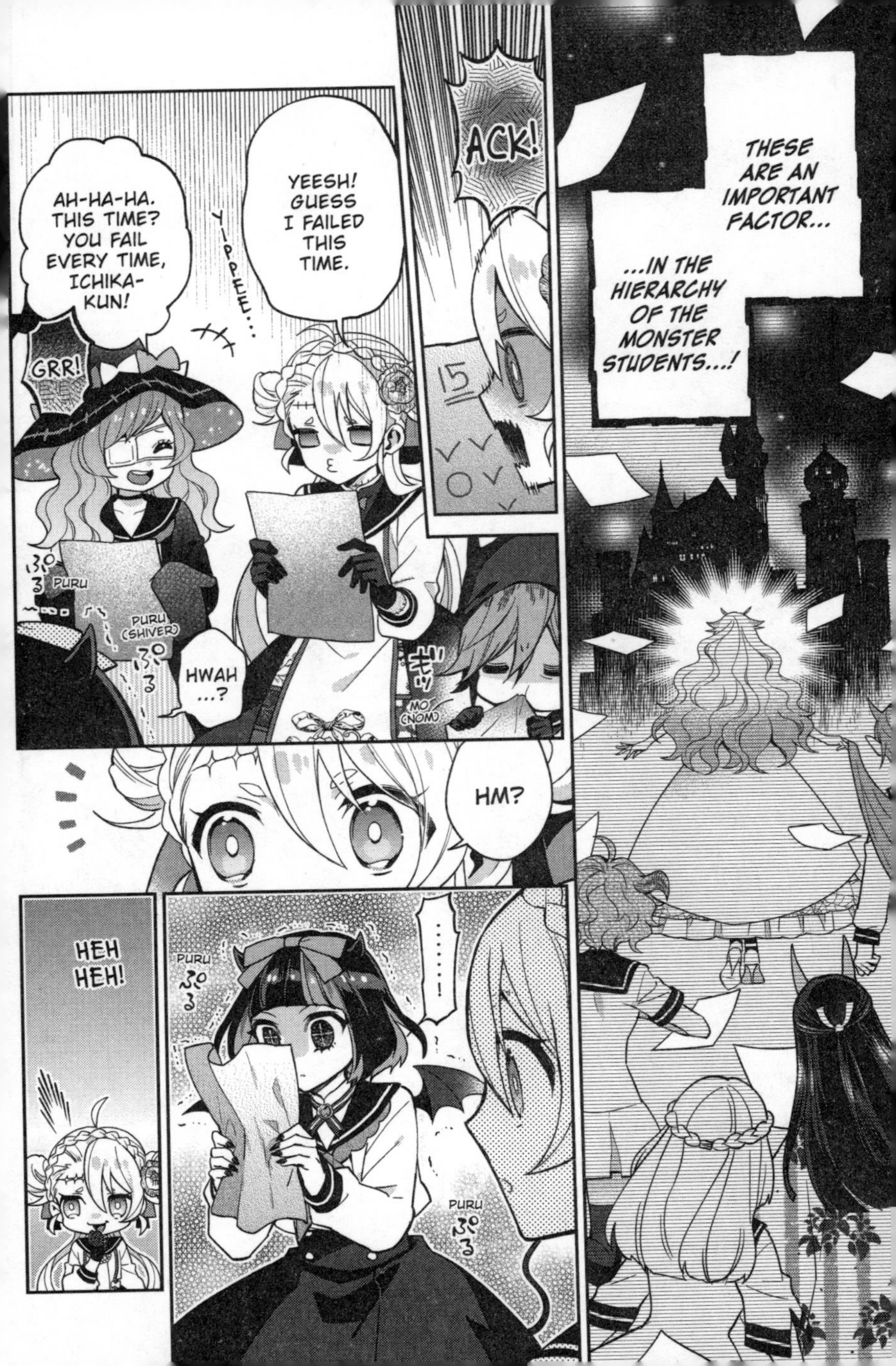

THESE ARE AN IMPORTANT FACTOR...
...IN THE HIERARCHY OF THE MONSTER STUDENTS...!
ACK!
15
YEESH! GUESS I FAILED THIS TIME.
YIPPEEE...
AH-HA-HA. THIS TIME? YOU FAIL EVERY TIME, ICHIKA-KUN!
GRR!
MO (NOM)
HWAH ...?
ぷる PURU (SHIVER)
ぷる PURU
HM?
......!
PURU ぷる
PURU ぷる
HEH HEH!

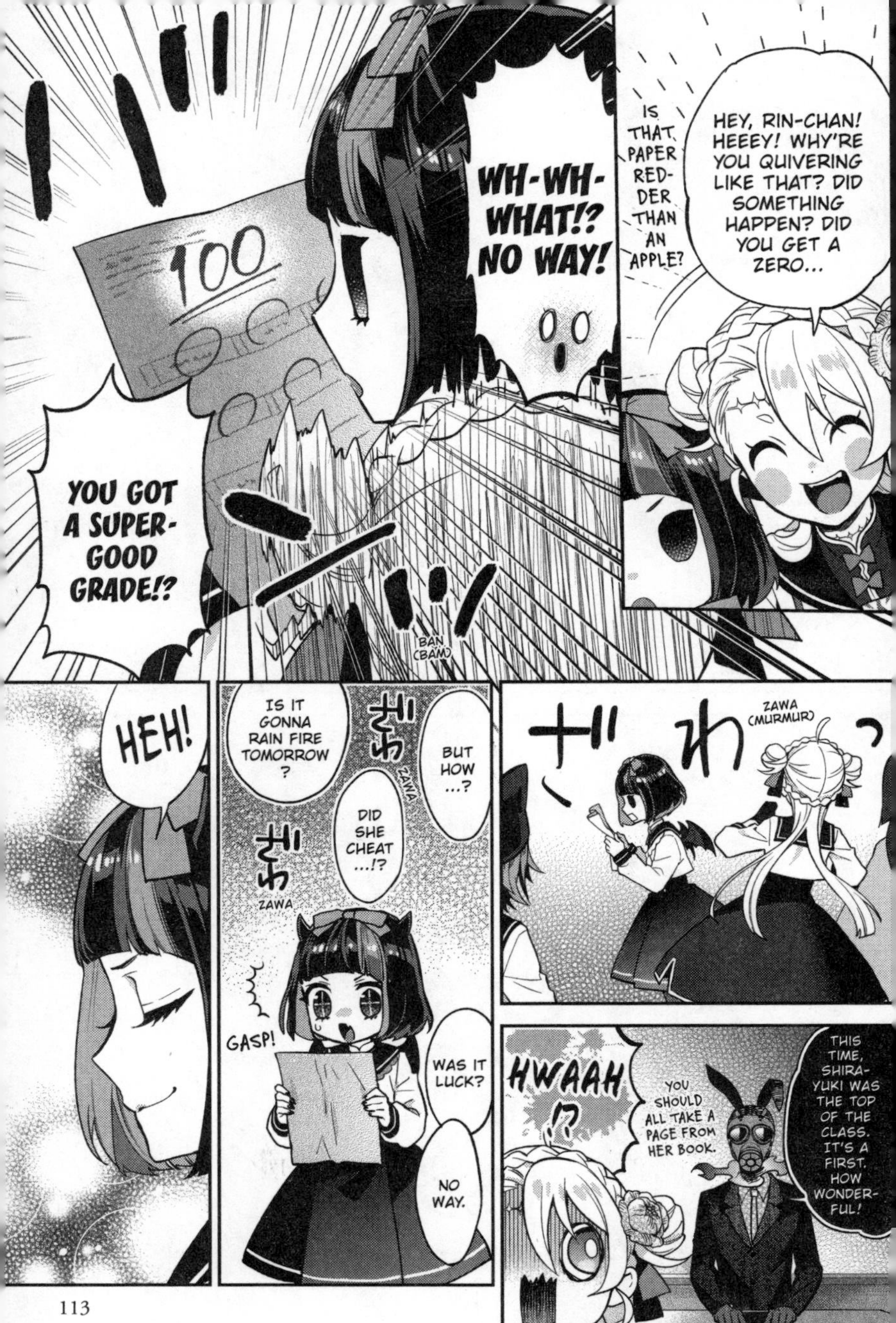
HEY, RIN-CHAN! HEEEY! WHY'RE YOU QUIVERING LIKE THAT? DID SOMETHING HAPPEN? DID YOU GET A ZERO...
IS THAT PAPER RED-DER THAN AN APPLE?
WH-WH-WHAT!? NO WAY!
100
YOU GOT A SUPER-GOOD GRADE!?
BAN (BAM)
ざわ
ZAWA (MURMUR)
THIS TIME, SHIRA-YUKI WAS THE TOP OF THE CLASS. IT'S A FIRST. HOW WONDER-FUL!
YOU SHOULD ALL TAKE A PAGE FROM HER BOOK.
HWAAH !?
ざわ
ZAWA
BUT HOW ...?
IS IT GONNA RAIN FIRE TOMORROW ?
DID SHE CHEAT ...!?
ざわ
ZAWA
GASP!
WAS IT LUCK?
NO WAY.
HEH!

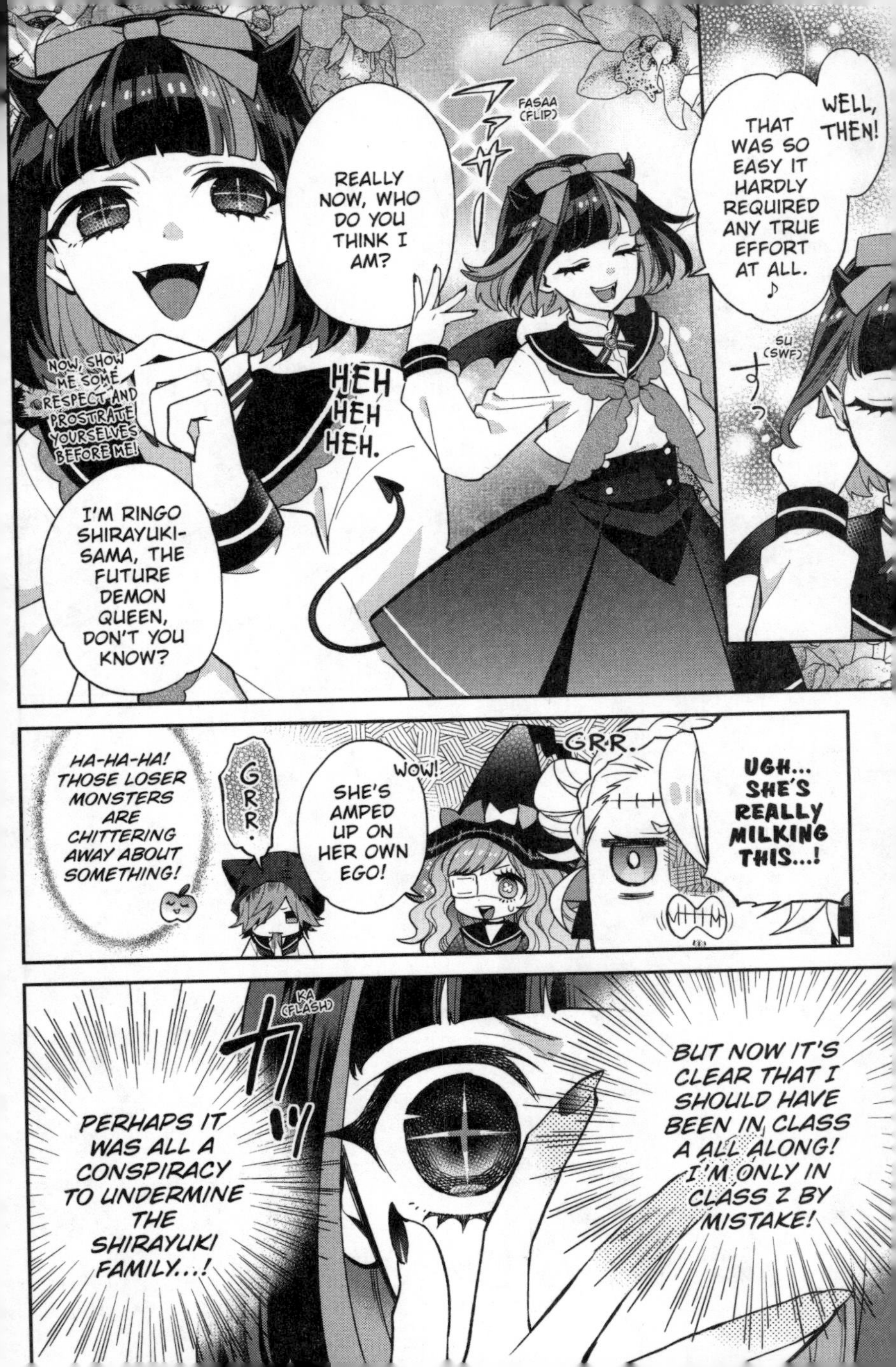
WELL, THEN!
THAT WAS SO EASY IT HARDLY REQUIRED ANY TRUE EFFORT AT ALL. ♪
SU (SWF)
FASAA (FLIP)
REALLY NOW, WHO DO YOU THINK I AM?
HEH HEH HEH.
NOW, SHOW ME SOME RESPECT AND PROSTRATE YOURSELVES BEFORE ME!
I'M RINGO SHIRAYUKI-SAMA, THE FUTURE DEMON QUEEN, DON'T YOU KNOW?
UGH... SHE'S REALLY MILKING THIS...!
GRR.
WOW!
SHE'S AMPED UP ON HER OWN EGO!
GRR.
HA-HA-HA! THOSE LOSER MONSTERS ARE CHITTERING AWAY ABOUT SOMETHING!
BUT NOW IT'S CLEAR THAT I SHOULD HAVE BEEN IN CLASS A ALL ALONG! I'M ONLY IN CLASS 2 BY MISTAKE!
KA (FLASH)
PERHAPS IT WAS ALL A CONSPIRACY TO UNDERMINE THE SHIRAYUKI FAMILY...!

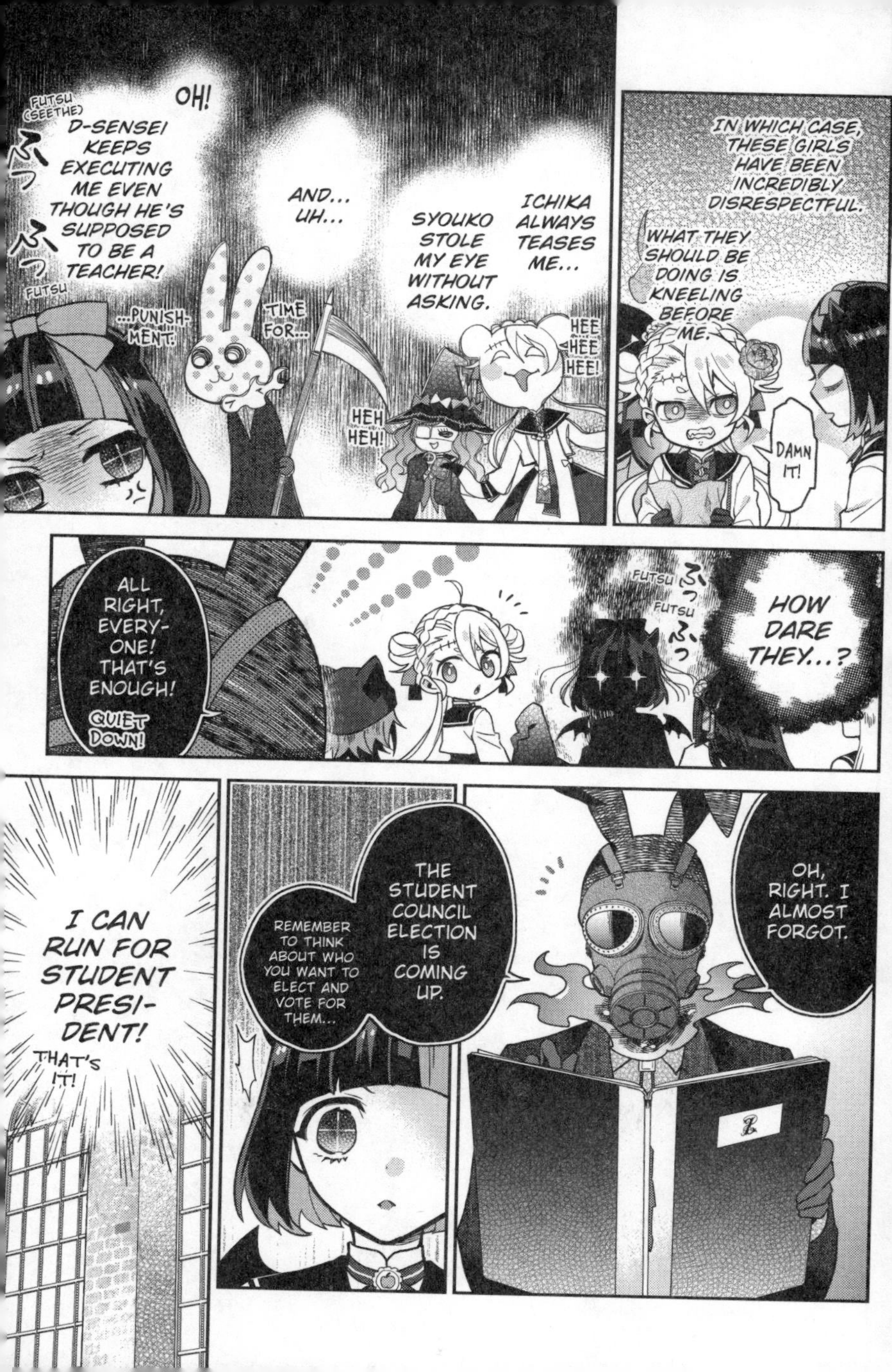
IN WHICH CASE, THESE GIRLS HAVE BEEN INCREDIBLY DISRESPECTFUL.
WHAT THEY SHOULD BE DOING IS KNEELING BEFORE ME.
DAMN IT!
ICHIKA ALWAYS TEASES ME...
SYOUKO STOLE MY EYE WITHOUT ASKING.
HEE HEE HEE!
HEH HEH!
AND... UH...
TIME FOR...
...PUNISHMENT.
OH!
FUTSU (SEETHE)
D-SENSEI KEEPS EXECUTING ME EVEN THOUGH HE'S SUPPOSED TO BE A TEACHER!
FUTSU
HOW DARE THEY...?
FUTSU
FUTSU
ALL RIGHT, EVERYONE! THAT'S ENOUGH!
QUIET DOWN!
OH, RIGHT. I ALMOST FORGOT.
THE STUDENT COUNCIL ELECTION IS COMING UP.
REMEMBER TO THINK ABOUT WHO YOU WANT TO ELECT AND VOTE FOR THEM...
I CAN RUN FOR STUDENT PRESIDENT!
THAT'S IT!

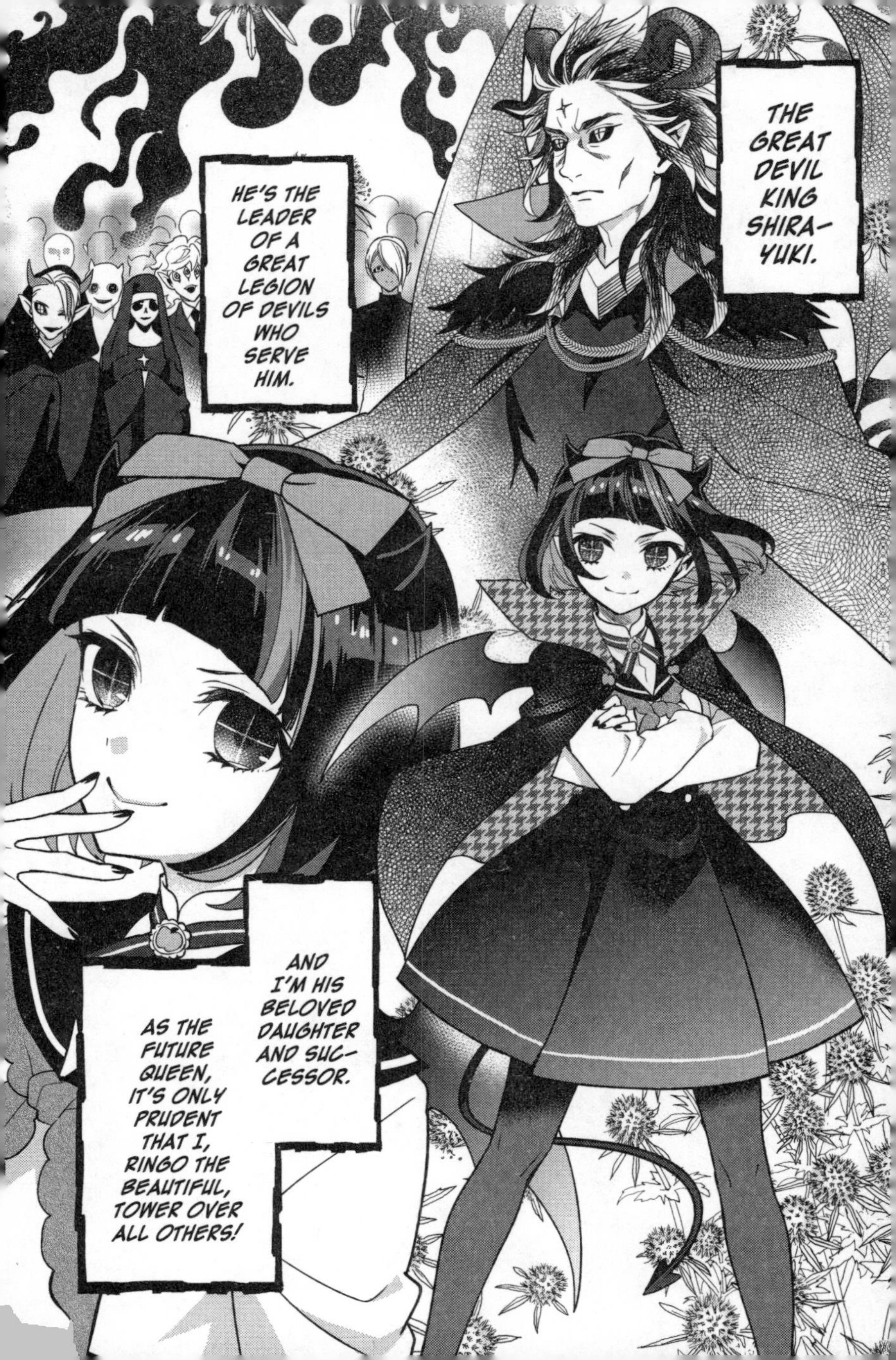
THE GREAT DEVIL KING SHIRA-YUKI.
HE'S THE LEADER OF A GREAT LEGION OF DEVILS WHO SERVE HIM.
AND I'M HIS BELOVED DAUGHTER AND SUC-CESSOR.
AS THE FUTURE QUEEN, IT'S ONLY PRUDENT THAT I, RINGO THE BEAUTIFUL, TOWER OVER ALL OTHERS!

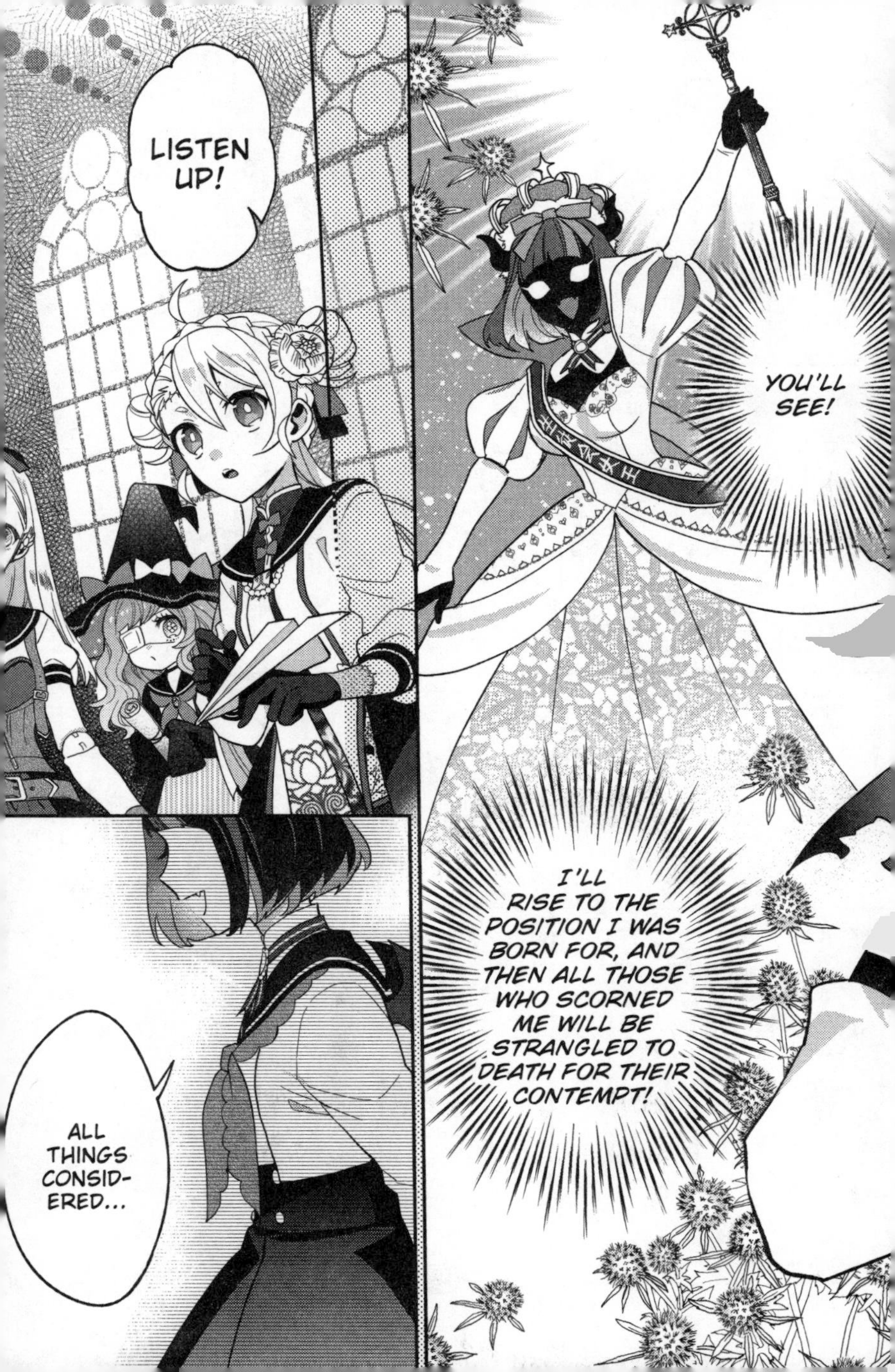
YOU'LL SEE!
I'LL RISE TO THE POSITION I WAS BORN FOR, AND THEN ALL THOSE WHO SCORNED ME WILL BE STRANGLED TO DEATH FOR THEIR CONTEMPT!
LISTEN UP!
ALL THINGS CONSID-ERED...

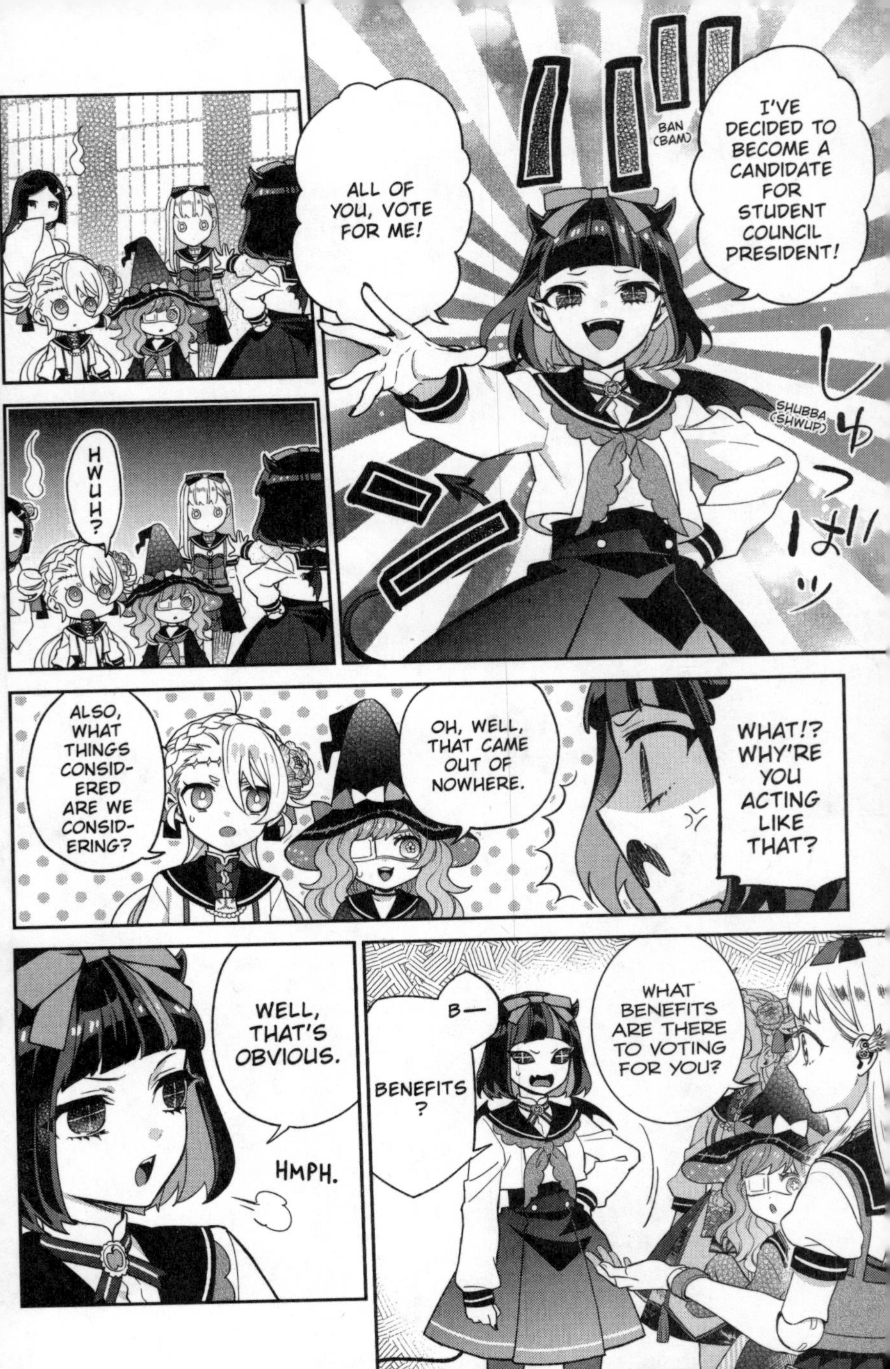
I'VE DECIDED TO BECOME A CANDIDATE FOR STUDENT COUNCIL PRESIDENT!
BAN (BAM)
ALL OF YOU, VOTE FOR ME!
しゅっぱッ
SHUBBA (SHWUP)
HWUH?
WHAT!? WHY'RE YOU ACTING LIKE THAT?
OH, WELL, THAT CAME OUT OF NOWHERE.
ALSO, WHAT THINGS CONSID-ERED ARE WE CONSID-ERING?
WHAT BENEFITS ARE THERE TO VOTING FOR YOU?
B—
BENEFITS?
WELL, THAT'S OBVIOUS.
HMPH.

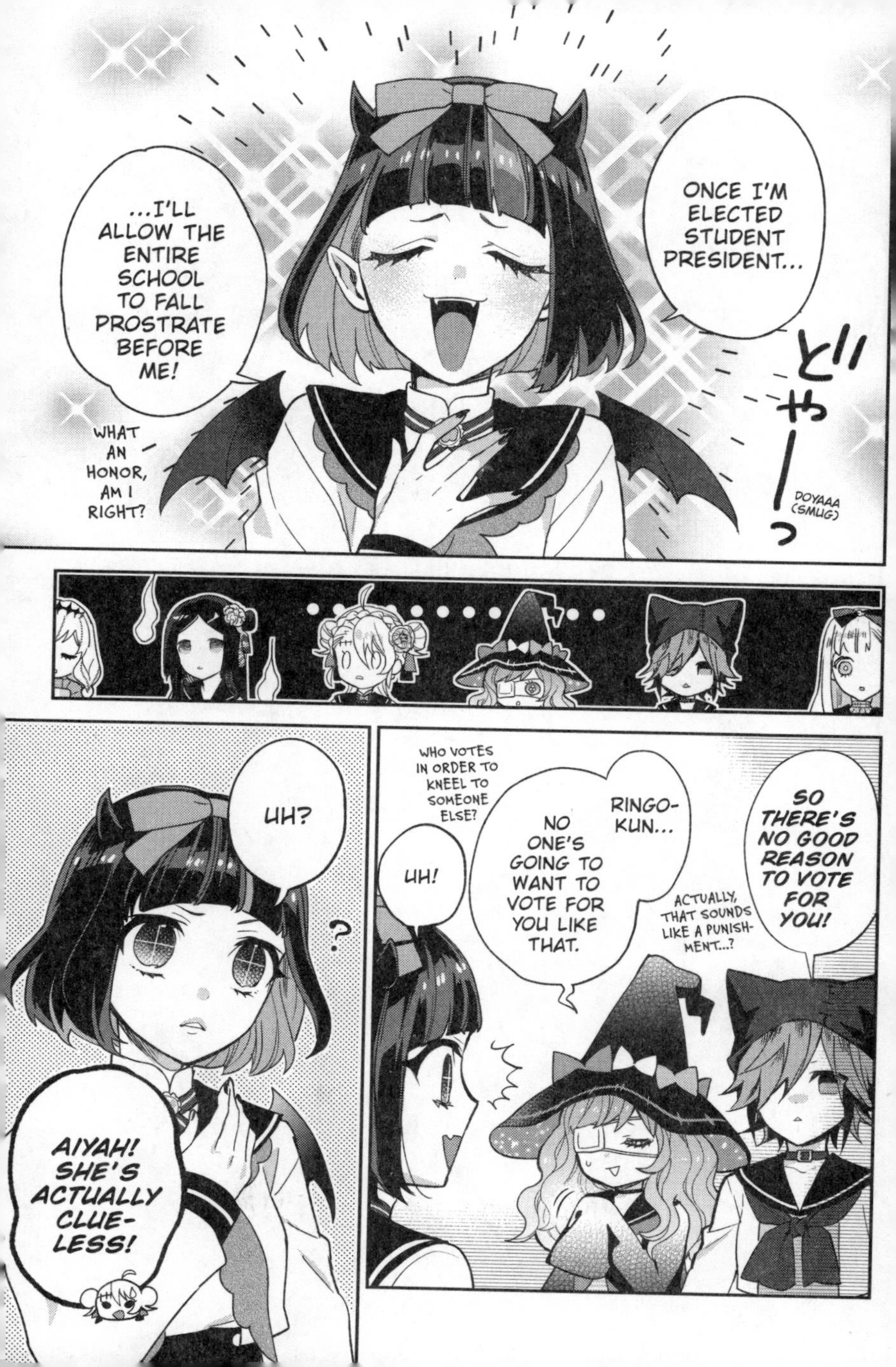
ONCE I'M ELECTED STUDENT PRESIDENT...
...I'LL ALLOW THE ENTIRE SCHOOL TO FALL PROSTRATE BEFORE ME!
WHAT AN HONOR, AM I RIGHT?
どやーっ
DOYAAA (SMUG)
SO THERE'S NO GOOD REASON TO VOTE FOR YOU!
ACTUALLY, THAT SOUNDS LIKE A PUNISHMENT...?
RINGO-KUN... NO ONE'S GOING TO WANT TO VOTE FOR YOU LIKE THAT.
WHO VOTES IN ORDER TO KNEEL TO SOMEONE ELSE?
UH!
UH?
?
AIYAH! SHE'S ACTUALLY CLUELESS!

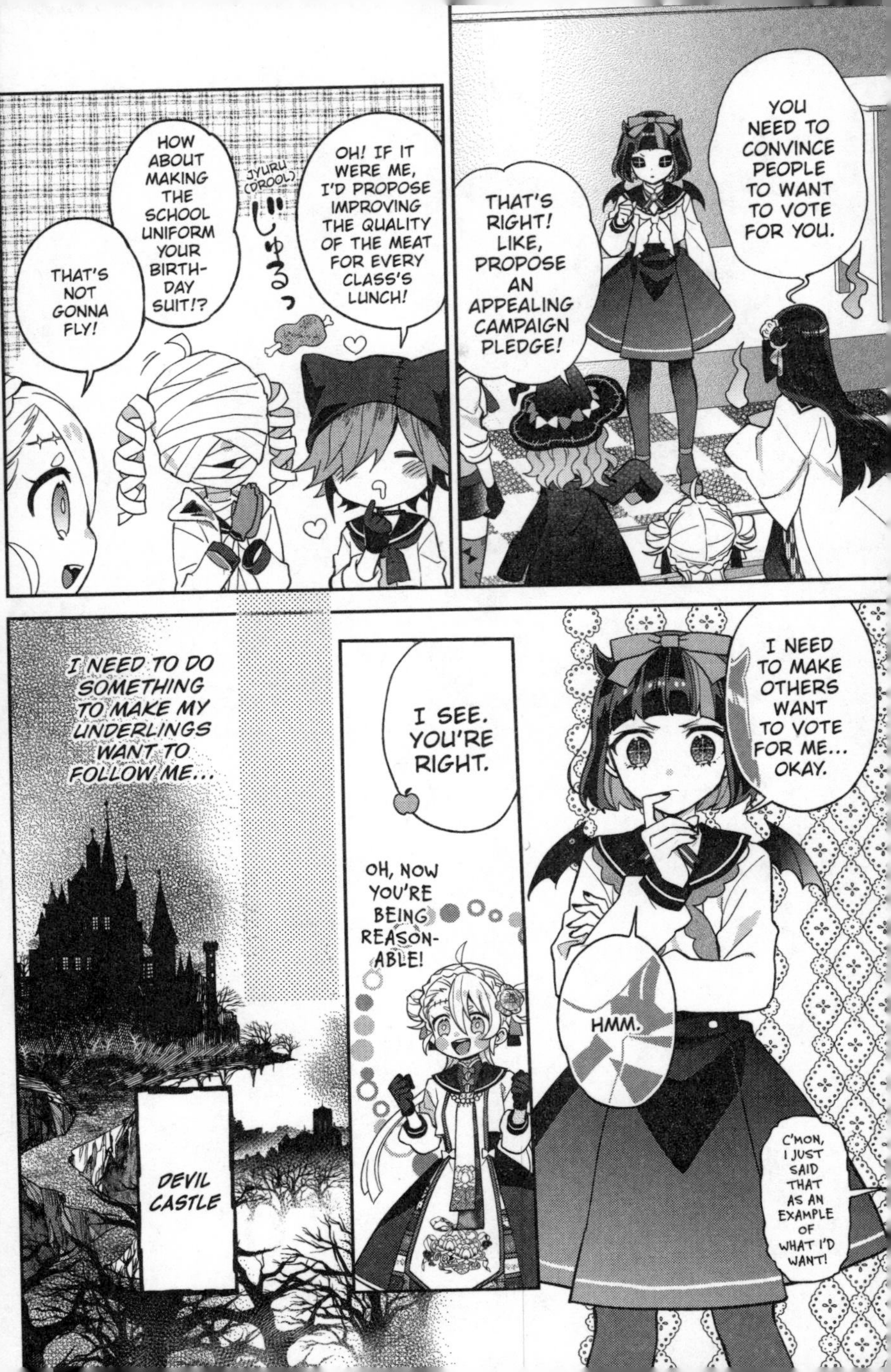
YOU NEED TO CONVINCE PEOPLE TO WANT TO VOTE FOR YOU.
THAT'S RIGHT! LIKE, PROPOSE AN APPEALING CAMPAIGN PLEDGE!
OH! IF IT WERE ME, I'D PROPOSE IMPROVING THE QUALITY OF THE MEAT FOR EVERY CLASS'S LUNCH!
JYURU (DROOL)
じゅるっ
HOW ABOUT MAKING THE SCHOOL UNIFORM YOUR BIRTH-DAY SUIT!?
THAT'S NOT GONNA FLY!
I NEED TO MAKE OTHERS WANT TO VOTE FOR ME... OKAY.
HMM.
C'MON, I JUST SAID THAT AS AN EXAMPLE OF WHAT I'D WANT!
I SEE. YOU'RE RIGHT.
OH, NOW YOU'RE BEING REASON-ABLE!
I NEED TO DO SOMETHING TO MAKE MY UNDERLINGS WANT TO FOLLOW ME...
DEVIL CASTLE

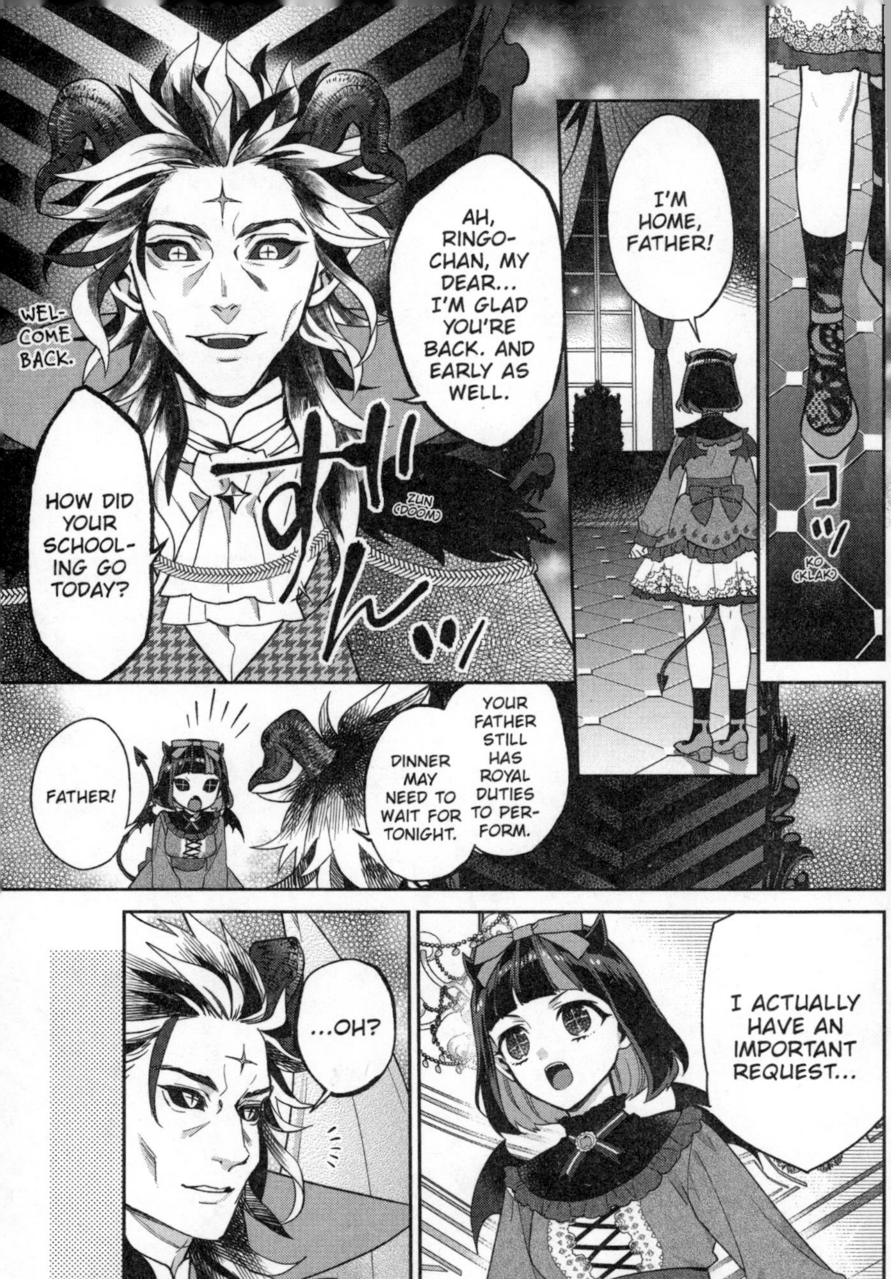
KO (KLAK)
I'M HOME, FATHER!
AH, RINGO-CHAN, MY DEAR... I'M GLAD YOU'RE BACK. AND EARLY AS WELL.
WEL-COME BACK.
HOW DID YOUR SCHOOL-ING GO TODAY?
ZUN (DOOM)
YOUR FATHER STILL HAS ROYAL DUTIES TO PER-FORM.
DINNER MAY NEED TO WAIT FOR TONIGHT.
FATHER!
I ACTUALLY HAVE AN IMPORTANT REQUEST...
...OH?

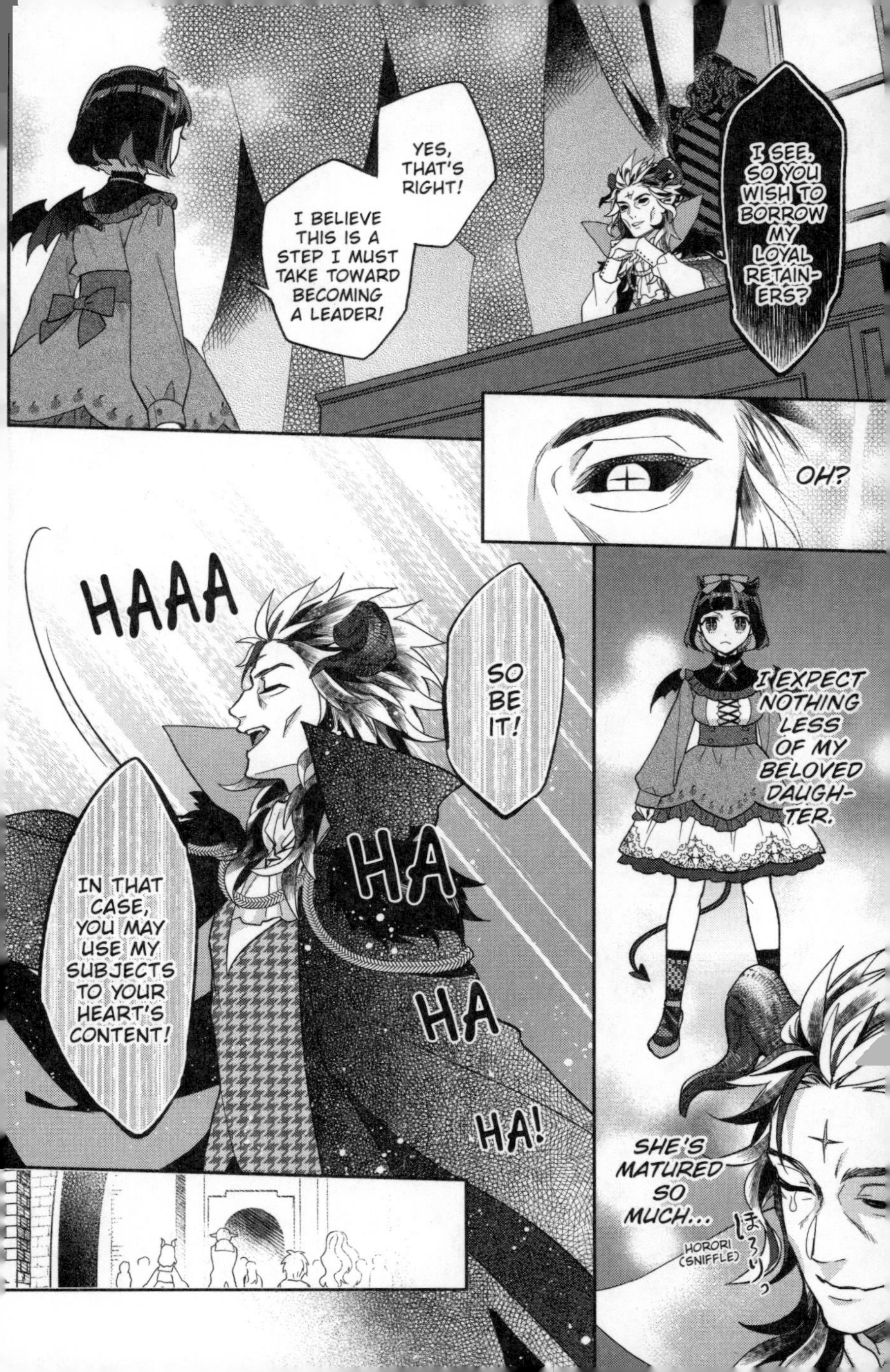
I SEE. SO YOU WISH TO BORROW MY LOYAL RETAINERS?
YES, THAT'S RIGHT!
I BELIEVE THIS IS A STEP I MUST TAKE TOWARD BECOMING A LEADER!
OH?
I EXPECT NOTHING LESS OF MY BELOVED DAUGHTER.
SHE'S MATURED SO MUCH...
ほろり
HORORI (SNIFFLE)
SO BE IT!
HAAA
HA
HA
HA!
IN THAT CASE, YOU MAY USE MY SUBJECTS TO YOUR HEART'S CONTENT!

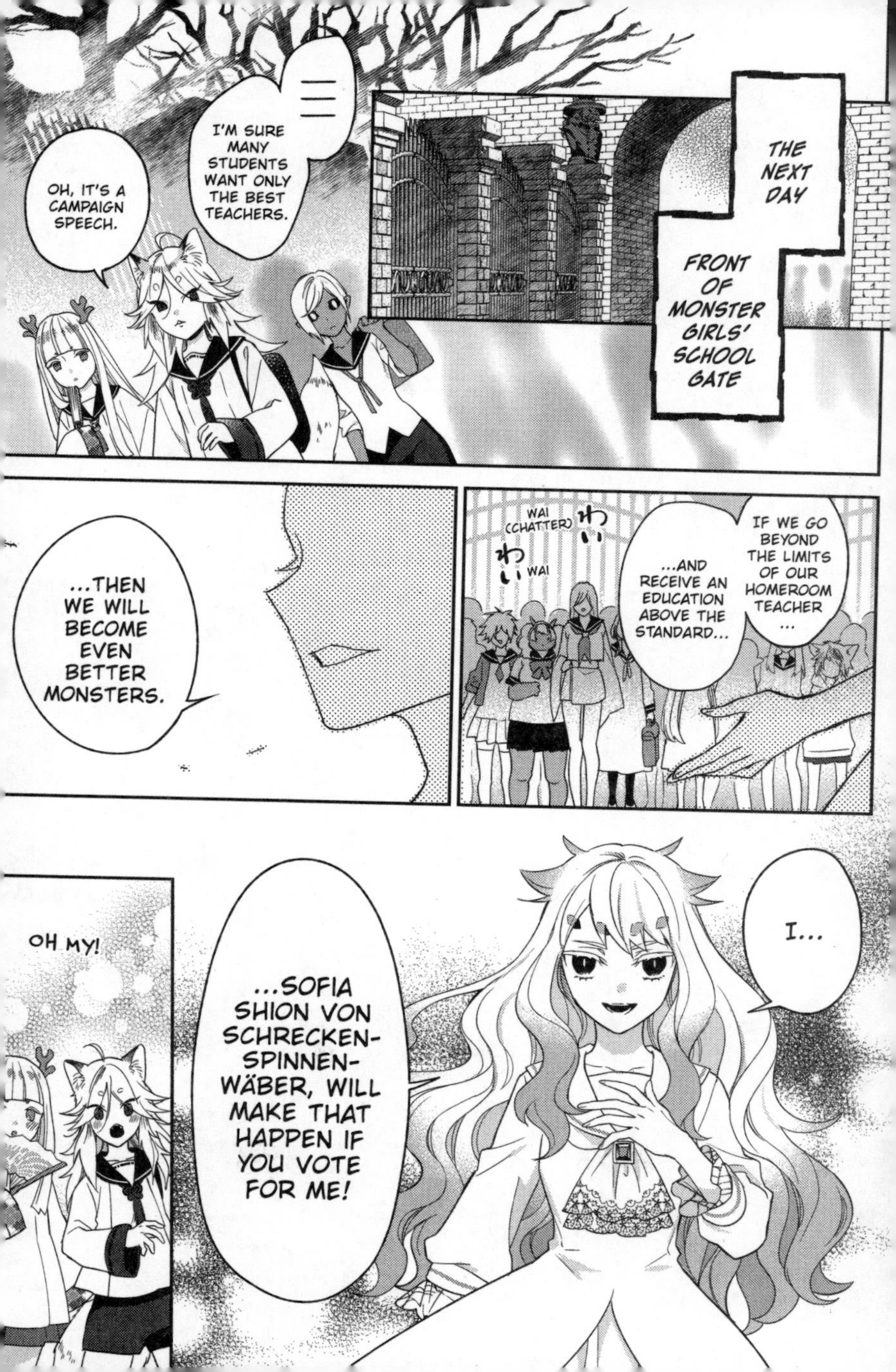
THE NEXT DAY
FRONT OF MONSTER GIRLS' SCHOOL GATE
—
I'M SURE MANY STUDENTS WANT ONLY THE BEST TEACHERS.
OH, IT'S A CAMPAIGN SPEECH.
IF WE GO BEYOND THE LIMITS OF OUR HOMEROOM TEACHER ...
...AND RECEIVE AN EDUCATION ABOVE THE STANDARD...
わい WAI (CHATTER)
わい WAI
...THEN WE WILL BECOME EVEN BETTER MONSTERS.
I...
...SOFIA SHION VON SCHRECKEN-SPINNEN-WÄBER, WILL MAKE THAT HAPPEN IF YOU VOTE FOR ME!
OH MY!

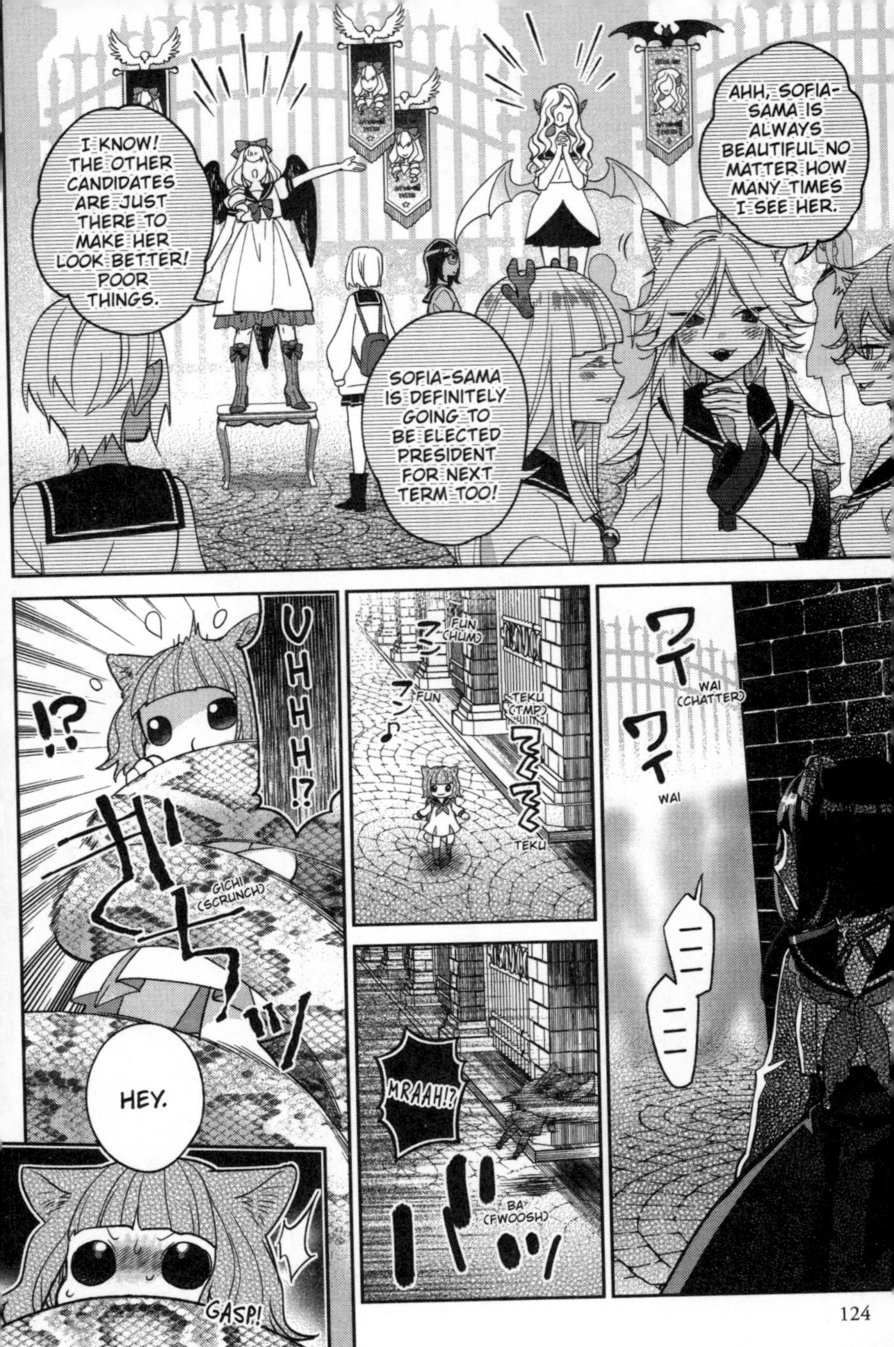
AHH, SOFIA-SAMA IS ALWAYS BEAUTIFUL NO MATTER HOW MANY TIMES I SEE HER.
I KNOW! THE OTHER CANDIDATES ARE JUST THERE TO MAKE HER LOOK BETTER! POOR THINGS.
SOFIA-SAMA IS DEFINITELY GOING TO BE ELECTED PRESIDENT FOR NEXT TERM TOO!
WAI (CHATTER)
WAI
―――
FUN (HUM)
FUN
TEKU (TMP)
TEKU
MRAAH!?
BA (FWOOSH)
UHHH!?
!?
GICHI (SCRUNCH)
HEY.
GASP!

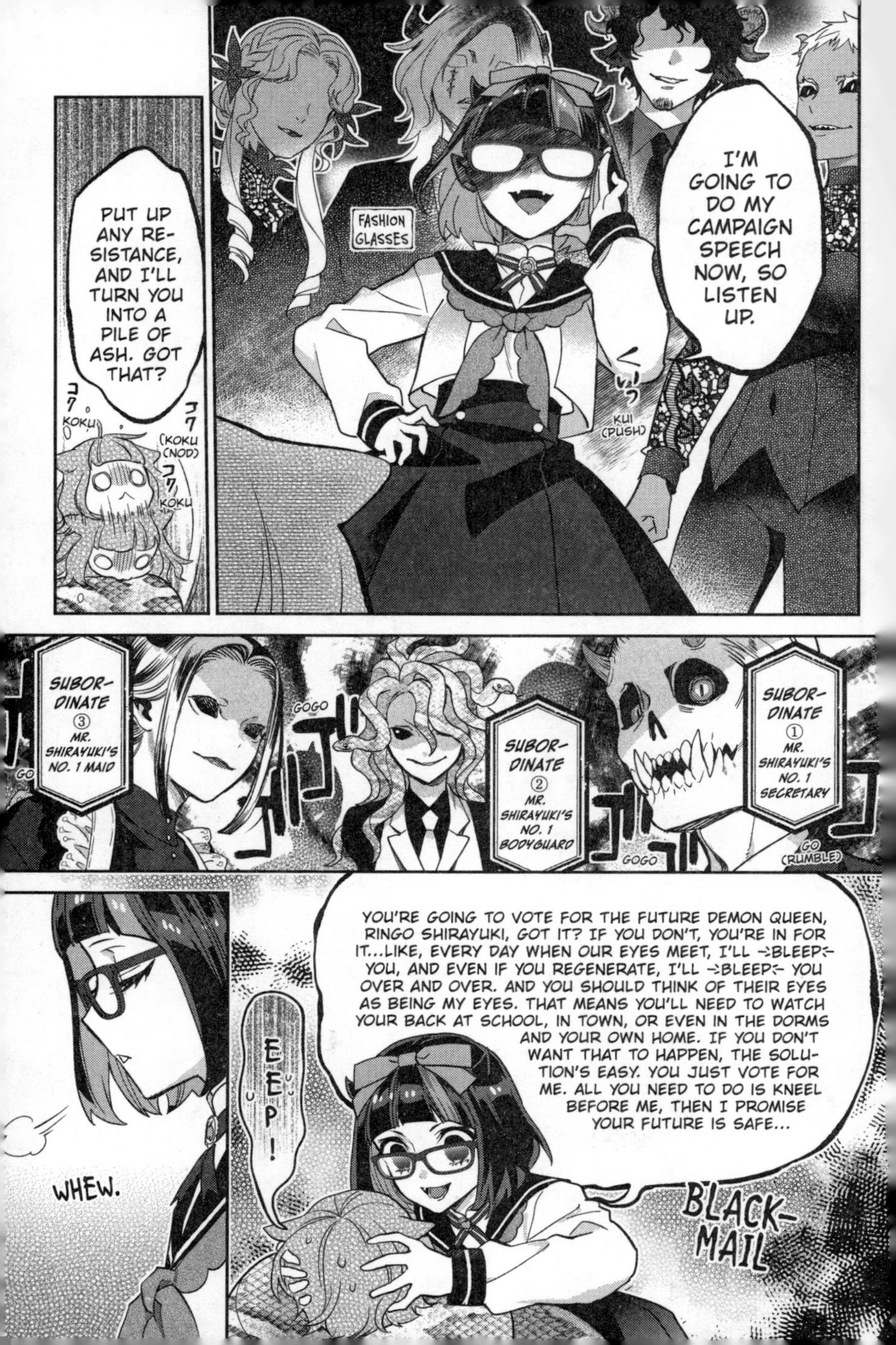
I'M GOING TO DO MY CAMPAIGN SPEECH NOW, SO LISTEN UP.
FASHION GLASSES
KUI (PUSH)
PUT UP ANY RE-SISTANCE, AND I'LL TURN YOU INTO A PILE OF ASH. GOT THAT?
KOKU (KOKU (NOD) KOKU
SUBOR-DINATE ① MR. SHIRAYUKI'S NO. 1 SECRETARY
GO (RUMBLE)
GOGO
SUBOR-DINATE ② MR. SHIRAYUKI'S NO. 1 BODYGUARD
GOGO
SUBOR-DINATE ③ MR. SHIRAYUKI'S NO. 1 MAID
GO
YOU'RE GOING TO VOTE FOR THE FUTURE DEMON QUEEN, RINGO SHIRAYUKI, GOT IT? IF YOU DON'T, YOU'RE IN FOR IT...LIKE, EVERY DAY WHEN OUR EYES MEET, I'LL ⇒BLEEP⇐ YOU, AND EVEN IF YOU REGENERATE, I'LL ⇒BLEEP⇐ YOU OVER AND OVER. AND YOU SHOULD THINK OF THEIR EYES AS BEING MY EYES. THAT MEANS YOU'LL NEED TO WATCH YOUR BACK AT SCHOOL, IN TOWN, OR EVEN IN THE DORMS AND YOUR OWN HOME. IF YOU DON'T WANT THAT TO HAPPEN, THE SOLU-TION'S EASY. YOU JUST VOTE FOR ME. ALL YOU NEED TO DO IS KNEEL BEFORE ME, THEN I PROMISE YOUR FUTURE IS SAFE...
BLACK-MAIL
EEP!
WHEW.

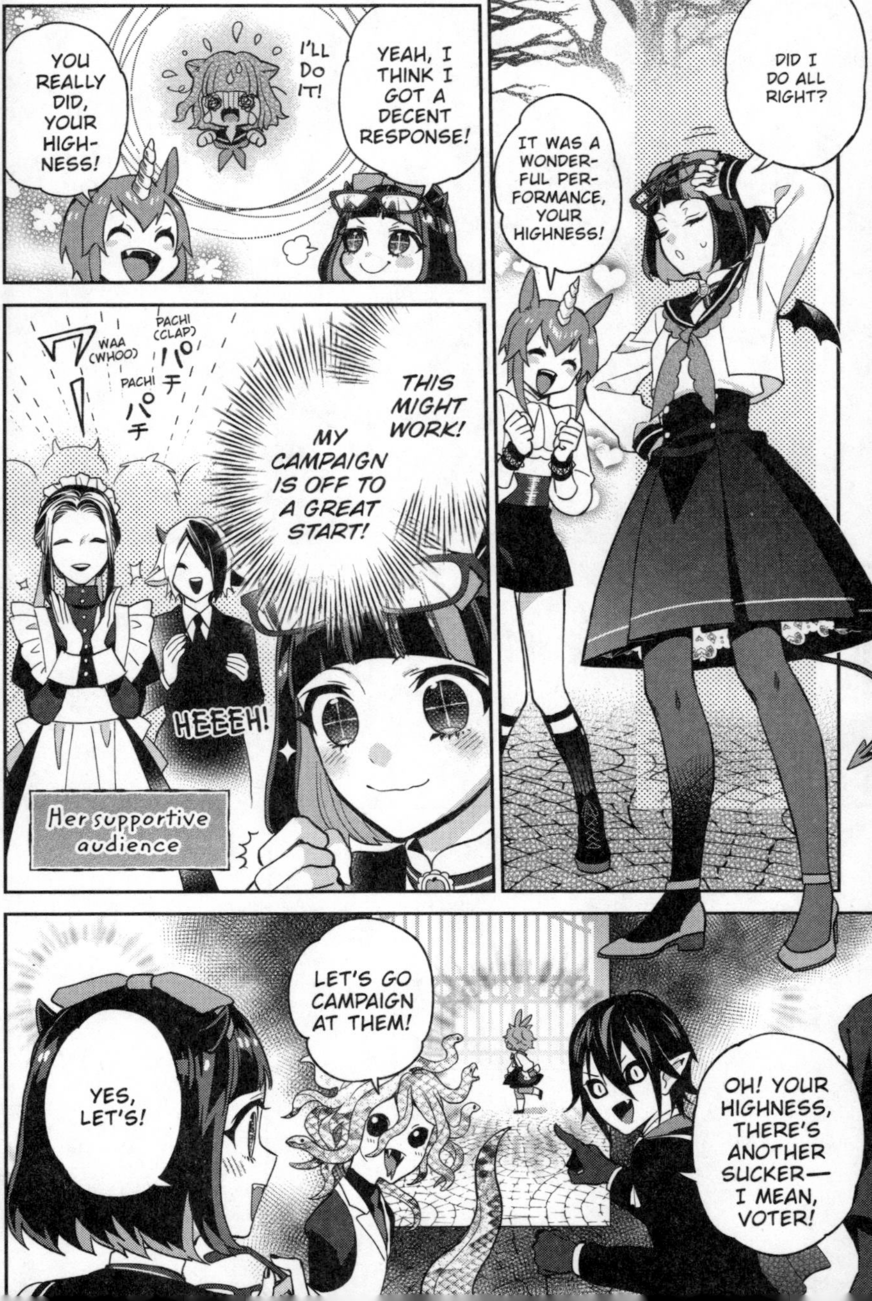
DID I DO ALL RIGHT?
IT WAS A WONDERFUL PERFORMANCE, YOUR HIGHNESS!
YEAH, I THINK I GOT A DECENT RESPONSE!
I'LL DO IT!
YOU REALLY DID, YOUR HIGHNESS!
THIS MIGHT WORK!
MY CAMPAIGN IS OFF TO A GREAT START!
PACHI (CLAP) パチ
PACHI パチ
WAA (WHOO) ワ
HEEEH!
Her supportive audience
OH! YOUR HIGHNESS, THERE'S ANOTHER SUCKER— I MEAN, VOTER!
LET'S GO CAMPAIGN AT THEM!
YES, LET'S!

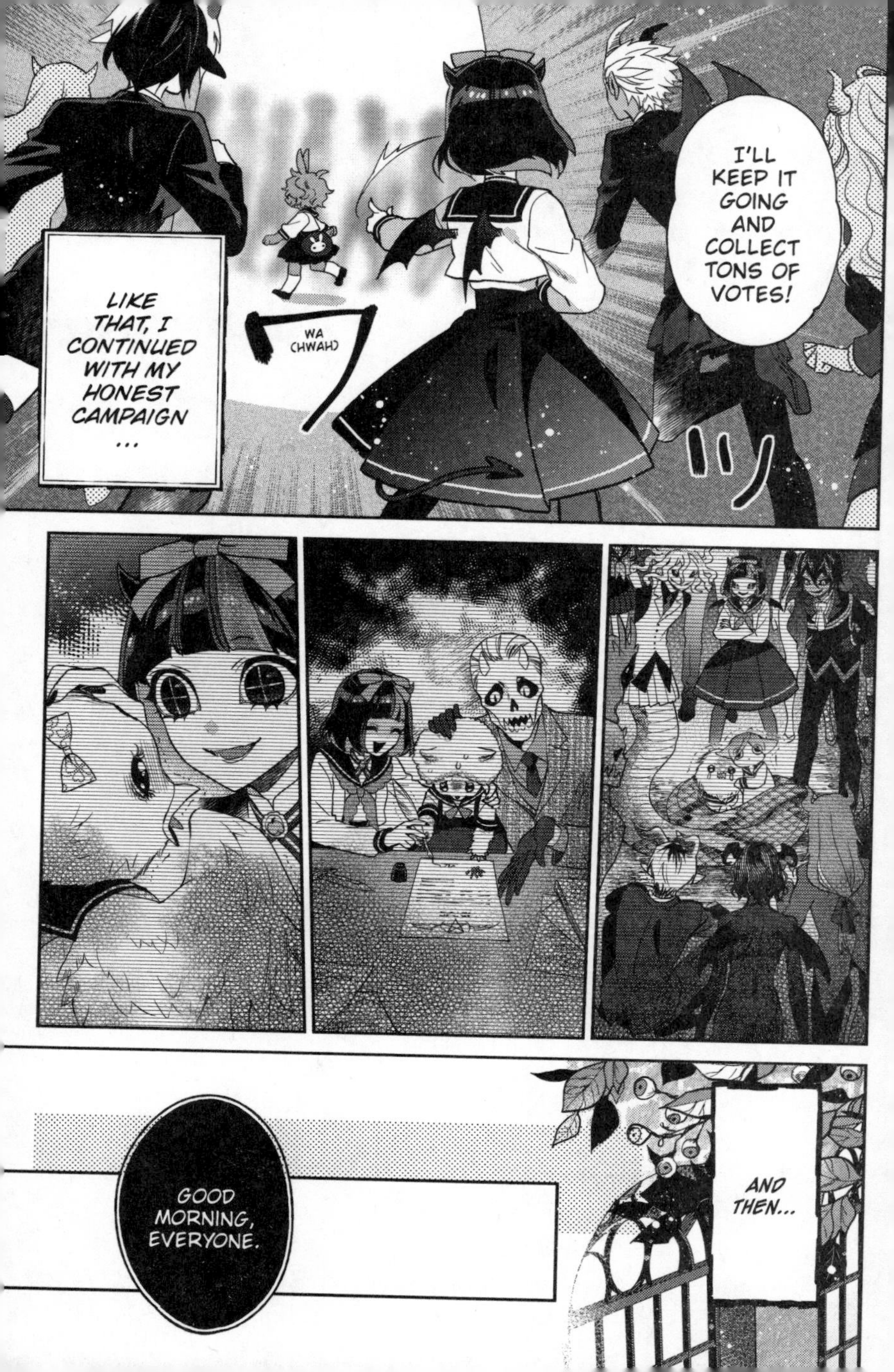
I'LL KEEP IT GOING AND COLLECT TONS OF VOTES!
WA (HWAH)
LIKE THAT, I CONTINUED WITH MY HONEST CAMPAIGN ...
AND THEN...
GOOD MORNING, EVERYONE.

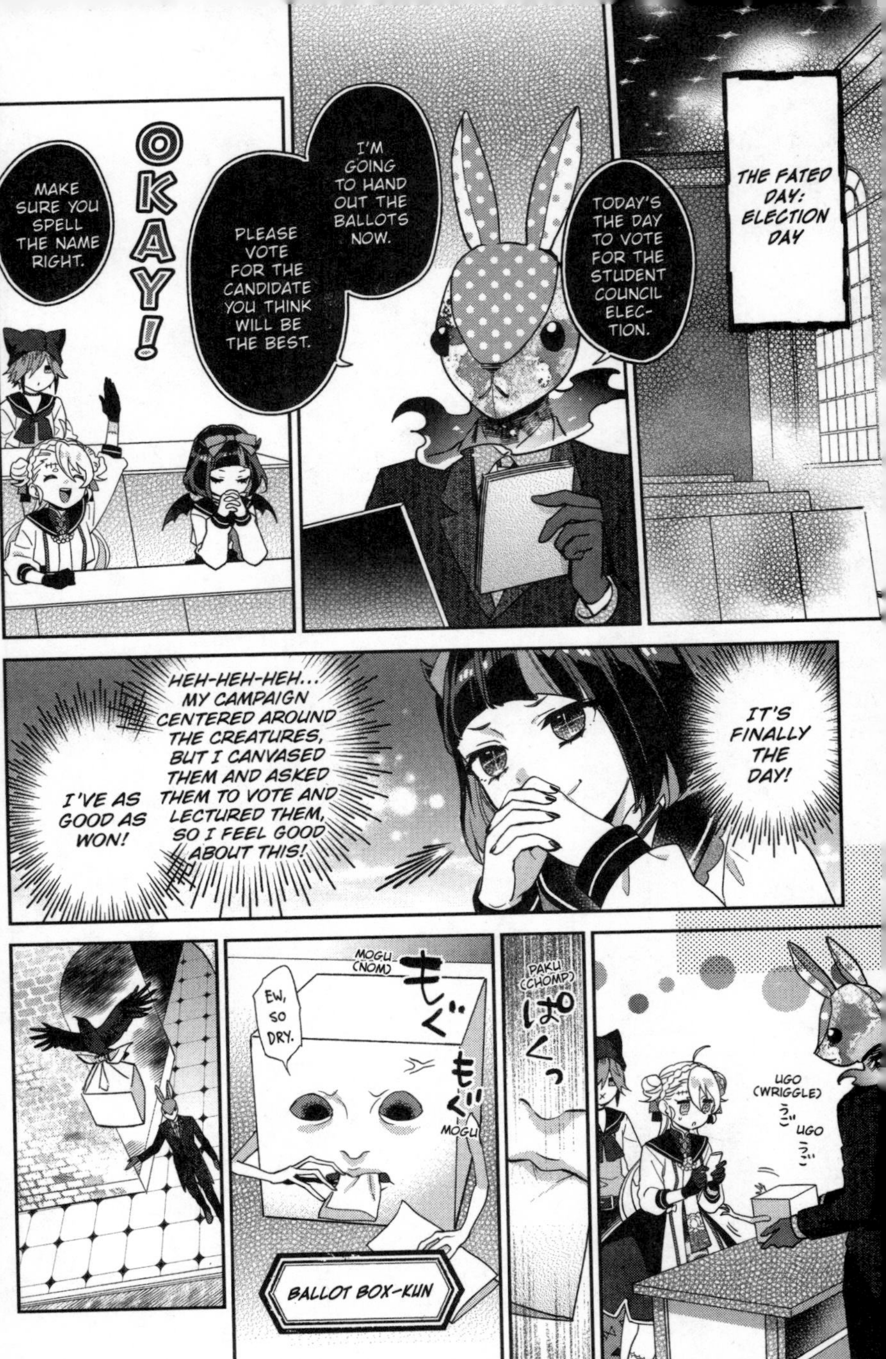
THE FATED DAY: ELECTION DAY
TODAY'S THE DAY TO VOTE FOR THE STUDENT COUNCIL ELEC-TION.
I'M GOING TO HAND OUT THE BALLOTS NOW.
PLEASE VOTE FOR THE CANDIDATE YOU THINK WILL BE THE BEST.
OKAY!
MAKE SURE YOU SPELL THE NAME RIGHT.
IT'S FINALLY THE DAY!
HEH-HEH-HEH... MY CAMPAIGN CENTERED AROUND THE CREATURES, BUT I CANVASED THEM AND ASKED THEM TO VOTE AND LECTURED THEM, SO I FEEL GOOD ABOUT THIS!
I'VE AS GOOD AS WON!
UGO (WRIGGLE)
うご
UGO
うご
PAKU (CHOMP)
ぱくっ
MOGU (NOM)
もぐ
もぐ
MOGU
EW, SO DRY.
BALLOT BOX-KUN

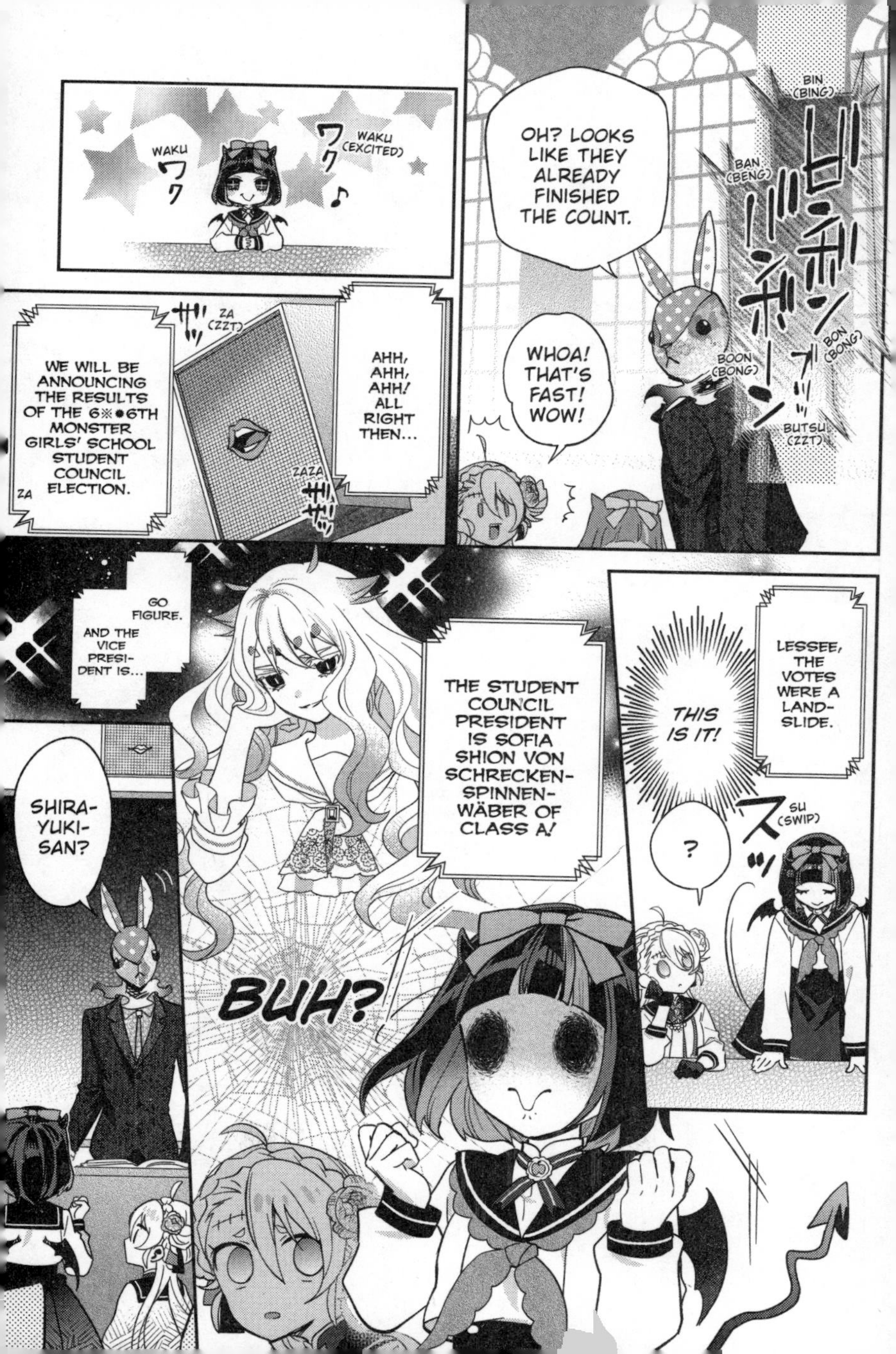
BIN (BING)
BAN (BENG)
BON (BONG)
BOON (BONG)
BUTSU (ZZT)
OH? LOOKS LIKE THEY ALREADY FINISHED THE COUNT.
WHOA! THAT'S FAST! WOW!
WAKU
WAKU (EXCITED)
ZA (ZZT)
AHH, AHH, AHH! ALL RIGHT THEN...
ZAZA
WE WILL BE ANNOUNCING THE RESULTS OF THE 6※●6TH MONSTER GIRLS' SCHOOL STUDENT COUNCIL ELECTION.
ZA
LESSEE, THE VOTES WERE A LANDSLIDE.
THIS IS IT!
SU (SWIP)
?
THE STUDENT COUNCIL PRESIDENT IS SOFIA SHION VON SCHRECKENSPINNENWÄBER OF CLASS A!
GO FIGURE.
AND THE VICE PRESIDENT IS...
BUH?
SHIRAYUKI-SAN?

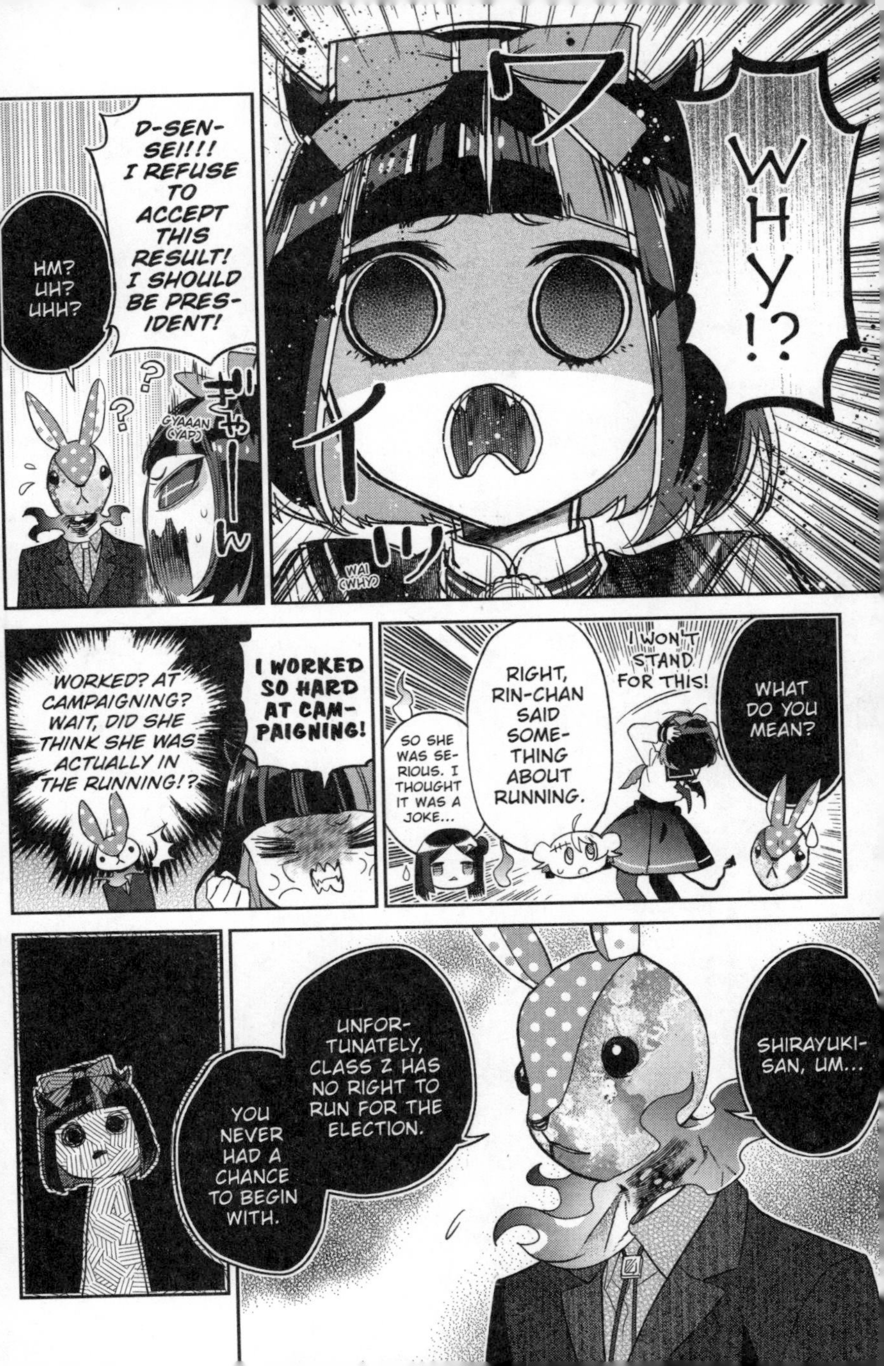
WHY!?
WAI (WHY)
D-SENSEI!!! I REFUSE TO ACCEPT THIS RESULT! I SHOULD BE PRESIDENT!
GYAAAN (YAP)
HM? UH? UHH?
WHAT DO YOU MEAN?
I WON'T STAND FOR THIS!
RIGHT, RIN-CHAN SAID SOMETHING ABOUT RUNNING.
SO SHE WAS SERIOUS. I THOUGHT IT WAS A JOKE...
I WORKED SO HARD AT CAMPAIGNING!
WORKED? AT CAMPAIGNING? WAIT, DID SHE THINK SHE WAS ACTUALLY IN THE RUNNING!?
SHIRAYUKI-SAN, UM...
UNFORTUNATELY, CLASS Z HAS NO RIGHT TO RUN FOR THE ELECTION.
YOU NEVER HAD A CHANCE TO BEGIN WITH.

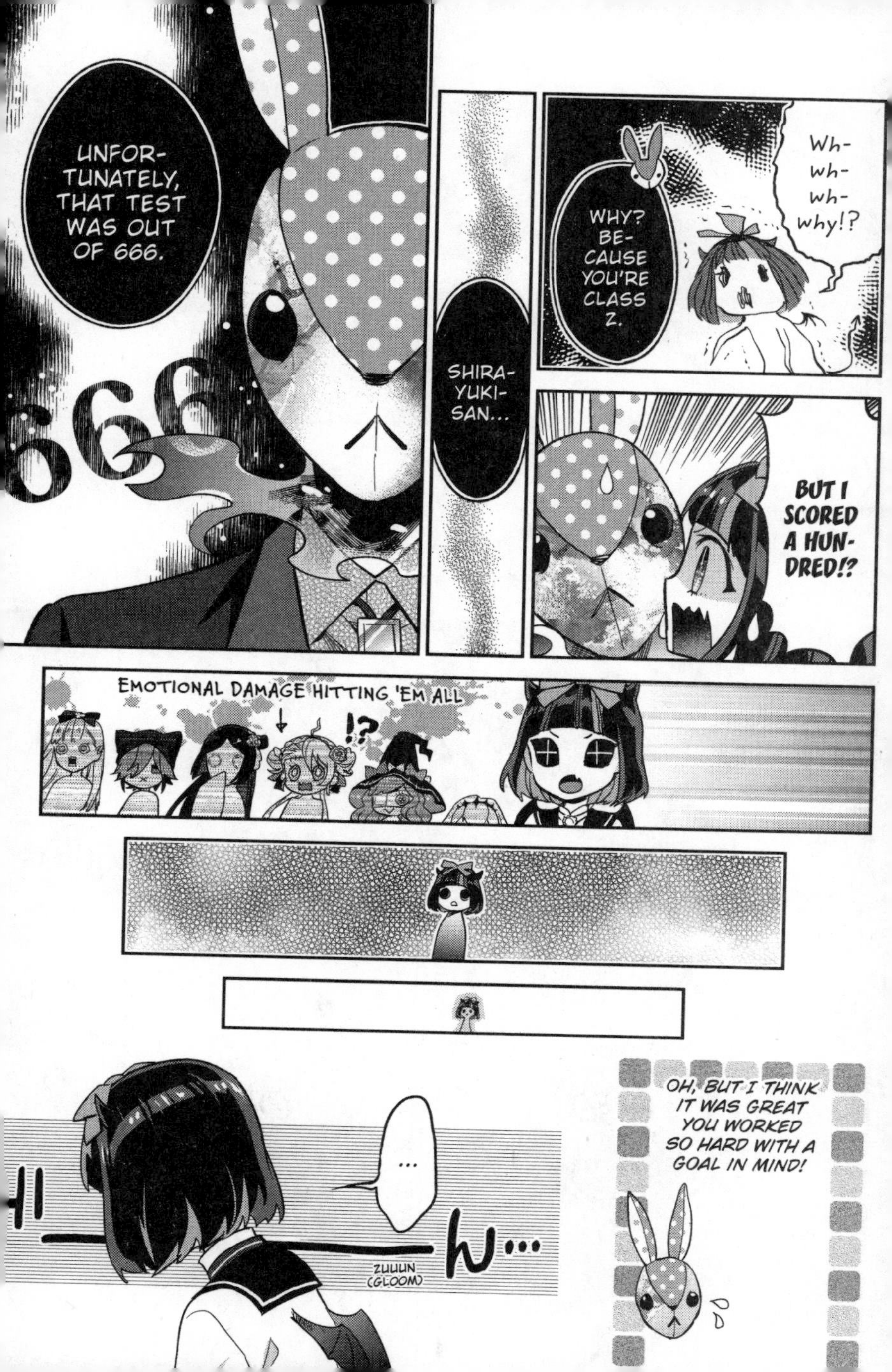
Wh-wh-wh-why!?
WHY? BE-CAUSE YOU'RE CLASS Z.
BUT I SCORED A HUN-DRED!?
SHIRA-YUKI-SAN...
UNFOR-TUNATELY, THAT TEST WAS OUT OF 666.
666
EMOTIONAL DAMAGE HITTING 'EM ALL
!?
OH, BUT I THINK IT WAS GREAT YOU WORKED SO HARD WITH A GOAL IN MIND!
...
H——h...
ZUUUN (GLOOM)

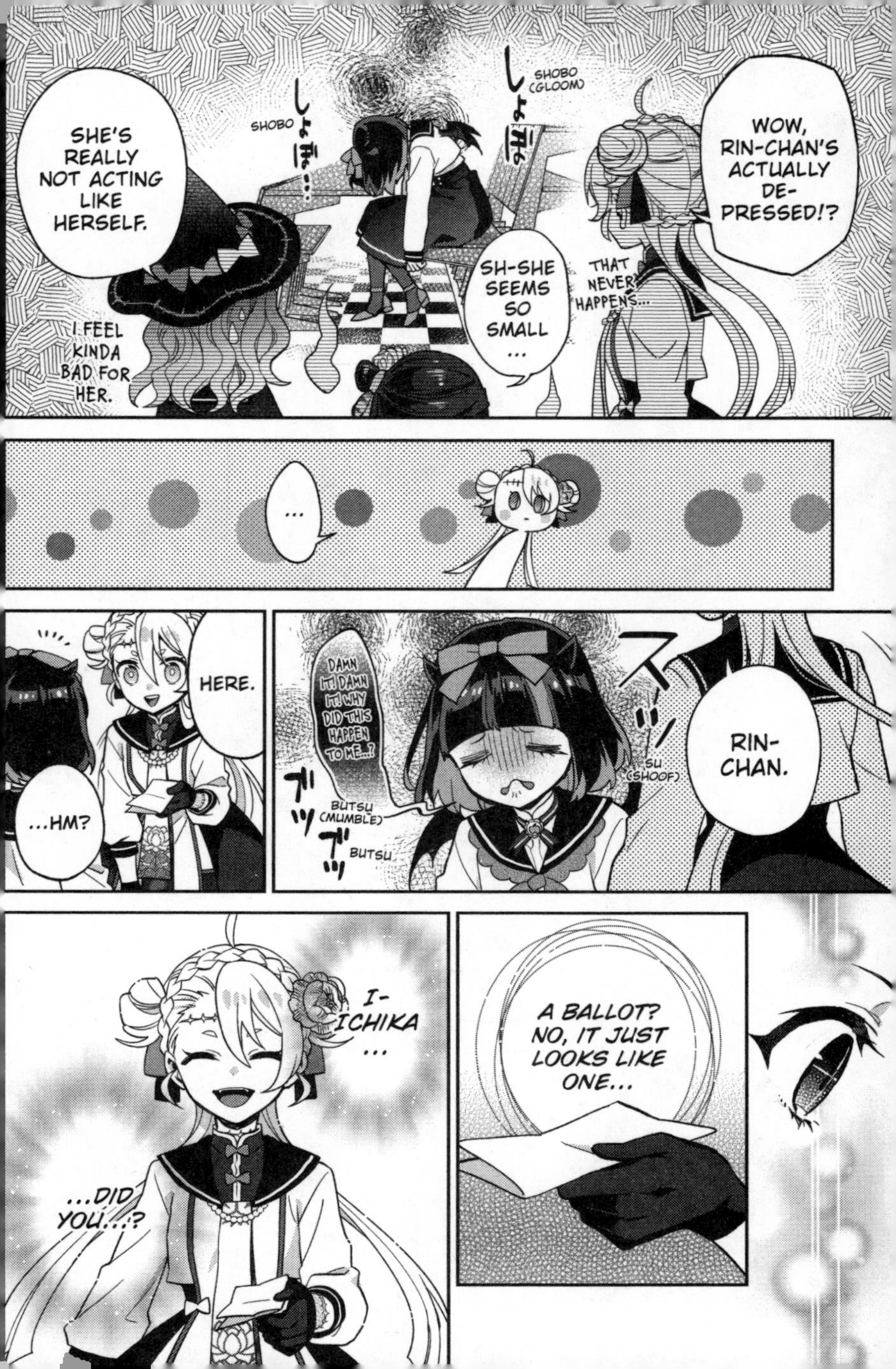
WOW, RIN-CHAN'S ACTUALLY DE-PRESSED!?
THAT NEVER HAPPENS...
SHOBO (GLOOM)
SHOBO
SH-SHE SEEMS SO SMALL ...
SHE'S REALLY NOT ACTING LIKE HERSELF.
I FEEL KINDA BAD FOR HER.
...
RIN-CHAN.
SU (SHOOF)
DAMN IT! DAMN IT! WHY DID THIS HAPPEN TO ME...?
BUTSU (MUMBLE)
BUTSU
HERE.
...HM?
A BALLOT? NO, IT JUST LOOKS LIKE ONE...
I-ICHIKA ...
...DID YOU...?

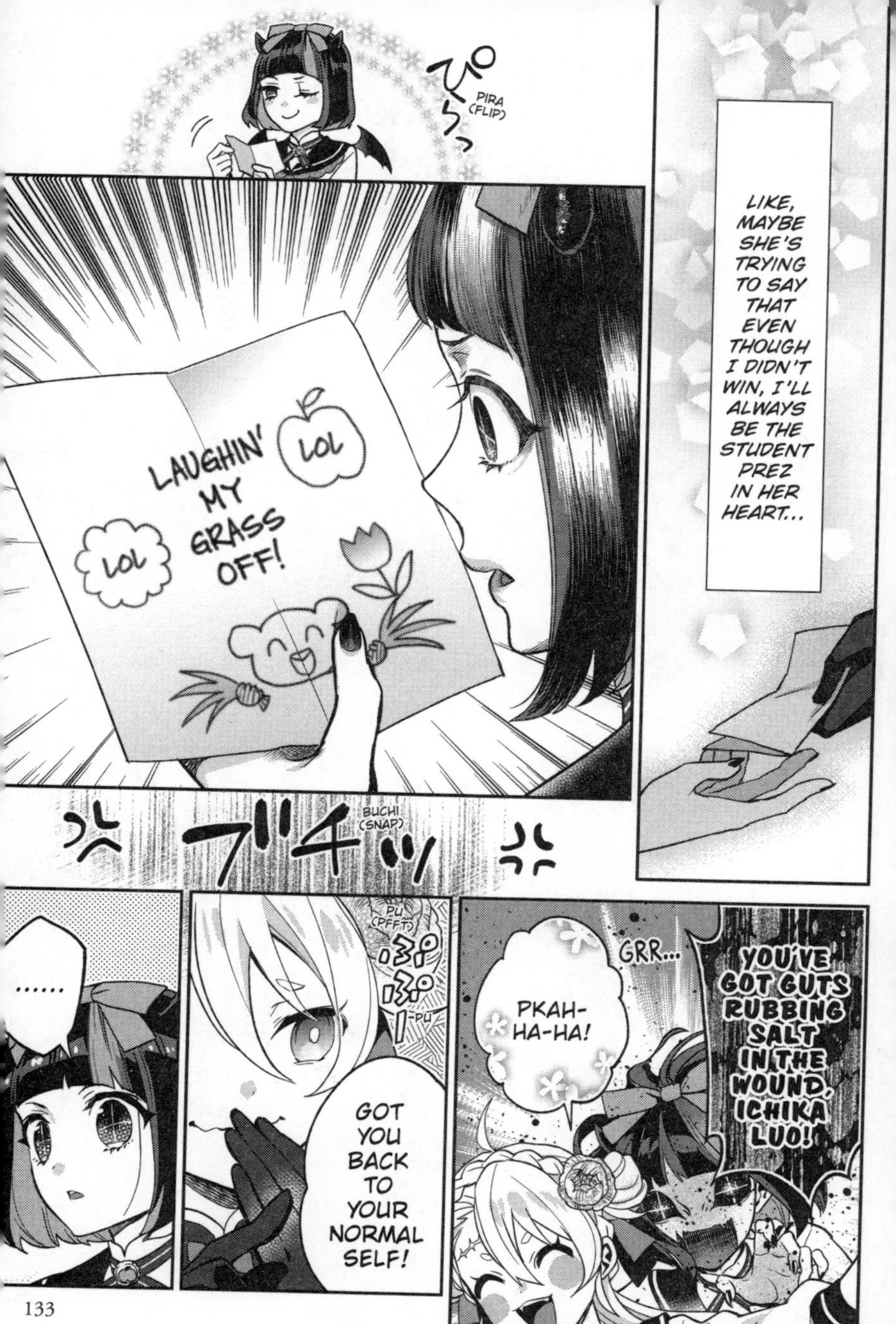
LIKE, MAYBE SHE'S TRYING TO SAY THAT EVEN THOUGH I DIDN'T WIN, I'LL ALWAYS BE THE STUDENT PREZ IN HER HEART...
PIRA (FLIP)
LAUGHIN' MY GRASS OFF!
LOL
LOL
BUCHI (SNAP)
YOU'VE GOT GUTS RUBBING SALT IN THE WOUND, ICHIKA LUO!
GRR...
PKAH-HA-HA!
PU (PFFT)
-PU
GOT YOU BACK TO YOUR NORMAL SELF!
......

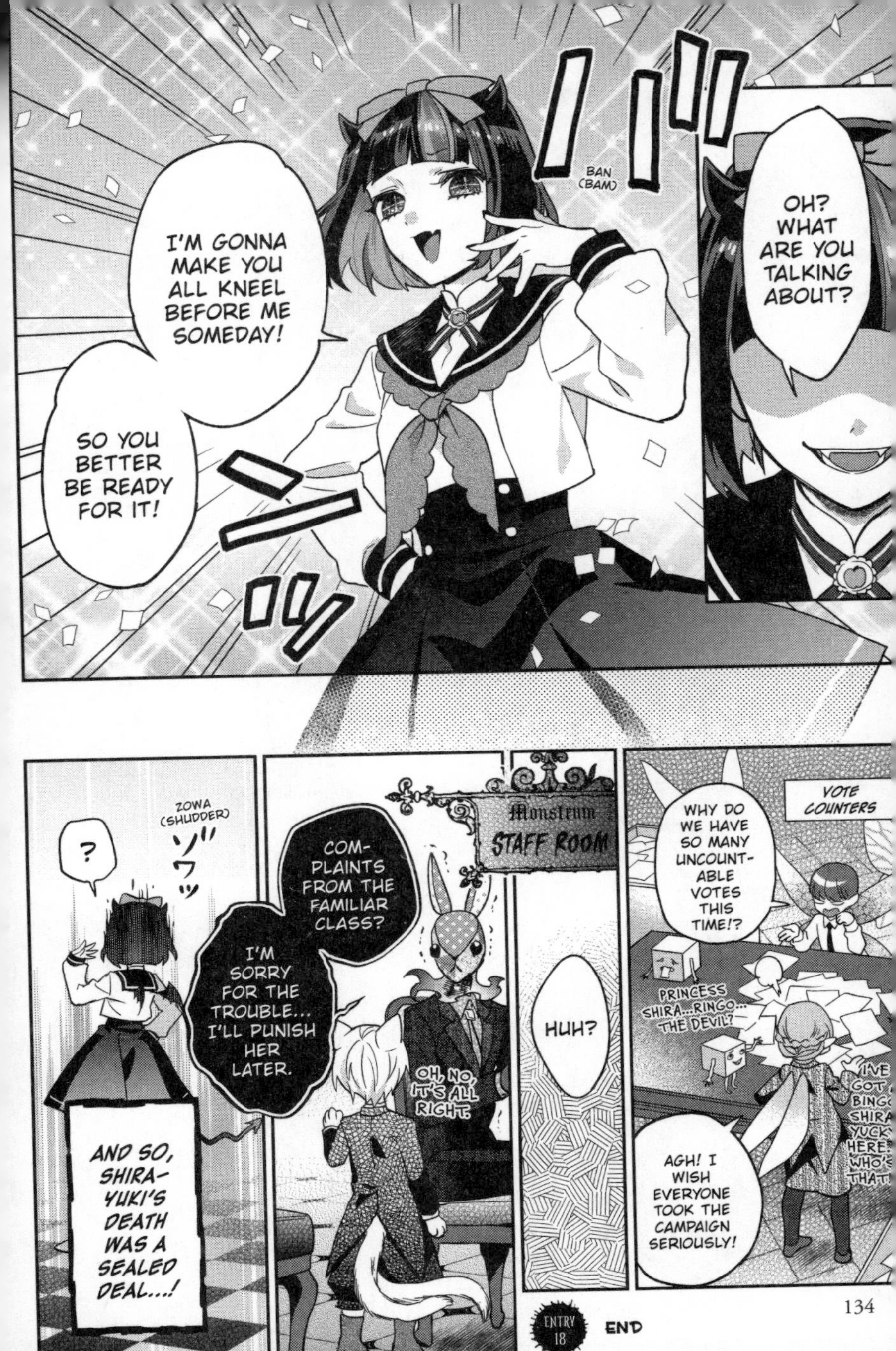
OH? WHAT ARE YOU TALKING ABOUT?
BAN (BAM)
I'M GONNA MAKE YOU ALL KNEEL BEFORE ME SOMEDAY!
SO YOU BETTER BE READY FOR IT!
VOTE COUNTERS
WHY DO WE HAVE SO MANY UNCOUNT-ABLE VOTES THIS TIME!?
PRINCESS SHIRA...RINGO... THE DEVIL?
AGH! I WISH EVERYONE TOOK THE CAMPAIGN SERIOUSLY!
HUH?
Monstrum STAFF ROOM
COM-PLAINTS FROM THE FAMILIAR CLASS?
I'M SORRY FOR THE TROUBLE... I'LL PUNISH HER LATER.
OH, NO, IT'S ALL RIGHT.
ZOWA (SHUDDER)
?
AND SO, SHIRA-YUKI'S DEATH WAS A SEALED DEAL...!
ENTRY 18 END

Monster Girls' School

Class Report

Monster Year: 20020 Month: Darkening Day: 124th **Homeroom** Class Z **Teacher** D **Teacher Species** Dullahan

Classes and such

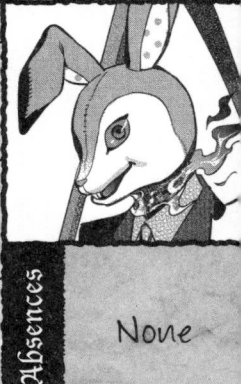

	Subject	Studied Material
1st Period	Magicmatics	As this class is devastatingly below average in magicmatics, I've decided to go back to the basics and review culling subtraction with them. There was once a monster couple that had one hundred children. However, the couple was poor and no matter how hard they worked to commit evil deeds, they could never provide for a hundred children. So, the couple kept twenty-one of the strongest-looking children and three children who had gruesome features, but sold the rest to a circus. A few days later, three of the children were returned from the circus because they were too wild and couldn't be controlled. Now then, how many monsters remain in the family? That was the problem and none of them got it right. According to them, "There's no way the couple would just take back the kids from the circus! They'd have a war!"
2nd Period	Magicmatics	Just as I did in first period, I had them review a concept which they should have already learned at the elementary level: additive haughtiness. The problem was, there was once a young and adored devil girl. The adults around her cherished her each day and sung her praises until the girl started to let it get to her head and she became so arrogant everyone hated her and wanted to kill her. However, for whatever reason, everyone continued to praise her. After ten years pass, how arrogant will she be? Shirayuki was the only one with the correct answer. She looked despicably smug, which earned her cold stares from her classmates.
3rd Period	PE	We were supposed to learn how to ride bicorns, a mount needed to hunt humans in wildlands and plains. I nearly doubted my eyes at the carelessness I witnessed. One student stood behind a bicorn and was summarily eviscerated upon being kicked. Another was pierced by a horn after attempting to take a bicorn's eye. Another was envious of another bicorn and student and sent the bicorns into a frenzy. In the end, none of them were able to ride their mounts. I was also left to reflect on my failings, as I wasn't able to stop one student from chopping off a bicorn's limbs and eating them.
4th Period	Art	They formed pairs and drew their partner's portrait. Though my students aren't terribly smart, many of them are horribly conceited and fights broke out among most of the pairs because of the ugly likenesses. After that, they decided to "split the difference" (whatever that means) and instead drew portraits of me. Each and every one of them was revoltingly ugly, but I believe I should accept and cherish each portrait regardless.
5th Period	Performing Arts	We learned how to hunt humans from a human movie that is also popular among children in the monster realm: Monsters' I●c. The monsters were too soft and kind and the movie wasn't accurate to real human hunting at all, so I can't see how it could possibly be useful. But it's part of the curriculum, so what else is there to be done? It seemed to resonate too well with my class, however, and I have some concerns for them.
6th Period	X	X

Absences	None
Tardies	Luo
Left Early	None
Permitted Absences	None

Special Mentions (Goals, worries, etc.)

It seems that a student from my class was "blackmailing students from another class over the student council election, which was quite an ordeal and caused much trouble. However, my students don't have the right to run for the election, so I believe that it wasn't a true problem in the end.

This week's executed students

Name and affiliation	Shirayuki (devil)
Method	Just smacked her around (Since she looked so pitiful)
Reason	Blackmail, coercion, and ignorance

→ Photo evidence section ←

SHOBO (GLOOM)
SHOBO
SH-SHE SEEMS SO SMALL ...

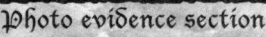

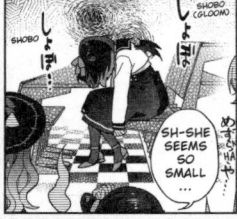

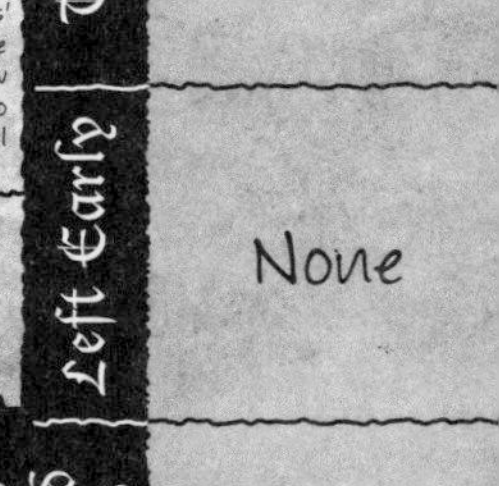

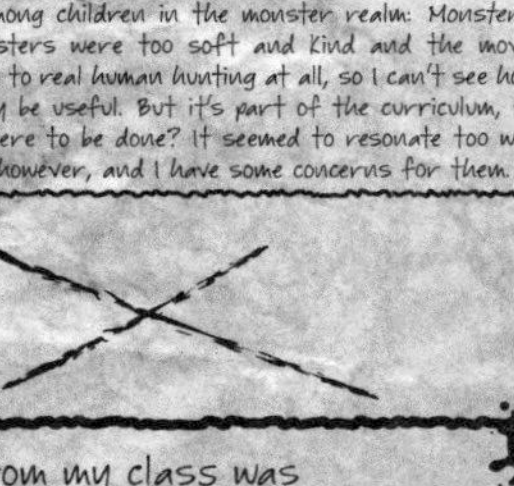

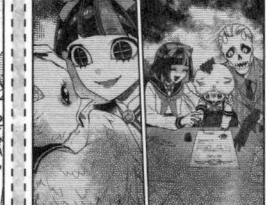

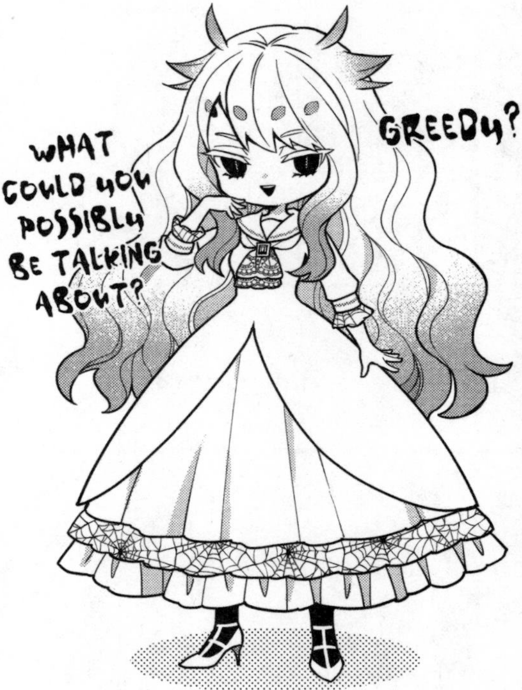
GREEDY?
WHAT COULD YOU POSSIBLY BE TALKING ABOUT?

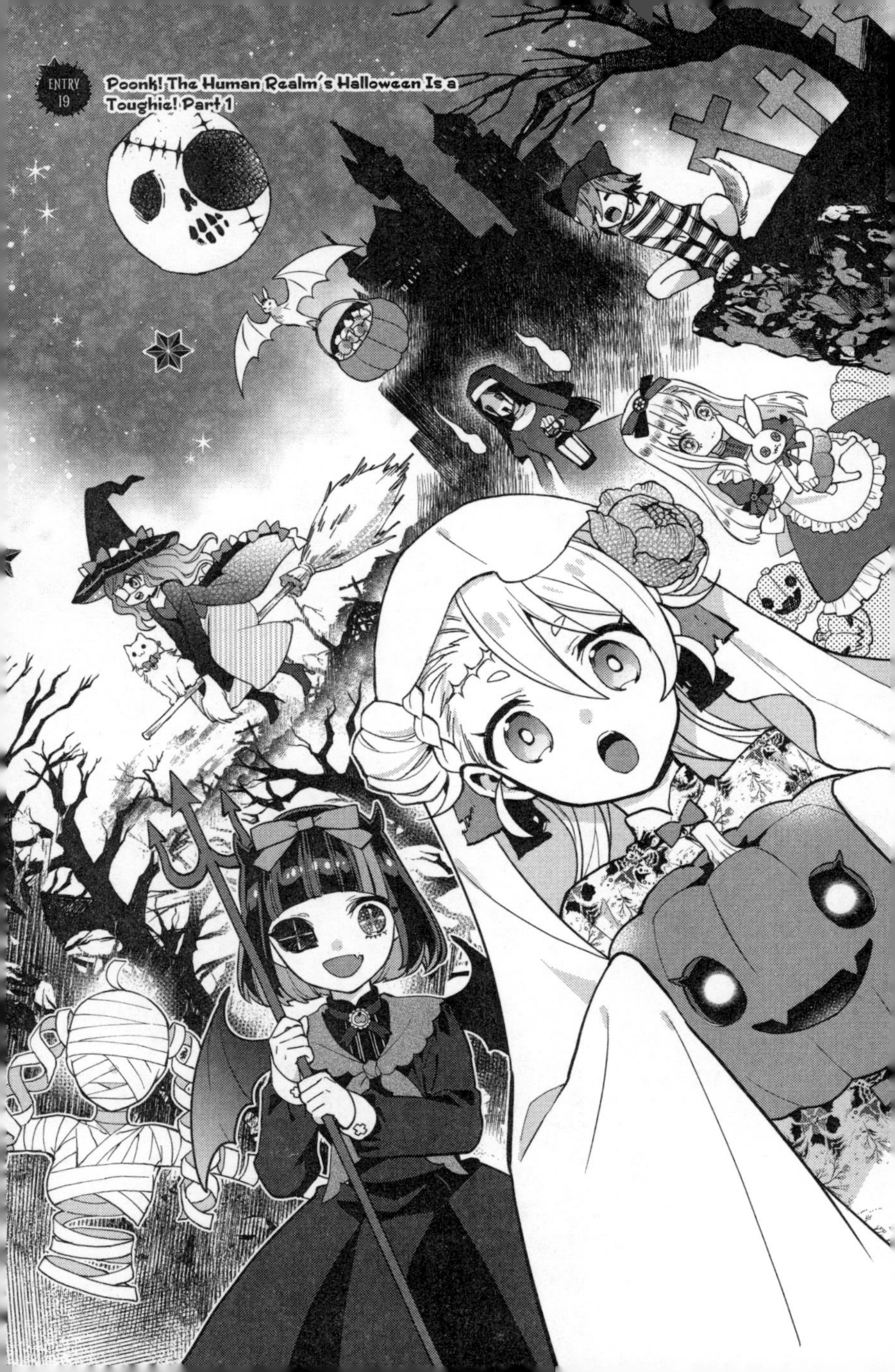
ENTRY 19
Poonk! The Human Realm's Halloween Is a Toughie! Part 1

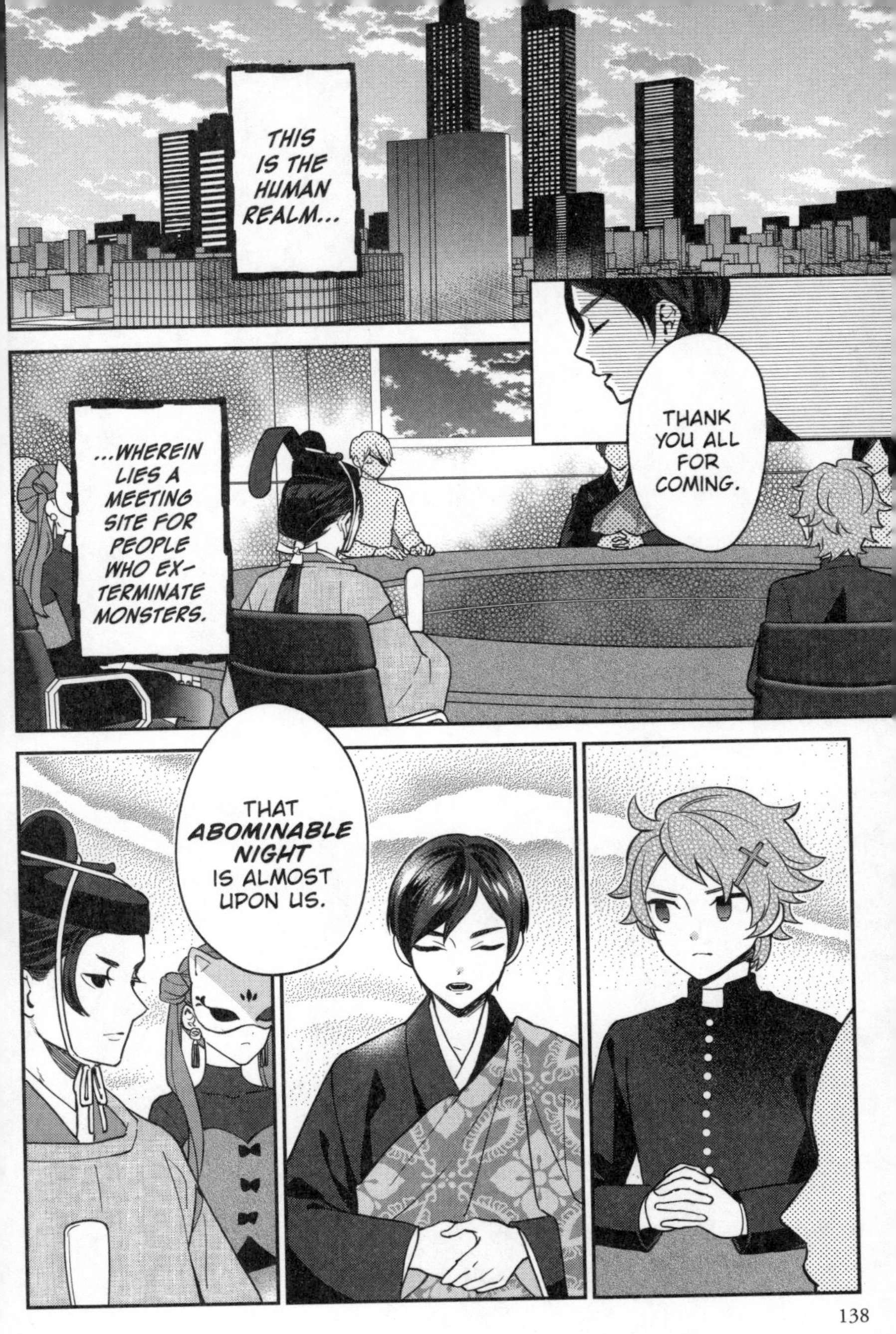
THIS IS THE HUMAN REALM...
THANK YOU ALL FOR COMING.
...WHEREIN LIES A MEETING SITE FOR PEOPLE WHO EX-TERMINATE MONSTERS.
THAT ***ABOMINABLE NIGHT*** IS ALMOST UPON US.

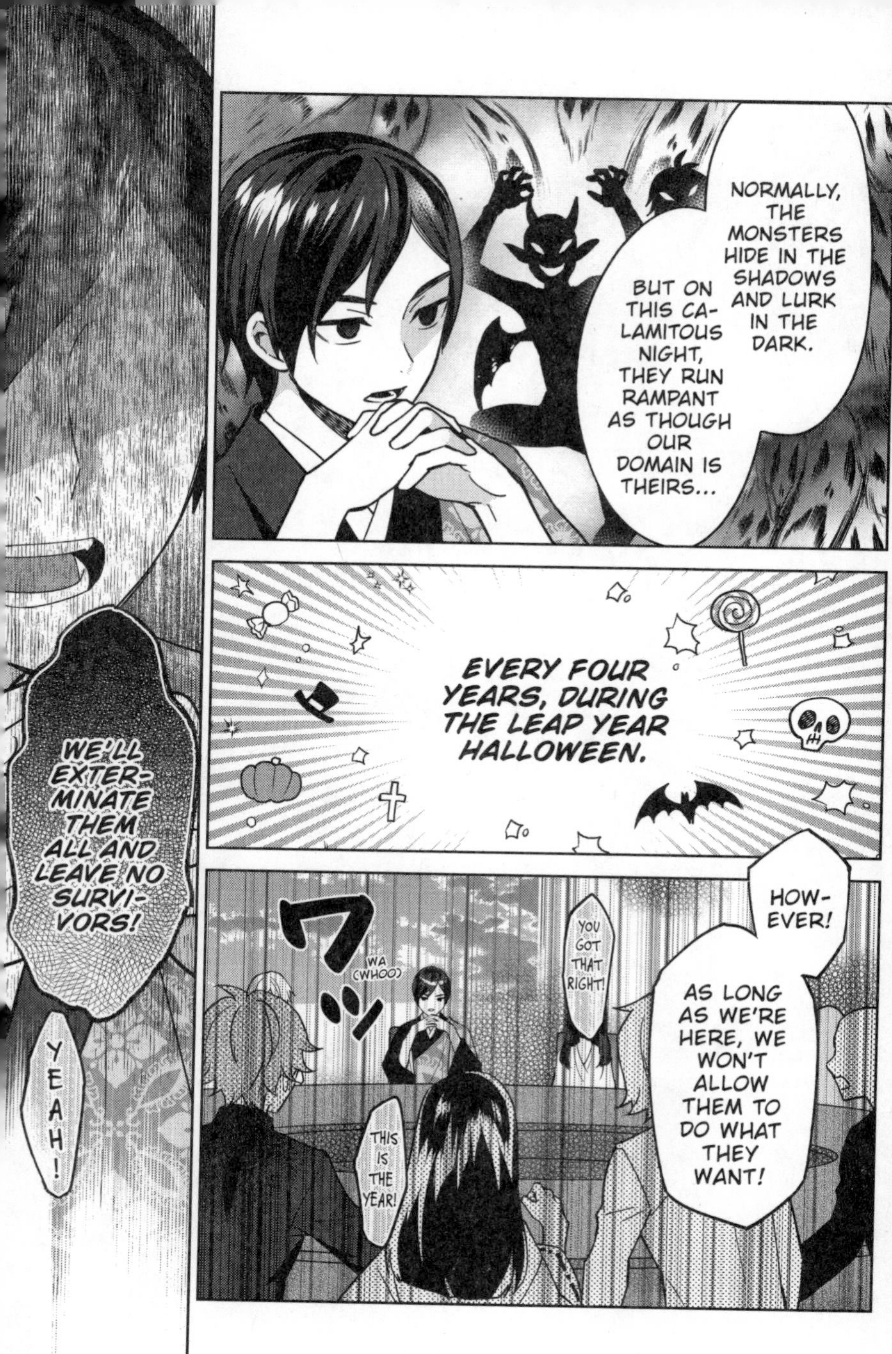
NORMALLY, THE MONSTERS HIDE IN THE SHADOWS AND LURK IN THE DARK.
BUT ON THIS CA-LAMITOUS NIGHT, THEY RUN RAMPANT AS THOUGH OUR DOMAIN IS THEIRS...
EVERY FOUR YEARS, DURING THE LEAP YEAR HALLOWEEN.
HOW-EVER!
AS LONG AS WE'RE HERE, WE WON'T ALLOW THEM TO DO WHAT THEY WANT!
YOU GOT THAT RIGHT!
WA (WHOO)
THIS IS THE YEAR!
WE'LL EXTER-MINATE THEM ALL AND LEAVE NO SURVI-VORS!
YEAH!

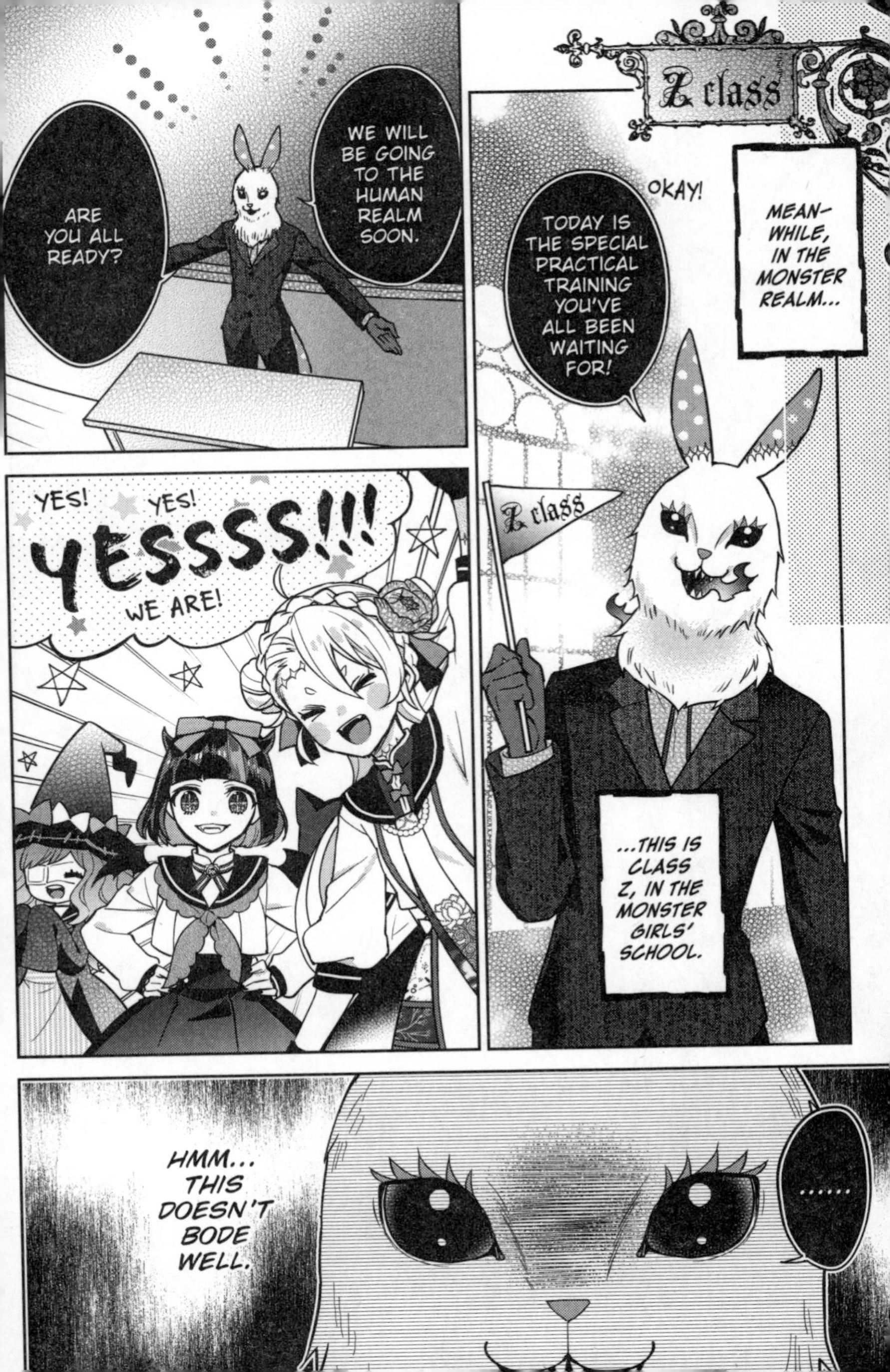
Z class
MEAN-WHILE, IN THE MONSTER REALM...
OKAY!
TODAY IS THE SPECIAL PRACTICAL TRAINING YOU'VE ALL BEEN WAITING FOR!
Z class
...THIS IS CLASS Z, IN THE MONSTER GIRLS' SCHOOL.
WE WILL BE GOING TO THE HUMAN REALM SOON.
ARE YOU ALL READY?
YES!
YES!
YESSSS!!!
WE ARE!
......
HMM... THIS DOESN'T BODE WELL.

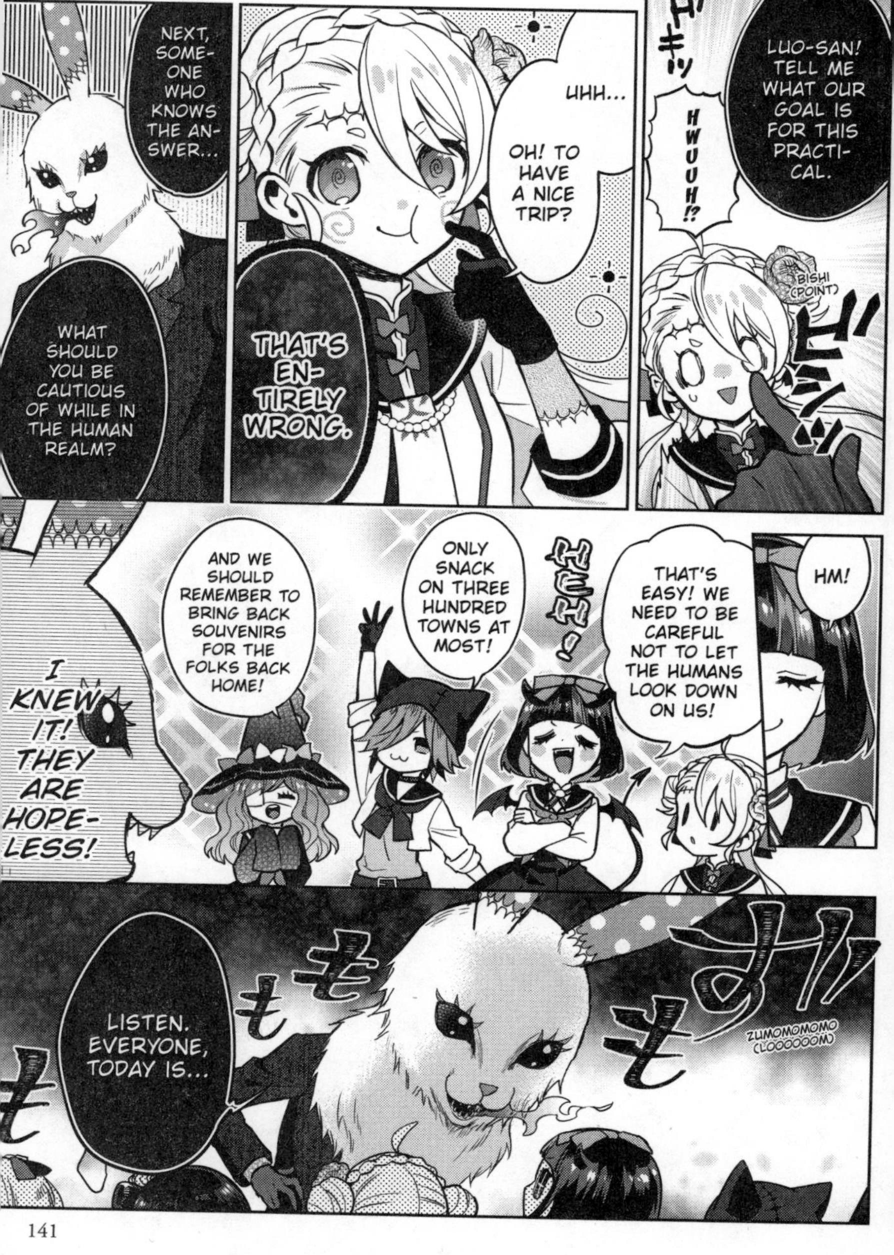
LUO-SAN! TELL ME WHAT OUR GOAL IS FOR THIS PRACTI-CAL.
DOKI (B-DMP)
HWUUUH!?
BISHI (POINT)
UHH...
OH! TO HAVE A NICE TRIP?
THAT'S EN-TIRELY WRONG.
NEXT, SOME-ONE WHO KNOWS THE AN-SWER...
WHAT SHOULD YOU BE CAUTIOUS OF WHILE IN THE HUMAN REALM?
HM!
THAT'S EASY! WE NEED TO BE CAREFUL NOT TO LET THE HUMANS LOOK DOWN ON US!
HEH!
ONLY SNACK ON THREE HUNDRED TOWNS AT MOST!
AND WE SHOULD REMEMBER TO BRING BACK SOUVENIRS FOR THE FOLKS BACK HOME!
I KNEW IT! THEY ARE HOPE-LESS!
ZUMOMOMOMO (LOOOOOOM)
LISTEN. EVERYONE, TODAY IS...

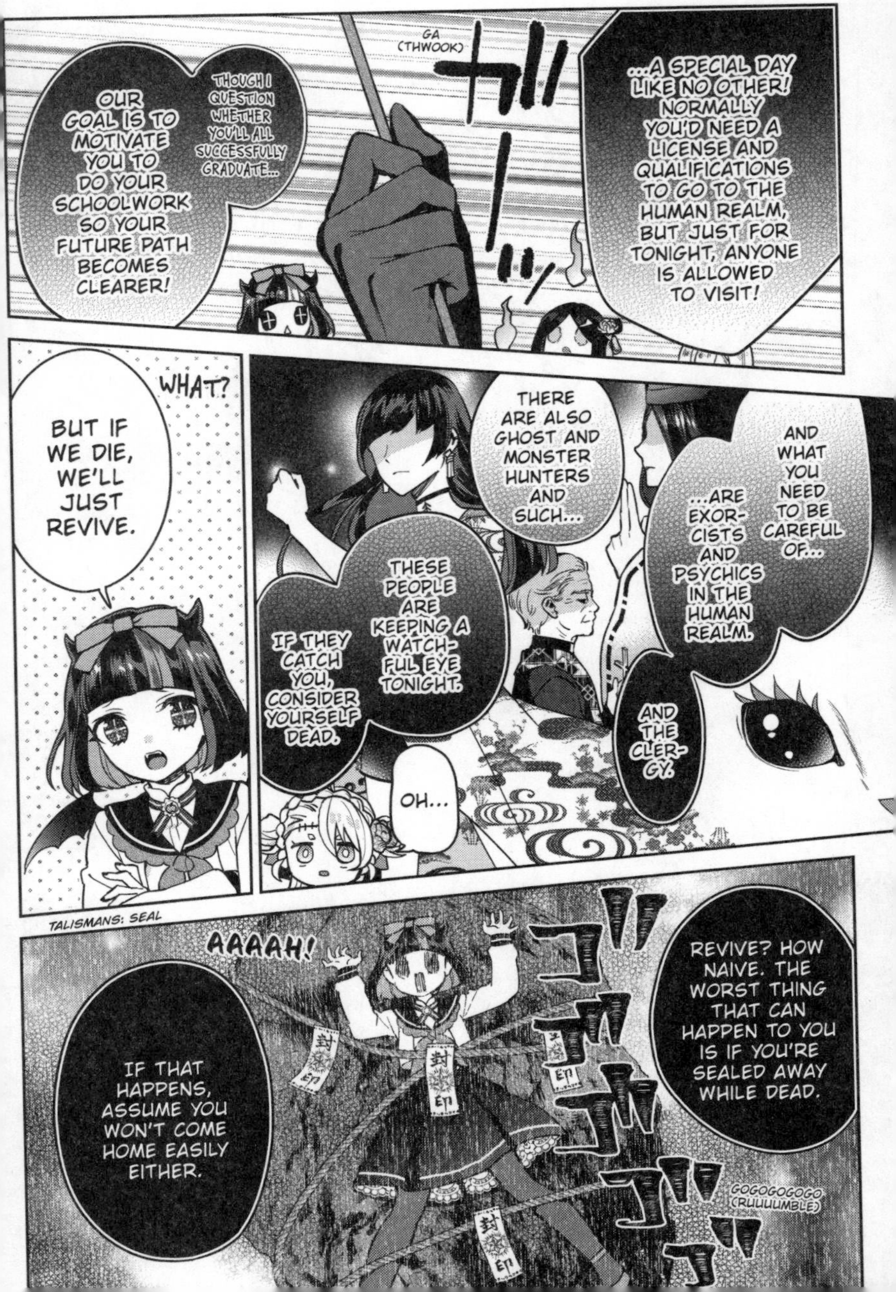
...A SPECIAL DAY LIKE NO OTHER! NORMALLY YOU'D NEED A LICENSE AND QUALIFICATIONS TO GO TO THE HUMAN REALM, BUT JUST FOR TONIGHT, ANYONE IS ALLOWED TO VISIT!
GA (THWOOK)
THOUGH I QUESTION WHETHER YOU'LL ALL SUCCESSFULLY GRADUATE...
OUR GOAL IS TO MOTIVATE YOU TO DO YOUR SCHOOLWORK SO YOUR FUTURE PATH BECOMES CLEARER!
AND WHAT YOU NEED TO BE CAREFUL OF...
...ARE EXORCISTS AND PSYCHICS IN THE HUMAN REALM.
THERE ARE ALSO GHOST AND MONSTER HUNTERS AND SUCH...
AND THE CLERGY.
THESE PEOPLE ARE KEEPING A WATCHFUL EYE TONIGHT.
IF THEY CATCH YOU, CONSIDER YOURSELF DEAD.
OH...
WHAT?
BUT IF WE DIE, WE'LL JUST REVIVE.
TALISMANS: SEAL
REVIVE? HOW NAIVE. THE WORST THING THAT CAN HAPPEN TO YOU IS IF YOU'RE SEALED AWAY WHILE DEAD.
AAAAH!
IF THAT HAPPENS, ASSUME YOU WON'T COME HOME EASILY EITHER.
GOGOGOGOGO (RUUUUMBLE)

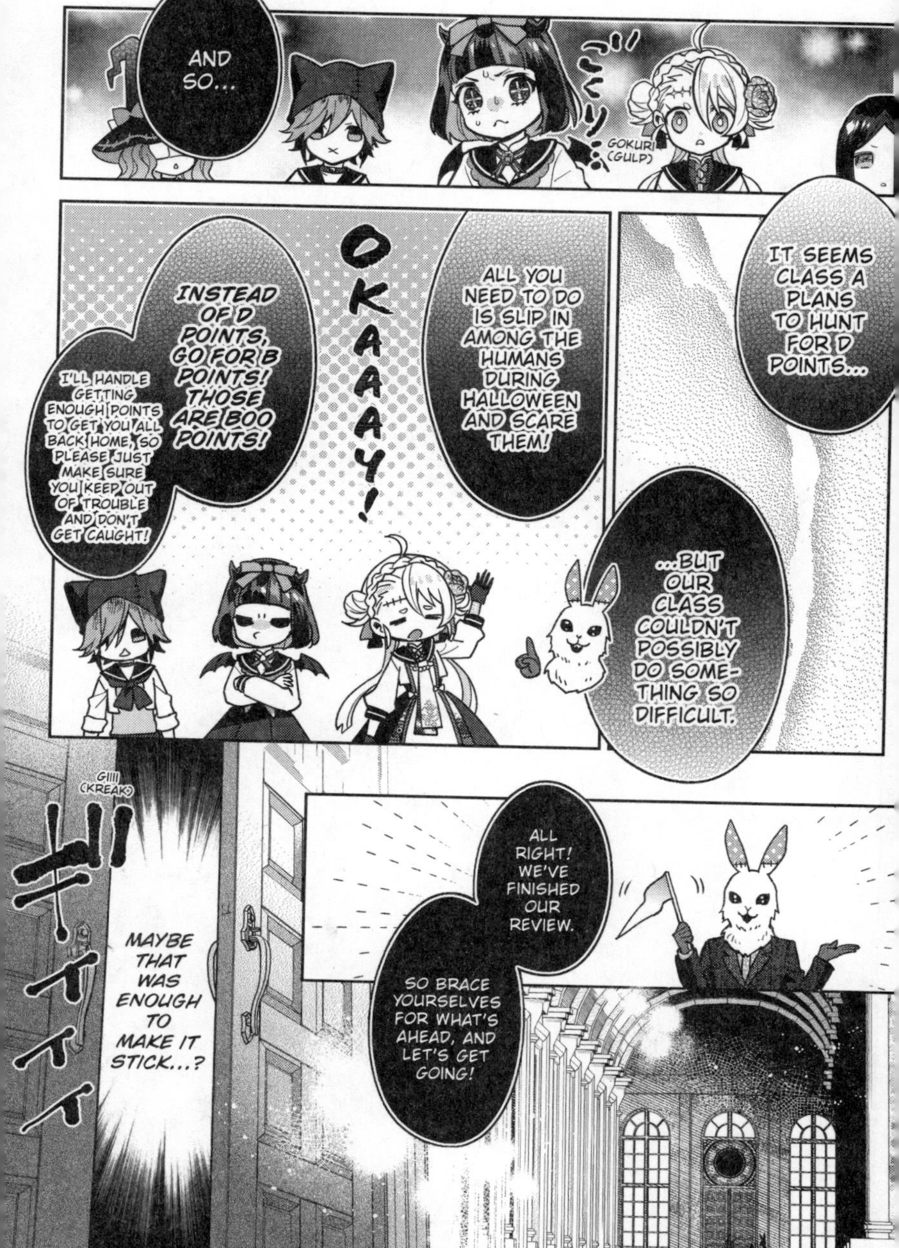
AND SO...
GOKURI (GULP)
IT SEEMS CLASS A PLANS TO HUNT FOR D POINTS...
...BUT OUR CLASS COULDN'T POSSIBLY DO SOME-THING SO DIFFICULT.
ALL YOU NEED TO DO IS SLIP IN AMONG THE HUMANS DURING HALLOWEEN AND SCARE THEM!
OKAAAY!
INSTEAD OF D POINTS, GO FOR B POINTS! THOSE ARE BOO POINTS!
I'LL HANDLE GETTING ENOUGH POINTS TO GET YOU ALL BACK HOME, SO PLEASE JUST MAKE SURE YOU KEEP OUT OF TROUBLE AND DON'T GET CAUGHT!
ALL RIGHT! WE'VE FINISHED OUR REVIEW.
SO BRACE YOURSELVES FOR WHAT'S AHEAD, AND LET'S GET GOING!
GIIII (KREAK)
MAYBE THAT WAS ENOUGH TO MAKE IT STICK...?

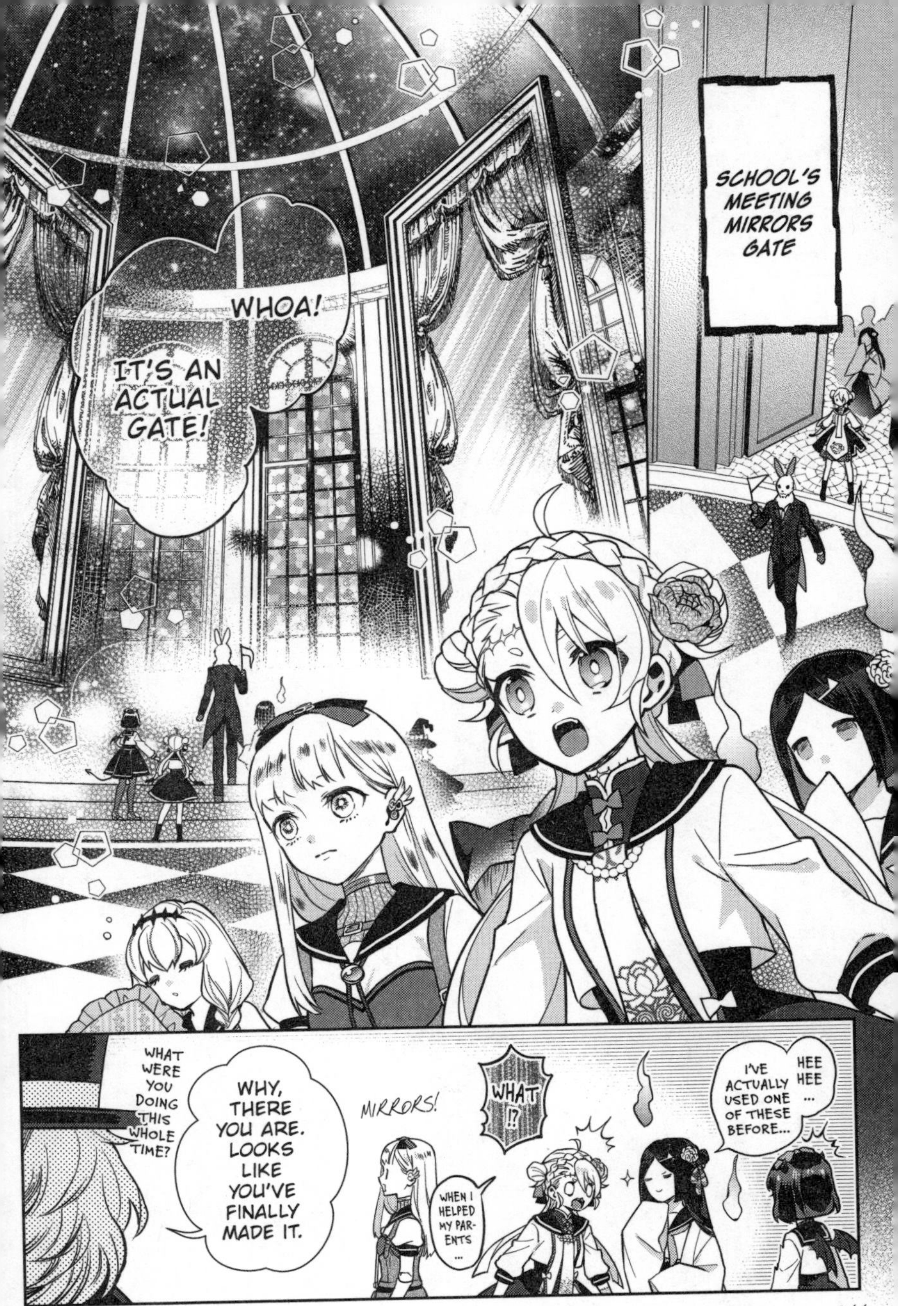
SCHOOL'S MEETING MIRRORS GATE
WHOA!
IT'S AN ACTUAL GATE!
HEE HEE ...
I'VE ACTUALLY USED ONE OF THESE BEFORE...
WHAT !?
WHEN I HELPED MY PAR- ENTS ...
MIRRORS!
WHY, THERE YOU ARE. LOOKS LIKE YOU'VE FINALLY MADE IT.
WHAT WERE YOU DOING THIS WHOLE TIME?

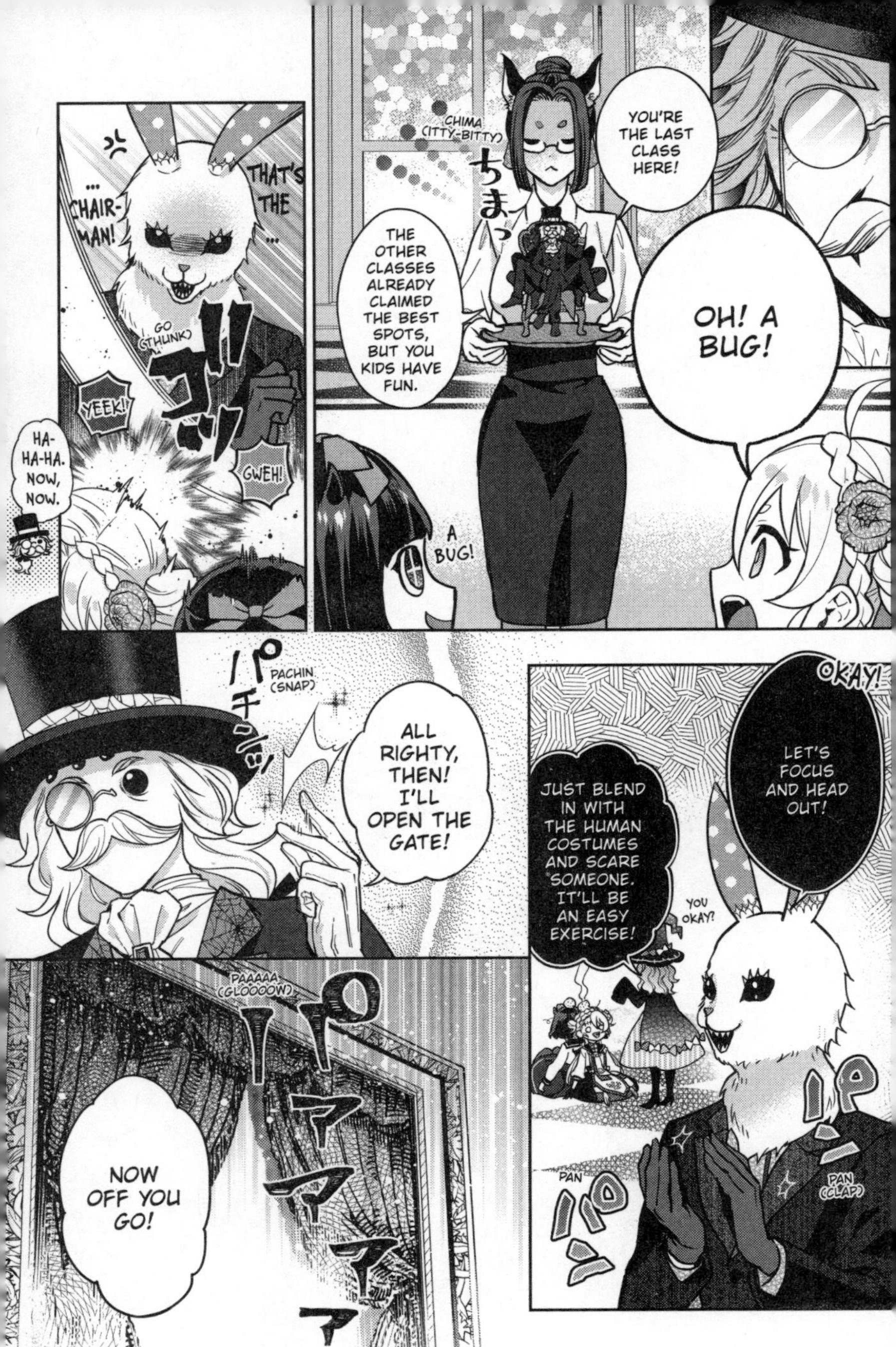
YOU'RE THE LAST CLASS HERE!
CHIMA (ITTY-BITTY)
ちまっ
THE OTHER CLASSES ALREADY CLAIMED THE BEST SPOTS, BUT YOU KIDS HAVE FUN.
OH! A BUG!
A BUG!
THAT'S THE ...
... CHAIR-MAN!
GO (THUNK)
YEEK!
GWEH!
HA-HA-HA. NOW, NOW.
OKAY!
LET'S FOCUS AND HEAD OUT!
JUST BLEND IN WITH THE HUMAN COSTUMES AND SCARE SOMEONE. IT'LL BE AN EASY EXERCISE!
YOU OKAY?
PAN
PAN (CLAP)
PACHIN (SNAP)
ALL RIGHTY, THEN! I'LL OPEN THE GATE!
PAAAAA (GLOOOOW)
NOW OFF YOU GO!

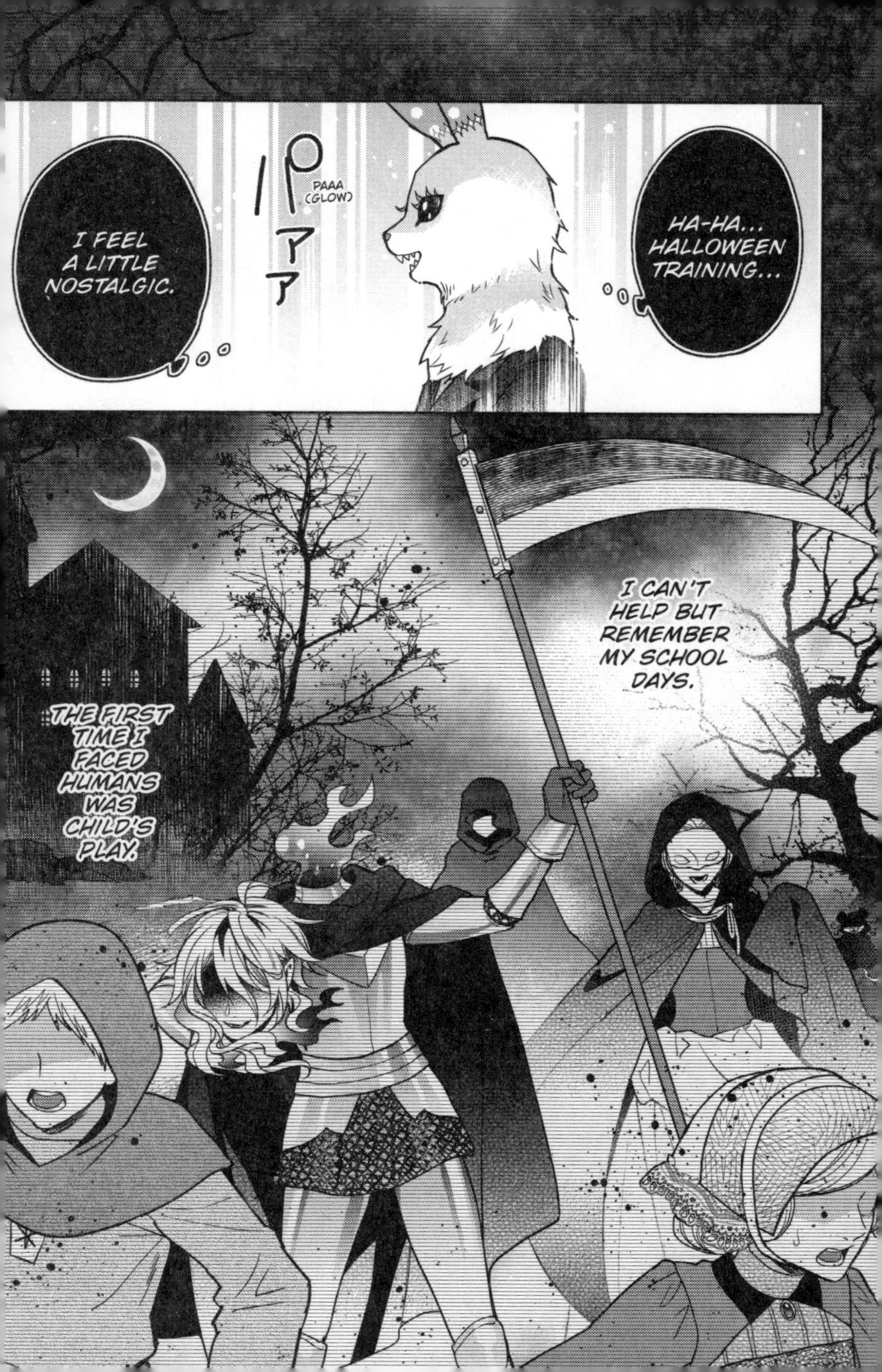
HA-HA... HALLOWEEN TRAINING...
パァァ
PAAA (GLOW)
I FEEL A LITTLE NOSTALGIC.
I CAN'T HELP BUT REMEMBER MY SCHOOL DAYS.
THE FIRST TIME I FACED HUMANS WAS CHILD'S PLAY.

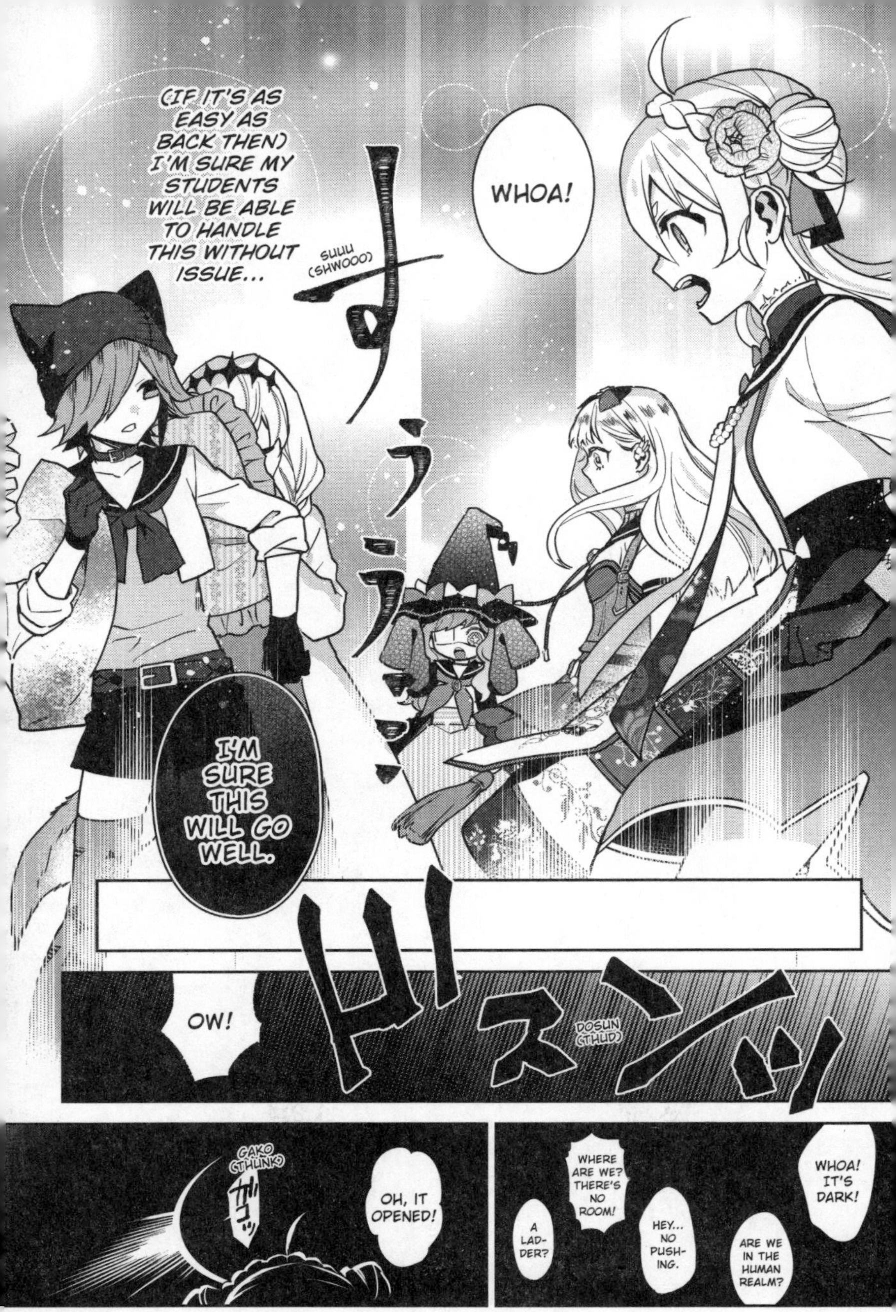
WHOA!
(IF IT'S AS EASY AS BACK THEN) I'M SURE MY STUDENTS WILL BE ABLE TO HANDLE THIS WITHOUT ISSUE...
SUUU (SHWOOO)
I'M SURE THIS WILL GO WELL.
DOSUN (THUD)
OW!
WHOA! IT'S DARK!
ARE WE IN THE HUMAN REALM?
WHERE ARE WE? THERE'S NO ROOM!
HEY... NO PUSH-ING.
A LAD-DER?
OH, IT OPENED!
GAKO (THUNK)

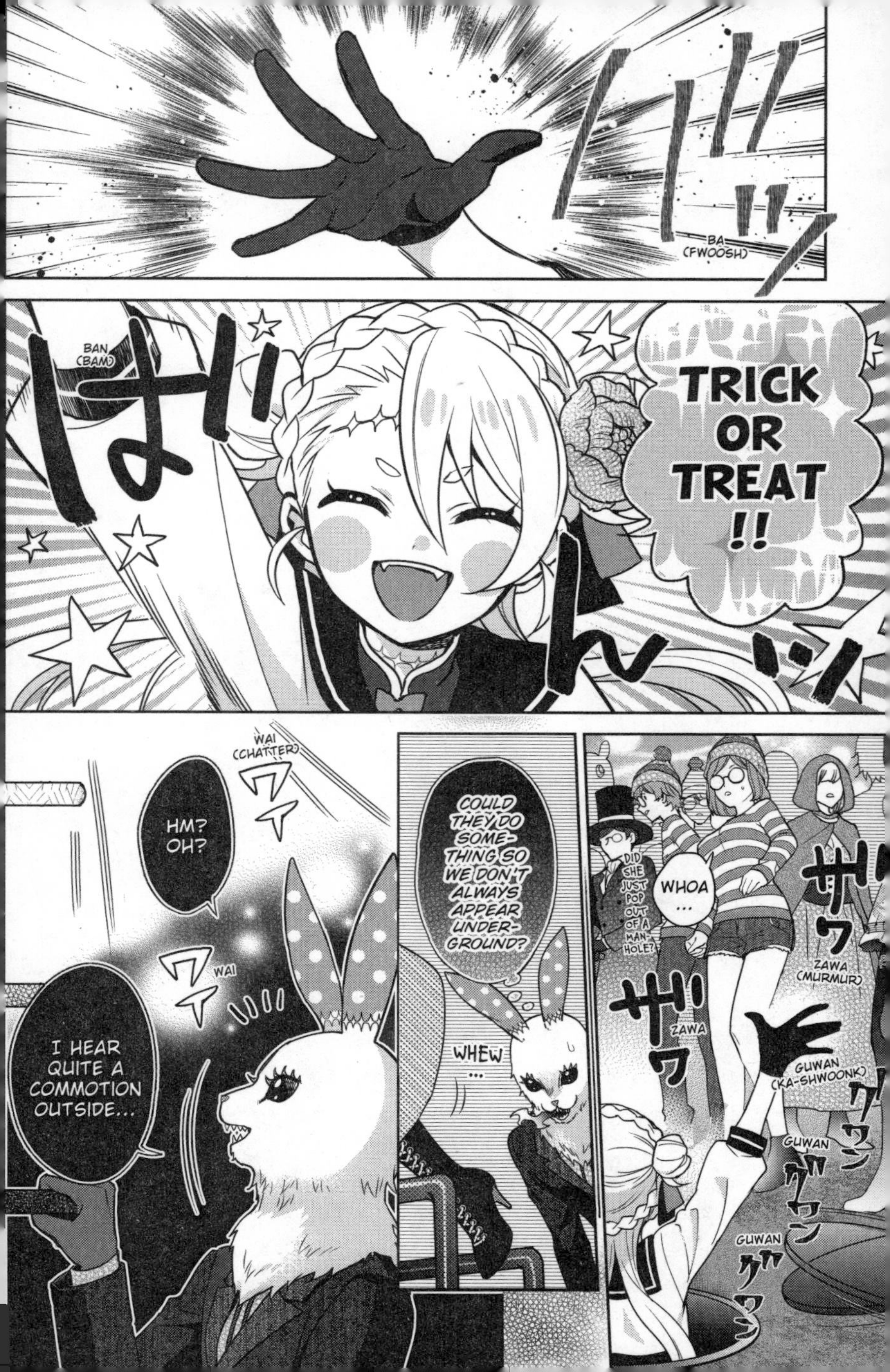
BA (FWOOSH)
TRICK OR TREAT !!
BAN (BAM)
ZAWA (MURMUR)
ZAWA
DID SHE JUST POP OUT OF A MAN-HOLE?
WHOA ...
GUWAN (KA-SHWOONK)
GUWAN
GUWAN
COULD THEY DO SOME-THING SO WE DON'T ALWAYS APPEAR UNDER-GROUND?
WHEW ...
WAI (CHATTER)
HM? OH?
WAI
I HEAR QUITE A COMMOTION OUTSIDE...

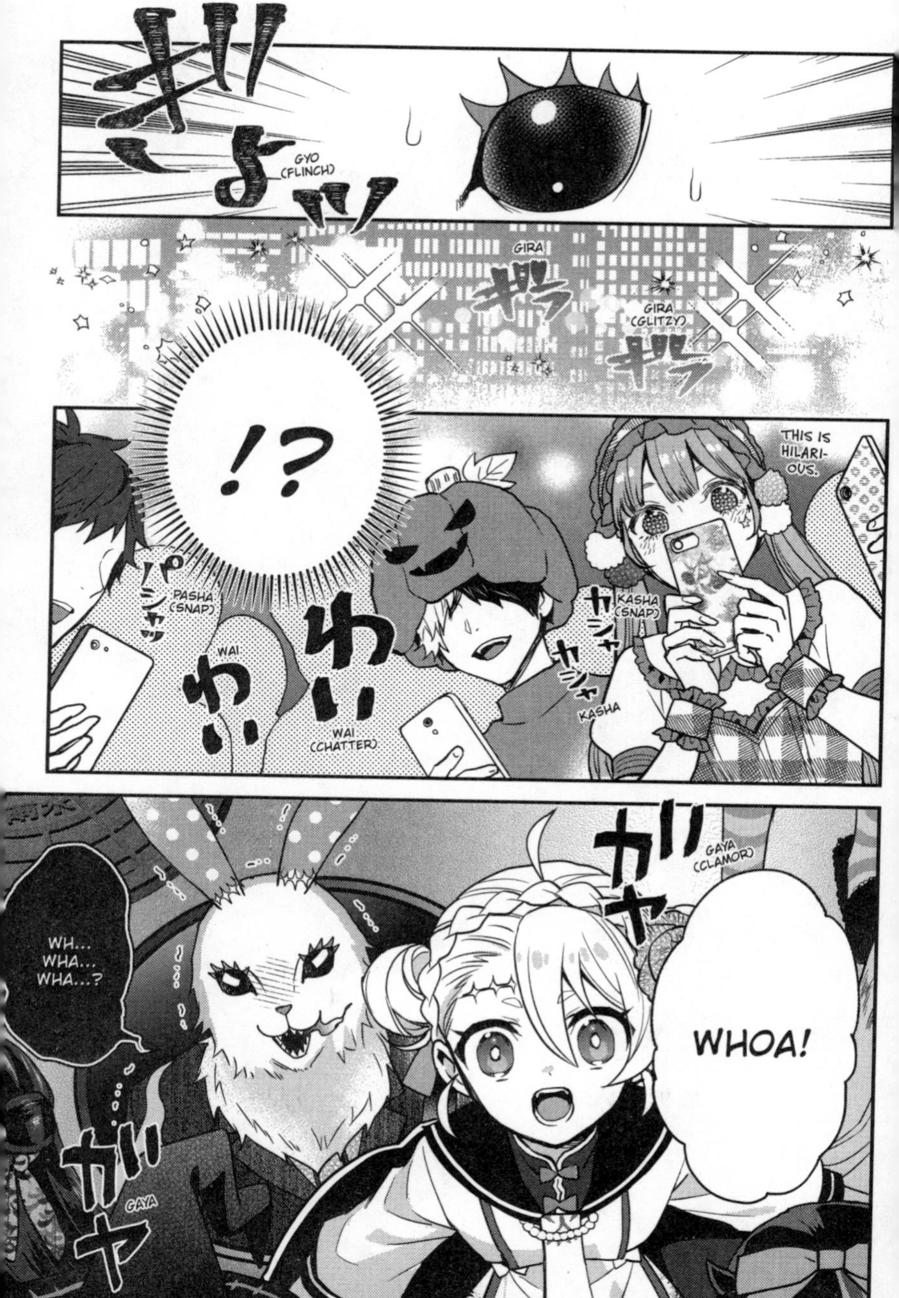
GYO (FLINCH)
GIRA
GIRA (GLITZY)
THIS IS HILARIOUS.
KASHA (SNAP)
KASHA
!?
WAI (CHATTER)
WAI
PASHA (SNAP)
GAYA (CLAMOR)
WHOA!
WH... WHA... WHA...?
GAYA

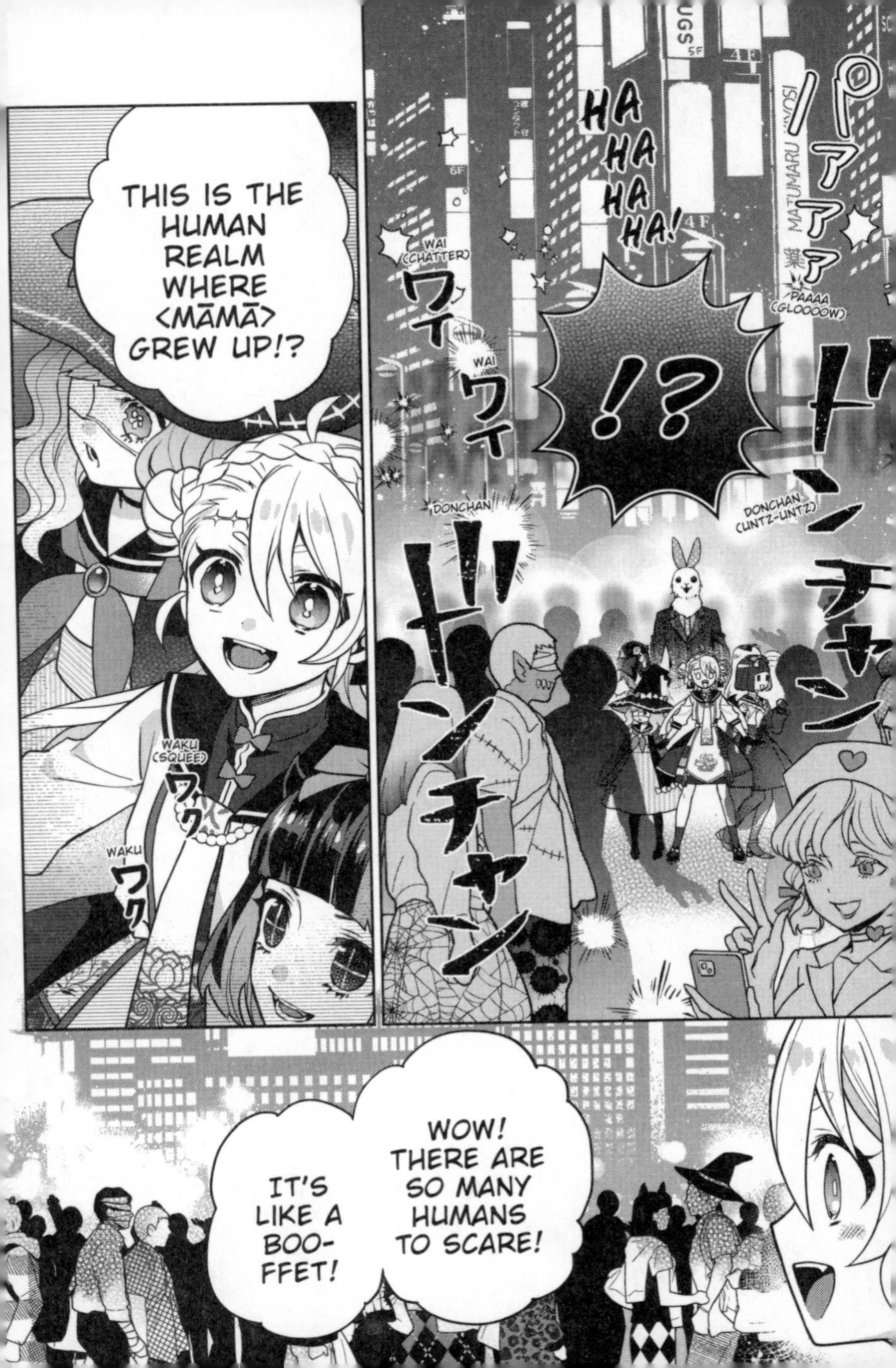
パァァァ
PAAAA (GLOOOOW)
MATUMARU KIYOSI
HA HA HA HA!
!?
ドンチャン
DONCHAN (UNTZ-UNTZ)
ドンチャン
DONCHAN
ワイ
WAI (CHATTER)
ワイ
WAI
THIS IS THE HUMAN REALM WHERE <MĀMĀ> GREW UP!?
ワク
WAKU (SQUEE)
ワク
WAKU
WOW! THERE ARE SO MANY HUMANS TO SCARE!
IT'S LIKE A BOO-FFET!

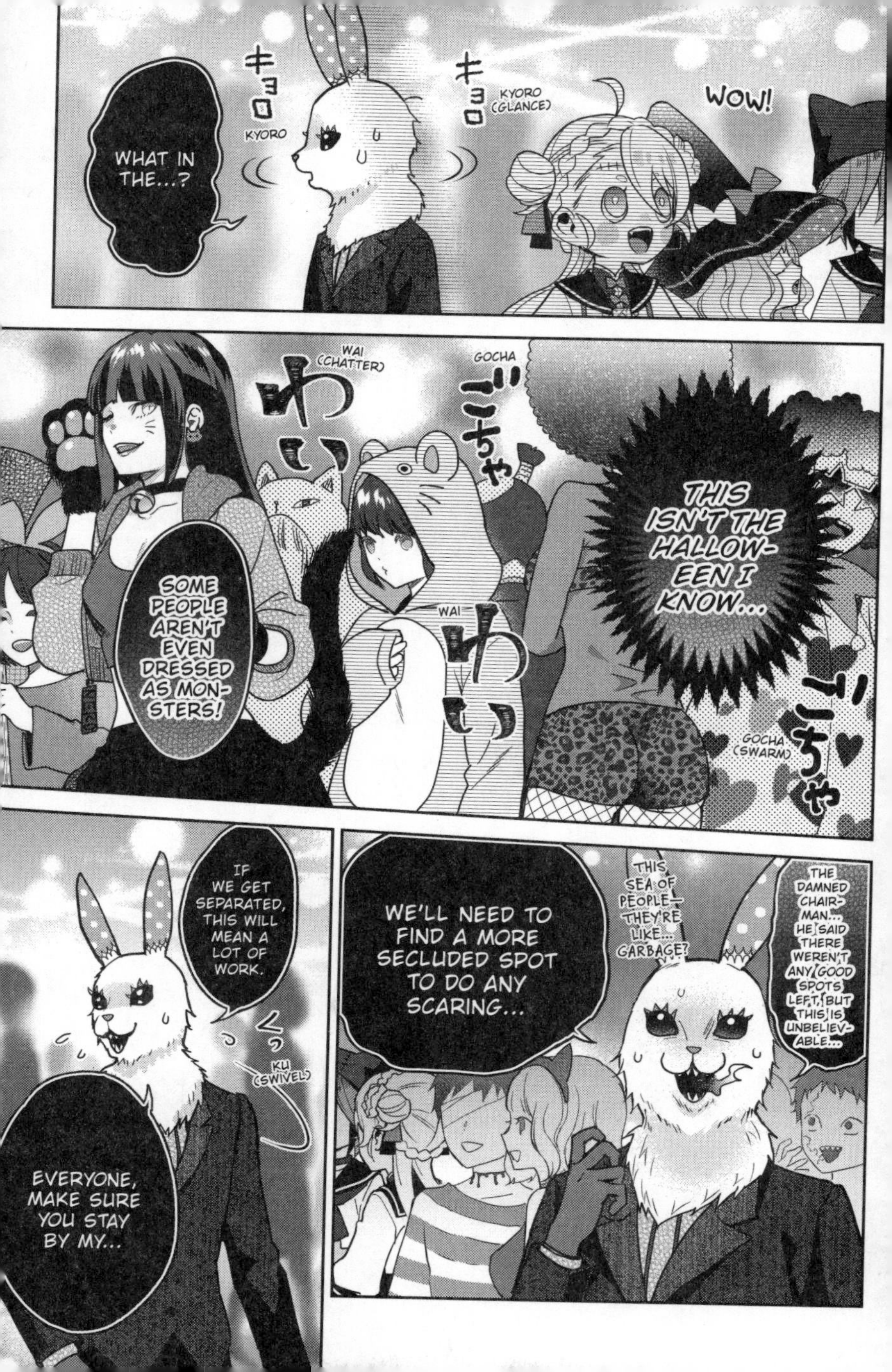
WOW!
キョロ
KYORO (GLANCE)
キョロ
KYORO
WHAT IN THE...?
ごちゃ
GOCHA (SWARM)
THIS ISN'T THE HALLOWEEN I KNOW...
ごちゃ
GOCHA
わい
WAI (CHATTER)
わい
WAI
SOME PEOPLE AREN'T EVEN DRESSED AS MONSTERS!
THE DAMNED CHAIRMAN... HE SAID THERE WEREN'T ANY GOOD SPOTS LEFT, BUT THIS IS UNBELIEVABLE...
THIS SEA OF PEOPLE—THEY'RE LIKE... GARBAGE?
WE'LL NEED TO FIND A MORE SECLUDED SPOT TO DO ANY SCARING...
IF WE GET SEPARATED, THIS WILL MEAN A LOT OF WORK.
KU (SWIVEL)
EVERYONE, MAKE SURE YOU STAY BY MY...

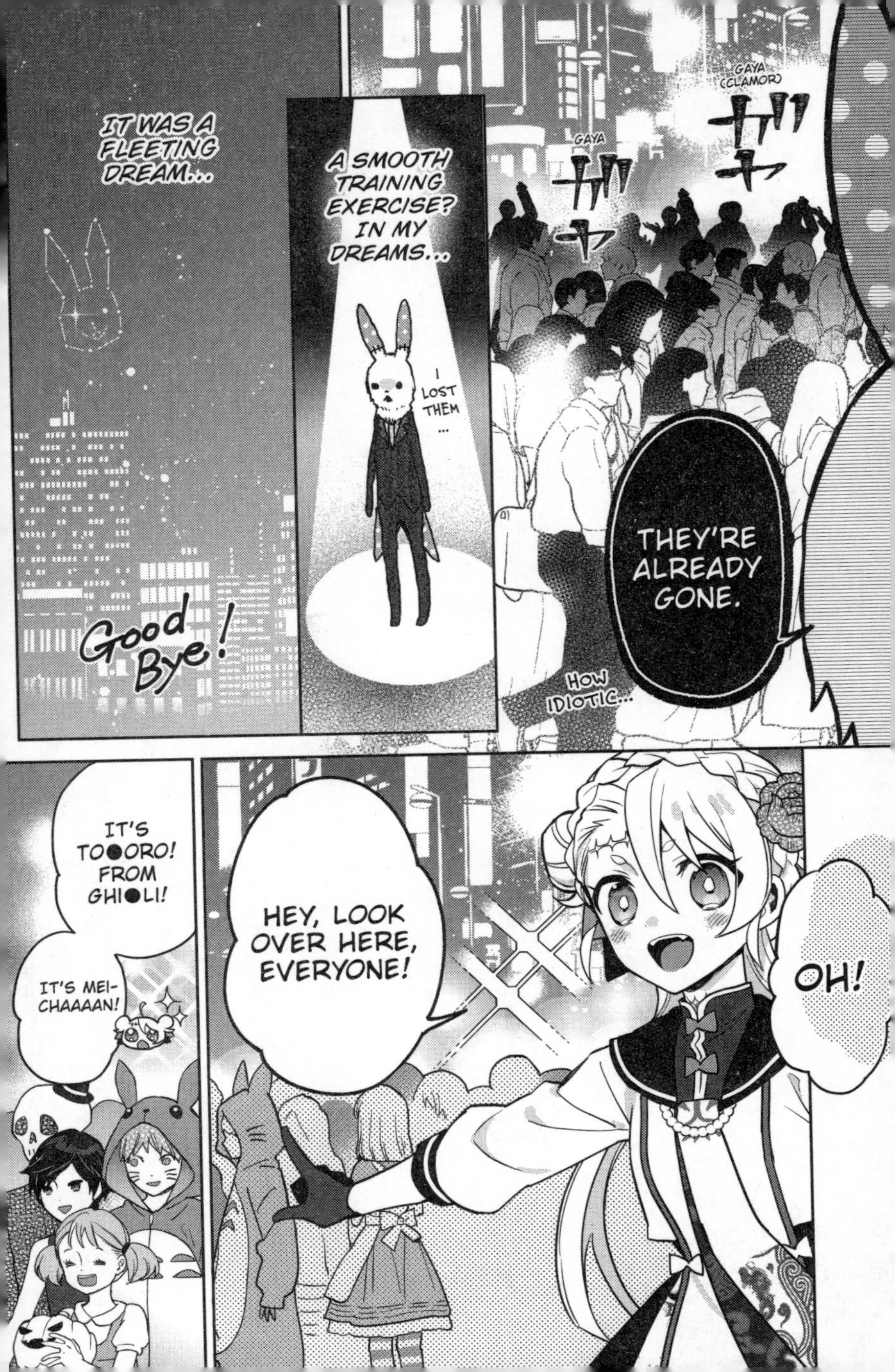
GAYA (CLAMOR)
GAYA
THEY'RE ALREADY GONE.
HOW IDIOTIC...
A SMOOTH TRAINING EXERCISE? IN MY DREAMS...
I LOST THEM...
IT WAS A FLEETING DREAM...
Good Bye!
OH!
HEY, LOOK OVER HERE, EVERYONE!
IT'S TO●ORO! FROM GHI●LI!
IT'S MEI-CHAAAAN!

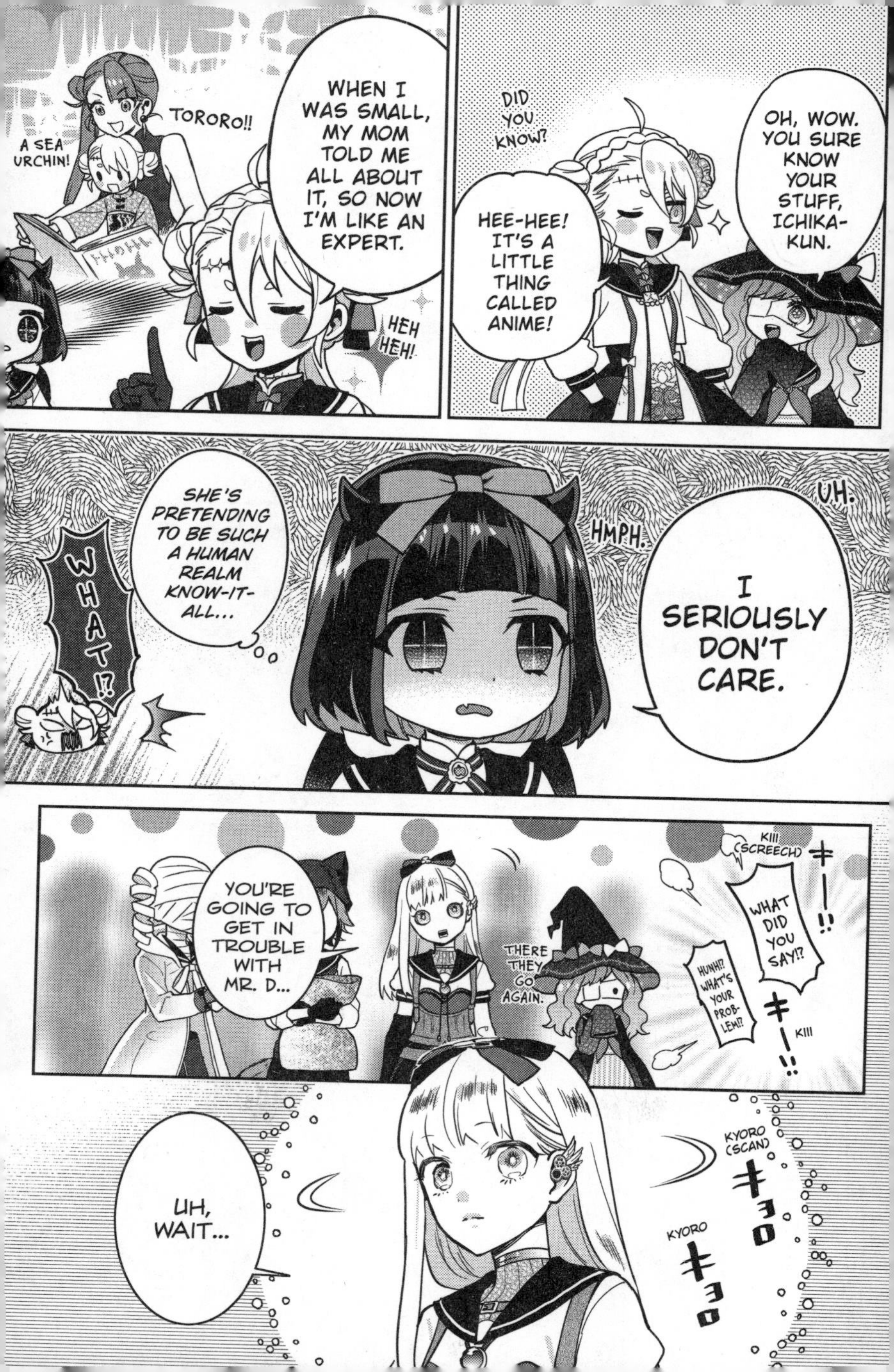
OH, WOW. YOU SURE KNOW YOUR STUFF, ICHIKA-KUN.
DID YOU KNOW?
HEE-HEE! IT'S A LITTLE THING CALLED ANIME!
WHEN I WAS SMALL, MY MOM TOLD ME ALL ABOUT IT, SO NOW I'M LIKE AN EXPERT.
HEH HEH!
TORORO!!
A SEA URCHIN!
UH.
HMPH.
I SERIOUSLY DON'T CARE.
SHE'S PRETENDING TO BE SUCH A HUMAN REALM KNOW-IT-ALL...
WHAT!?
KIII (SCREECH)
WHAT DID YOU SAY!?
HUNH!? WHAT'S YOUR PROB-LEM!?
KIII
THERE THEY GO AGAIN.
YOU'RE GOING TO GET IN TROUBLE WITH MR. D...
KYORO (SCAN)
KYORO
UH, WAIT...

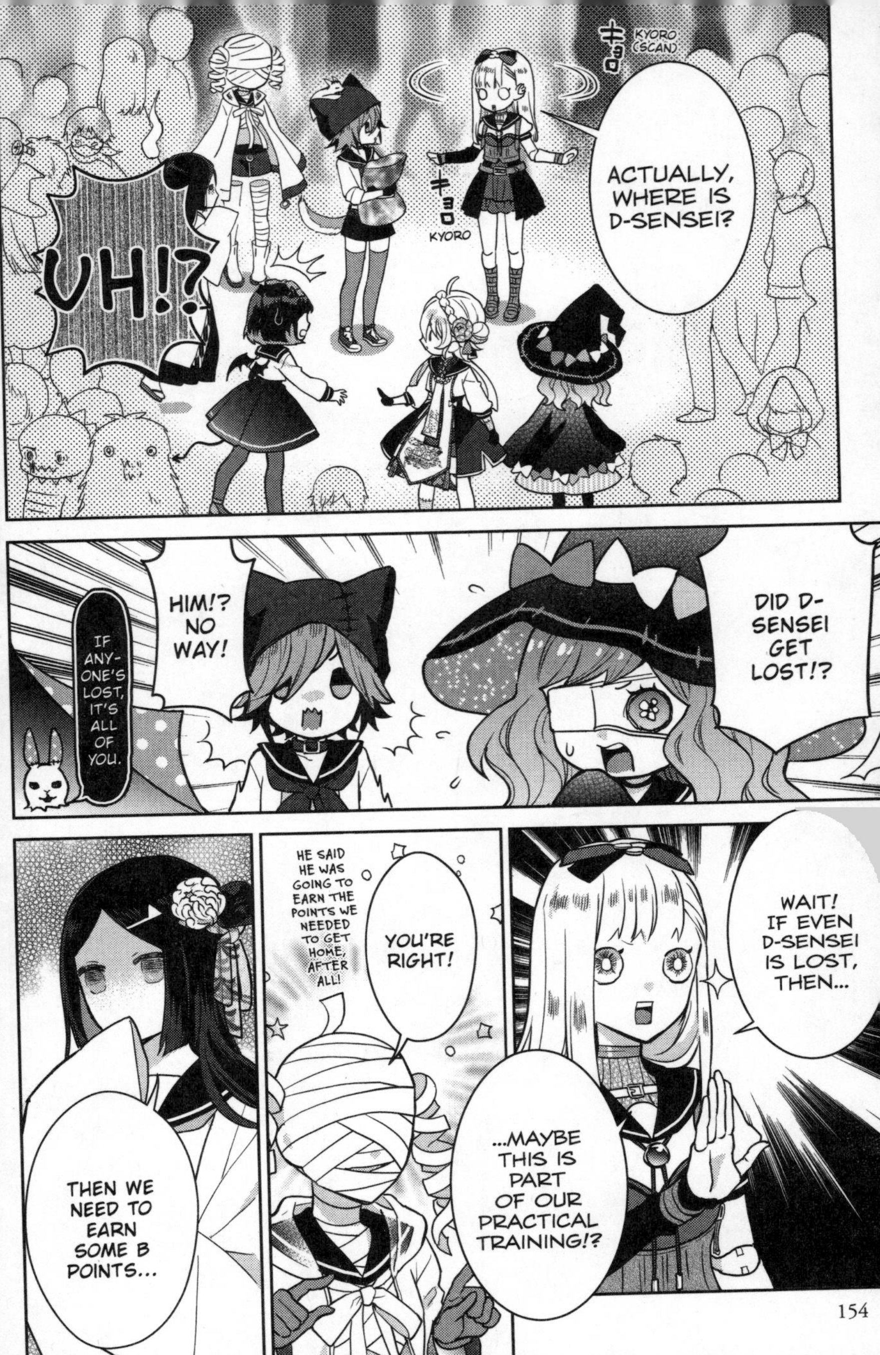

キョロ
KYORO (SCAN)
ACTUALLY, WHERE IS D-SENSEI?
キョロ
KYORO
UH!?
DID D-SENSEI GET LOST!?
HIM!? NO WAY!
IF ANYONE'S LOST, IT'S ALL OF YOU.
WAIT! IF EVEN D-SENSEI IS LOST, THEN...
...MAYBE THIS IS PART OF OUR PRACTICAL TRAINING!?
YOU'RE RIGHT!
HE SAID HE WAS GOING TO EARN THE POINTS WE NEEDED TO GET HOME, AFTER ALL!
THEN WE NEED TO EARN SOME B POINTS...

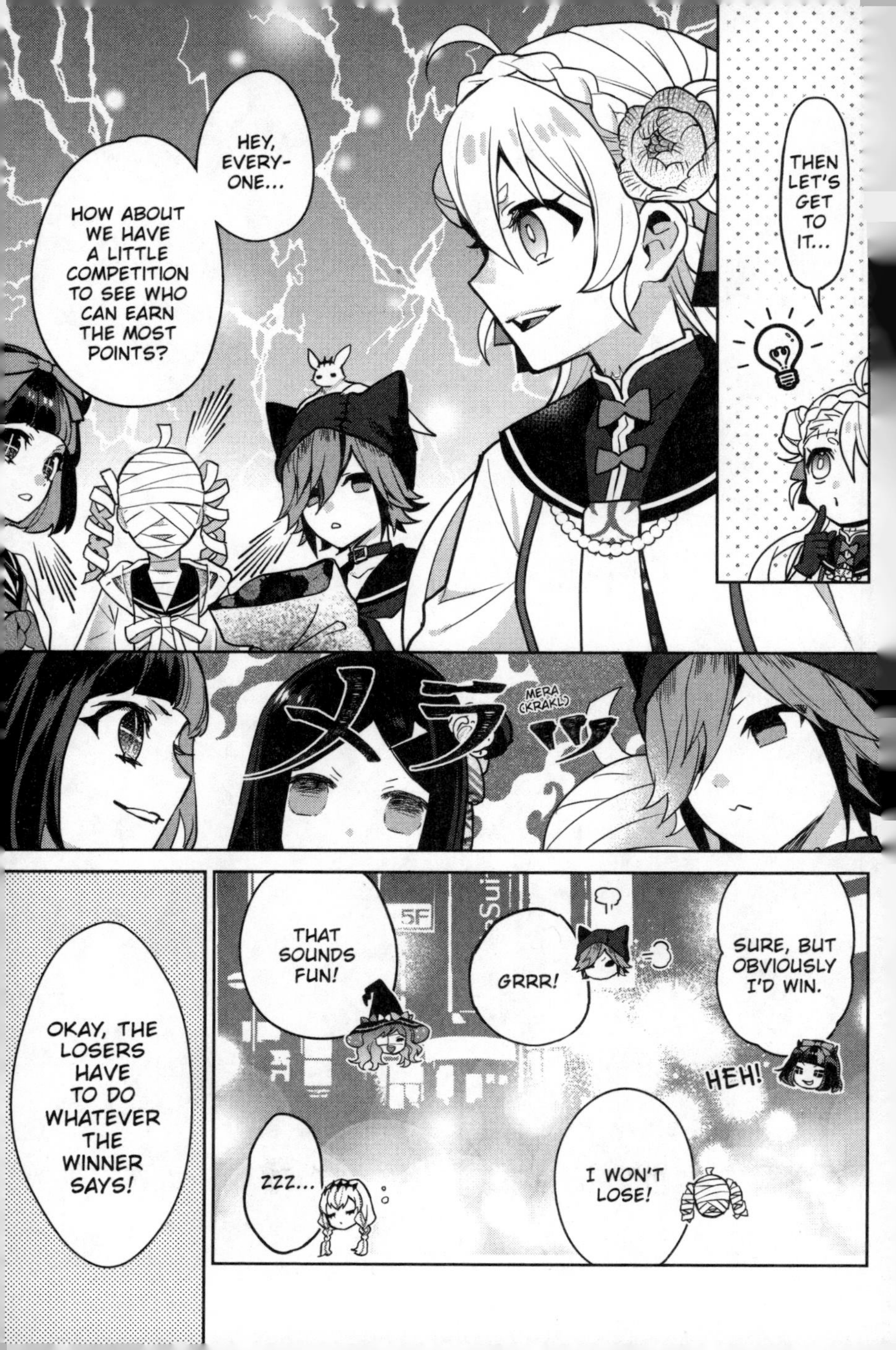
THEN LET'S GET TO IT...
HEY, EVERY-ONE...
HOW ABOUT WE HAVE A LITTLE COMPETITION TO SEE WHO CAN EARN THE MOST POINTS?
MERA (KRAKL)
SURE, BUT OBVIOUSLY I'D WIN.
HEH!
GRRR!
THAT SOUNDS FUN!
I WON'T LOSE!
ZZZ...
OKAY, THE LOSERS HAVE TO DO WHATEVER THE WINNER SAYS!

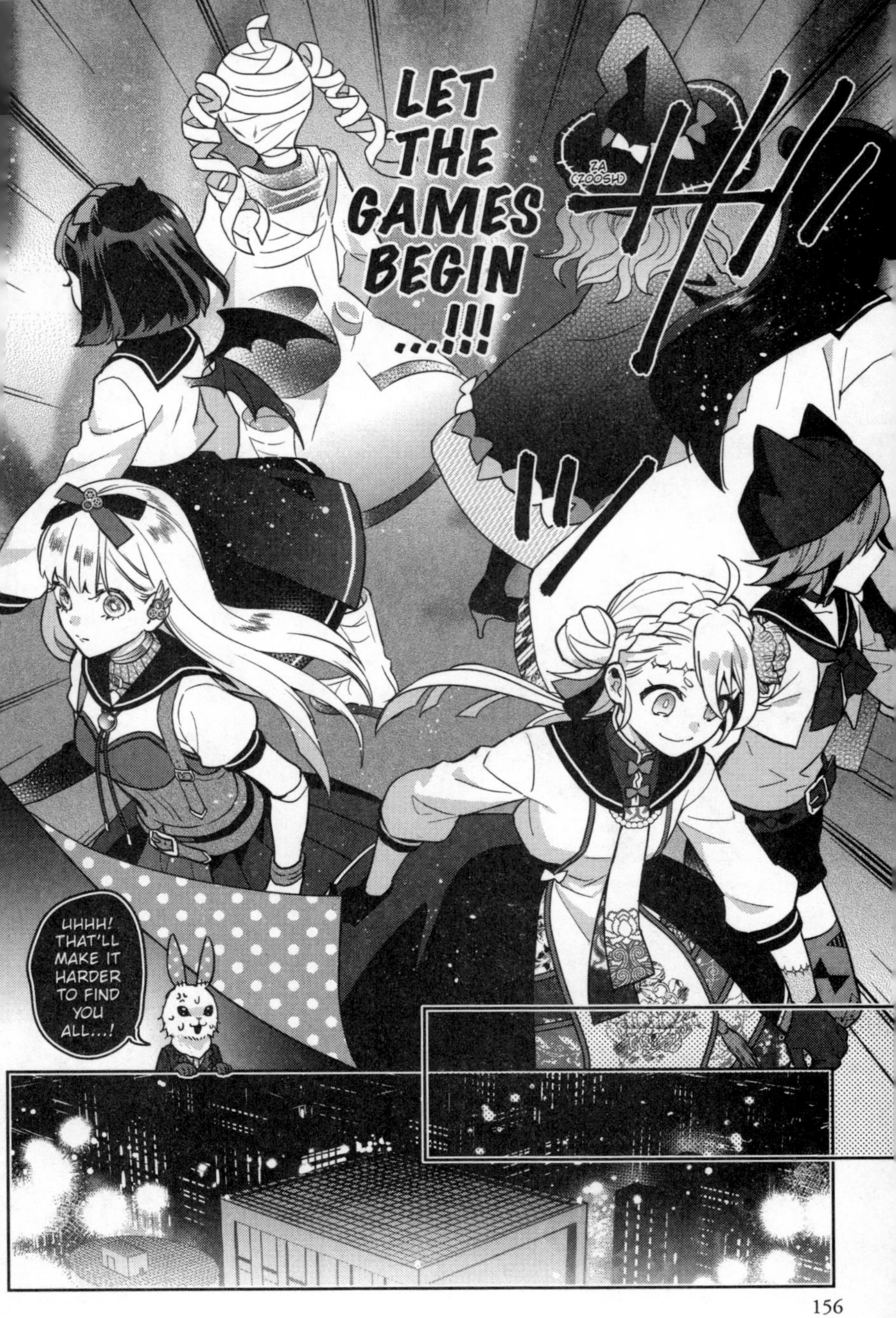
ZA (ZOOSH)
LET THE GAMES BEGIN ...!!!
UHHH! THAT'LL MAKE IT HARDER TO FIND YOU ALL...!

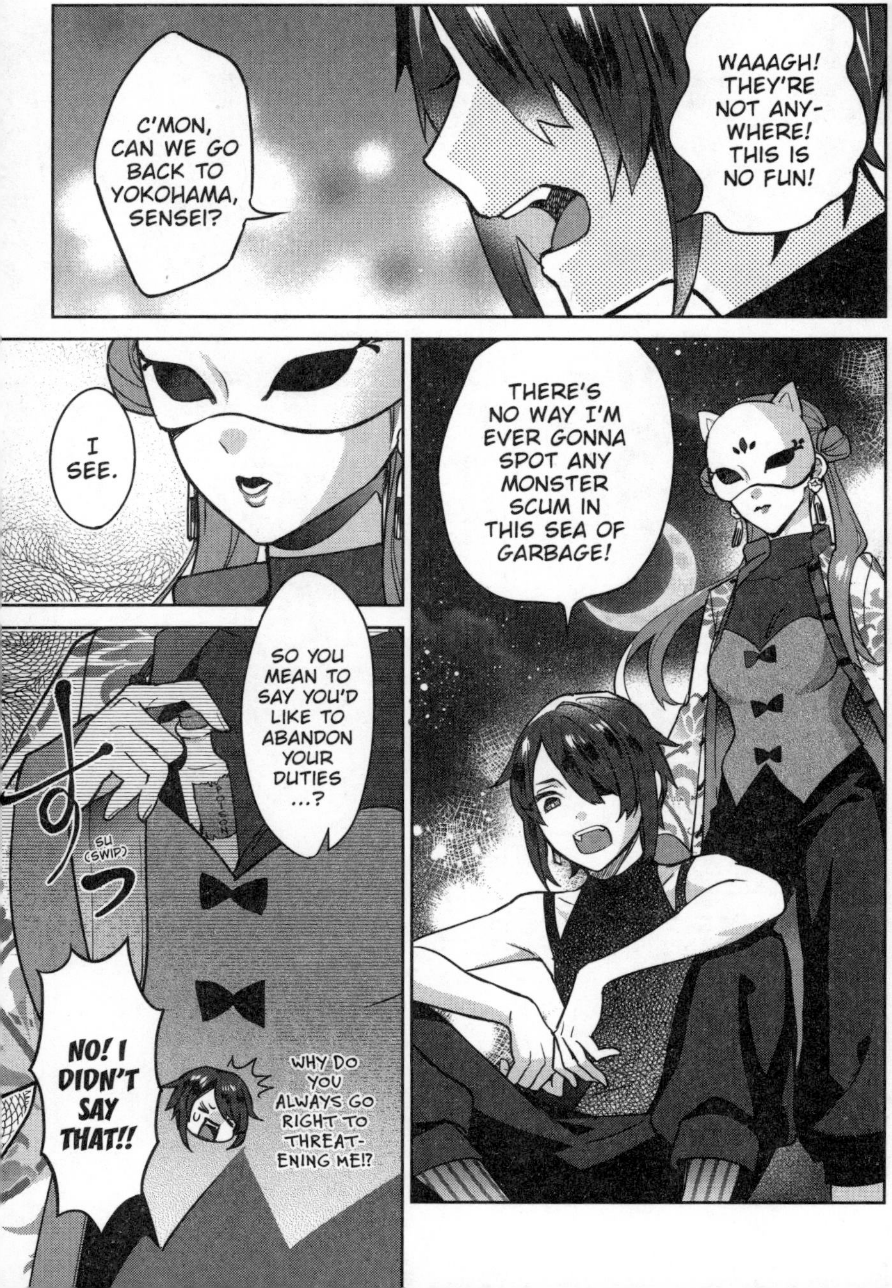
WAAAGH! THEY'RE NOT ANY-WHERE! THIS IS NO FUN!
C'MON, CAN WE GO BACK TO YOKOHAMA, SENSEI?
THERE'S NO WAY I'M EVER GONNA SPOT ANY MONSTER SCUM IN THIS SEA OF GARBAGE!
I SEE.
SO YOU MEAN TO SAY YOU'D LIKE TO ABANDON YOUR DUTIES ...?
SU (SWIP)
NO! I DIDN'T SAY THAT!!
WHY DO YOU ALWAYS GO RIGHT TO THREAT-ENING ME!?

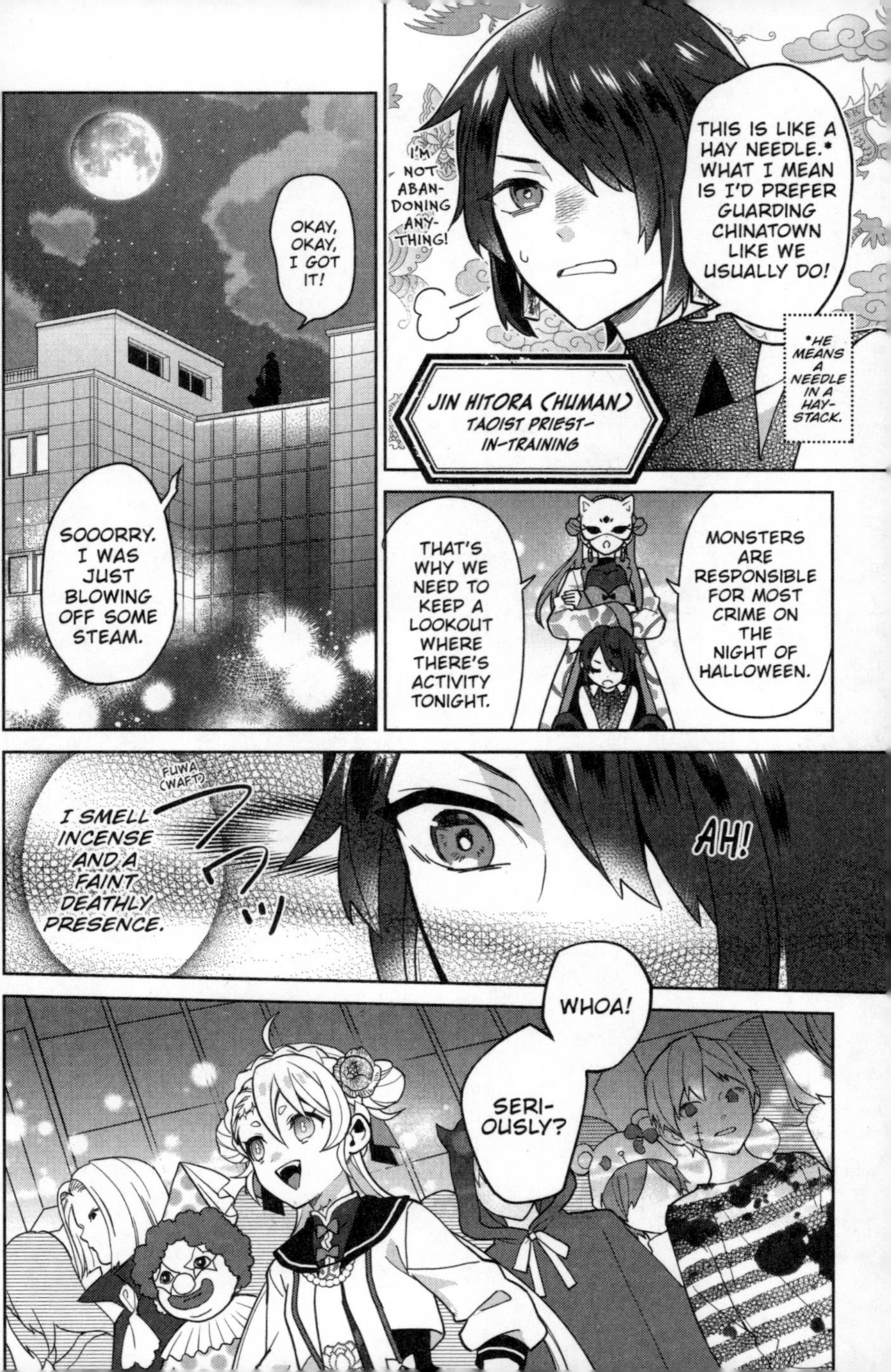
THIS IS LIKE A HAY NEEDLE.* WHAT I MEAN IS I'D PREFER GUARDING CHINATOWN LIKE WE USUALLY DO!
I'M NOT ABAN-DONING ANY-THING!
JIN HITORA (HUMAN) TAOIST PRIEST-IN-TRAINING
*HE MEANS A NEEDLE IN A HAY-STACK.
OKAY, OKAY, I GOT IT!
SOOORRY. I WAS JUST BLOWING OFF SOME STEAM.
MONSTERS ARE RESPONSIBLE FOR MOST CRIME ON THE NIGHT OF HALLOWEEN.
THAT'S WHY WE NEED TO KEEP A LOOKOUT WHERE THERE'S ACTIVITY TONIGHT.
AH!
FUWA (WAFT)
I SMELL INCENSE AND A FAINT DEATHLY PRESENCE.
WHOA!
SERI-OUSLY?

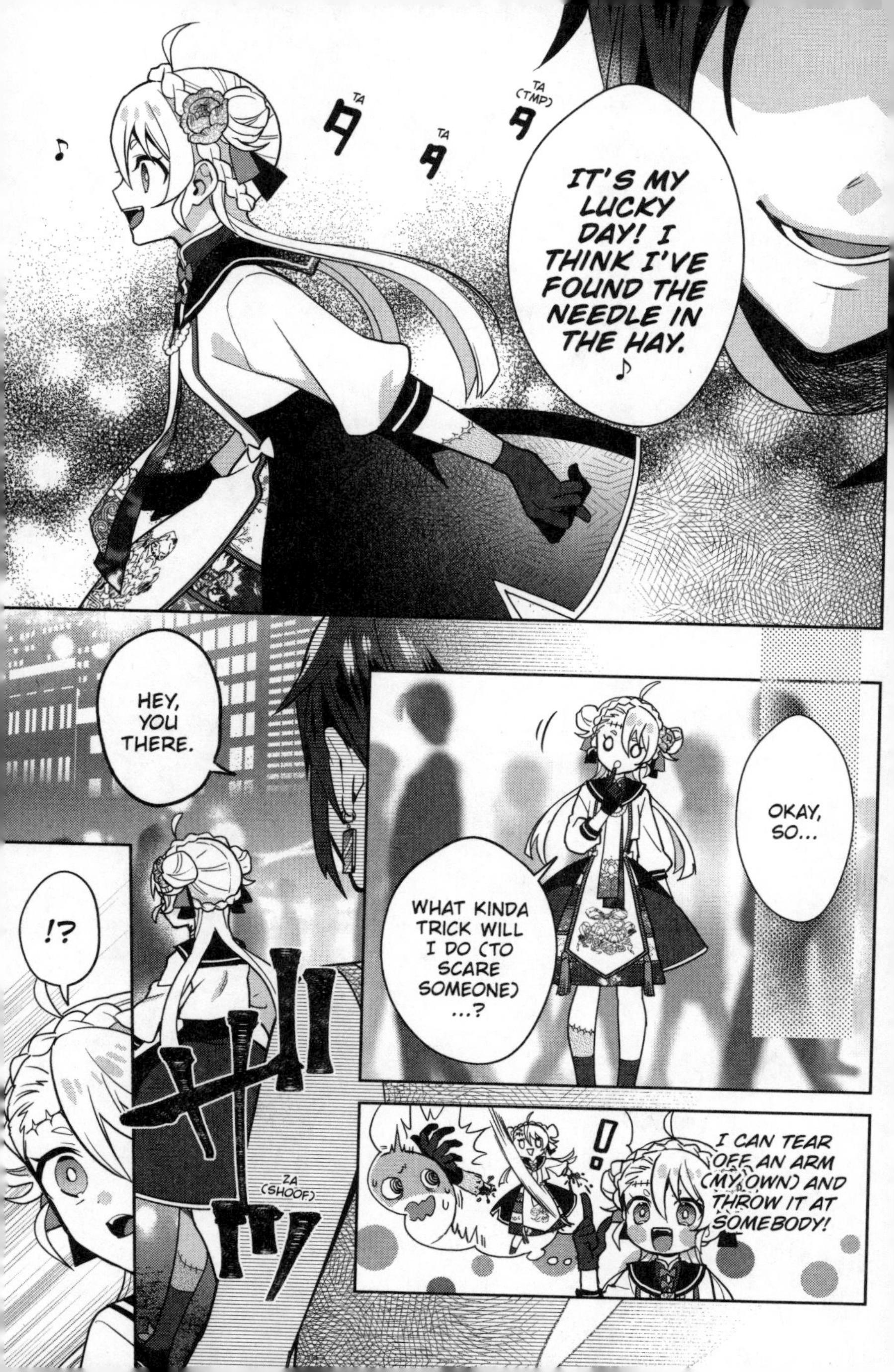

TA (TMP)
TA
TA
♪
IT'S MY LUCKY DAY! I THINK I'VE FOUND THE NEEDLE IN THE HAY. ♪
OKAY, SO...
WHAT KINDA TRICK WILL I DO (TO SCARE SOMEONE) ...?
I CAN TEAR OFF AN ARM (MY OWN) AND THROW IT AT SOMEBODY!
!
HEY, YOU THERE.
!?
ZA (SHOOF)

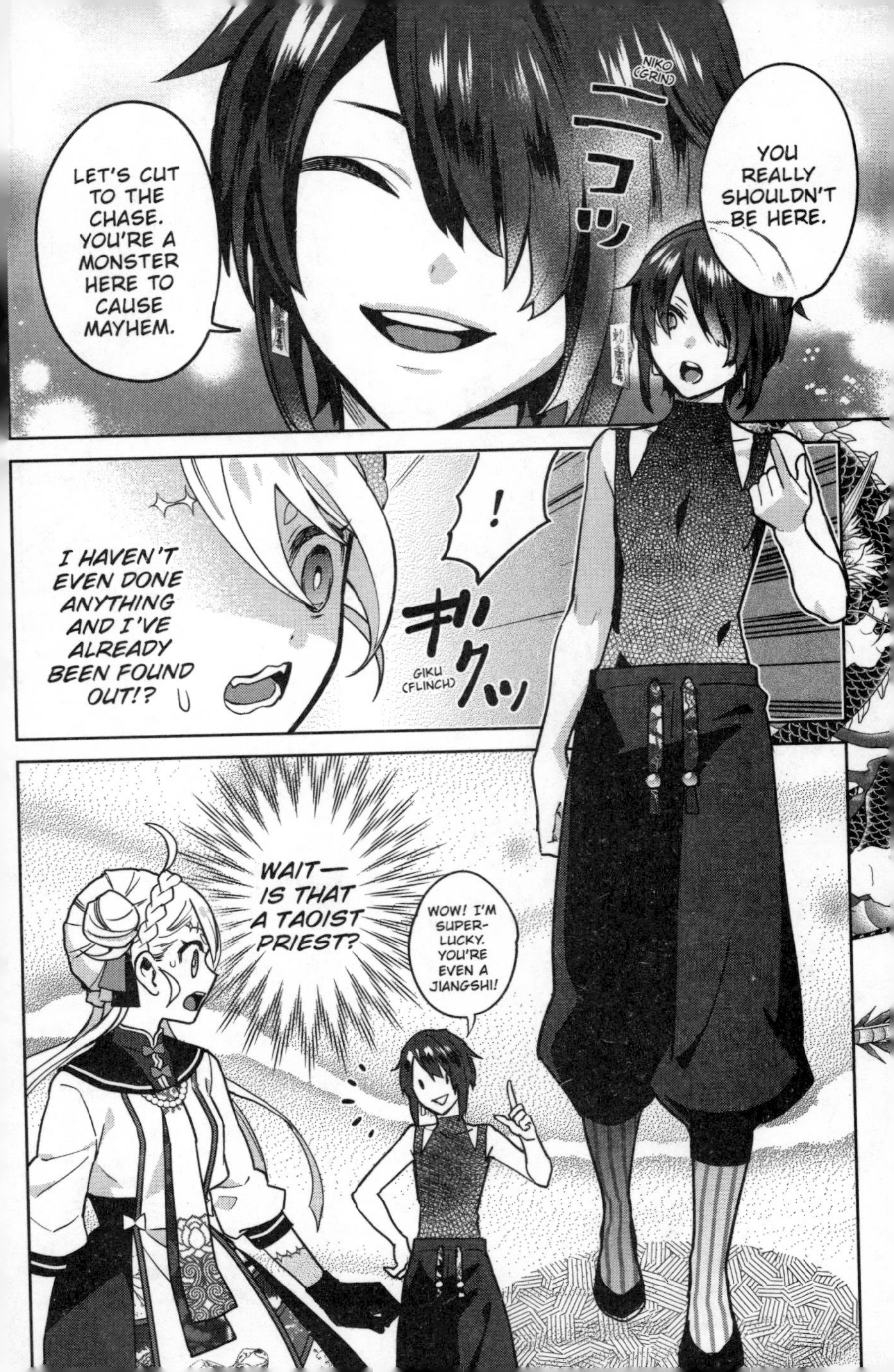
YOU REALLY SHOULDN'T BE HERE.
NIKO (GRIN)
LET'S CUT TO THE CHASE. YOU'RE A MONSTER HERE TO CAUSE MAYHEM.
!
GIKU (FLINCH)
I HAVEN'T EVEN DONE ANYTHING AND I'VE ALREADY BEEN FOUND OUT!?
WOW! I'M SUPER-LUCKY. YOU'RE EVEN A JIANGSHI!
WAIT— IS THAT A TAOIST PRIEST?

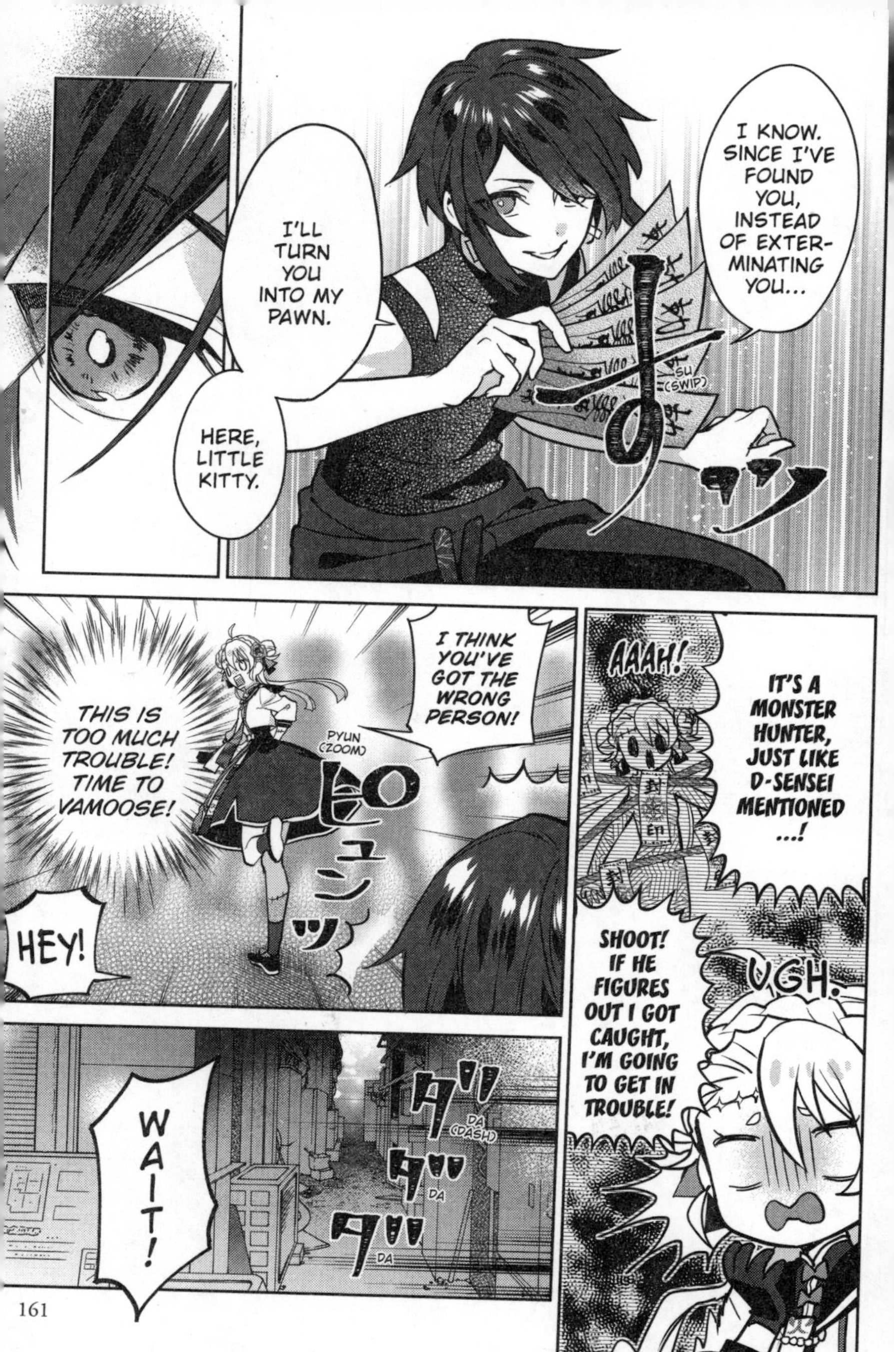
I KNOW. SINCE I'VE FOUND YOU, INSTEAD OF EXTER-MINATING YOU...
SU (SWIP)
I'LL TURN YOU INTO MY PAWN.
HERE, LITTLE KITTY.
AAAH!
IT'S A MONSTER HUNTER, JUST LIKE D-SENSEI MENTIONED ...!
UGH.
SHOOT! IF HE FIGURES OUT I GOT CAUGHT, I'M GOING TO GET IN TROUBLE!
I THINK YOU'VE GOT THE WRONG PERSON!
THIS IS TOO MUCH TROUBLE! TIME TO VAMOOSE!
PYUN (ZOOM)
HEY!
WAIT!
DA (DASH)
DA
DA

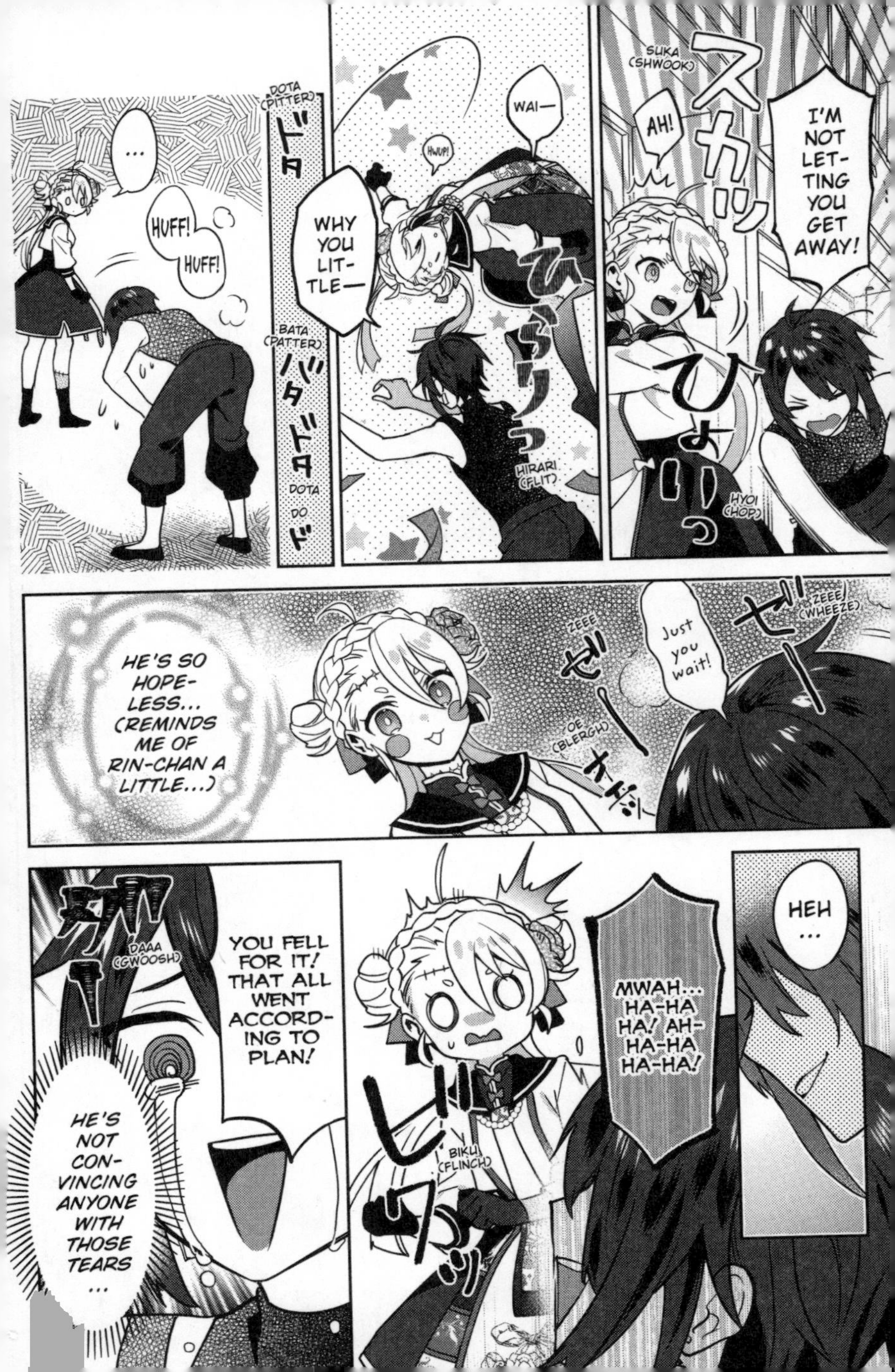

I'M NOT LETTING YOU GET AWAY!
スカッ
SUKA (SHWOOK)
AH!
ひょいっ
HYOI (HOP)
WAI—
HWUP!
WHY YOU LITTLE—
ひらりっ
HIRARI (FLIT)
ドタ
DOTA (PITTER)
バタドタド
BATA (PATTER)
DOTA
DO
...
HUFF!
HUFF!
ゼー
ZEEE (WHEEZE)
Just you wait!
ゼー
ZEEE
オェ
OE (BLERGH)
HE'S SO HOPELESS... (REMINDS ME OF RIN-CHAN A LITTLE...)
HEH ...
MWAH... HA-HA HA! AH-HA-HA HA-HA!
ビクッ
BIKU (FLINCH)
ダー
DAAA (GWOOSH)
YOU FELL FOR IT! THAT ALL WENT ACCORDING TO PLAN!
HE'S NOT CONVINCING ANYONE WITH THOSE TEARS ...

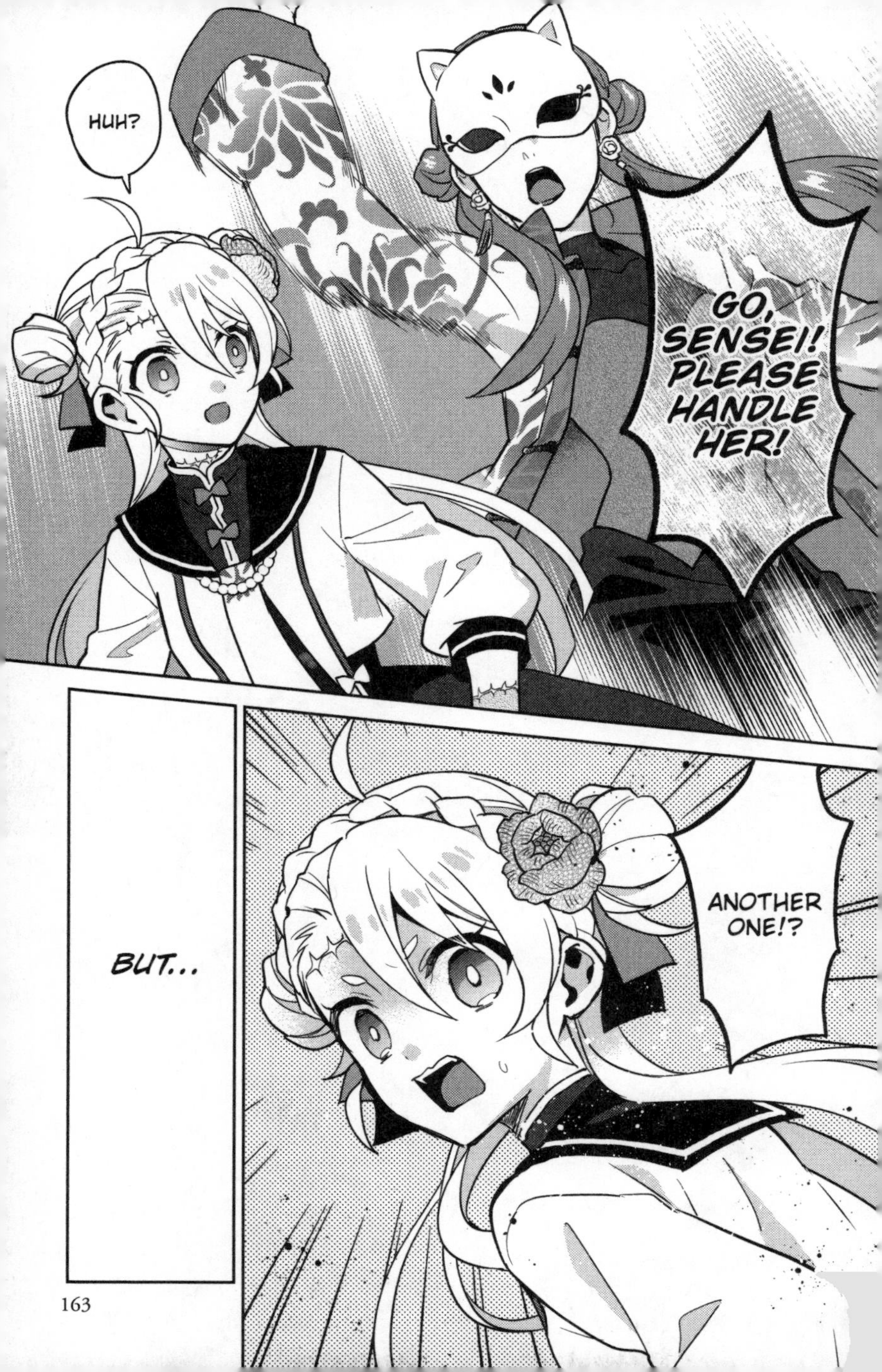
GO, SENSEI! PLEASE HANDLE HER!
HUH?
ANOTHER ONE!?
BUT...

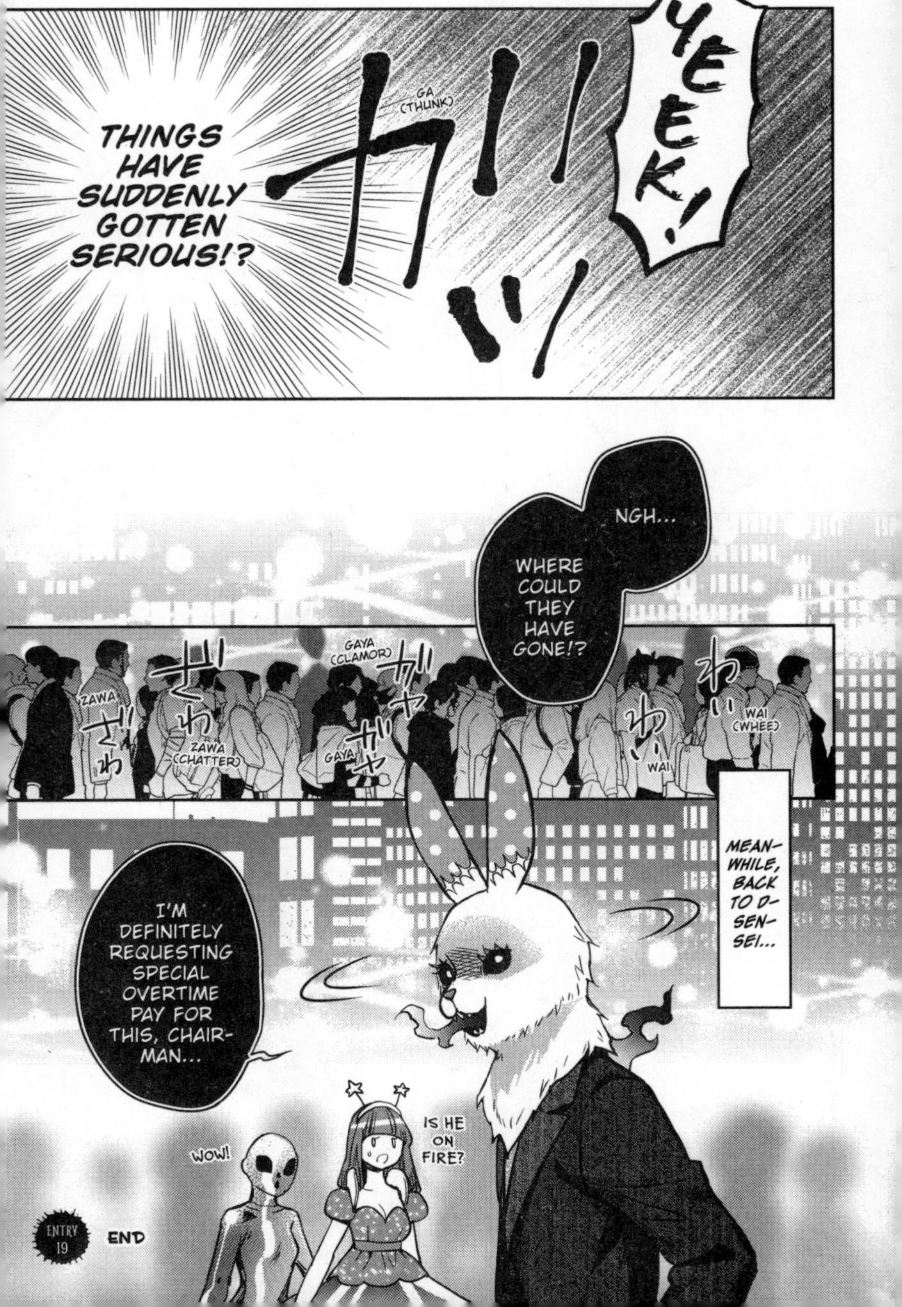
YEEK!
ガッ
GA (THUNK)
THINGS HAVE SUDDENLY GOTTEN SERIOUS!?
NGH...
WHERE COULD THEY HAVE GONE!?
わいわい
WAI (WHEE)
WAI
ガヤガヤ
GAYA (CLAMOR)
GAYA
ざわざわ
ZAWA (CHATTER)
ZAWA
MEAN-WHILE, BACK TO D-SEN-SEI...
I'M DEFINITELY REQUESTING SPECIAL OVERTIME PAY FOR THIS, CHAIR-MAN...
IS HE ON FIRE?
WOW!
ENTRY 19 END

The Illustrated Guide to Monster Girls

Supplemental Lesson Manga ENTRY 2

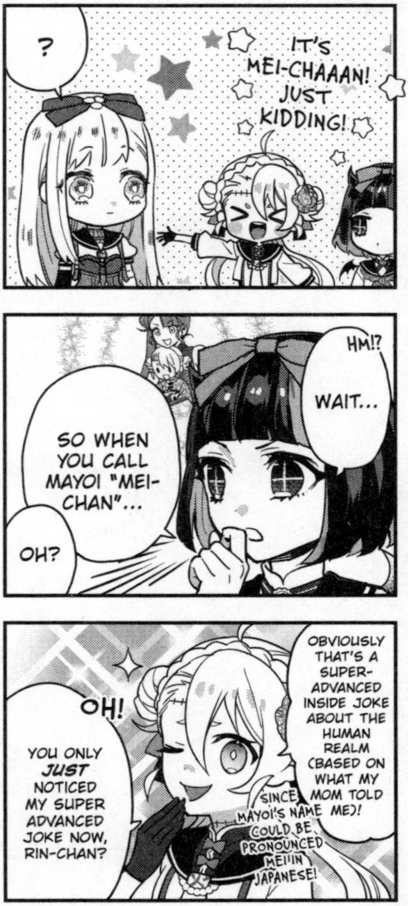
IT'S MEI-CHAAAN! JUST KIDDING!
?
HM!?
WAIT...
SO WHEN YOU CALL MAYOI "MEI-CHAN"...
OH?
OBVIOUSLY THAT'S A SUPER-ADVANCED INSIDE JOKE ABOUT THE HUMAN REALM (BASED ON WHAT MY MOM TOLD ME)!
OH!
YOU ONLY JUST NOTICED MY SUPER ADVANCED JOKE NOW, RIN-CHAN?
SINCE MAYOI'S NAME COULD BE PRONOUNCED MEI IN JAPANESE!
NO, I JUST THOUGHT YOU WERE ILLITER-ATE TOO.
WHAT!? OF COURSE NOT!

Supplemental Lesson Manga ENTRY 3

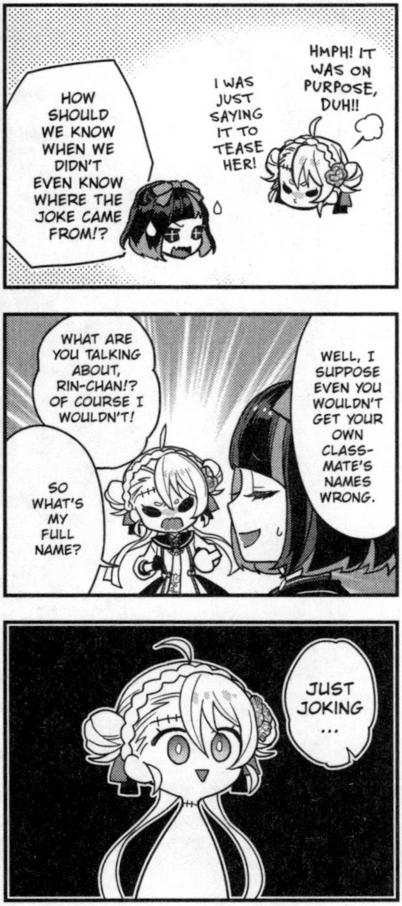
HMPH! IT WAS ON PURPOSE, DUH!!
I WAS JUST SAYING IT TO TEASE HER!
HOW SHOULD WE KNOW WHEN WE DIDN'T EVEN KNOW WHERE THE JOKE CAME FROM!?
WELL, I SUPPOSE EVEN YOU WOULDN'T GET YOUR OWN CLASS-MATE'S NAMES WRONG.
WHAT ARE YOU TALKING ABOUT, RIN-CHAN!? OF COURSE I WOULDN'T!
SO WHAT'S MY FULL NAME?
JUST JOKING...
RIN-CHAN... SHIRO... YUKI?
YOU'VE GOT TO BE KID-DING!

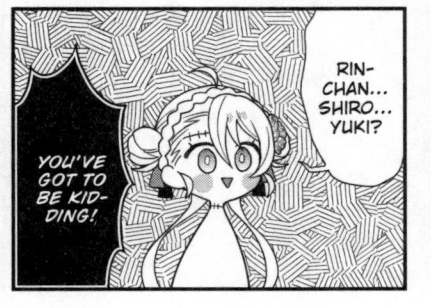

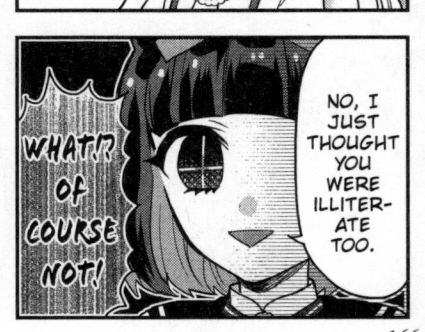

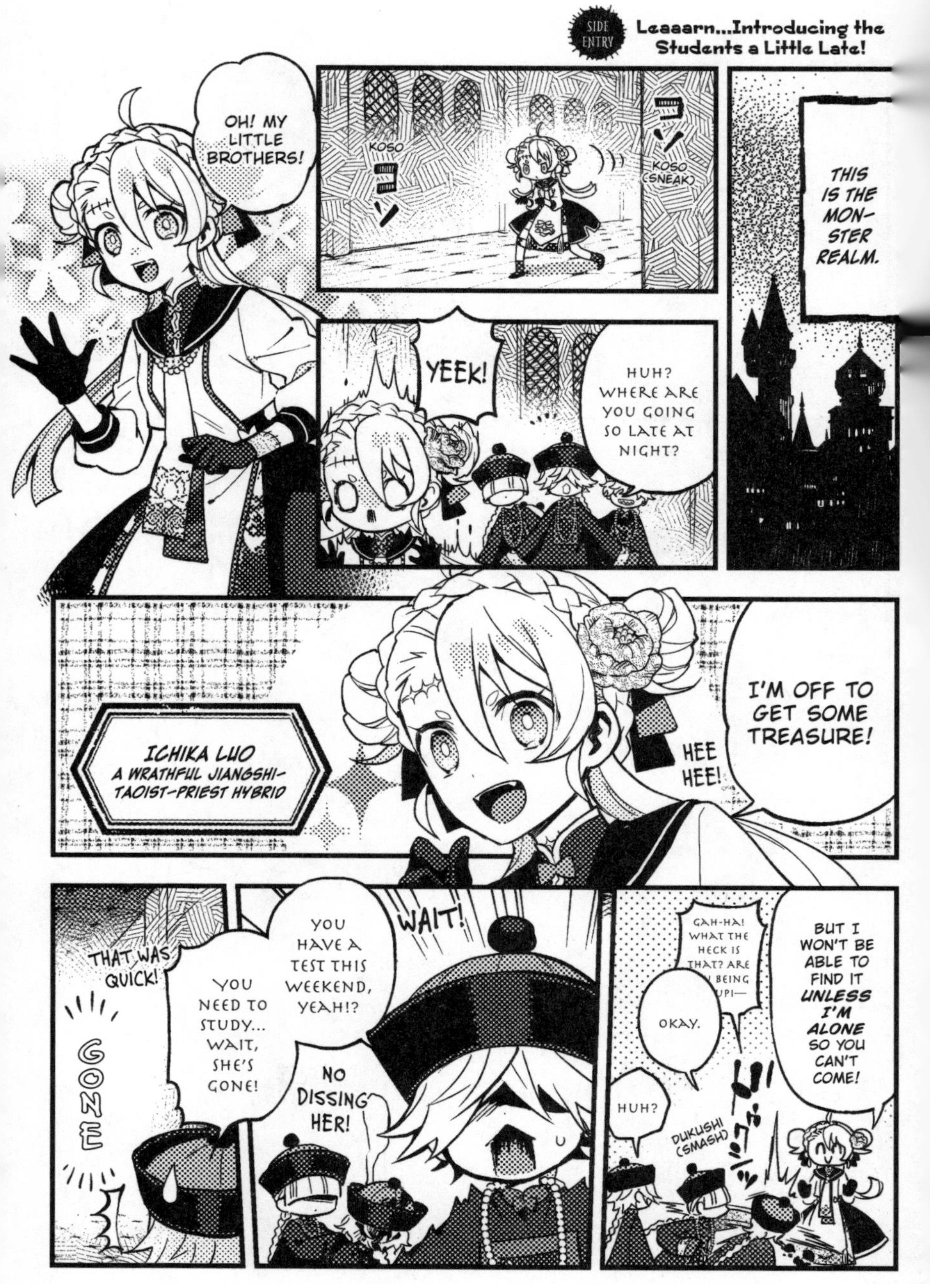
THIS IS THE MON-STER REALM.
KOSO (SNEAK)
KOSO
YEEK!
HUH? WHERE ARE YOU GOING SO LATE AT NIGHT?
OH! MY LITTLE BROTHERS!
I'M OFF TO GET SOME TREASURE!
HEE HEE!
ICHIKA LUO
A WRATHFUL JIANGSHI-TAOIST-PRIEST HYBRID
BUT I WON'T BE ABLE TO FIND IT UNLESS I'M ALONE SO YOU CAN'T COME!
OKAY.
HUH?
DUKUSHI (SMASH)
WAIT!
YOU HAVE A TEST THIS WEEKEND, YEAH!?
NO DISSING HER!
YOU NEED TO STUDY... WAIT, SHE'S GONE!
THAT WAS QUICK!
GONE

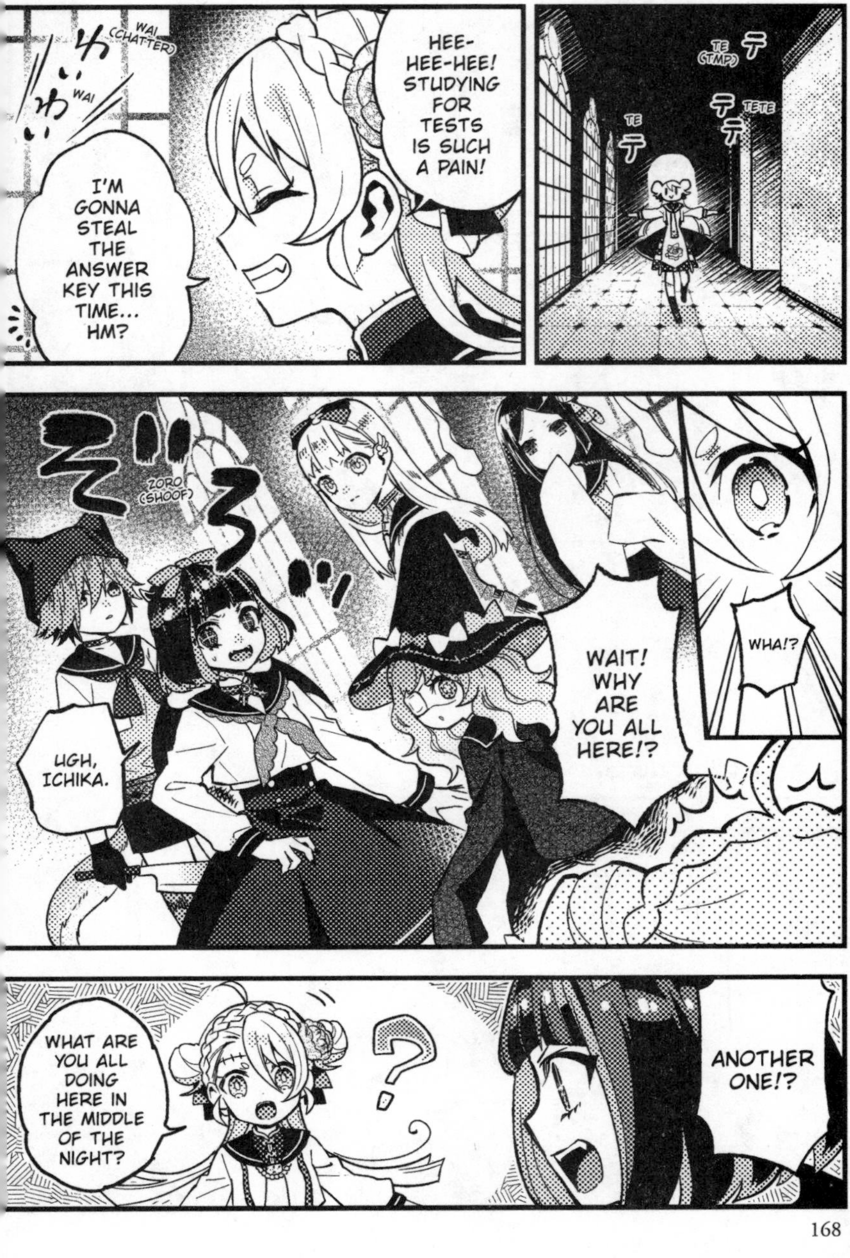
TE (TMP)
TETE
TE
HEE-HEE-HEE! STUDYING FOR TESTS IS SUCH A PAIN!
WAI (CHATTER)
WAI
I'M GONNA STEAL THE ANSWER KEY THIS TIME... HM?
WHA!?
WAIT! WHY ARE YOU ALL HERE!?
ZORO (SHOOF)
UGH, ICHIKA.
ANOTHER ONE!?
WHAT ARE YOU ALL DOING HERE IN THE MIDDLE OF THE NIGHT?

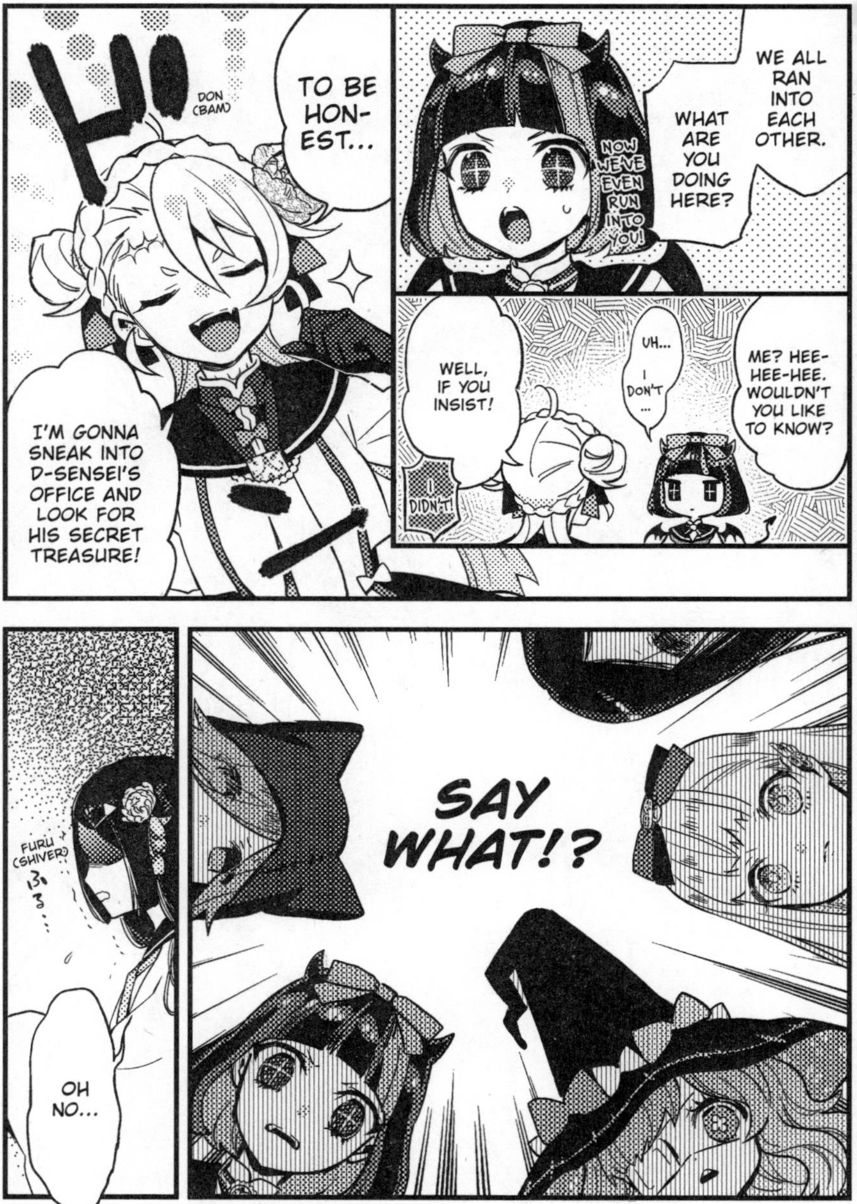
WE ALL RAN INTO EACH OTHER.
NOW WE'VE EVEN RUN INTO YOU!
WHAT ARE YOU DOING HERE?
ME? HEE-HEE-HEE. WOULDN'T YOU LIKE TO KNOW?
UH... I DON'T ...
WELL, IF YOU INSIST!
I DIDN'T!
TO BE HON-EST...
DON (BAM)
I'M GONNA SNEAK INTO D-SENSEI'S OFFICE AND LOOK FOR HIS SECRET TREASURE!
SAY WHAT!?
FURU (SHIVER)
ふる…
OH NO...

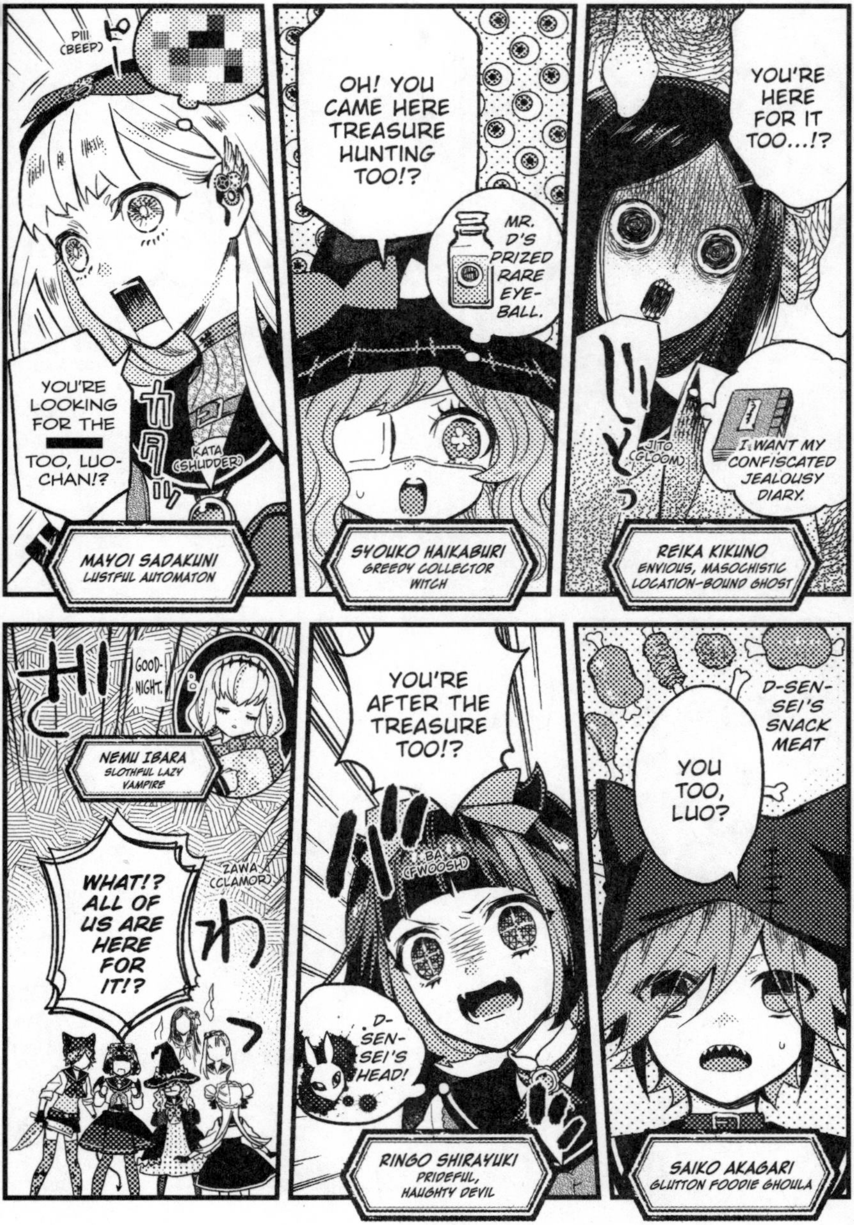
YOU'RE HERE FOR IT TOO...!?
JITO (GLOOM)
I WANT MY CONFISCATED JEALOUSY DIARY.
REIKA KIKUNO
ENVIOUS, MASOCHISTIC LOCATION-BOUND GHOST
OH! YOU CAME HERE TREASURE HUNTING TOO!?
MR. D'S PRIZED RARE EYE-BALL.
SYOUKO HAIKABURI
GREEDY COLLECTOR WITCH
PIII (BEEP)
YOU'RE LOOKING FOR THE [redacted] TOO, LUO-CHAN!?
KATA (SHUDDER)
MAYOI SADAKUNI
LUSTFUL AUTOMATON
D-SEN-SEI'S SNACK MEAT
YOU TOO, LUO?
SAIKO AKAGARI
GLUTTON FOODIE GHOULA
YOU'RE AFTER THE TREASURE TOO!?
BA (FWOOSH)
D-SEN-SEI'S HEAD!
RINGO SHIRAYUKI
PRIDEFUL, HAUGHTY DEVIL
GOOD-NIGHT.
NEMU IBARA
SLOTHFUL LAZY VAMPIRE
ZAWA (CLAMOR)
WHAT!? ALL OF US ARE HERE FOR IT!?

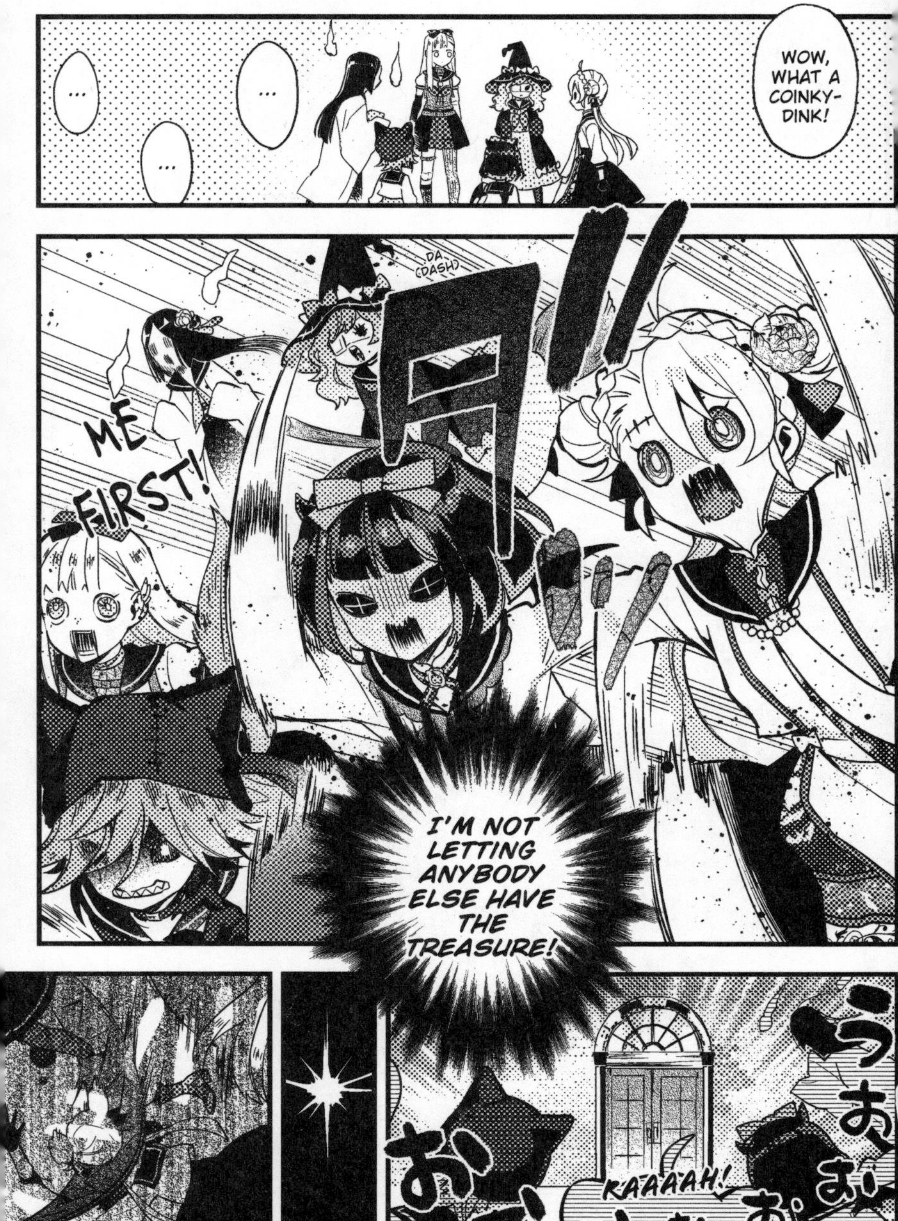
WOW, WHAT A COINKY-DINK!
...
...
...
DA (DASH)
ME FIRST!
I'M NOT LETTING ANYBODY ELSE HAVE THE TREASURE!
KAAAAH!

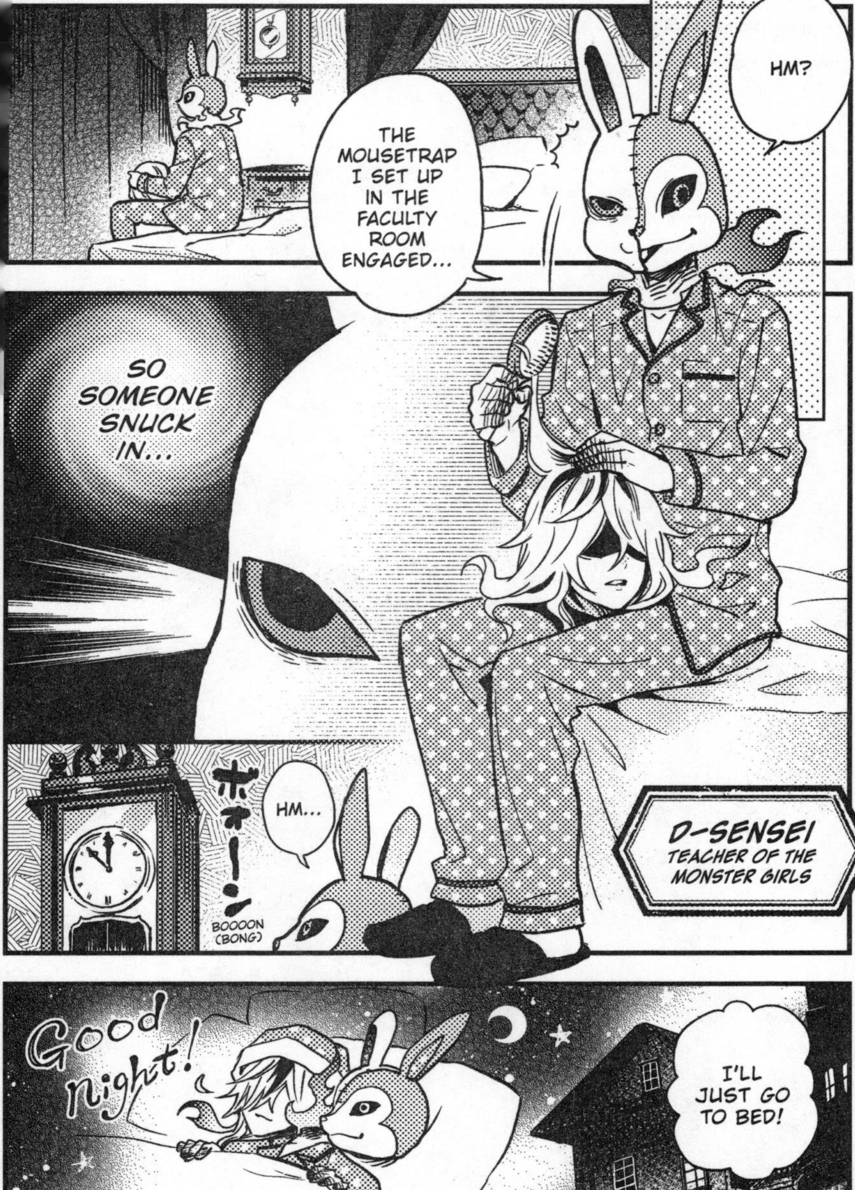
HM?
THE MOUSETRAP I SET UP IN THE FACULTY ROOM ENGAGED...
D-SENSEI
TEACHER OF THE MONSTER GIRLS
SO SOMEONE SNUCK IN...
HM...
ボオーン
BOOOON (BONG)
I'LL JUST GO TO BED!
Good night!

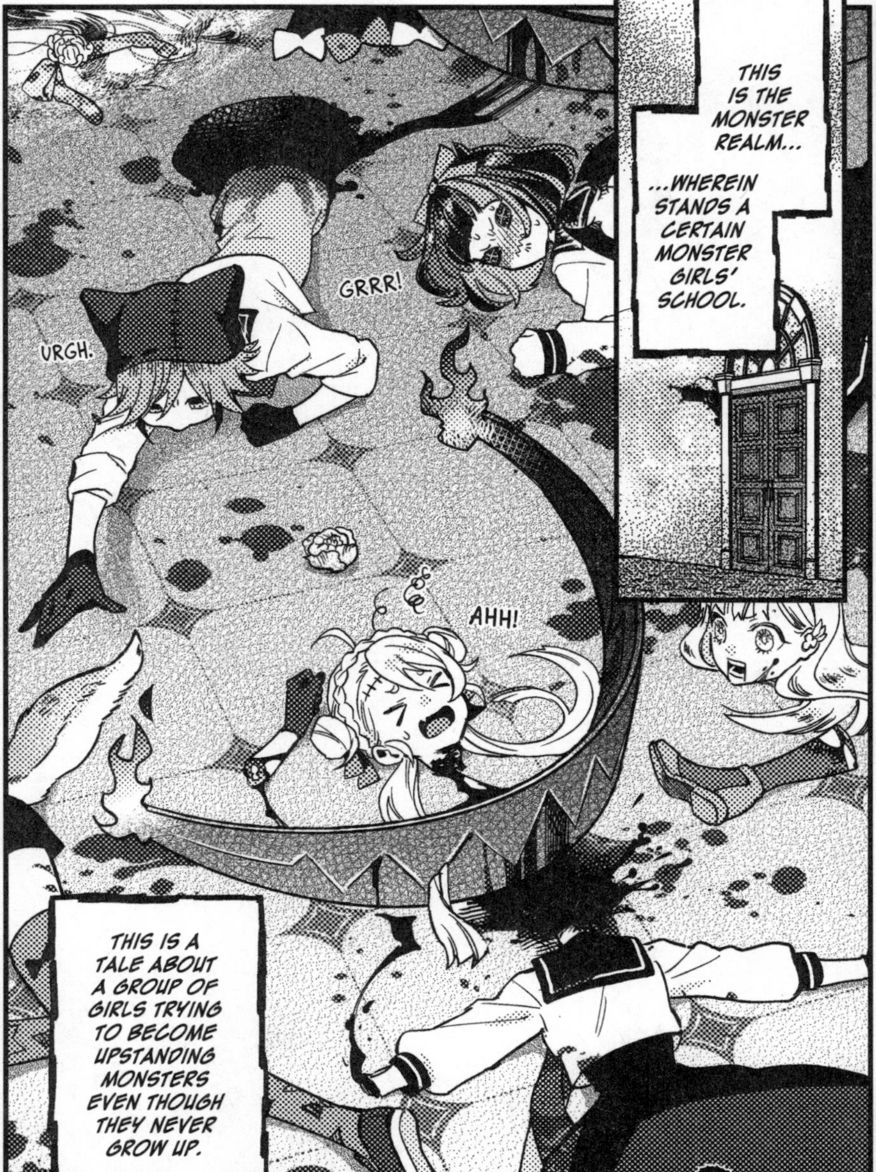
THIS IS THE MONSTER REALM...
...WHEREIN STANDS A CERTAIN MONSTER GIRLS' SCHOOL.
GRRR!
URGH.
AHH!
THIS IS A TALE ABOUT A GROUP OF GIRLS TRYING TO BECOME UPSTANDING MONSTERS EVEN THOUGH THEY NEVER GROW UP.
SIDE ENTRY
END

Illustrated Guide to Monster Girls continued in Vol. 4

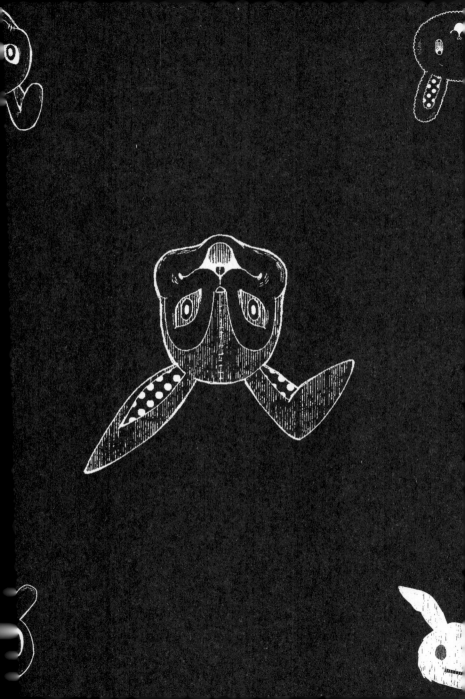

TRANSLATION NOTES

PAGE 13
A *jiangshi*, sometimes called a "hopping vampire," is a monster in Chinese folklore that steals the chi from its victims. They are said to hop because their bodies are stiff from rigor mortis.

A **Taoist priest** is one who practices Taoism, a philosophy and religion in China. They are said to guide *jiangshi* home for a proper burial.

PAGE 14
The Japanese character for **Utsuro** means "void" or "emptiness."

PAGE 21
"I want everyone to really see me! ♪" is a parody of the Japanese lyrics of the song "Let it Go" from the movie *Frozen*.

PAGE 33
In **"Crackle Mountain,"** a raccoon dog tricks a man into eating his wife by cooking her in a stew.

PAGE 38
The Japanese characters for **Tamako** mean "spirit child."

PAGE 39
Kaidou is Japanese for the boundary between the two worlds.

PAGE 44
"Hitting the seabed is making our business see red..." is *kaitei kyuugyou* in the original Japanese. It's a play on the phrase *kaiten kyuugyou*, meaning "The shop is open but has no business," but *kaiten* ("opening shop") is replaced with *kaitei* ("seabed").

PAGE 45
A **kappa** is a Japanese yokai monster appearing in folklore and literature, known for holding water in the top of its head like a dish. They are said to live in rivers or ponds and to like to drag people into the water.

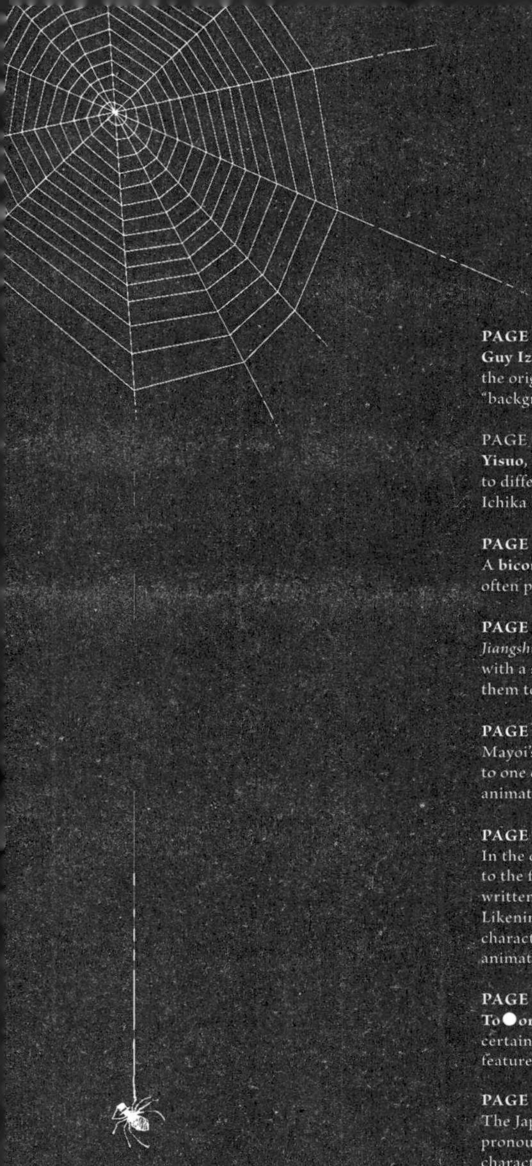

PAGE 52
Guy Izanobody is named Mobu Nohito in the original Japanese, which is a pun meaning "background/unimportant character."

PAGE 62
Yisuo, **Yiwan**, and **Yibing**'s names are all references to different mahjong tiles, playing into the theme of Ichika being a monster from Chinese folklore.

PAGE 67
A **bicorn** is a mythical two-horned creature that is often portrayed as a horse.

PAGE 79
Jiangshi are portrayed to have **talismans** imbued with a spell stuck on their heads to make it easier for them to move.

PAGE 103
Mayoi's line, "**My eye! My eye!**" sounds very similar to one delivered by a villain from a famous Japanese animated movie about a castle high up in the sky.

PAGE 151
In the original Japanese, D-sensei makes reference to the fact the Japanese word for crowd (*hitogomi*) is written with the words for "**people**" and "**garbage**." Likening people to garbage is also a well-known characteristic of a villain from a famous Japanese animated film about a castle high up in the sky.

PAGE 152
To●oro from Ghi●li refers to a character in a certain other popular Japanese animated film that features a girl named Mei.

PAGE 166
The Japanese character for **Mayoi** can be pronounced as *mayoi* or ***mei***. Most Japanese characters have two readings, one deriving from the Chinese pronunciation and one from the Japanese reading, depending on the context.

So I'm a Spider, So What?

I'M GONNA SURVIVE——JUST WATCH ME!

I was your average, everyday high school girl, but now I've been reborn in a magical world...as a spider?! How am I supposed to survive in this big, scary dungeon as one of the weakest monsters? I gotta figure out the rules to this QUICK, or I'll be kissing my short second life good-bye...

MANGA VOL. 1-12

LIGHT NOVEL VOL. 1-16

AVAILABLE NOW!

YOU CAN ALSO KEEP UP WITH THE MANGA SIMUL-PUB EVERY MONTH ONLINE!

ENJOY EVERYTHING.

Join Yotsuba as she delights in the
things many of us take for granted
in this Eisner-nominated series.

VOLUMES 1-15
AVAILABLE NOW!

Visit our website at www.yenpress.com.

Hello! This is YOTSUBA!

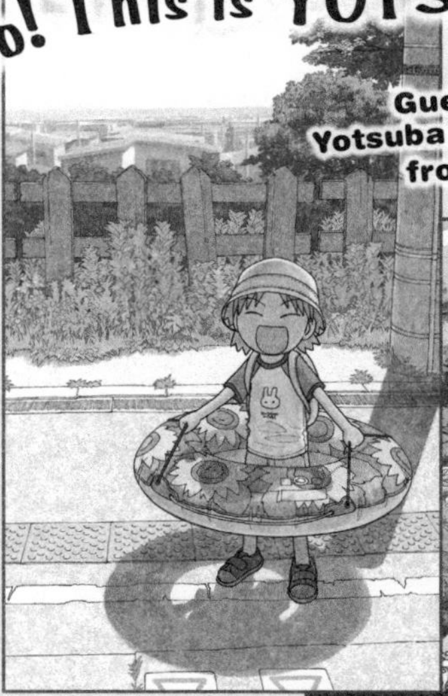

Guess what? Guess what?
Yotsuba and Daddy just moved here from waaaay over there!

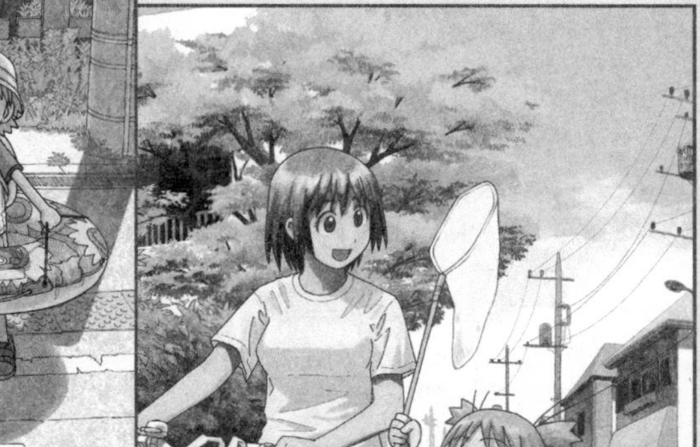

And Yotsuba met these nice people next door and made new friends to play with!

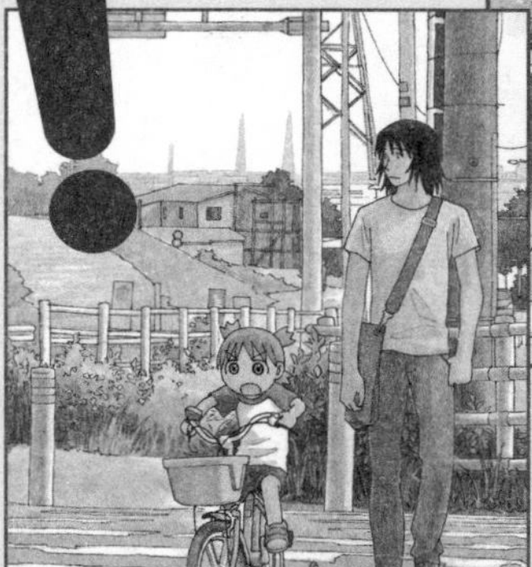

The pretty one took Yotsuba on a bike ride!
(Whoooa! There was a big hill!)

And Ena's a good drawer!
(Almost as good as Yotsuba!)

And their mom always gives Yotsuba ice cream!
(Yummy!)

And...
And...
OHHHH!

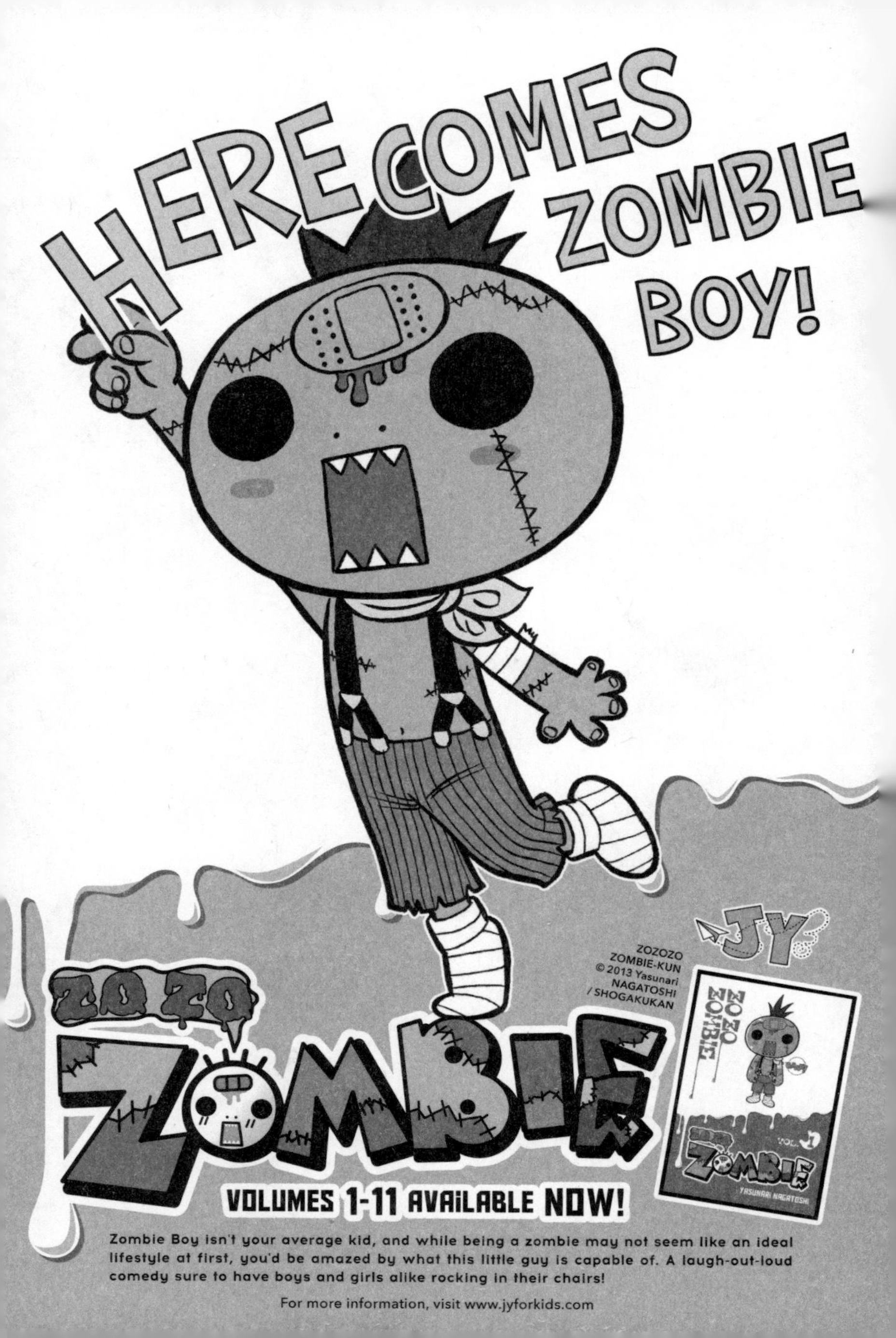
HERE COMES ZOMBIE BOY!
ZOZOZO ZOMBIE-KUN © 2013 Yasunari NAGATOSHI / SHOGAKUKAN
ZO ZO ZOMBIE
VOLUMES 1-11 AVAILABLE NOW!
Zombie Boy isn't your average kid, and while being a zombie may not seem like an ideal lifestyle at first, you'd be amazed by what this little guy is capable of. A laugh-out-loud comedy sure to have boys and girls alike rocking in their chairs!
For more information, visit www.jyforkids.com

The Illustrated Guide to Monster Girls 3

SUZU AKEKO

Translation: Jan Cash ✳ Lettering: Alexis Eckerman

This book is a work of fiction. Names, characters, places, and incidents are the product of the author's imagination or are used fictitiously. Any resemblance to actual events, locales, or persons, living or dead, is coincidental.

KAIBUTSU SHOJO ZUKAN Vol.3
©Suzu Akeko 2020
First published in Japan in 2020 by KADOKAWA CORPORATION, Tokyo.
English translation rights arranged with KADOKAWA CORPORATION, Tokyo
through TUTTLE-MORI AGENCY, INC., Tokyo.

Yen Press
150 West 30th Street, 19th Floor
New York, NY 10001

Visit us at yenpress.com ✳ facebook.com/yenpress ✳ twitter.com/yenpress
✳ yenpress.tumblr.com ✳ instagram.com/yenpress

First Yen Press Edition: April 2024

Edited by Yen Press Editorial: Carl Li
Designed by Yen Press Design: Wendy Chan

Yen Press is an imprint of Yen Press, LLC.
The Yen Press name and logo are trademarks of Yen Press, LLC.

The publisher is not responsible for websites (or their content) that are not owned by the publisher.

Library of Congress Control Number: 2023938735

ISBNs: 978-1-9753-6310-3 (paperback)
978-1-9753-6311-0 (eBook)

1 3 5 7 9 10 8 6 4 2

WOR

Printed in the United States of America